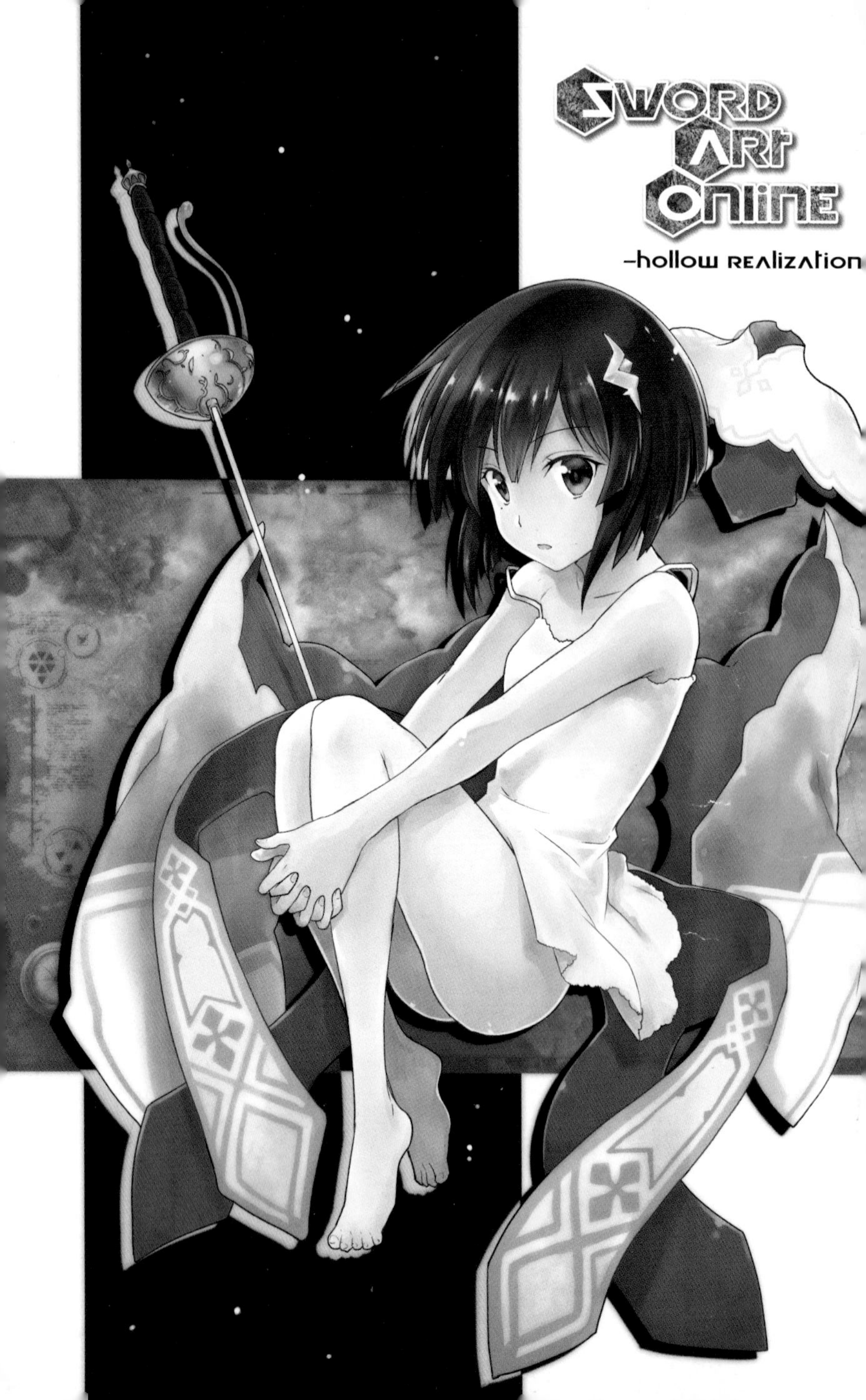
SWORD ART ONLINE
-hollow REALIZATION

SWORD ART ONLINE
—HOLLOW REALIZATION—

001

CONTENTS.

#01: Ainground

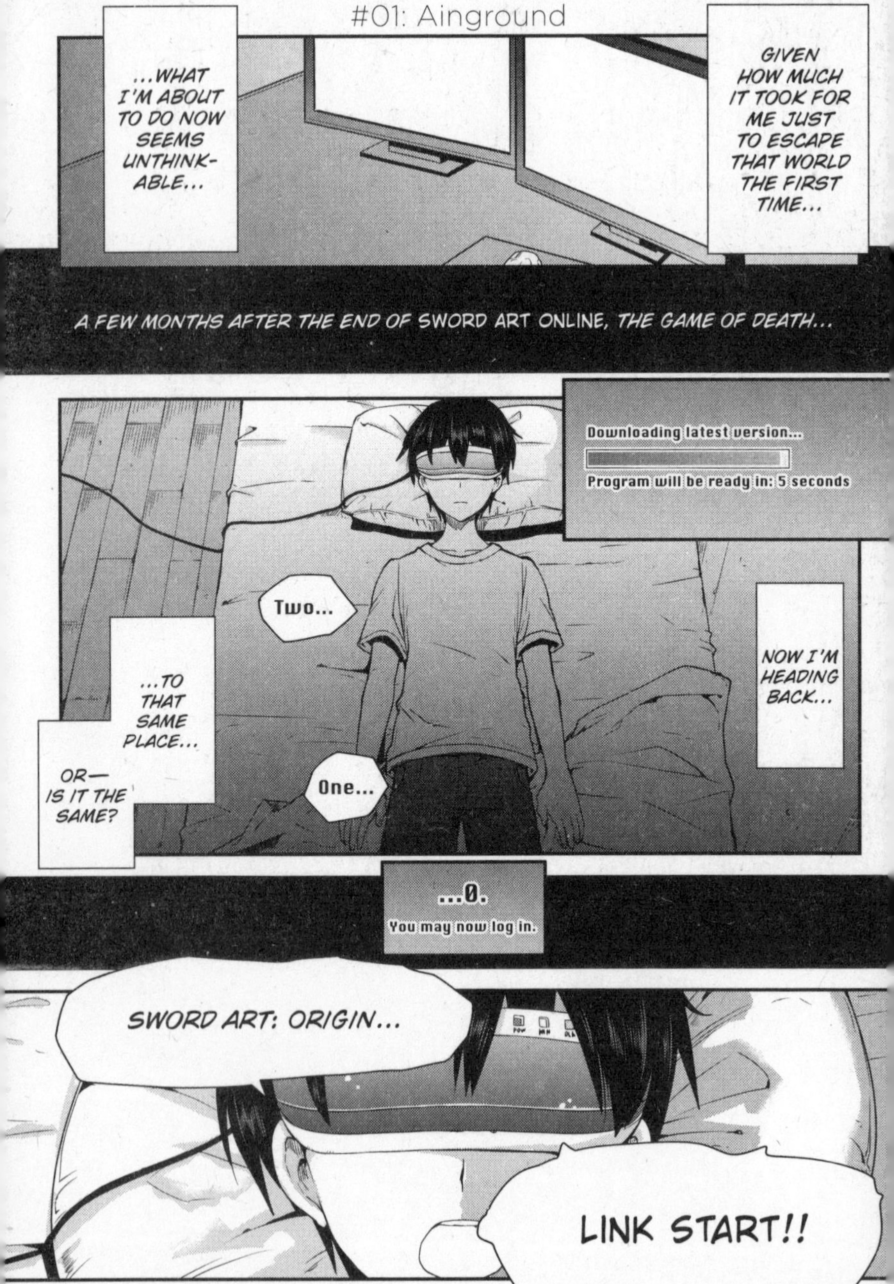
GIVEN HOW MUCH IT TOOK FOR ME JUST TO ESCAPE THAT WORLD THE FIRST TIME...
...WHAT I'M ABOUT TO DO NOW SEEMS UNTHINKABLE...
A FEW MONTHS AFTER THE END OF SWORD ART ONLINE, THE GAME OF DEATH...
Downloading latest version...
Program will be ready in: 5 seconds
NOW I'M HEADING BACK...
Two...
...TO THAT SAME PLACE...
One...
OR— IS IT THE SAME?
...0.
You may now log in.
SWORD ART: ORIGIN...
LINK START!!

IT MIGHT LOOK FAMILIAR...
BUT THIS NEW VRMMO IS VERY DIFFERENT...!

WELCOME TO AINGROUND!

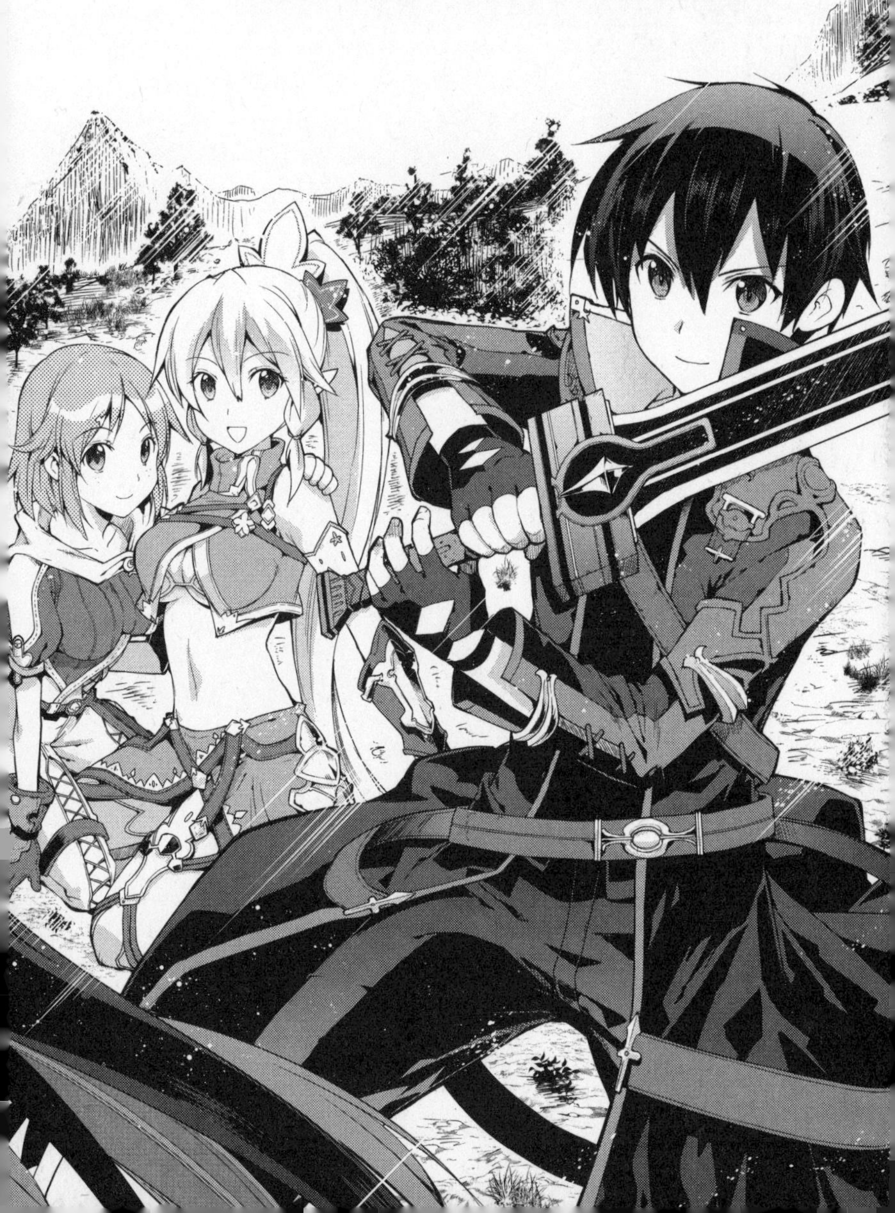

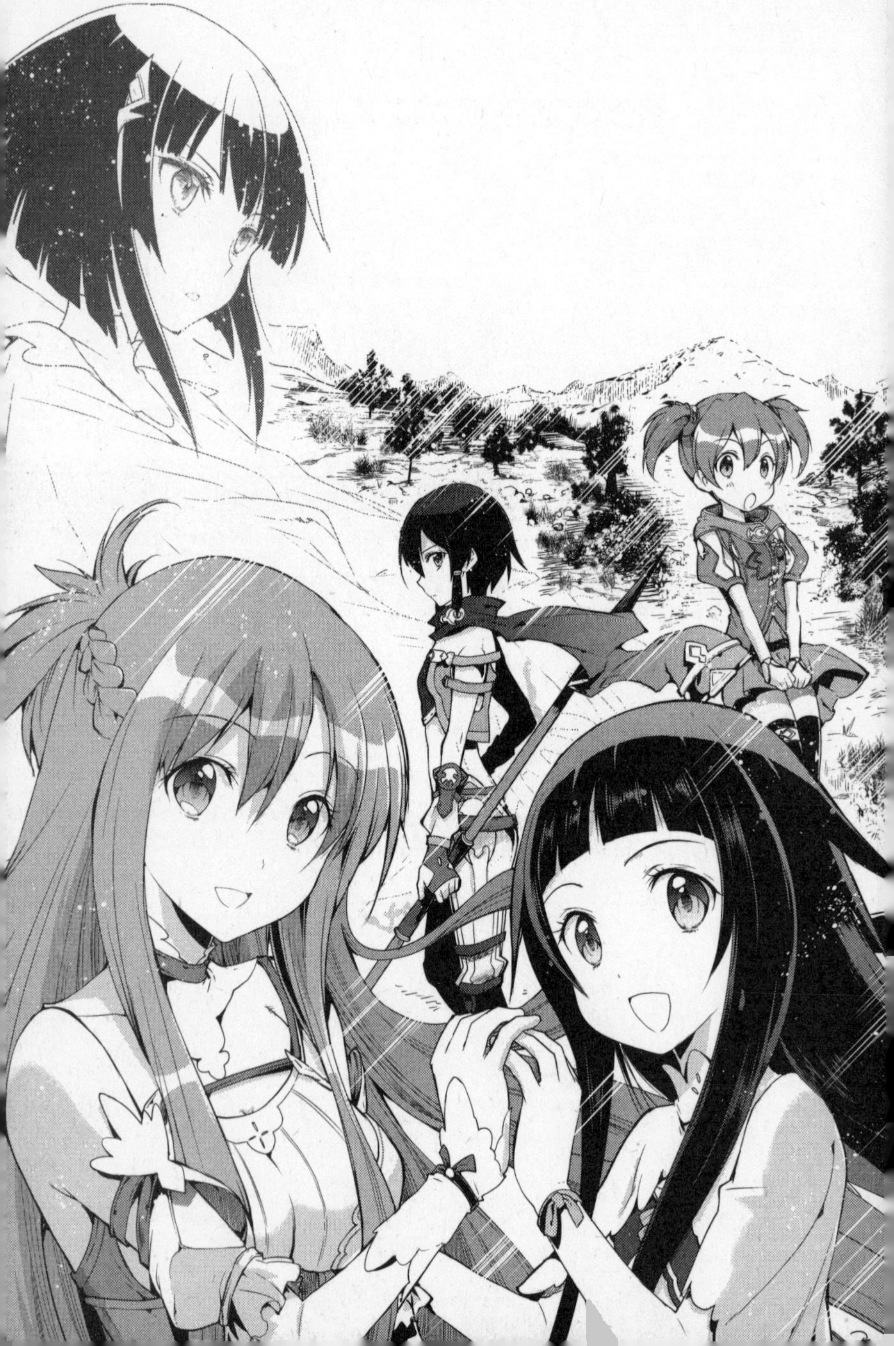

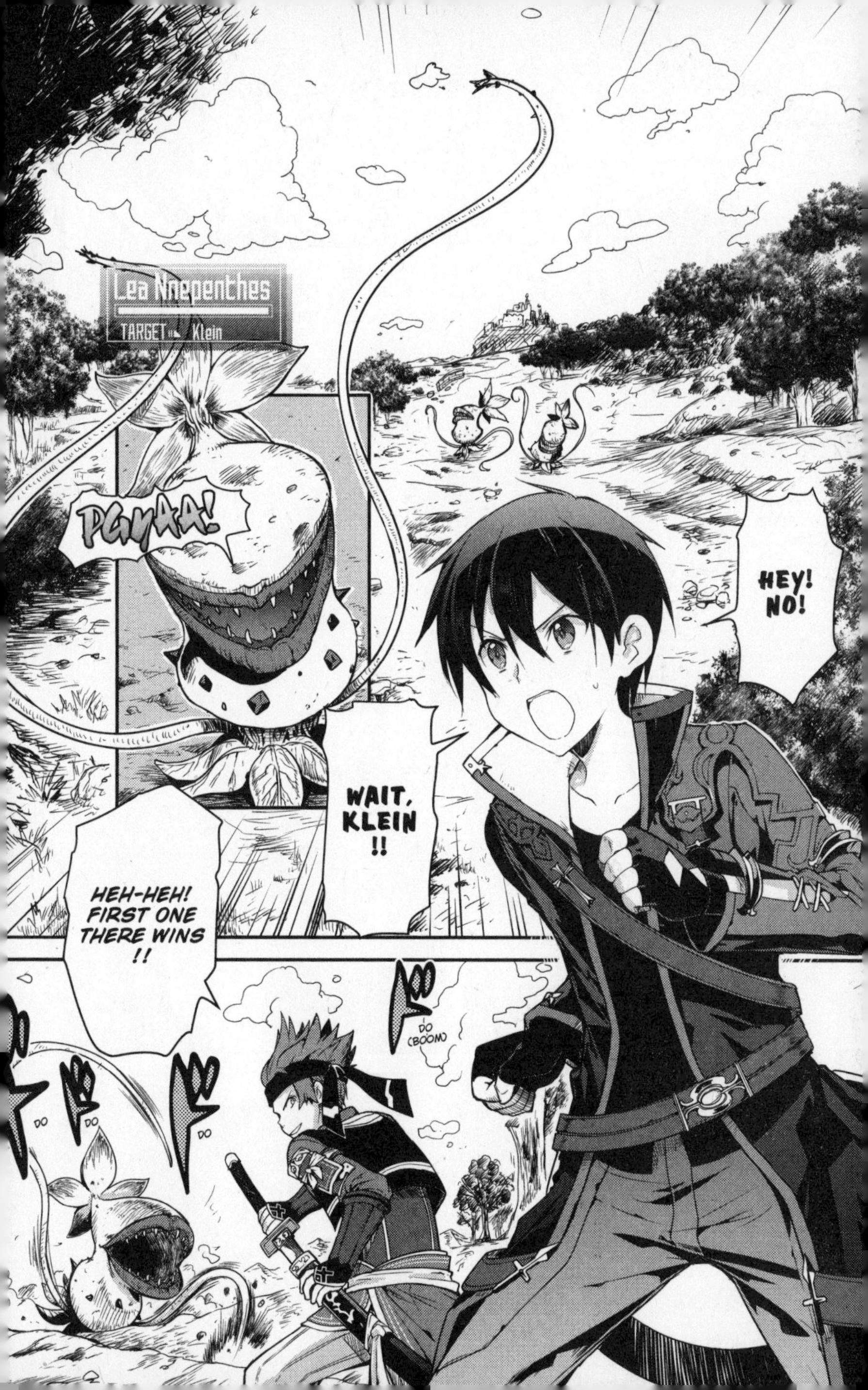
Lea Nnepenthes
TARGET Klein
PGYAA!
HEY! NO!
WAIT, KLEIN!!
HEH-HEH! FIRST ONE THERE WINS!!
DO (BOOM)
DO
DO
DO

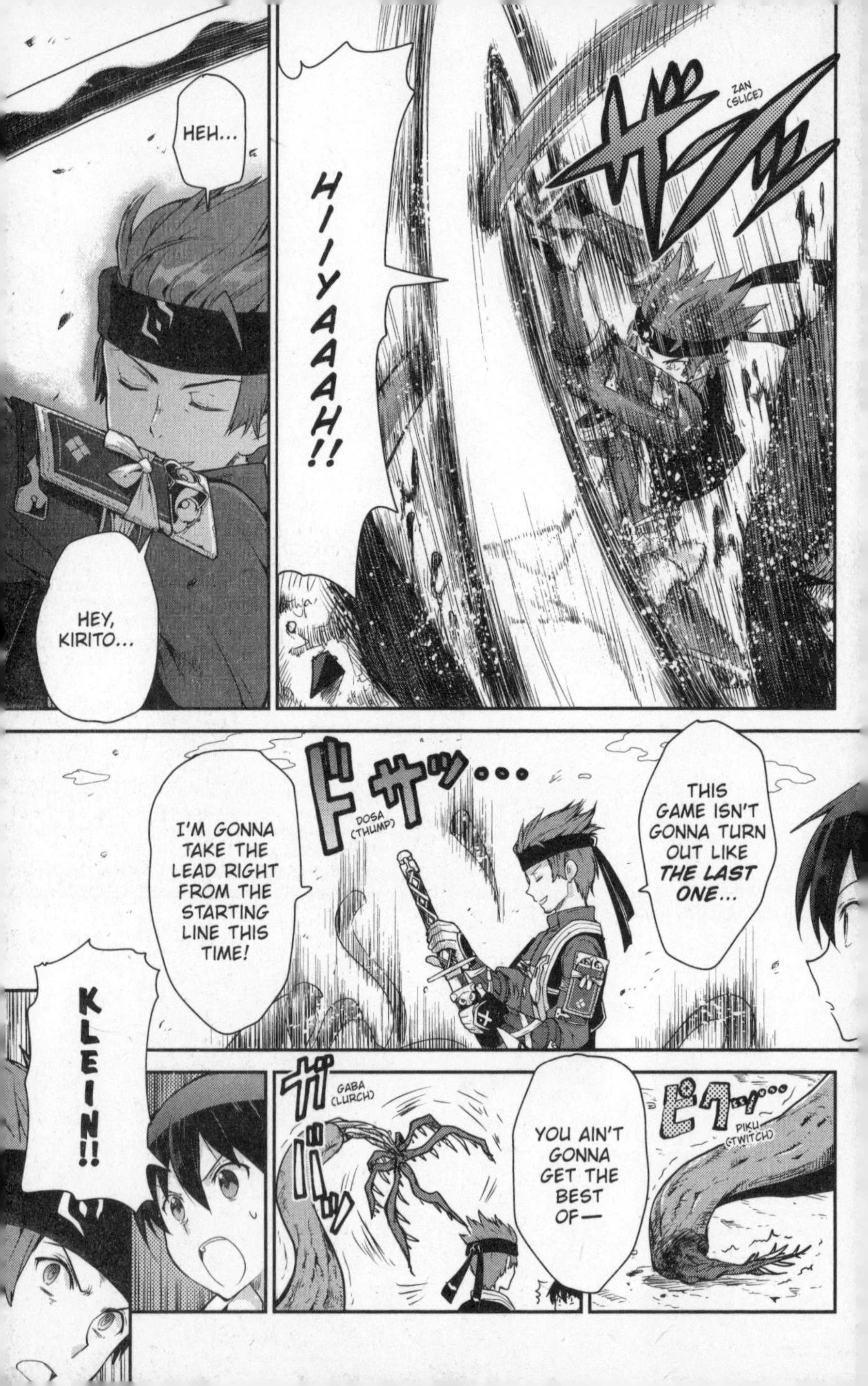
ZAN (SLICE)
HIIYAAAH!!
HEH...
HEY, KIRITO...
THIS GAME ISN'T GONNA TURN OUT LIKE *THE LAST ONE*...
DOSA (THUMP)
I'M GONNA TAKE THE LEAD RIGHT FROM THE STARTING LINE THIS TIME!
PIKU (TWITCH)
YOU AIN'T GONNA GET THE BEST OF—
GABA (LURCH)
KLEIN!!

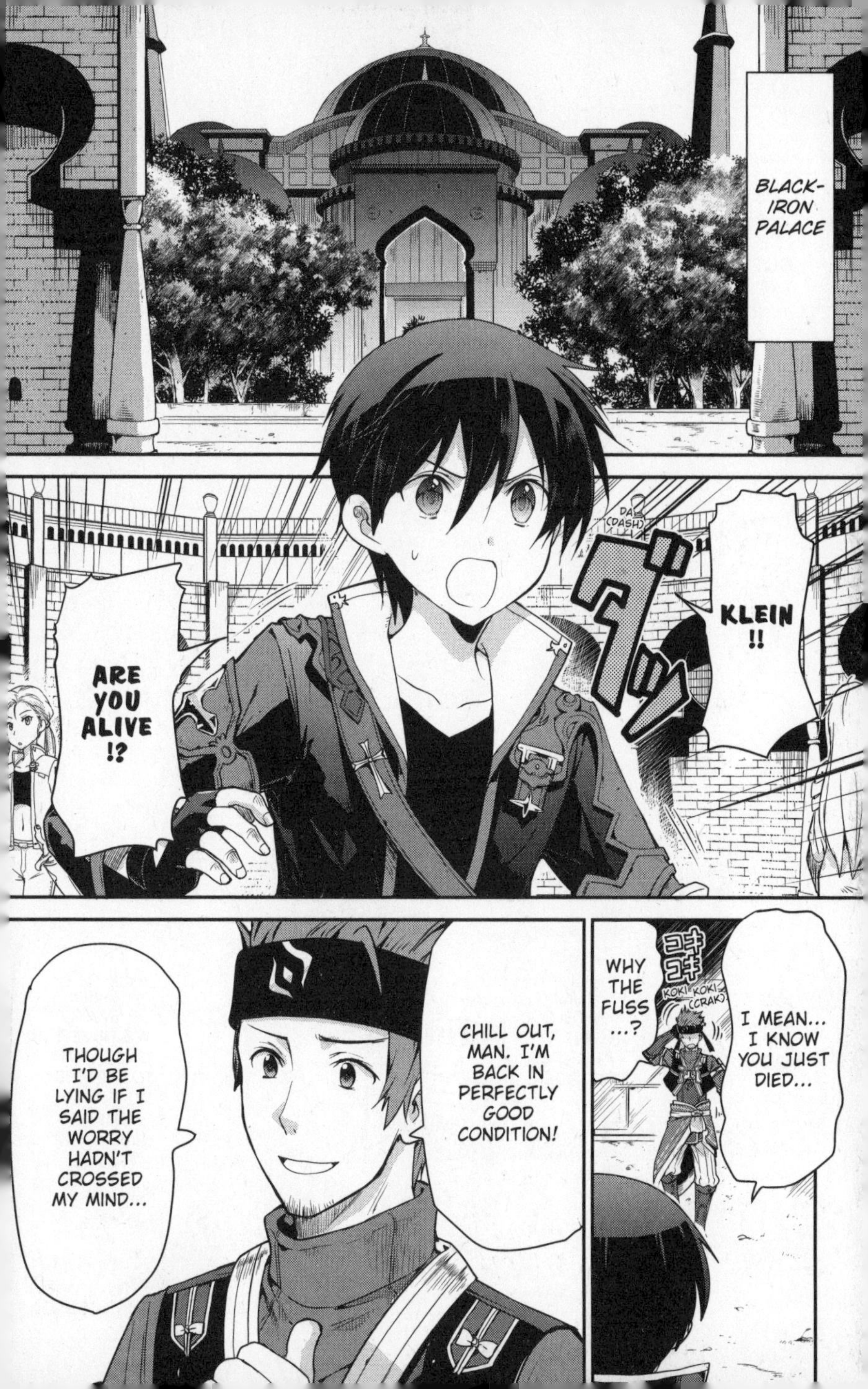
BLACK-IRON PALACE
KLEIN !!
DA (DASH)
ARE YOU ALIVE !?
I MEAN... I KNOW YOU JUST DIED...
WHY THE FUSS ...?
KOKI KOKI (CRAK)
CHILL OUT, MAN. I'M BACK IN PERFECTLY GOOD CONDITION!
THOUGH I'D BE LYING IF I SAID THE WORRY HADN'T CROSSED MY MIND...

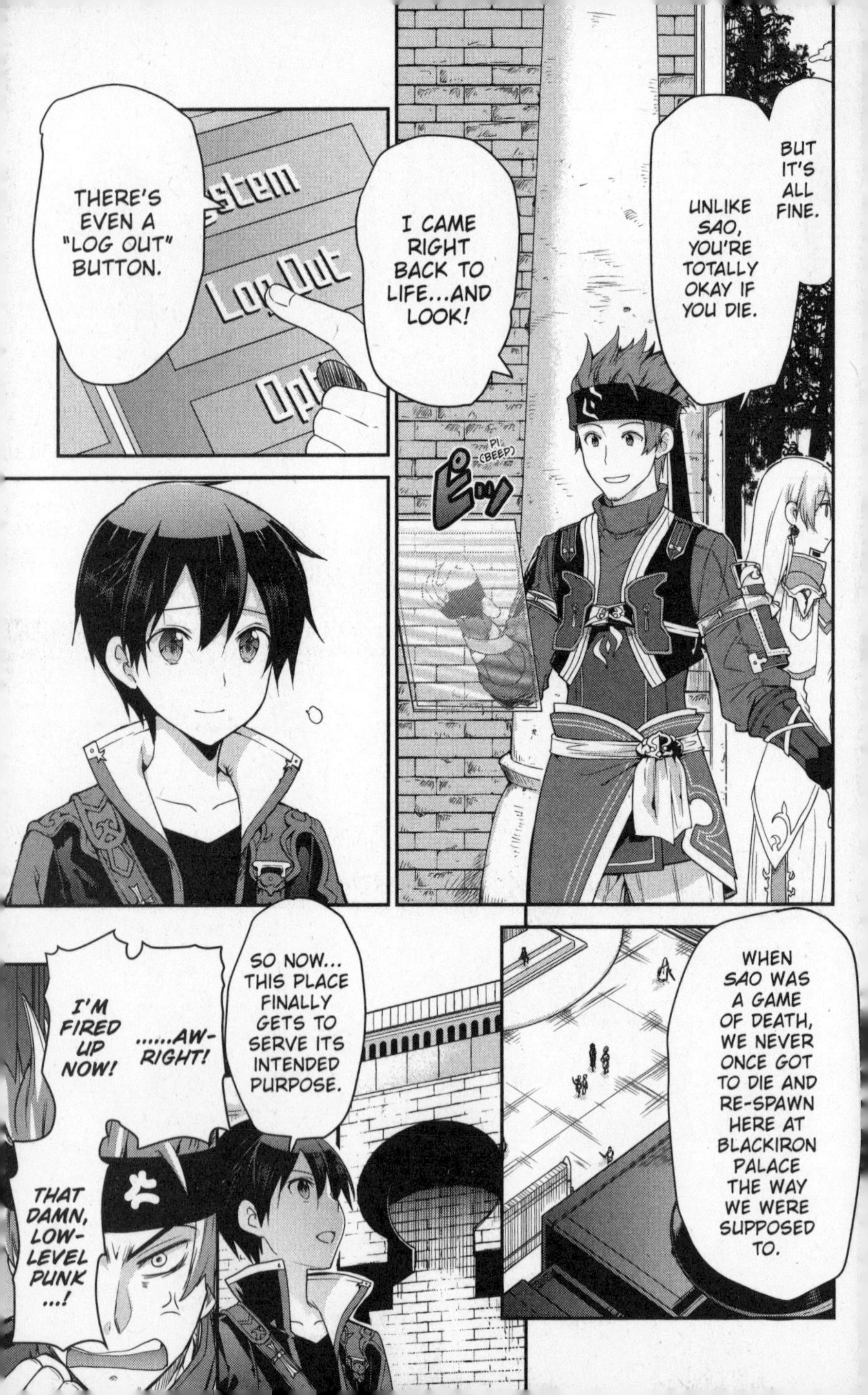
BUT IT'S ALL FINE.
UNLIKE SAO, YOU'RE TOTALLY OKAY IF YOU DIE.
I CAME RIGHT BACK TO LIFE...AND LOOK!
PI (BEEP)
THERE'S EVEN A "LOG OUT" BUTTON.
Log Out
WHEN SAO WAS A GAME OF DEATH, WE NEVER ONCE GOT TO DIE AND RE-SPAWN HERE AT BLACKIRON PALACE THE WAY WE WERE SUPPOSED TO.
SO NOW... THIS PLACE FINALLY GETS TO SERVE ITS INTENDED PURPOSE.
......AW-RIGHT!
I'M FIRED UP NOW!
THAT DAMN, LOW-LEVEL PUNK...!

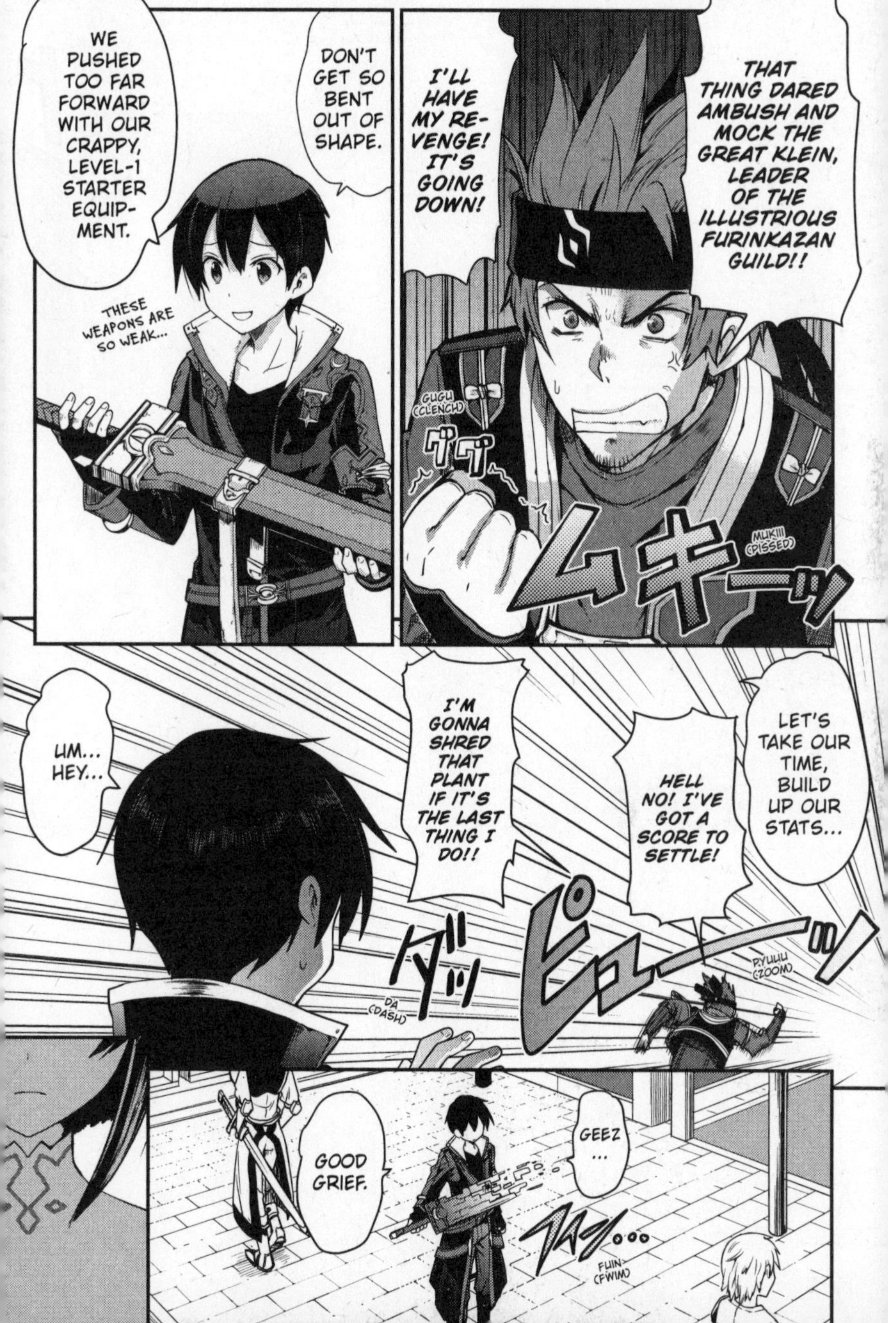
THAT THING DARED AMBUSH AND MOCK THE GREAT KLEIN, LEADER OF THE ILLUSTRIOUS FURINKAZAN GUILD!!
I'LL HAVE MY RE-VENGE! IT'S GOING DOWN!
GUGU (CLENCH)
MUKIII (PISSED)
DON'T GET SO BENT OUT OF SHAPE.
WE PUSHED TOO FAR FORWARD WITH OUR CRAPPY, LEVEL-1 STARTER EQUIPMENT.
THESE WEAPONS ARE SO WEAK...
LET'S TAKE OUR TIME, BUILD UP OUR STATS...
HELL NO! I'VE GOT A SCORE TO SETTLE!
I'M GONNA SHRED THAT PLANT IF IT'S THE LAST THING I DO!!
PYUUU (ZOOM)
DA (DASH)
UM... HEY...
GEEZ...
GOOD GRIEF.
FUIN (FWIM)

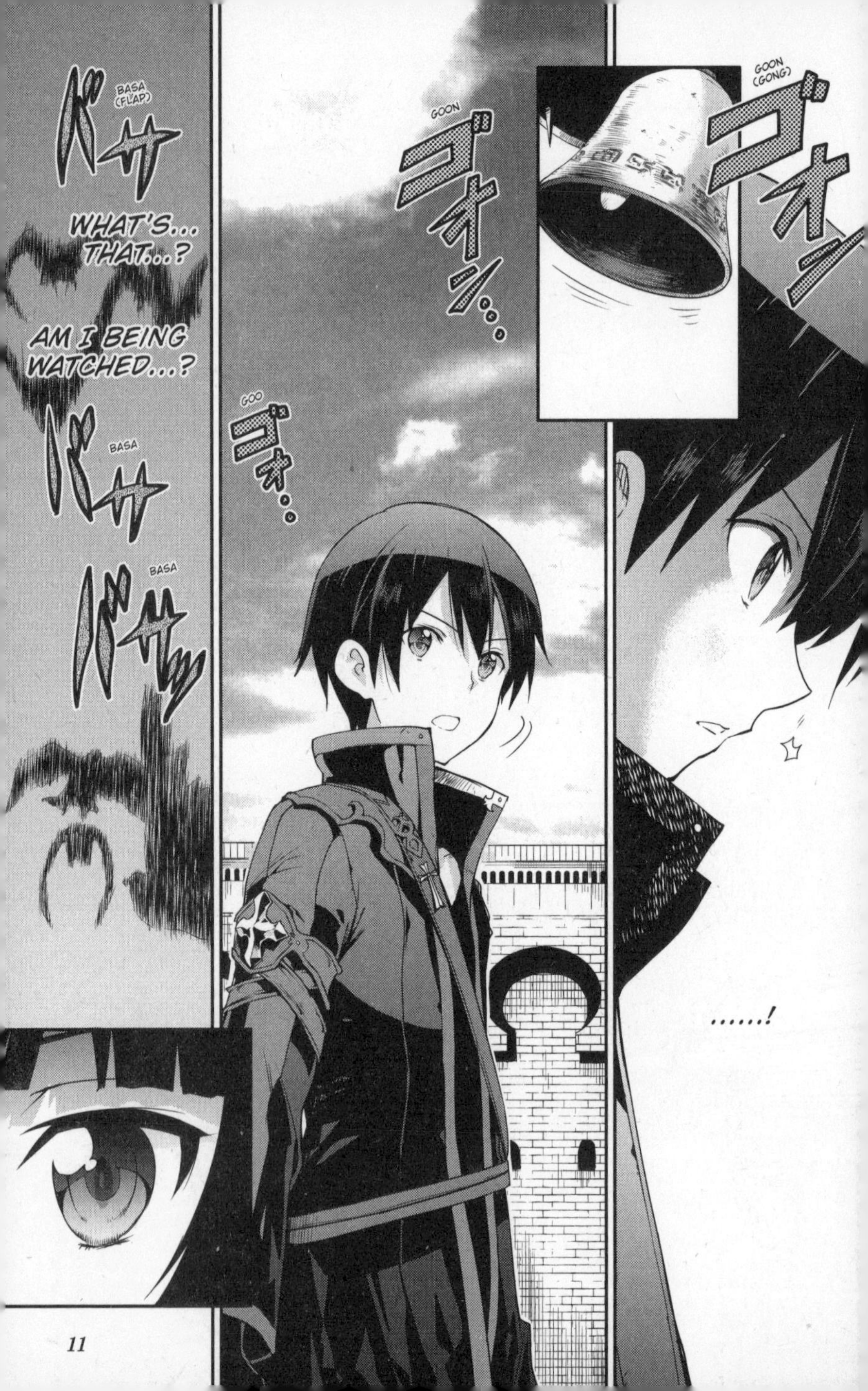
GOON (GONG)
ゴォン
......!
GOON
ゴォン...
GOO
ゴォ..
BASA (FLAP)
バサ
WHAT'S... THAT...?
AM I BEING WATCHED...?
BASA
バサ
BASA
バサッ

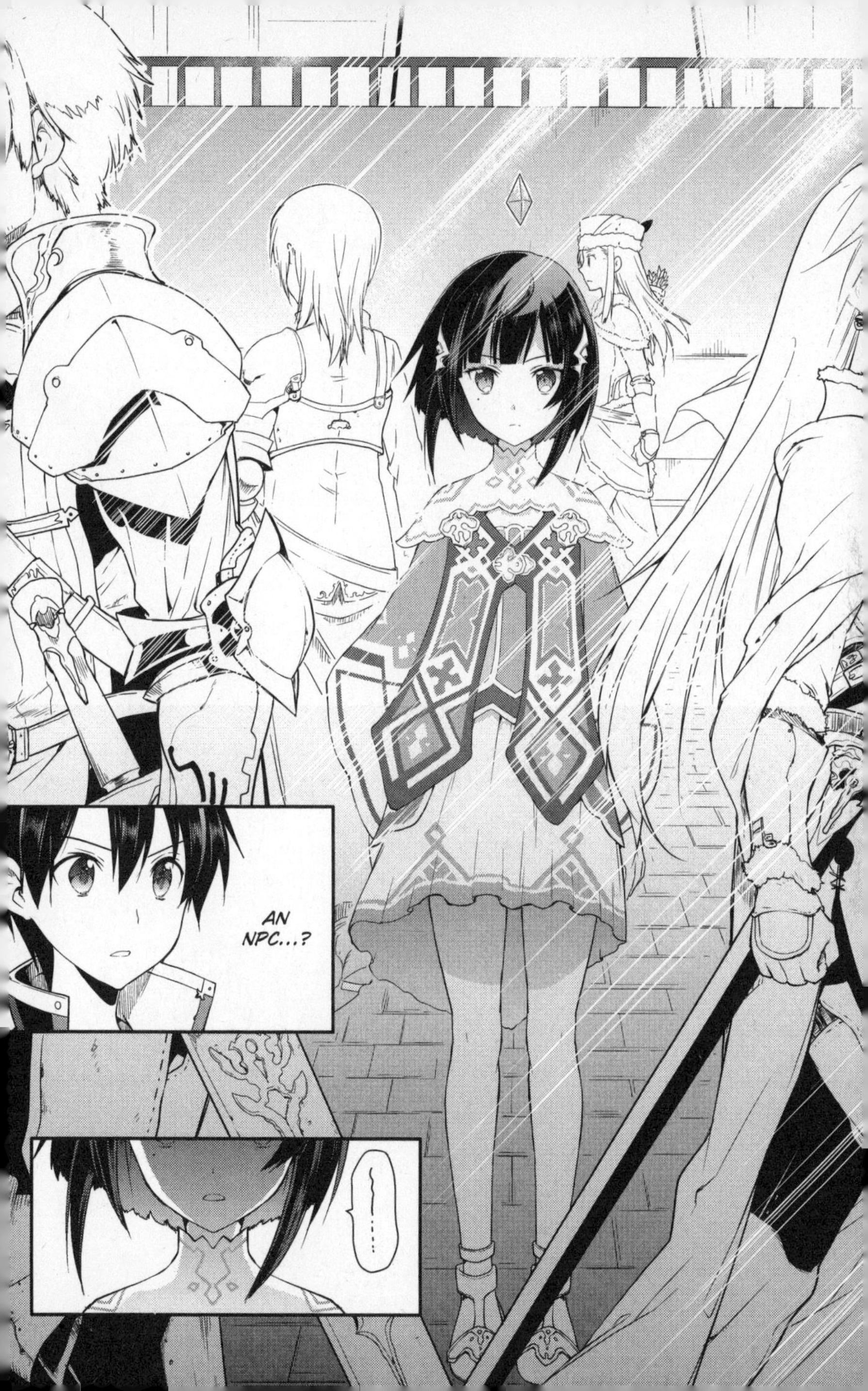
AN NPC...?
......!

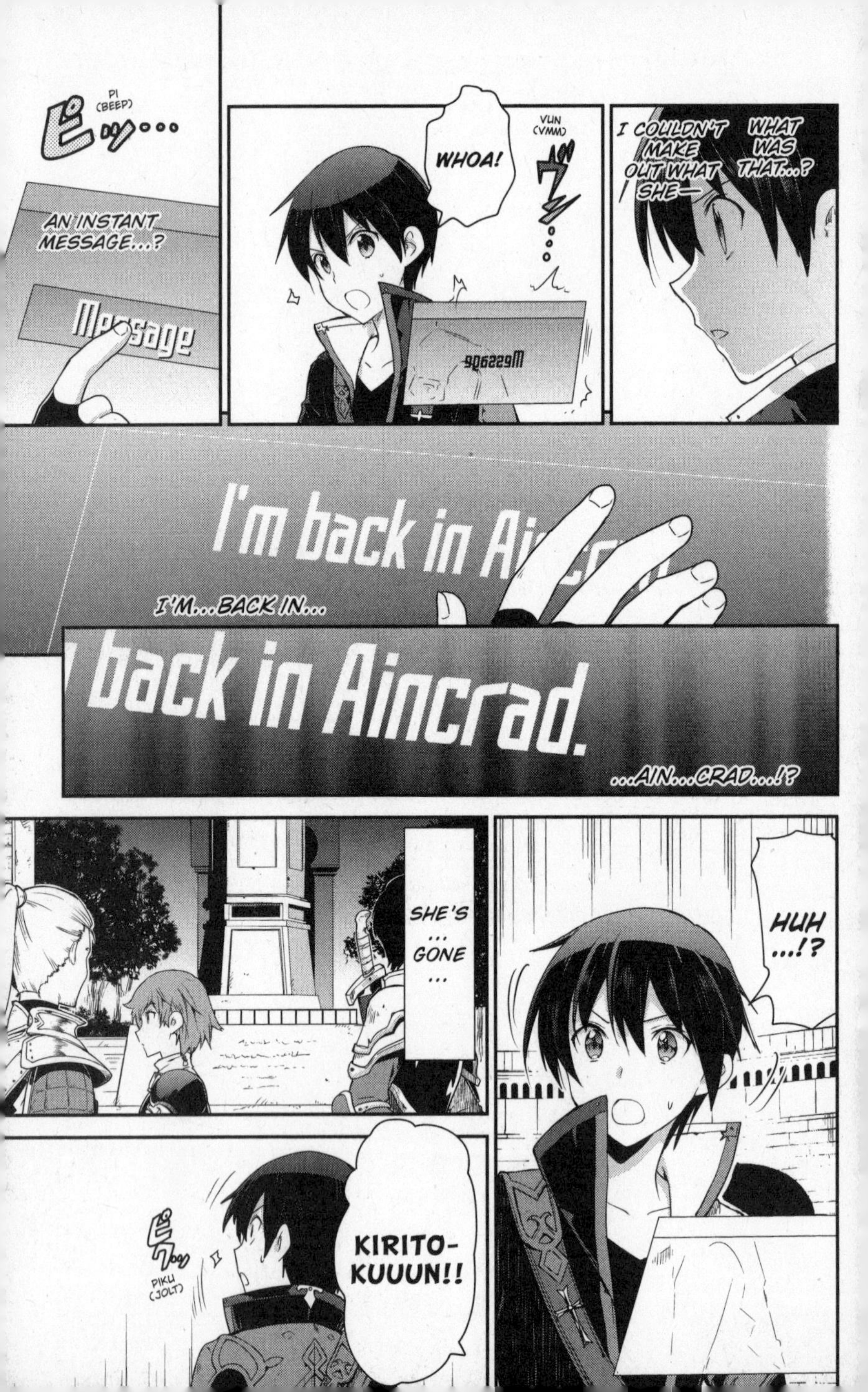
WHAT WAS THAT...?
I COULDN'T MAKE OUT WHAT SHE—
VUN (VMM)
WHOA!
PI (BEEP)
AN INSTANT MESSAGE...?
Message
I'm back in Ai
I'M...BACK IN...
back in Aincrad.
...AIN...CRAD...!?
HUH...!?
SHE'S... GONE...
KIRITO-KUUUN!!
PIKU (JOLT)

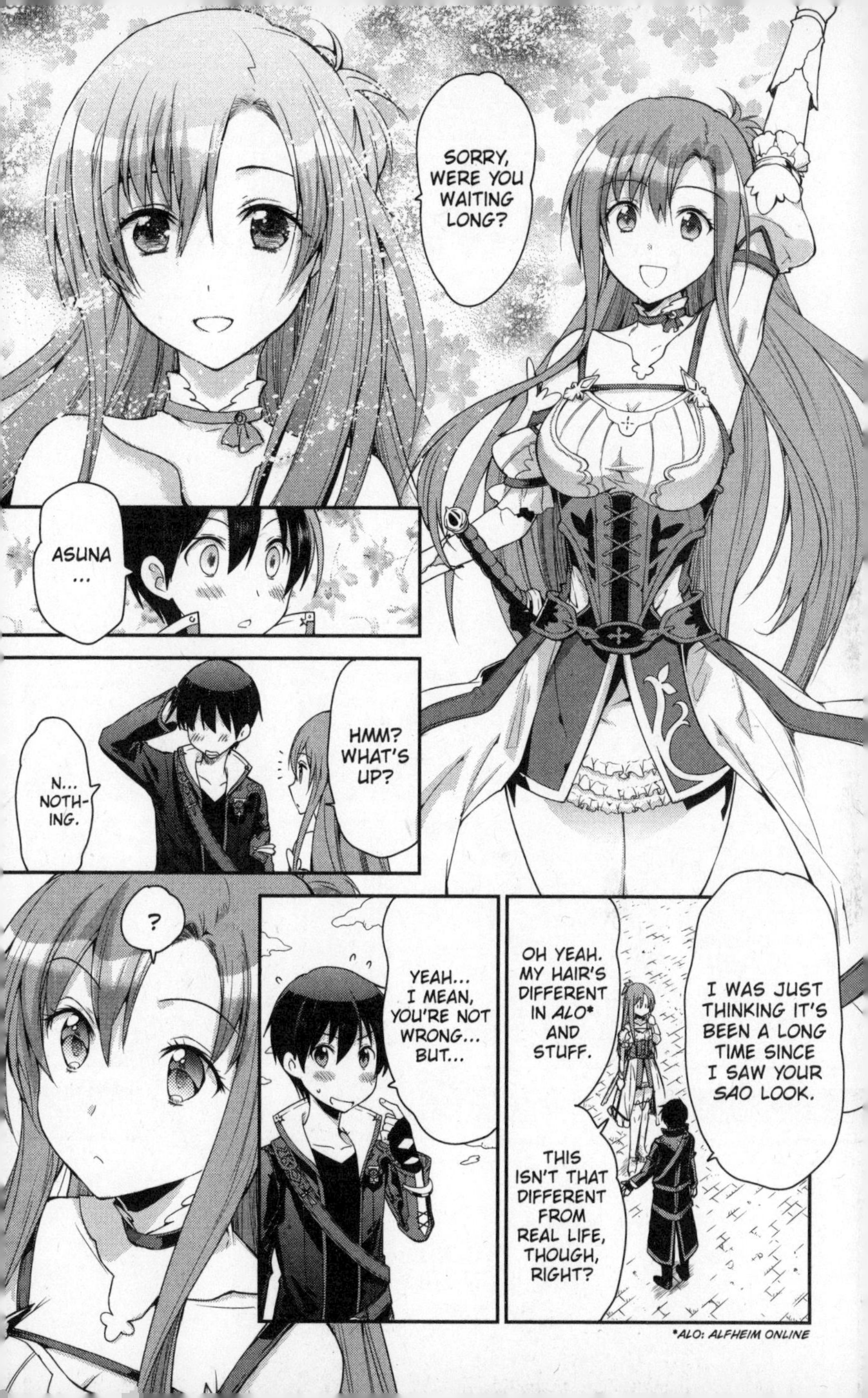
SORRY, WERE YOU WAITING LONG?
ASUNA ...
HMM? WHAT'S UP?
N... NOTHING.
I WAS JUST THINKING IT'S BEEN A LONG TIME SINCE I SAW YOUR SAO LOOK.
OH YEAH. MY HAIR'S DIFFERENT IN *ALO** AND STUFF.
THIS ISN'T THAT DIFFERENT FROM REAL LIFE, THOUGH, RIGHT?
YEAH... I MEAN, YOU'RE NOT WRONG... BUT...
?

**ALO: ALFHEIM ONLINE*

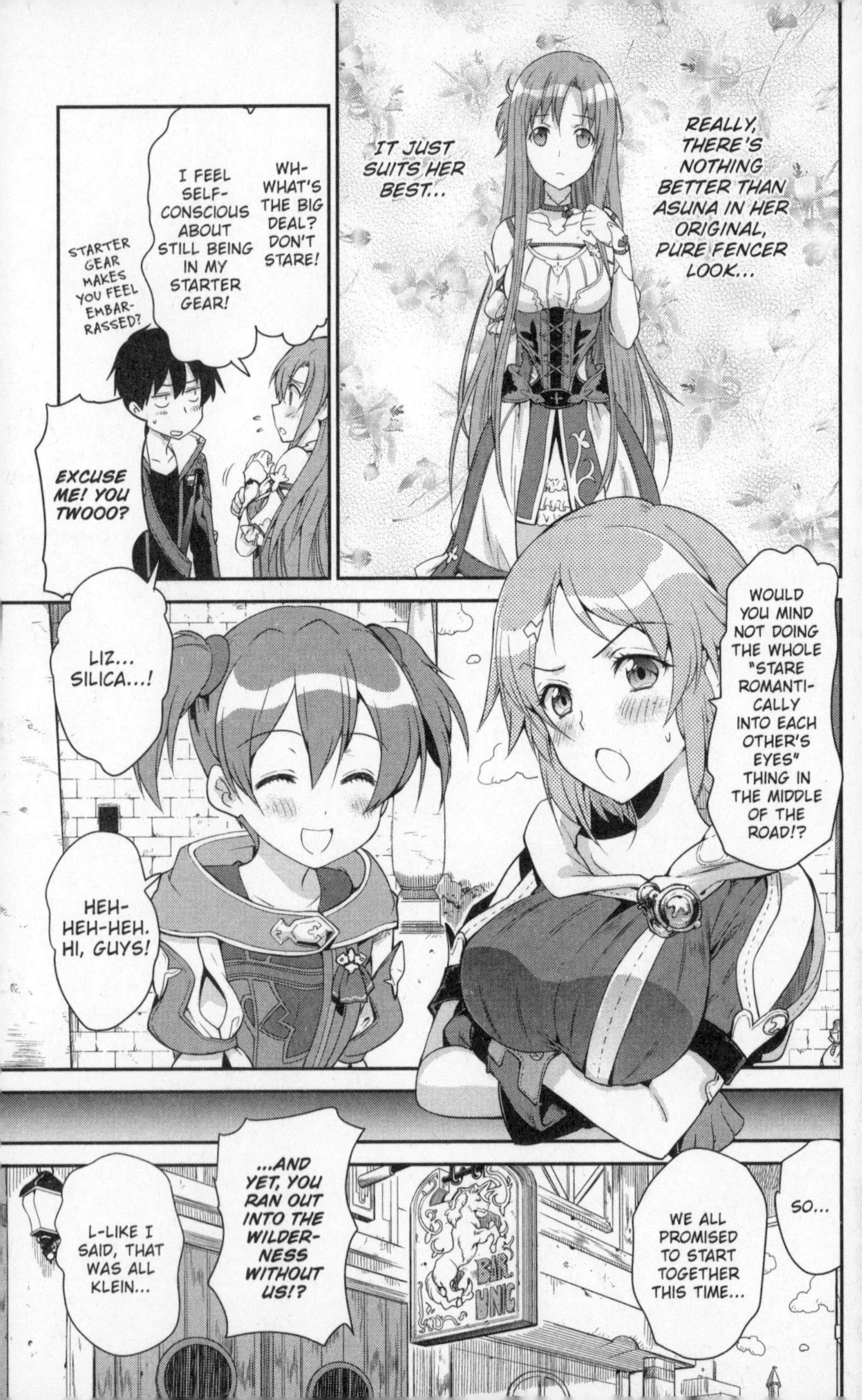
REALLY, THERE'S NOTHING BETTER THAN ASUNA IN HER ORIGINAL, PURE FENCER LOOK...
IT JUST SUITS HER BEST...
WH- WHAT'S THE BIG DEAL? DON'T STARE!
I FEEL SELF-CONSCIOUS ABOUT STILL BEING IN MY STARTER GEAR!
STARTER GEAR MAKES YOU FEEL EMBARRASSED?
EXCUSE ME! YOU TWOOO?
WOULD YOU MIND NOT DOING THE WHOLE "STARE ROMANTICALLY INTO EACH OTHER'S EYES" THING IN THE MIDDLE OF THE ROAD!?
LIZ... SILICA...!
HEH-HEH-HEH. HI, GUYS!
SO...
WE ALL PROMISED TO START TOGETHER THIS TIME...
...AND YET, YOU RAN OUT INTO THE WILDERNESS WITHOUT US!?
L-LIKE I SAID, THAT WAS ALL KLEIN...

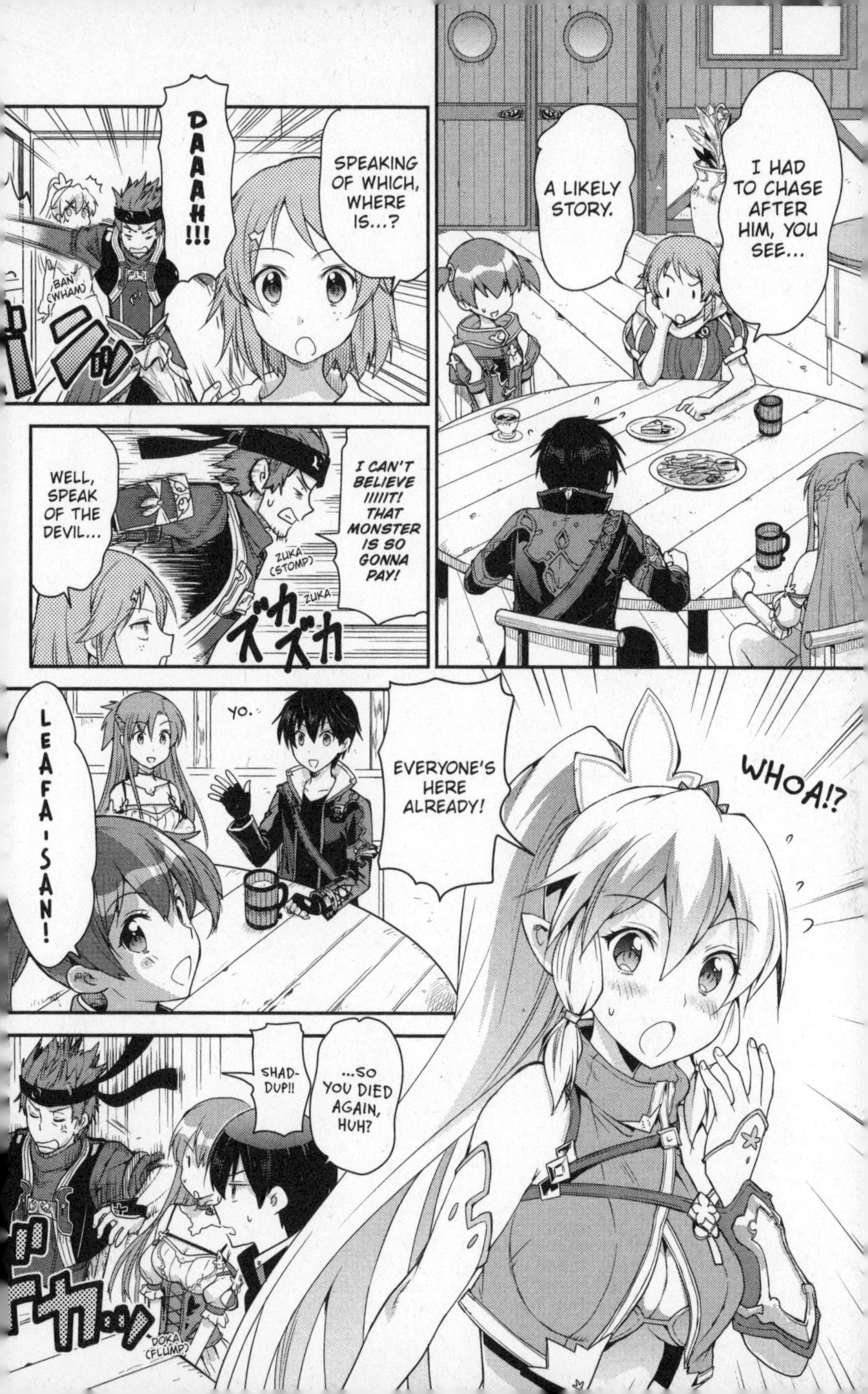
I HAD TO CHASE AFTER HIM, YOU SEE...
A LIKELY STORY.
SPEAKING OF WHICH, WHERE IS...?
DAAAAH!!!
BAN (WHAM)
I CAN'T BELIEVE IIIIIIT! THAT MONSTER IS SO GONNA PAY!
WELL, SPEAK OF THE DEVIL...
ZUKA (STOMP)
ZUKA
ズカズカ
WHOA!?
EVERYONE'S HERE ALREADY!
YO.
LEAFA-SAN!
...SO YOU DIED AGAIN, HUH?
SHAD-DUP!!
DOKA (FLUMP)

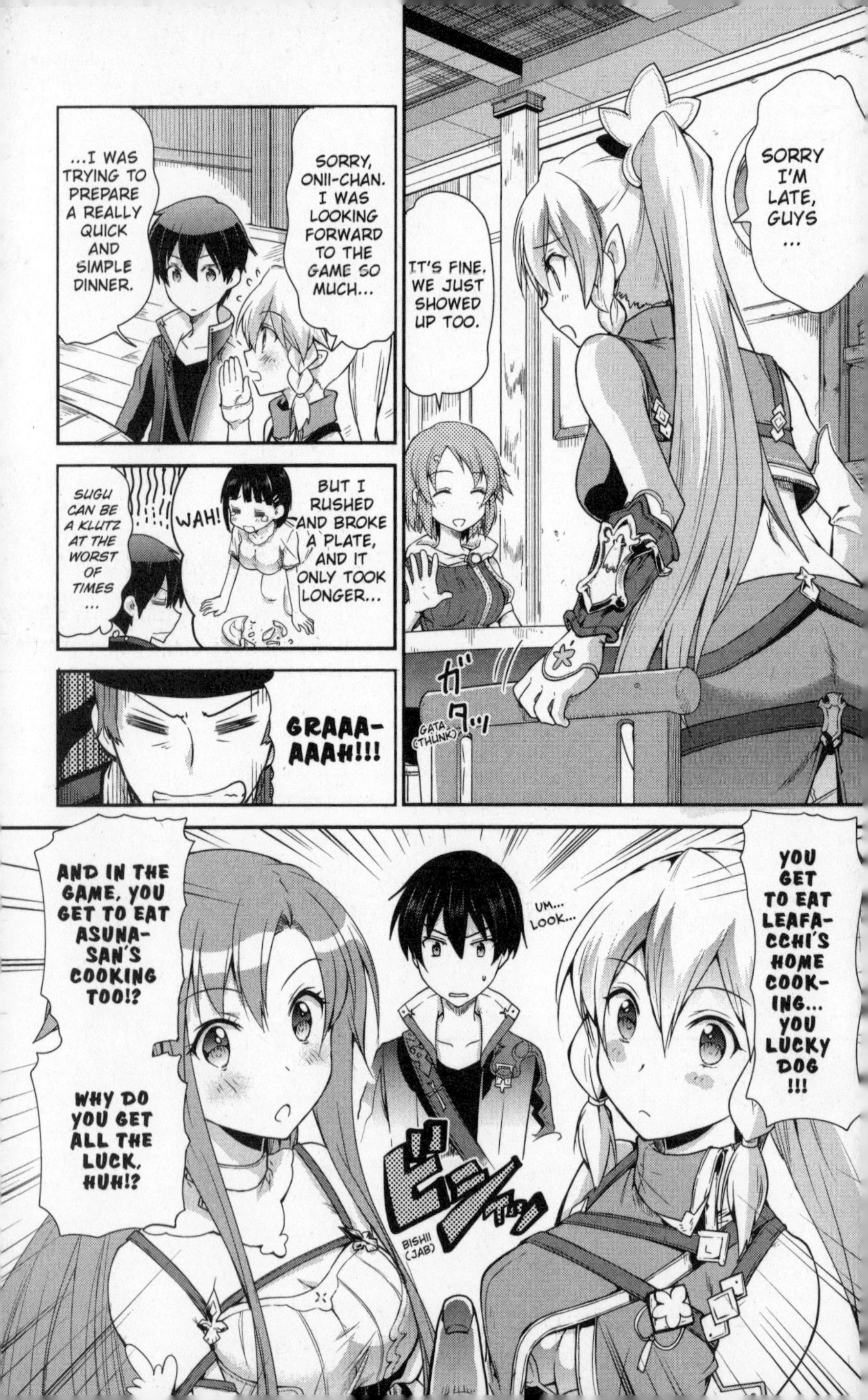
SORRY I'M LATE, GUYS ...
IT'S FINE. WE JUST SHOWED UP TOO.
ガタッ
GATA (THUNK)
SORRY, ONII-CHAN. I WAS LOOKING FORWARD TO THE GAME SO MUCH...
...I WAS TRYING TO PREPARE A REALLY QUICK AND SIMPLE DINNER.
BUT I RUSHED AND BROKE A PLATE, AND IT ONLY TOOK LONGER...
WAH!
SUGU CAN BE A KLUTZ AT THE WORST OF TIMES ...
GRAAAAAAH!!!
YOU GET TO EAT LEAFACCHI'S HOME COOKING... YOU LUCKY DOG!!!
UM... LOOK...
AND IN THE GAME, YOU GET TO EAT ASUNA-SAN'S COOKING TOO!?
WHY DO YOU GET ALL THE LUCK, HUH!?
BISHII (JAB)

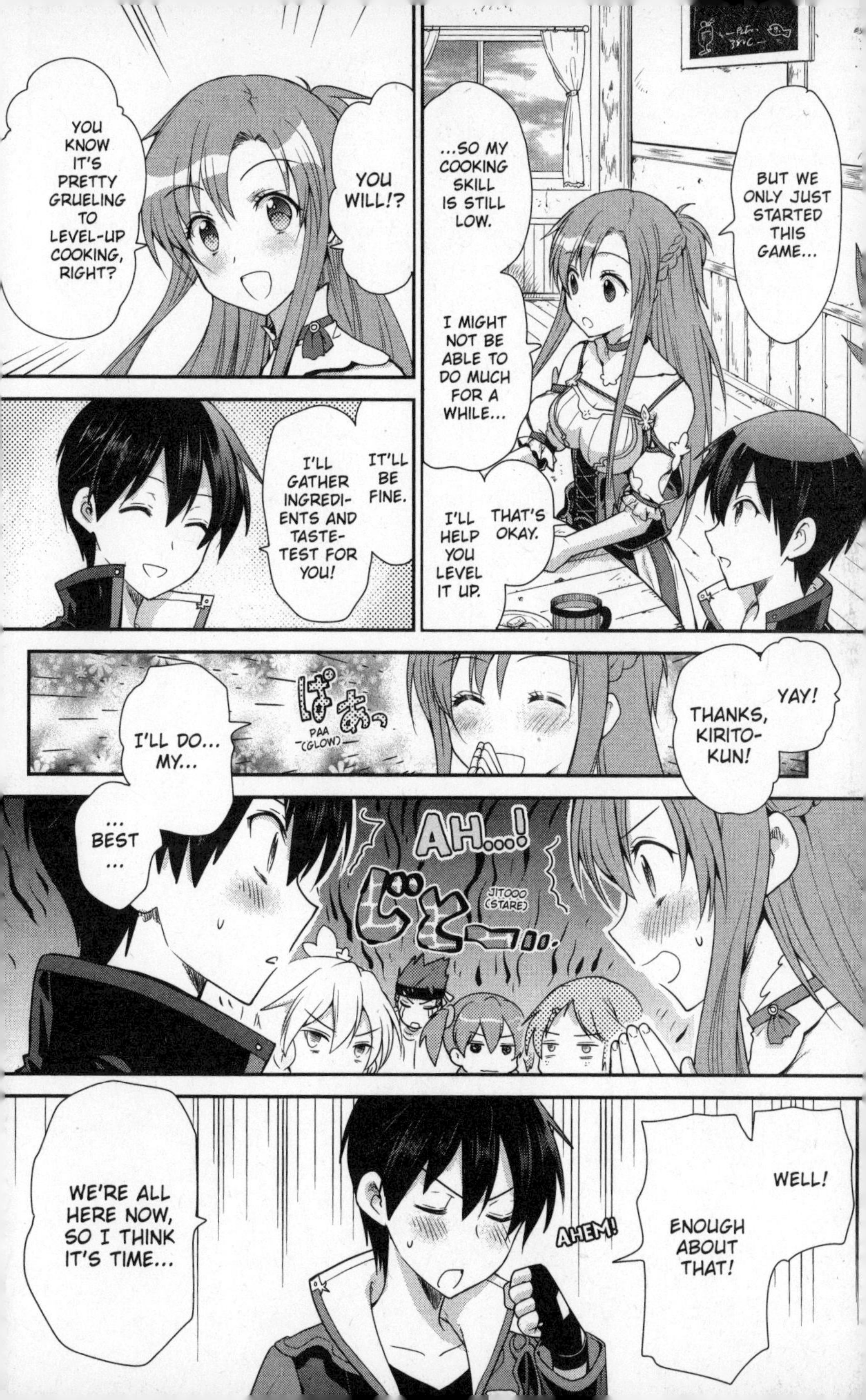
BUT WE ONLY JUST STARTED THIS GAME...
...SO MY COOKING SKILL IS STILL LOW.
I MIGHT NOT BE ABLE TO DO MUCH FOR A WHILE...
THAT'S OKAY.
I'LL HELP YOU LEVEL IT UP.
YOU WILL!?
YOU KNOW IT'S PRETTY GRUELING TO LEVEL-UP COOKING, RIGHT?
IT'LL BE FINE.
I'LL GATHER INGREDIENTS AND TASTE-TEST FOR YOU!
YAY!
THANKS, KIRITO-KUN!
ぱあっ
PAA (GLOW)
I'LL DO... MY...
... BEST ...
AH...!
じとーっ..
JITOOO (STARE)
WELL!
ENOUGH ABOUT THAT!
AHEM!
WE'RE ALL HERE NOW, SO I THINK IT'S TIME...

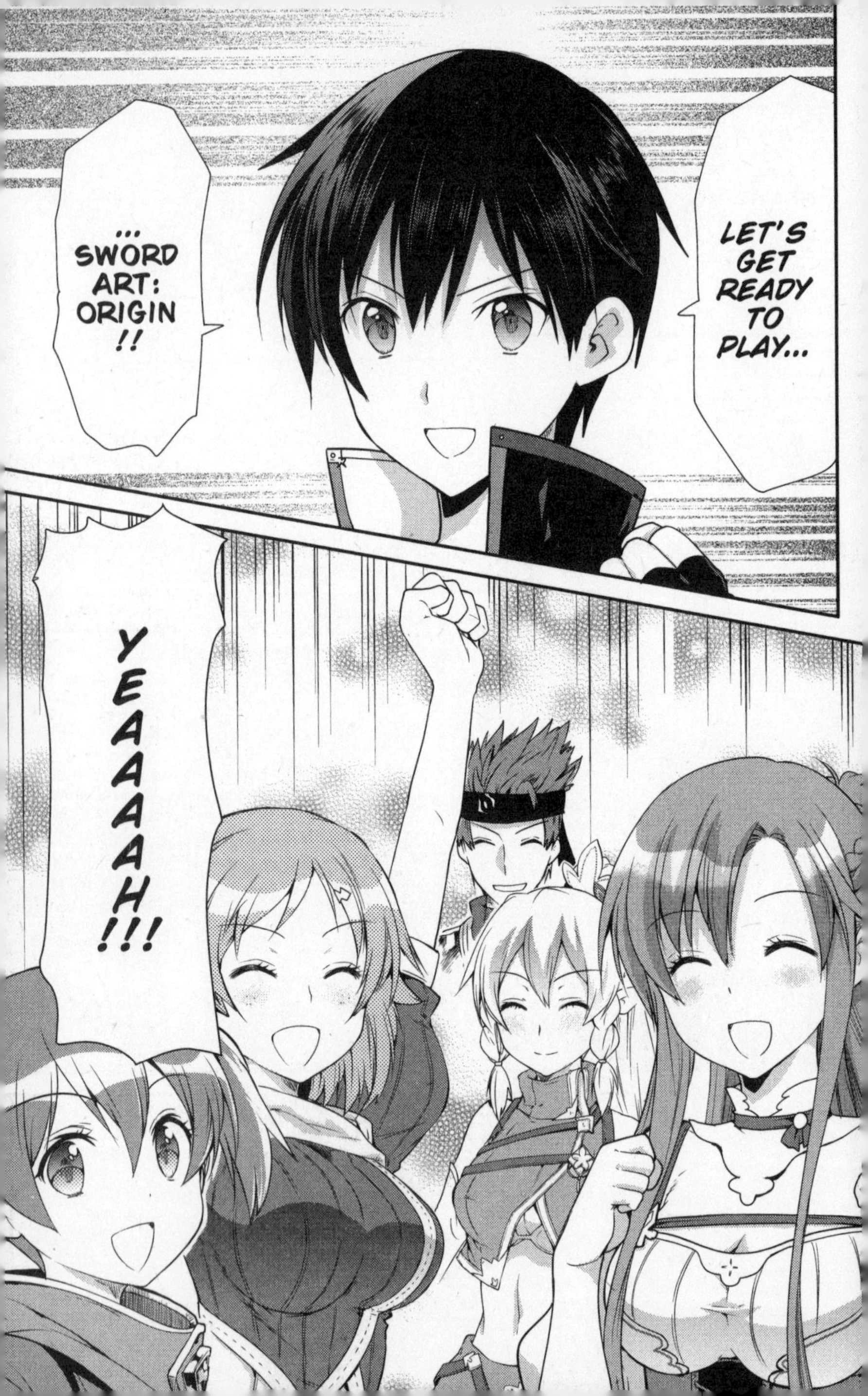
LET'S GET READY TO PLAY...
...SWORD ART: ORIGIN!!
YEAAAAAH!!!

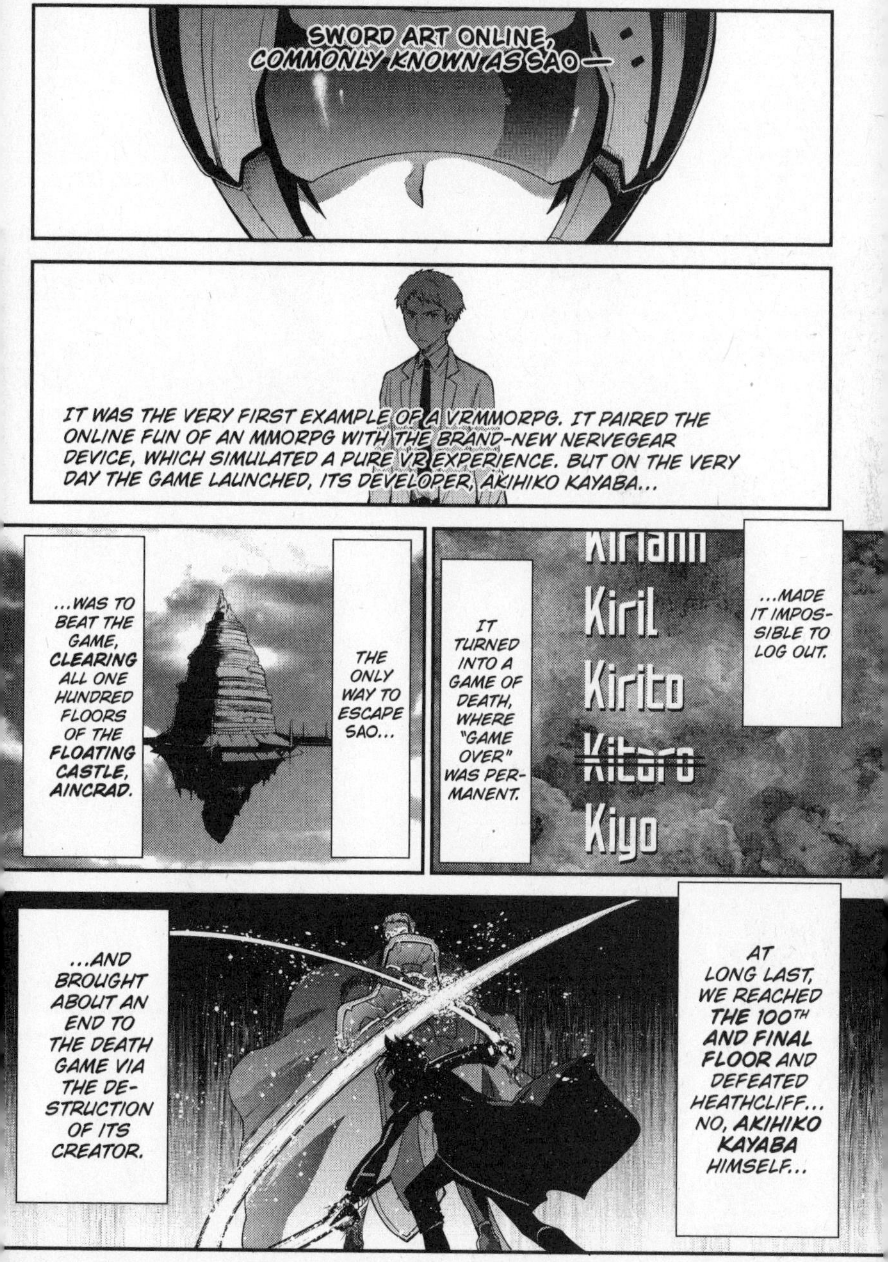
SWORD ART ONLINE, COMMONLY KNOWN AS SAO—
IT WAS THE VERY FIRST EXAMPLE OF A VRMMORPG. IT PAIRED THE ONLINE FUN OF AN MMORPG WITH THE BRAND-NEW NERVEGEAR DEVICE, WHICH SIMULATED A PURE VR EXPERIENCE. BUT ON THE VERY DAY THE GAME LAUNCHED, ITS DEVELOPER, AKIHIKO KAYABA...
...MADE IT IMPOSSIBLE TO LOG OUT.
Kiril
Kirito
Kitaro
Kiyo
IT TURNED INTO A GAME OF DEATH, WHERE "GAME OVER" WAS PERMANENT.
THE ONLY WAY TO ESCAPE SAO...
...WAS TO BEAT THE GAME, CLEARING ALL ONE HUNDRED FLOORS OF THE FLOATING CASTLE, AINCRAD.
AT LONG LAST, WE REACHED THE 100TH AND FINAL FLOOR AND DEFEATED HEATHCLIFF... NO, AKIHIKO KAYABA HIMSELF...
...AND BROUGHT ABOUT AN END TO THE DEATH GAME VIA THE DESTRUCTION OF ITS CREATOR.

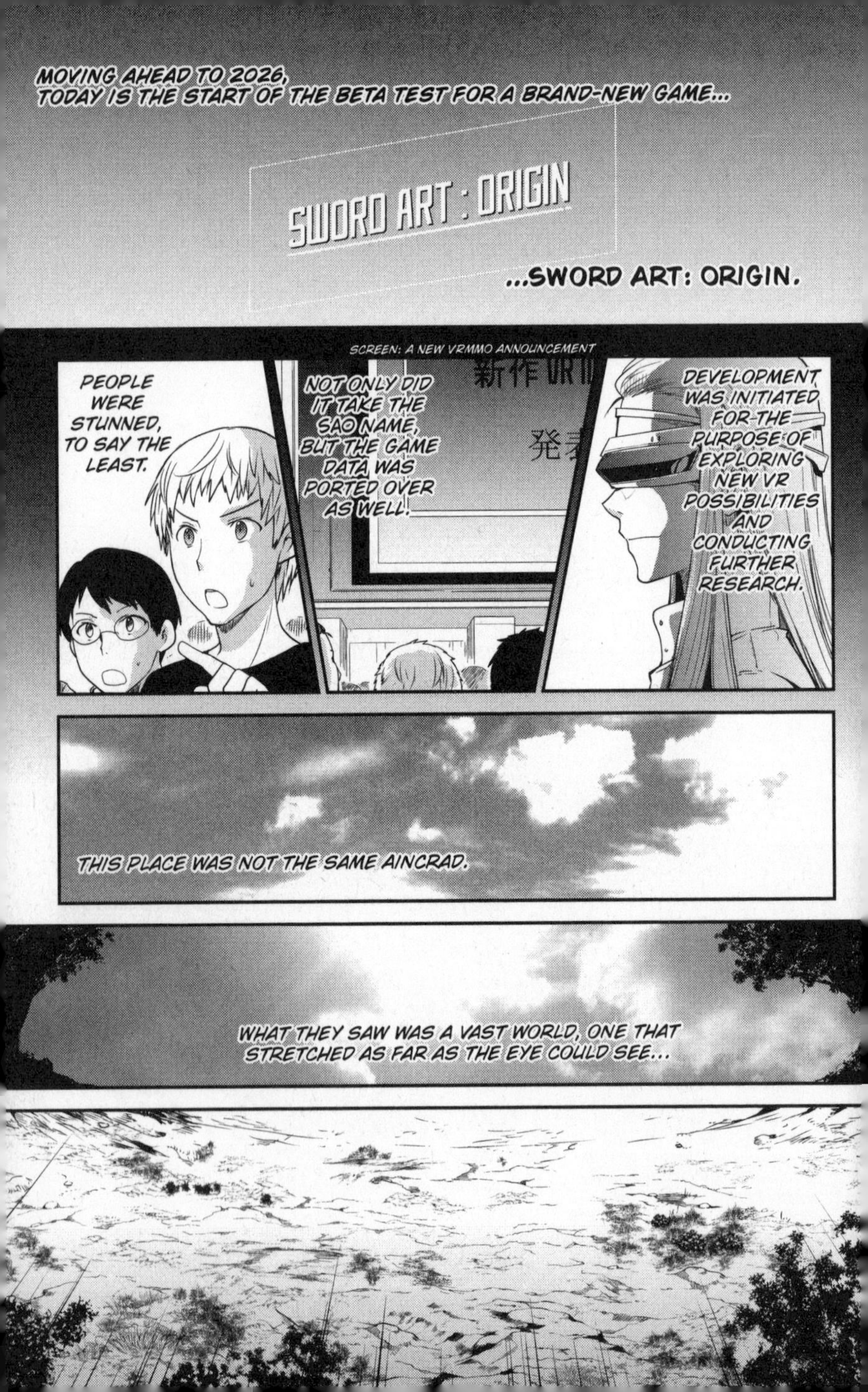
MOVING AHEAD TO 2026,
TODAY IS THE START OF THE BETA TEST FOR A BRAND-NEW GAME...
SWORD ART : ORIGIN
...SWORD ART: ORIGIN.
SCREEN: A NEW VRMMO ANNOUNCEMENT
DEVELOPMENT WAS INITIATED FOR THE PURPOSE OF EXPLORING NEW VR POSSIBILITIES AND CONDUCTING FURTHER RESEARCH.
NOT ONLY DID IT TAKE THE SAO NAME, BUT THE GAME DATA WAS PORTED OVER AS WELL.
PEOPLE WERE STUNNED, TO SAY THE LEAST.
THIS PLACE WAS NOT THE SAME AINCRAD.
WHAT THEY SAW WAS A VAST WORLD, ONE THAT STRETCHED AS FAR AS THE EYE COULD SEE...

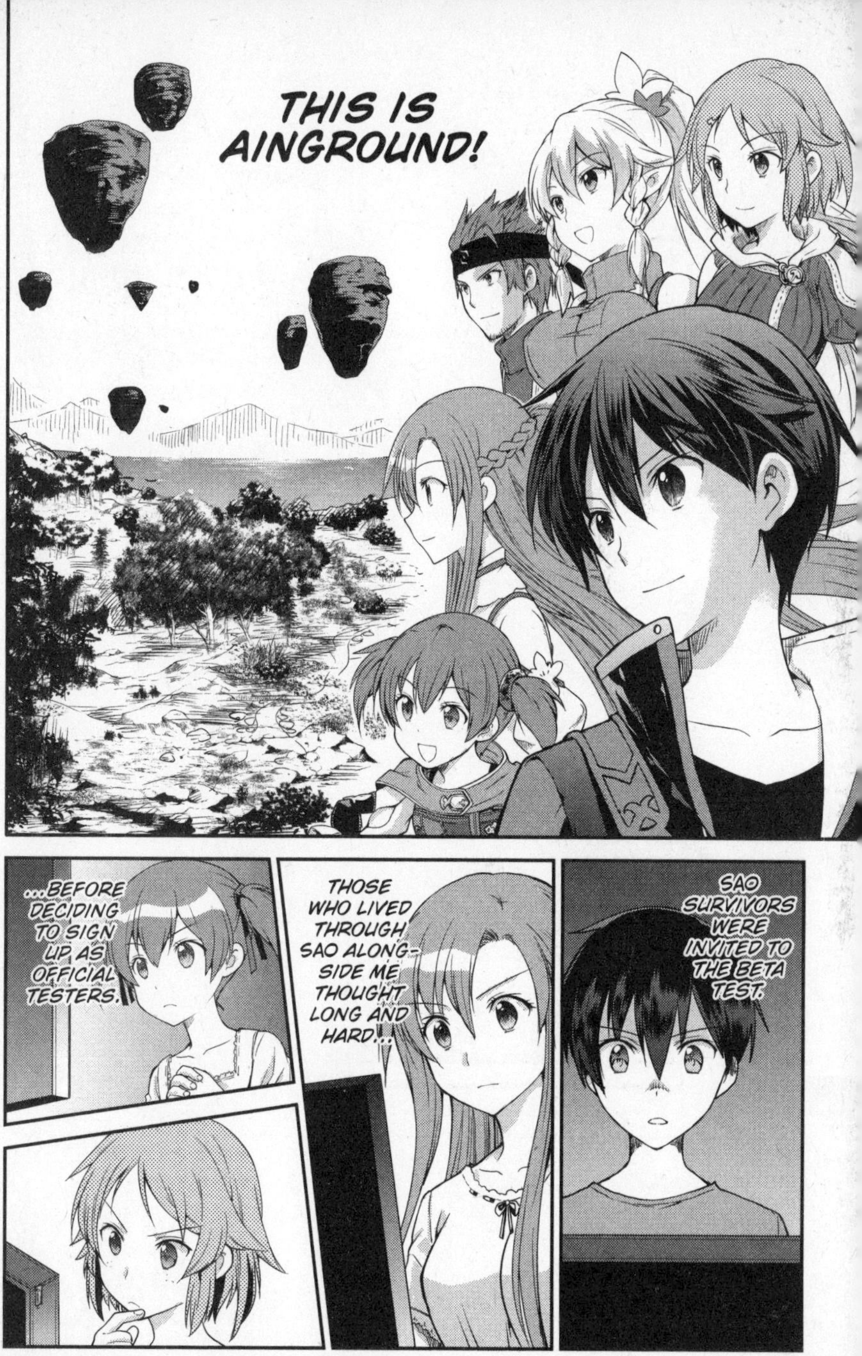
THIS IS AINGROUND!
SAO SURVIVORS WERE INVITED TO THE BETA TEST.
THOSE WHO LIVED THROUGH SAO ALONGSIDE ME THOUGHT LONG AND HARD...
...BEFORE DECIDING TO SIGN UP AS OFFICIAL TESTERS.

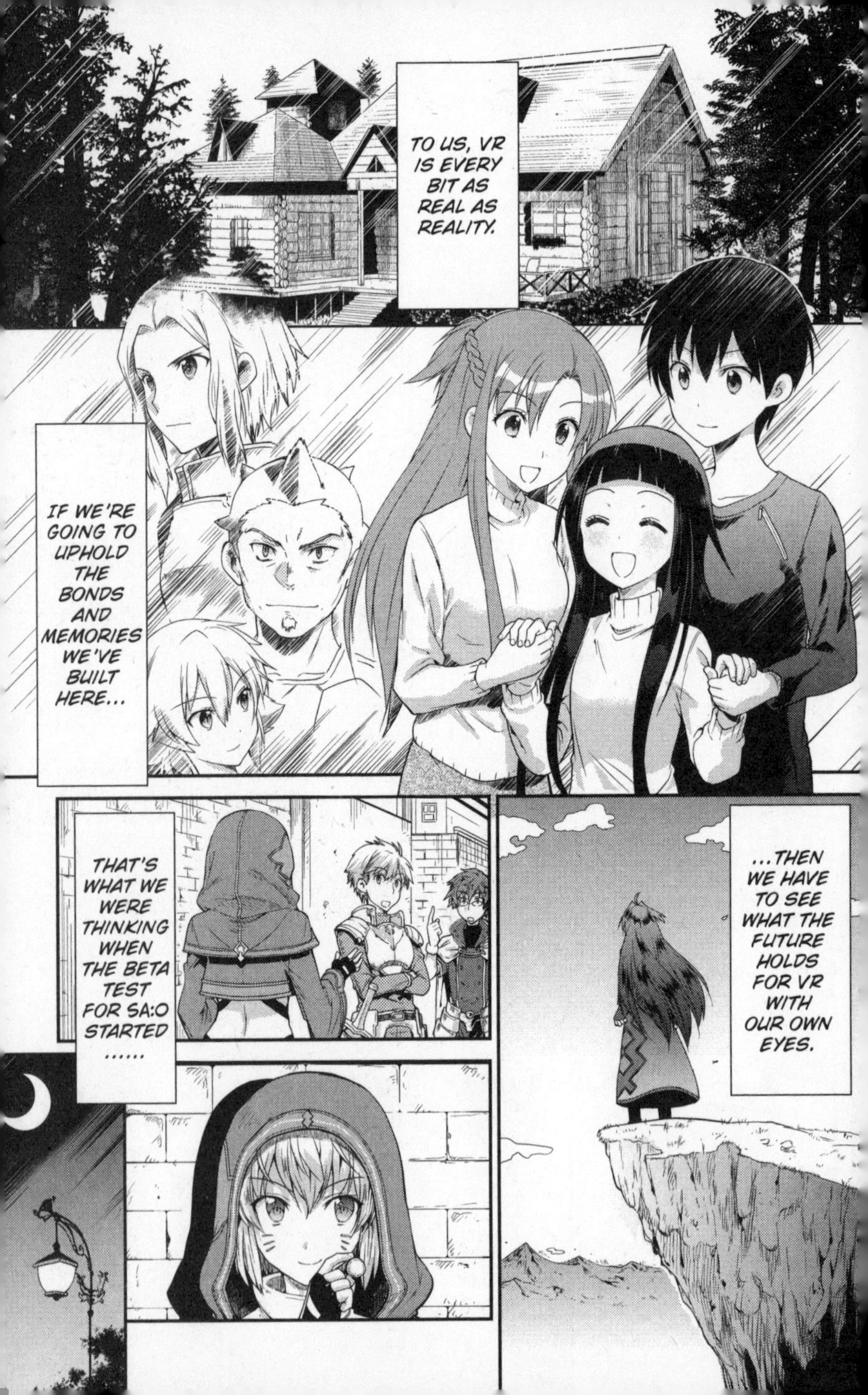
TO US, VR IS EVERY BIT AS REAL AS REALITY.
IF WE'RE GOING TO UPHOLD THE BONDS AND MEMORIES WE'VE BUILT HERE...
...THEN WE HAVE TO SEE WHAT THE FUTURE HOLDS FOR VR WITH OUR OWN EYES.
THAT'S WHAT WE WERE THINKING WHEN THE BETA TEST FOR SA:O STARTED......

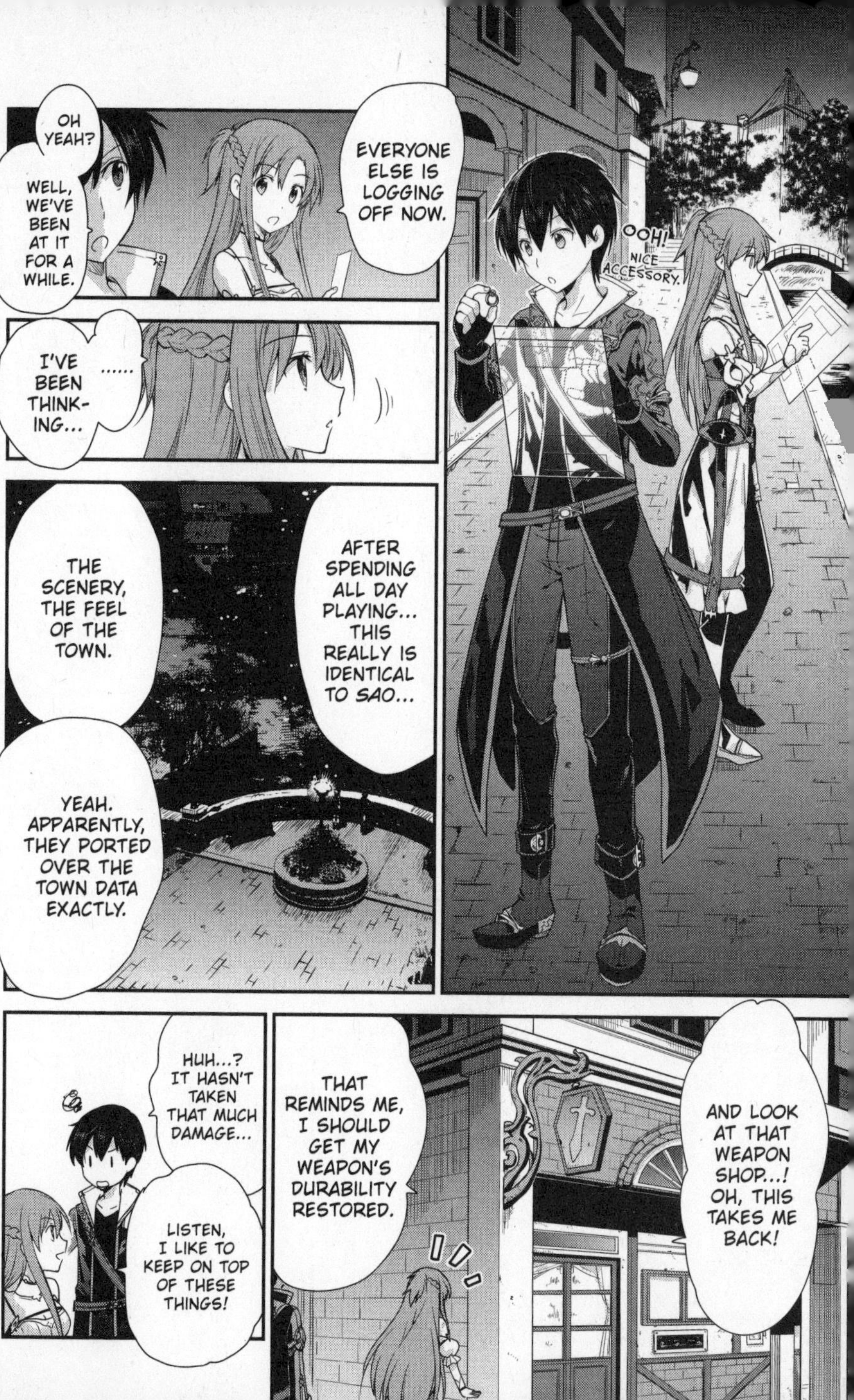
OOH! NICE ACCESSORY.
EVERYONE ELSE IS LOGGING OFF NOW.
OH YEAH?
WELL, WE'VE BEEN AT IT FOR A WHILE.
......
I'VE BEEN THINKING...
AFTER SPENDING ALL DAY PLAYING... THIS REALLY IS IDENTICAL TO SAO...
THE SCENERY, THE FEEL OF THE TOWN.
YEAH. APPARENTLY, THEY PORTED OVER THE TOWN DATA EXACTLY.
AND LOOK AT THAT WEAPON SHOP...! OH, THIS TAKES ME BACK!
THAT REMINDS ME, I SHOULD GET MY WEAPON'S DURABILITY RESTORED.
HUH...? IT HASN'T TAKEN THAT MUCH DAMAGE...
LISTEN, I LIKE TO KEEP ON TOP OF THESE THINGS!

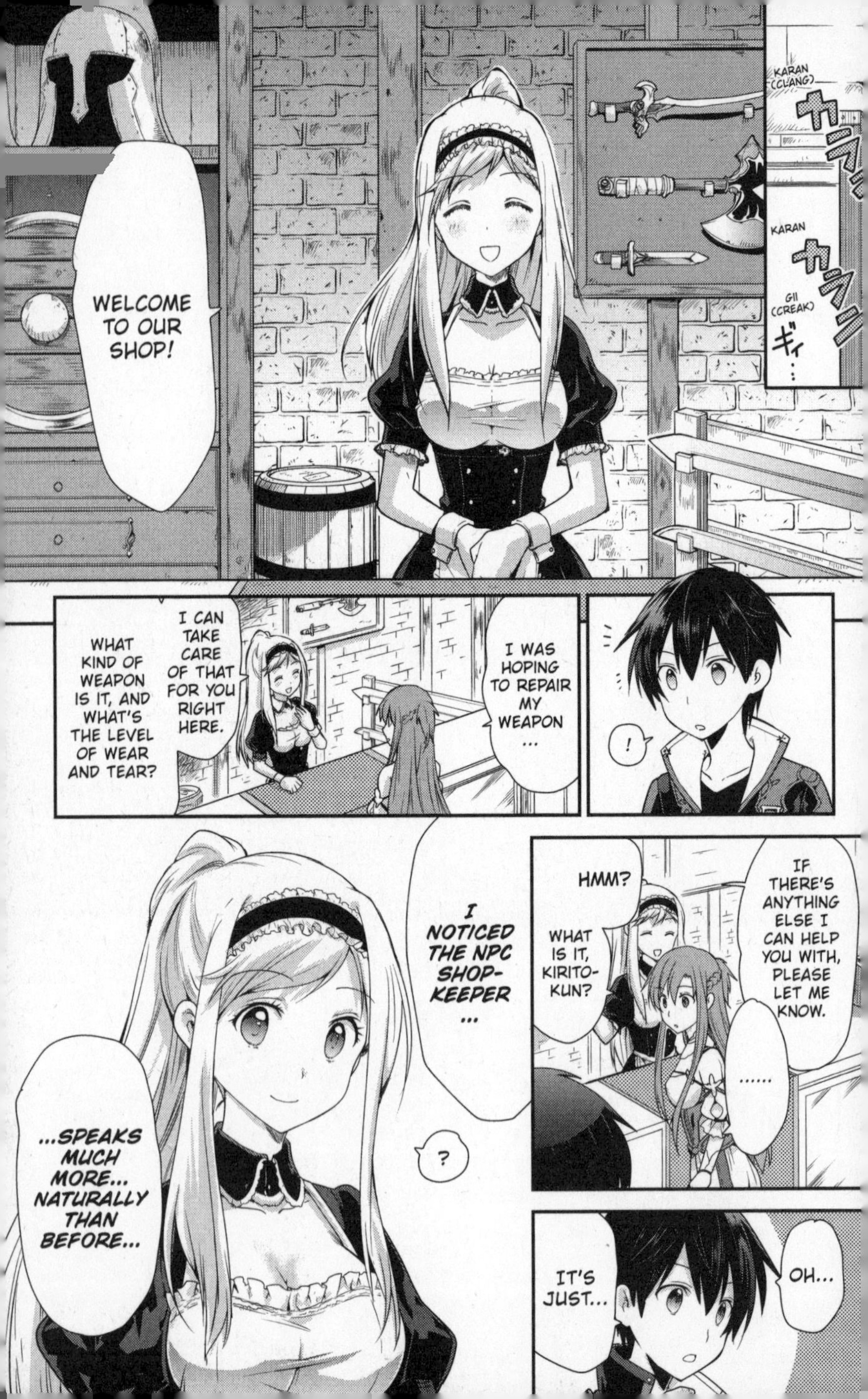
KARAN (CLANG)
カラン
KARAN
カラン
GII (CREAK)
ギィ…
WELCOME TO OUR SHOP!
!
I WAS HOPING TO REPAIR MY WEAPON ...
I CAN TAKE CARE OF THAT FOR YOU RIGHT HERE.
WHAT KIND OF WEAPON IS IT, AND WHAT'S THE LEVEL OF WEAR AND TEAR?
IF THERE'S ANYTHING ELSE I CAN HELP YOU WITH, PLEASE LET ME KNOW.
......
HMM?
WHAT IS IT, KIRITO-KUN?
OH...
IT'S JUST...
I NOTICED THE NPC SHOP-KEEPER ...
?
...SPEAKS MUCH MORE... NATURALLY THAN BEFORE...

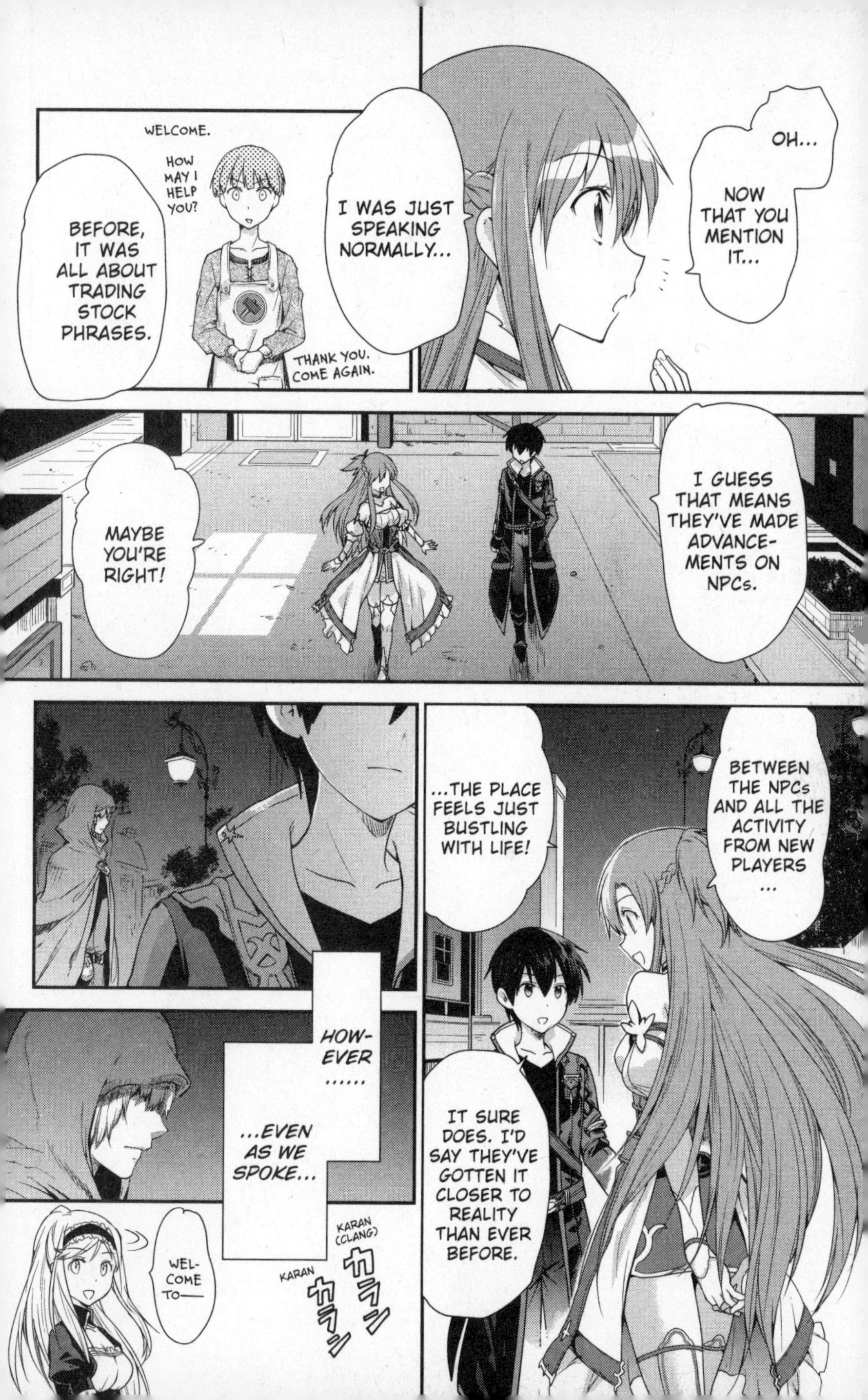
OH...
NOW THAT YOU MENTION IT...
I WAS JUST SPEAKING NORMALLY...
WELCOME.
HOW MAY I HELP YOU?
BEFORE, IT WAS ALL ABOUT TRADING STOCK PHRASES.
THANK YOU. COME AGAIN.
I GUESS THAT MEANS THEY'VE MADE ADVANCE-MENTS ON NPCs.
MAYBE YOU'RE RIGHT!
BETWEEN THE NPCs AND ALL THE ACTIVITY FROM NEW PLAYERS ...
...THE PLACE FEELS JUST BUSTLING WITH LIFE!
IT SURE DOES. I'D SAY THEY'VE GOTTEN IT CLOSER TO REALITY THAN EVER BEFORE.
HOW-EVER ......
...EVEN AS WE SPOKE...
KARAN (CLANG)
カラン
KARAN
カラン
WEL-COME TO—

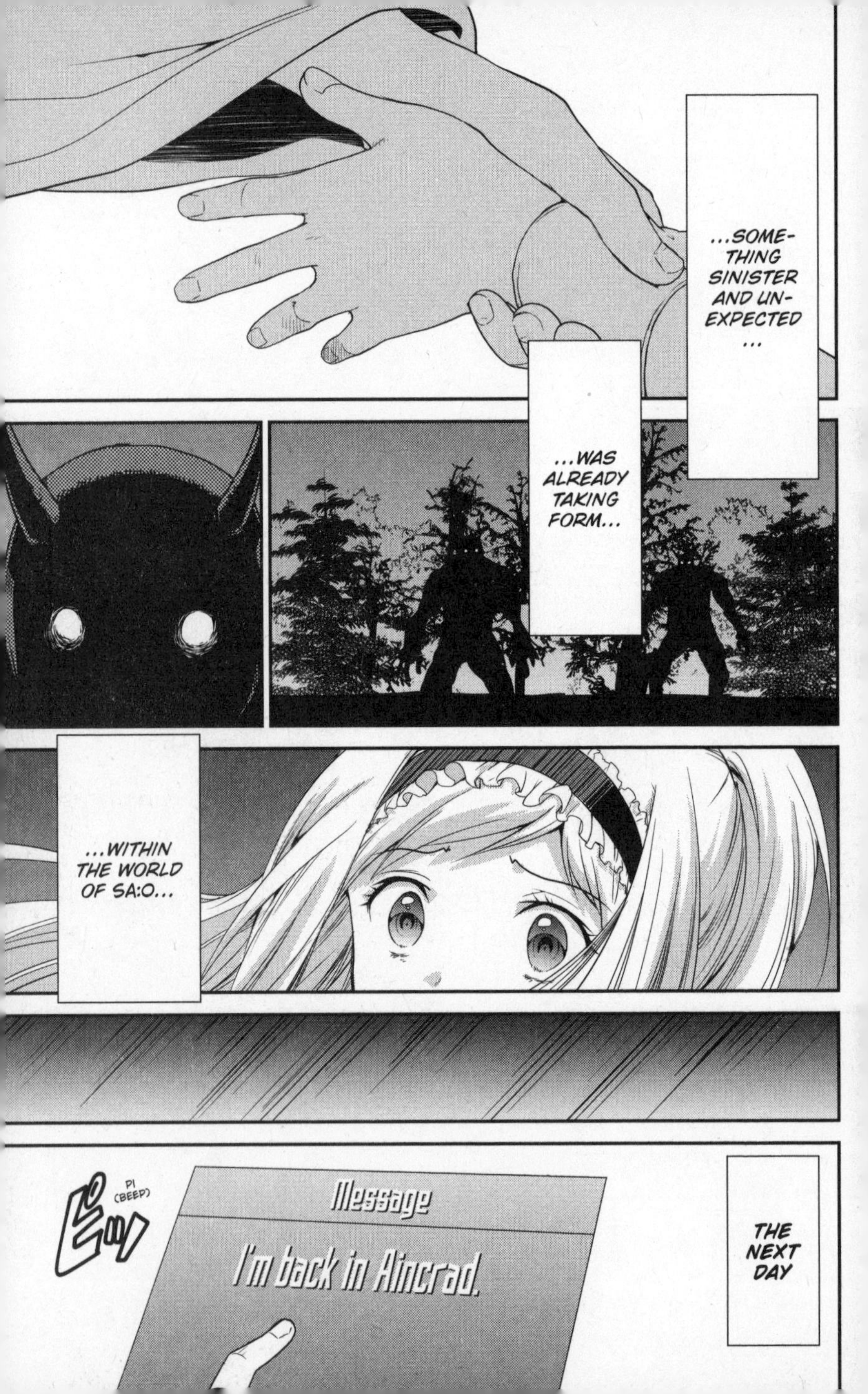
...SOME-THING SINISTER AND UN-EXPECTED ...
...WAS ALREADY TAKING FORM...
...WITHIN THE WORLD OF SA:O...
THE NEXT DAY
Message
I'm back in Aincrad.
PI (BEEP)

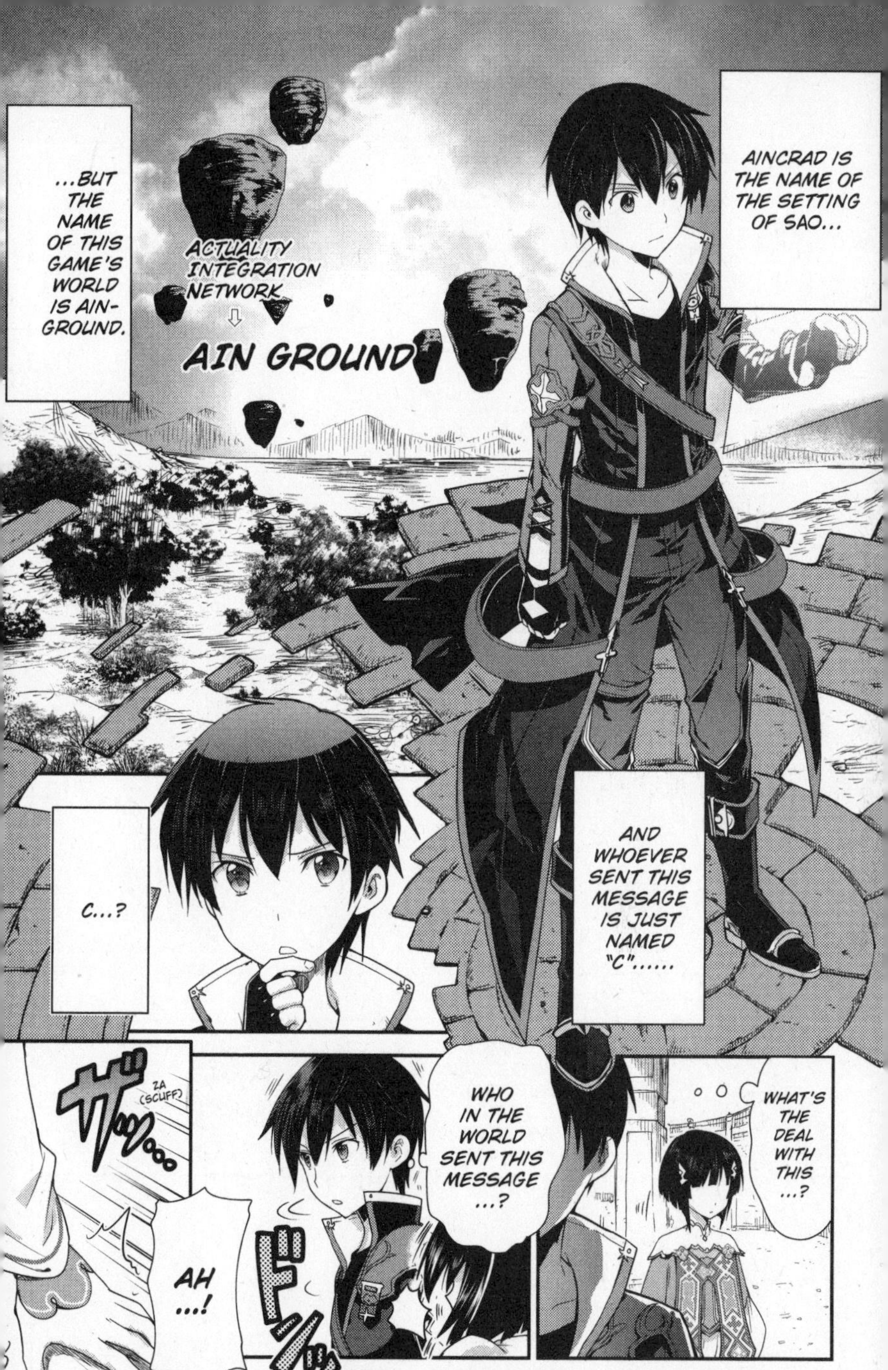
AINCRAD IS THE NAME OF THE SETTING OF SAO...
...BUT THE NAME OF THIS GAME'S WORLD IS AIN-GROUND.
ACTUALITY INTEGRATION NETWORK
⇩
AIN GROUND
AND WHOEVER SENT THIS MESSAGE IS JUST NAMED "C"......
C...?
WHAT'S THE DEAL WITH THIS ...?
WHO IN THE WORLD SENT THIS MESSAGE ...?
DON (THUMP)
ZA (SCUFF)
AH ...!

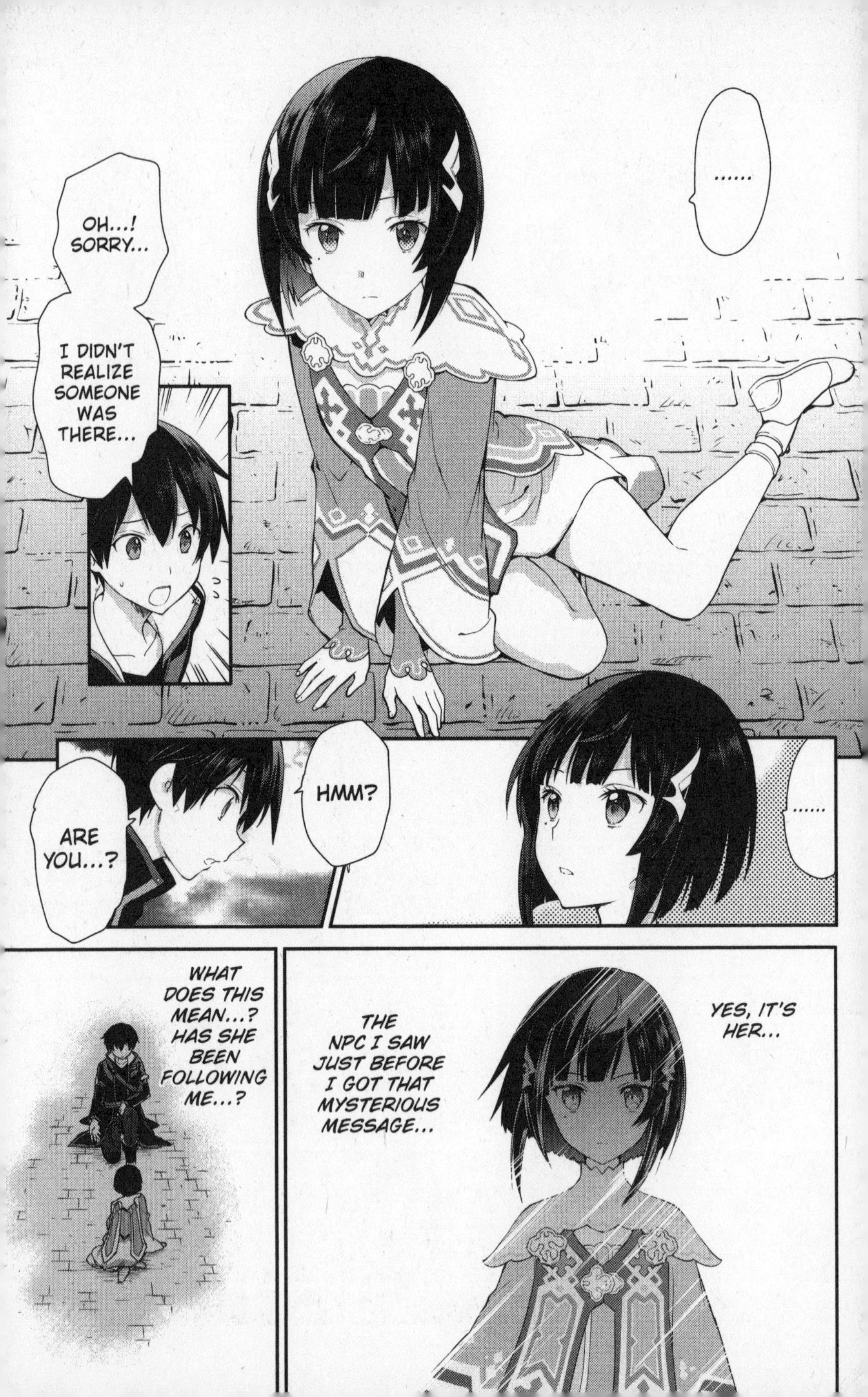
......
OH...! SORRY...
I DIDN'T REALIZE SOMEONE WAS THERE...
......
HMM?
ARE YOU...?
YES, IT'S HER...
THE NPC I SAW JUST BEFORE I GOT THAT MYSTERIOUS MESSAGE...
WHAT DOES THIS MEAN...? HAS SHE BEEN FOLLOWING ME...?

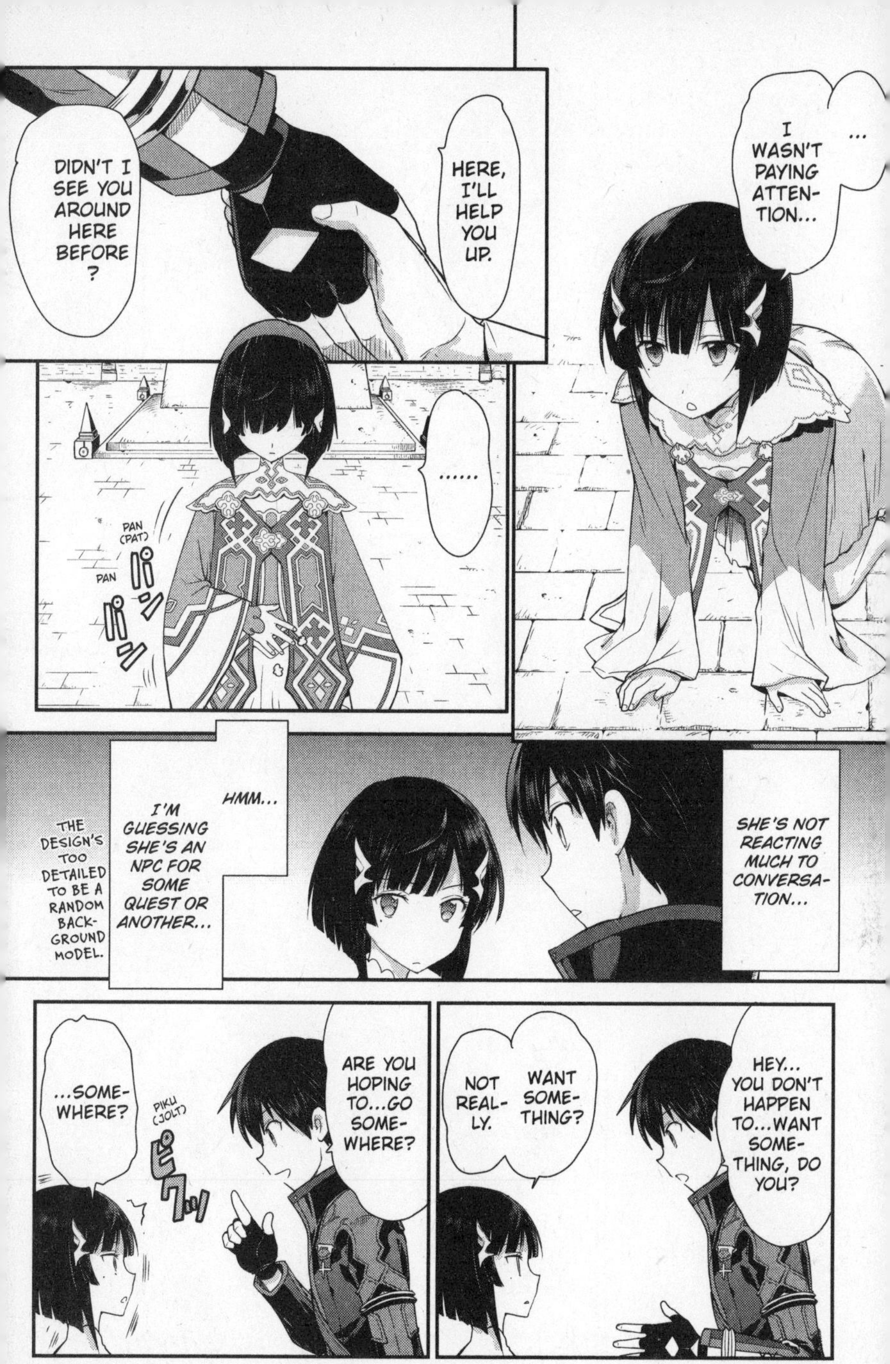
...
I WASN'T PAYING ATTENTION...
HERE, I'LL HELP YOU UP.
DIDN'T I SEE YOU AROUND HERE BEFORE?
......
PAN (PAT)
PAN
SHE'S NOT REACTING MUCH TO CONVERSATION...
HMM...
I'M GUESSING SHE'S AN NPC FOR SOME QUEST OR ANOTHER...
THE DESIGN'S TOO DETAILED TO BE A RANDOM BACKGROUND MODEL.
HEY... YOU DON'T HAPPEN TO...WANT SOMETHING, DO YOU?
WANT SOMETHING?
NOT REALLY.
ARE YOU HOPING TO...GO SOMEWHERE?
PIKU (JOLT)
...SOMEWHERE?

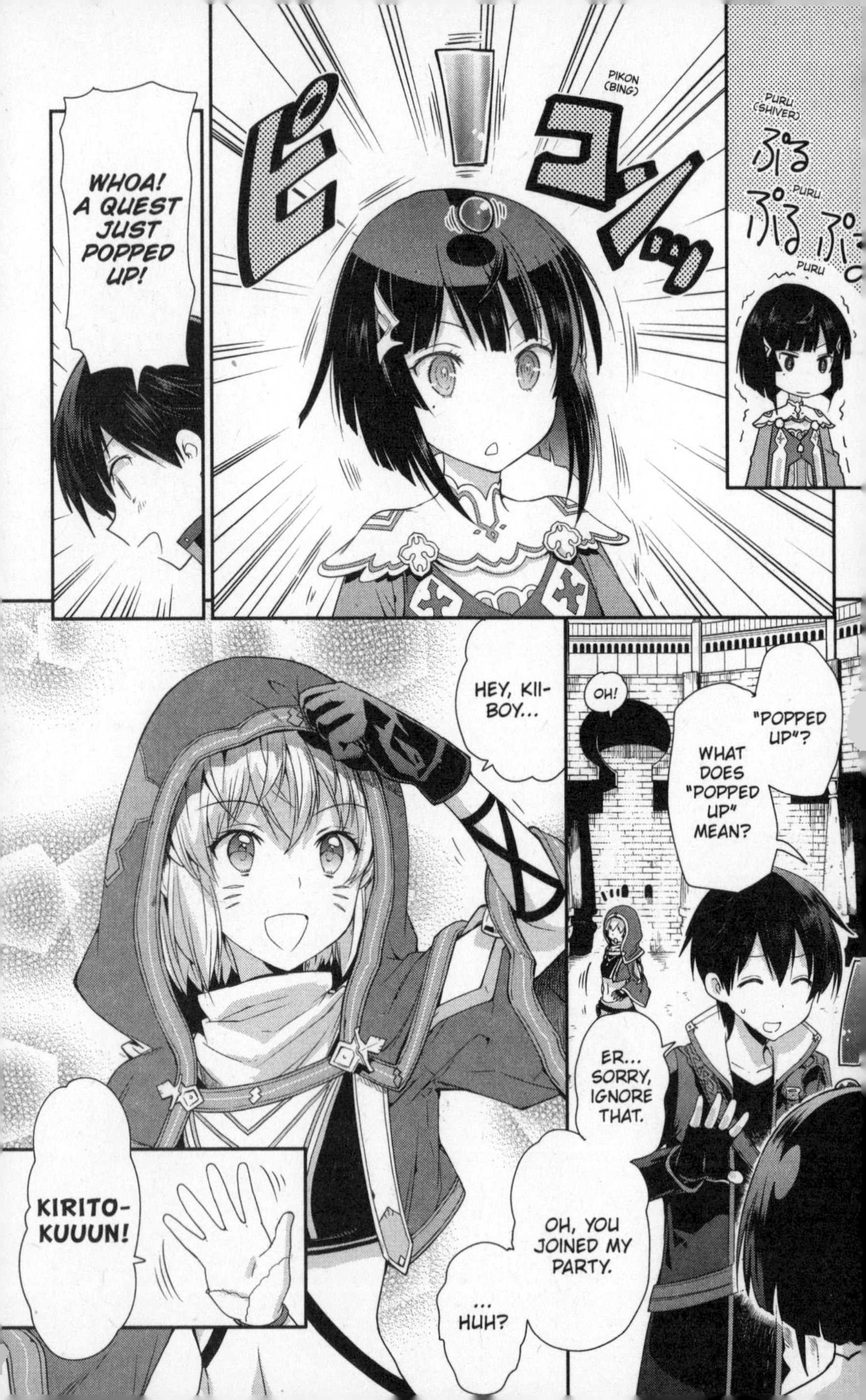
PURU (SHIVER)
ぷる
PURU
ぷる
ぷ
PURU
PIKON (BING)
ピコン！
WHOA! A QUEST JUST POPPED UP!
OH!
"POPPED UP"?
WHAT DOES "POPPED UP" MEAN?
ER... SORRY, IGNORE THAT.
OH, YOU JOINED MY PARTY.
...HUH?
HEY, KII-BOY...
KIRITO-KUUUN!

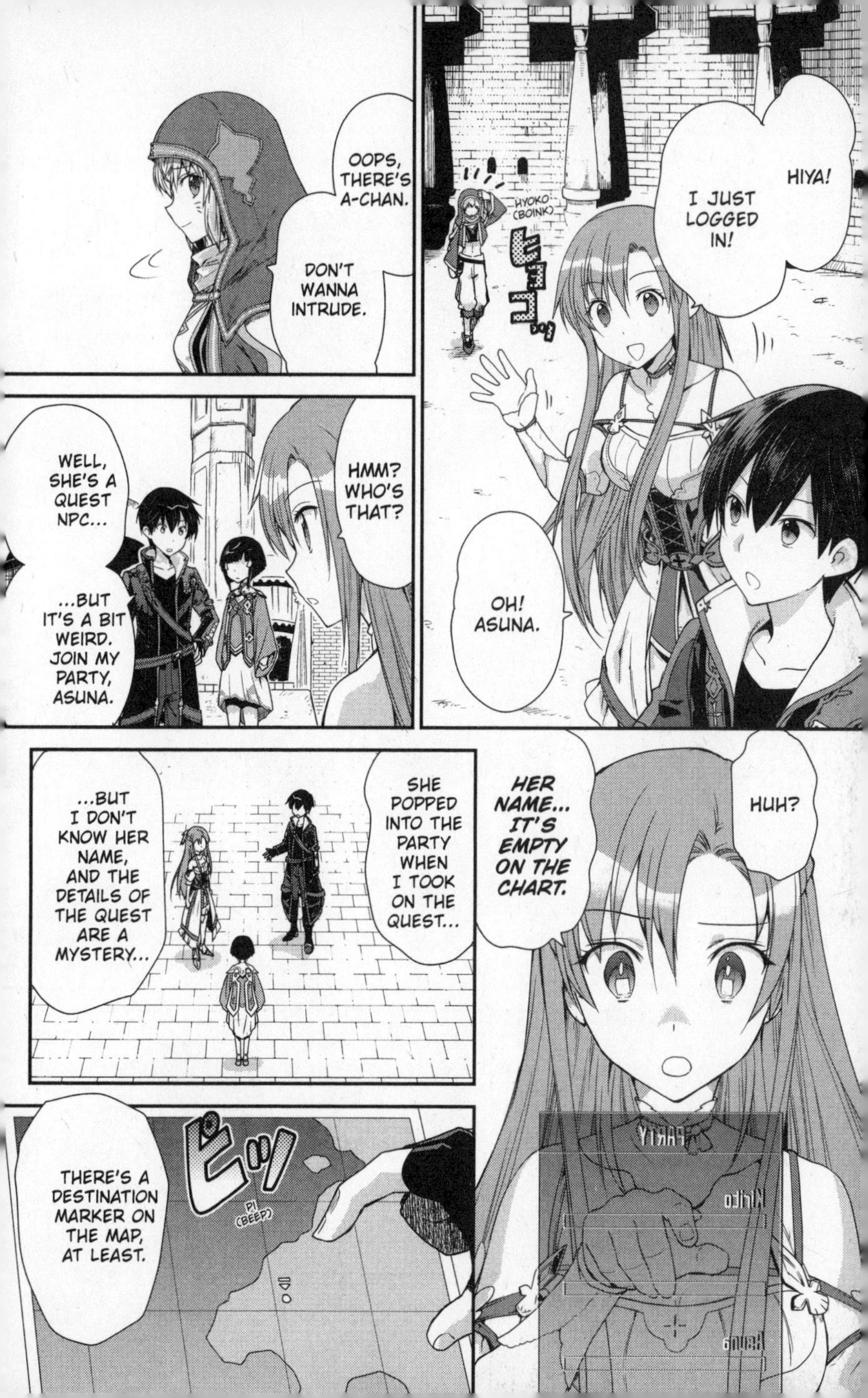
HIYA! I JUST LOGGED IN!
HYOKO (BOINK)
OH! ASUNA.
OOPS, THERE'S A-CHAN.
DON'T WANNA INTRUDE.
HMM? WHO'S THAT?
WELL, SHE'S A QUEST NPC...
...BUT IT'S A BIT WEIRD. JOIN MY PARTY, ASUNA.
HUH?
HER NAME... IT'S EMPTY ON THE CHART.
SHE POPPED INTO THE PARTY WHEN I TOOK ON THE QUEST...
...BUT I DON'T KNOW HER NAME, AND THE DETAILS OF THE QUEST ARE A MYSTERY...
PI (BEEP)
THERE'S A DESTINATION MARKER ON THE MAP, AT LEAST.

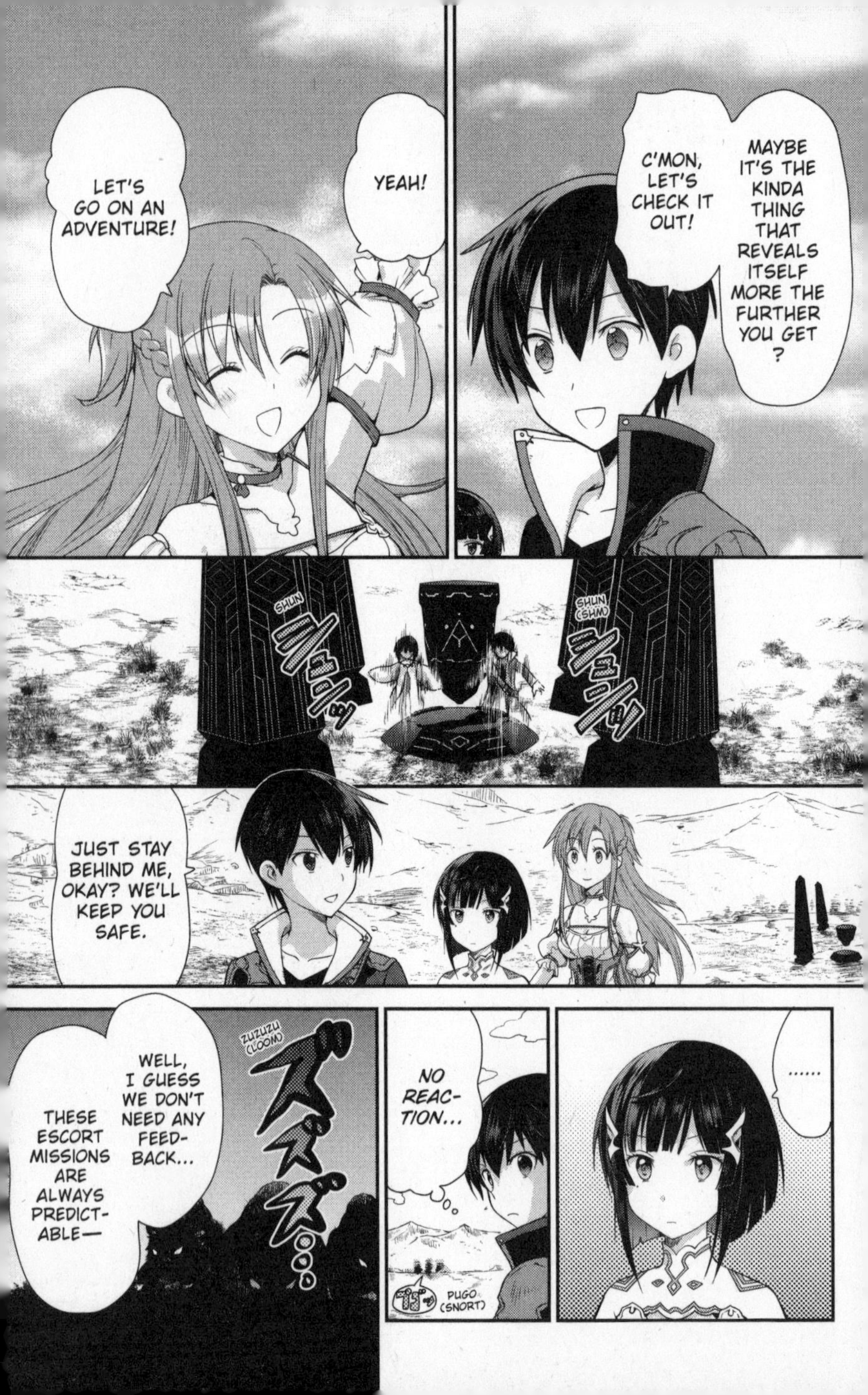
MAYBE IT'S THE KINDA THING THAT REVEALS ITSELF MORE THE FURTHER YOU GET?
C'MON, LET'S CHECK IT OUT!
YEAH!
LET'S GO ON AN ADVENTURE!
SHUN (SHM)
SHUN
JUST STAY BEHIND ME, OKAY? WE'LL KEEP YOU SAFE.
......
NO REACTION...
PUGO (SNORT)
ZUZUZU (LOOM)
WELL, I GUESS WE DON'T NEED ANY FEEDBACK...
THESE ESCORT MISSIONS ARE ALWAYS PREDICTABLE—

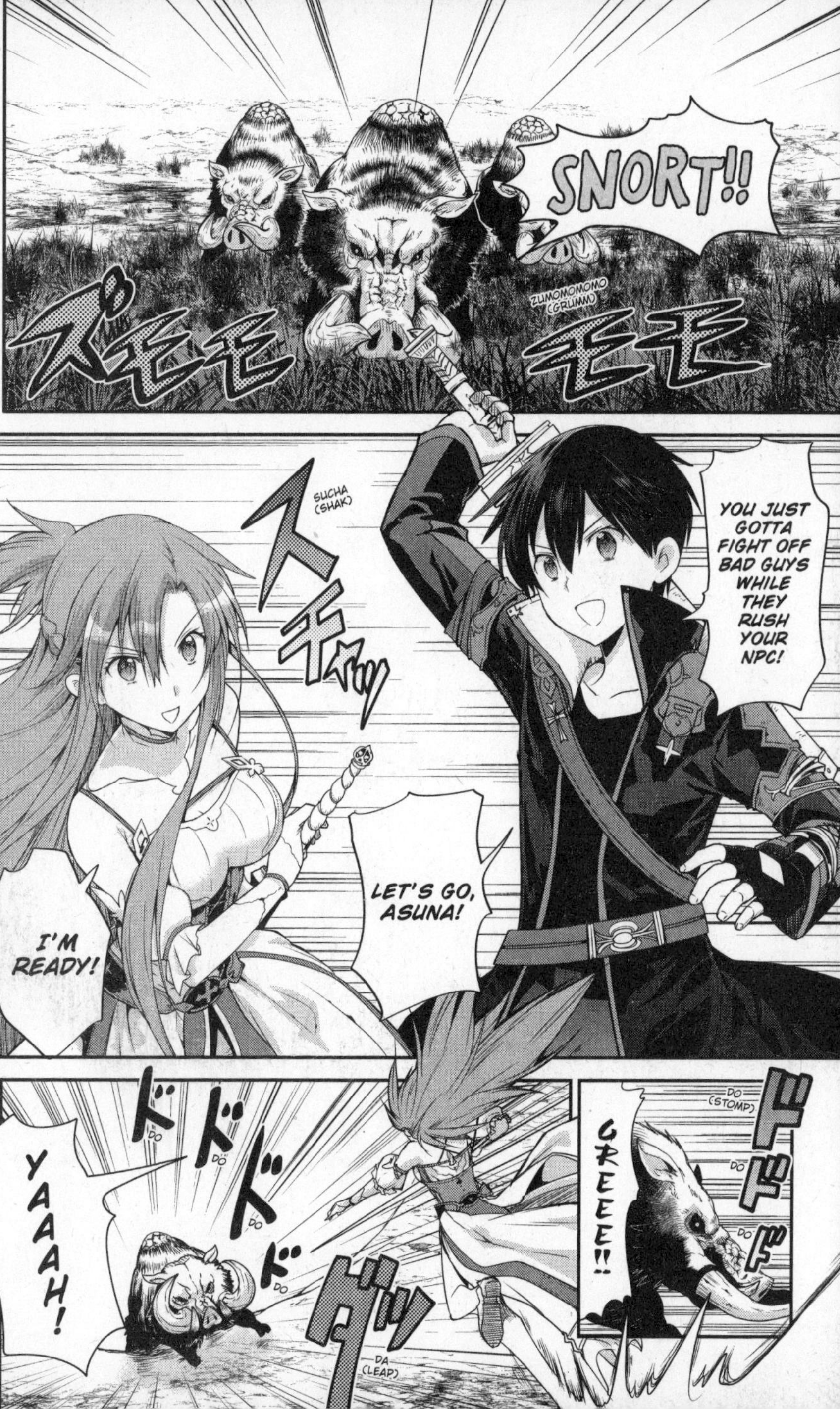
SNORT!!
ZUMOMOMOMO (GRUMM)
ズモモ モモ
YOU JUST GOTTA FIGHT OFF BAD GUYS WHILE THEY RUSH YOUR NPC!
SUCHA (SHAK)
スチャッ
LET'S GO, ASUNA!
I'M READY!
DO (STOMP)
ドドド
GREEEE!!
ドドドド
YAAAAH!
ダッ
DA (LEAP)

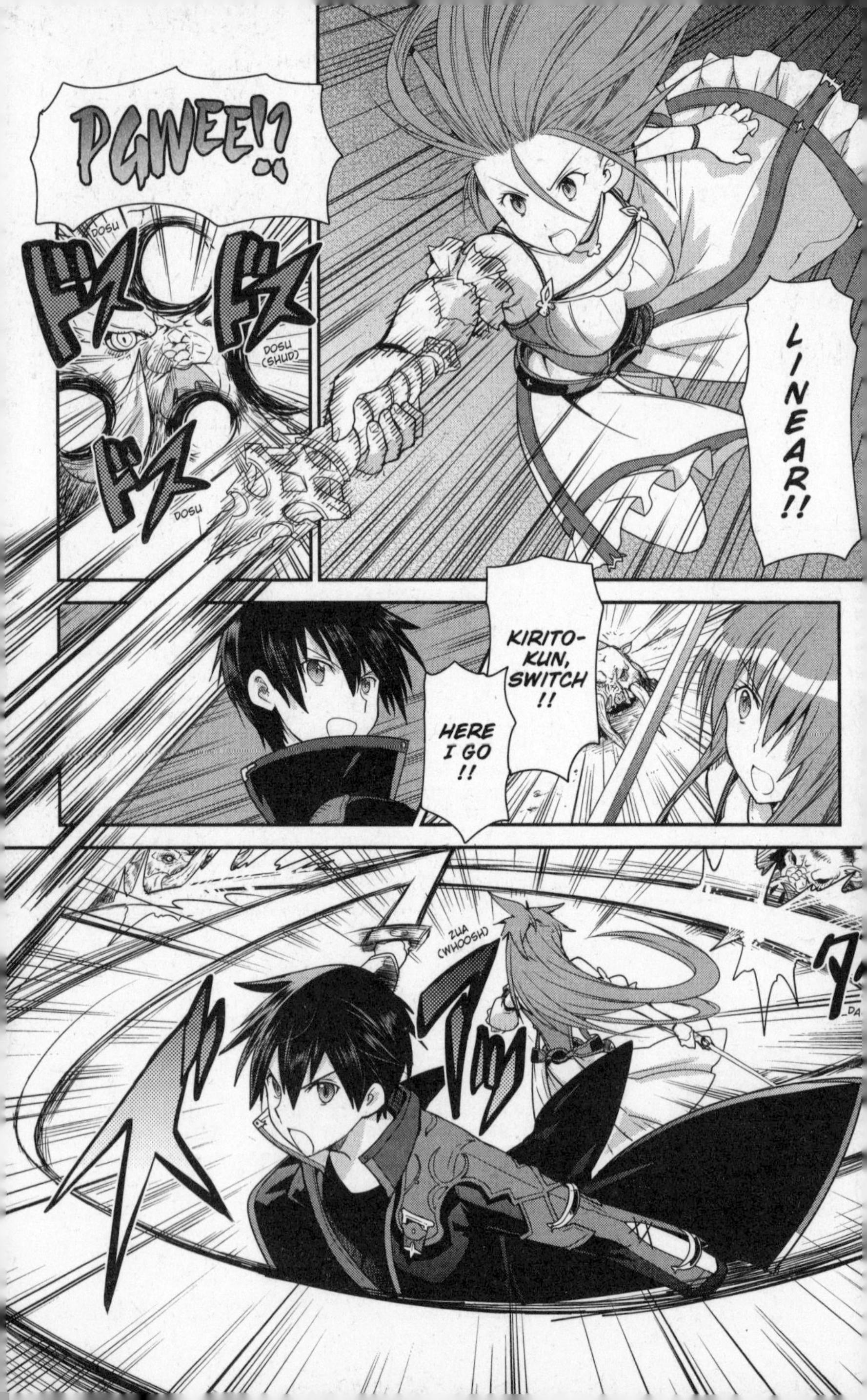
LINEAR!!
PGWEE!?
DOSU
DOSU (SHUD)
DOSU
KIRITO-KUN, SWITCH!!
HERE I GO!!
ZUA (WHOOSH)
DA

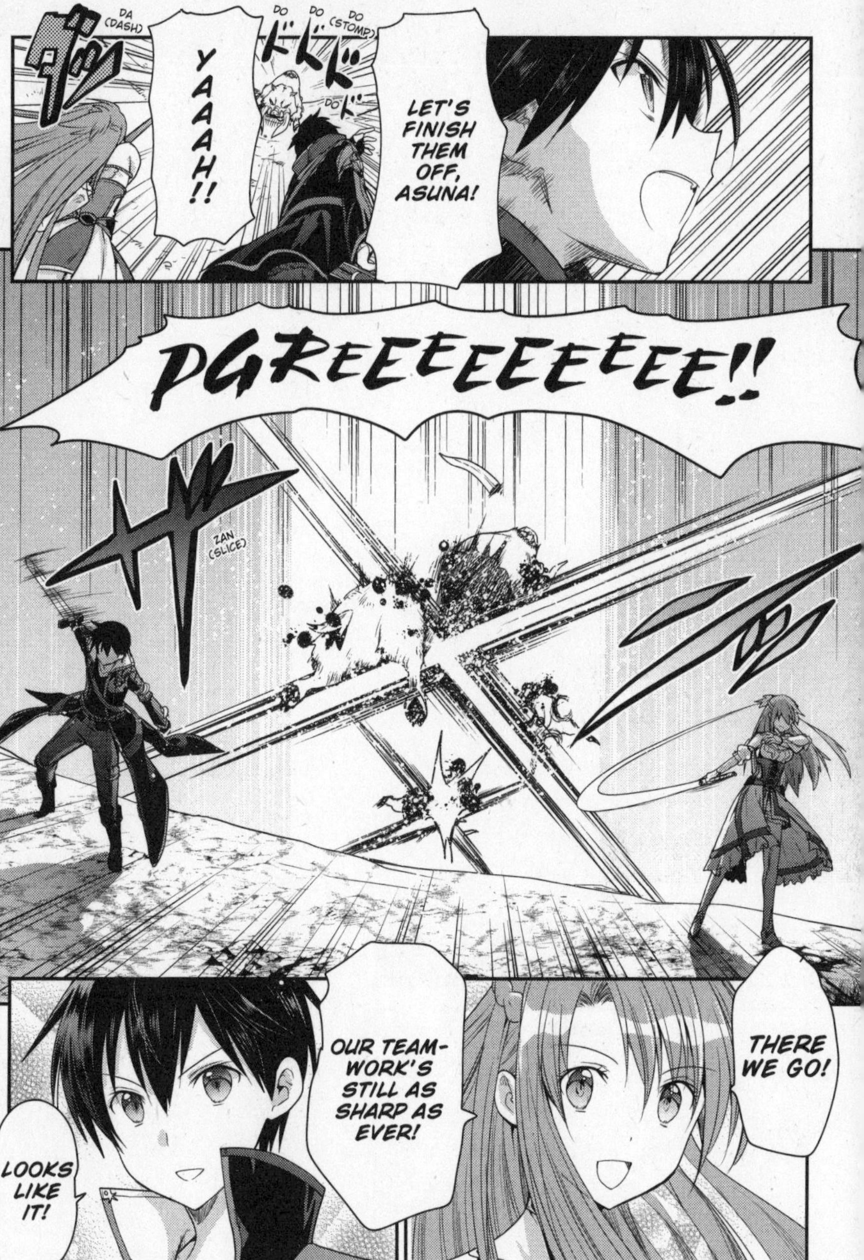
LET'S FINISH THEM OFF, ASUNA!
DO DO DO (STOMP)
DO
YAAAAH!!
DA (DASH)
PGREEEEEEEEE!!
ZAN (SLICE)
THERE WE GO!
OUR TEAM-WORK'S STILL AS SHARP AS EVER!
LOOKS LIKE IT!

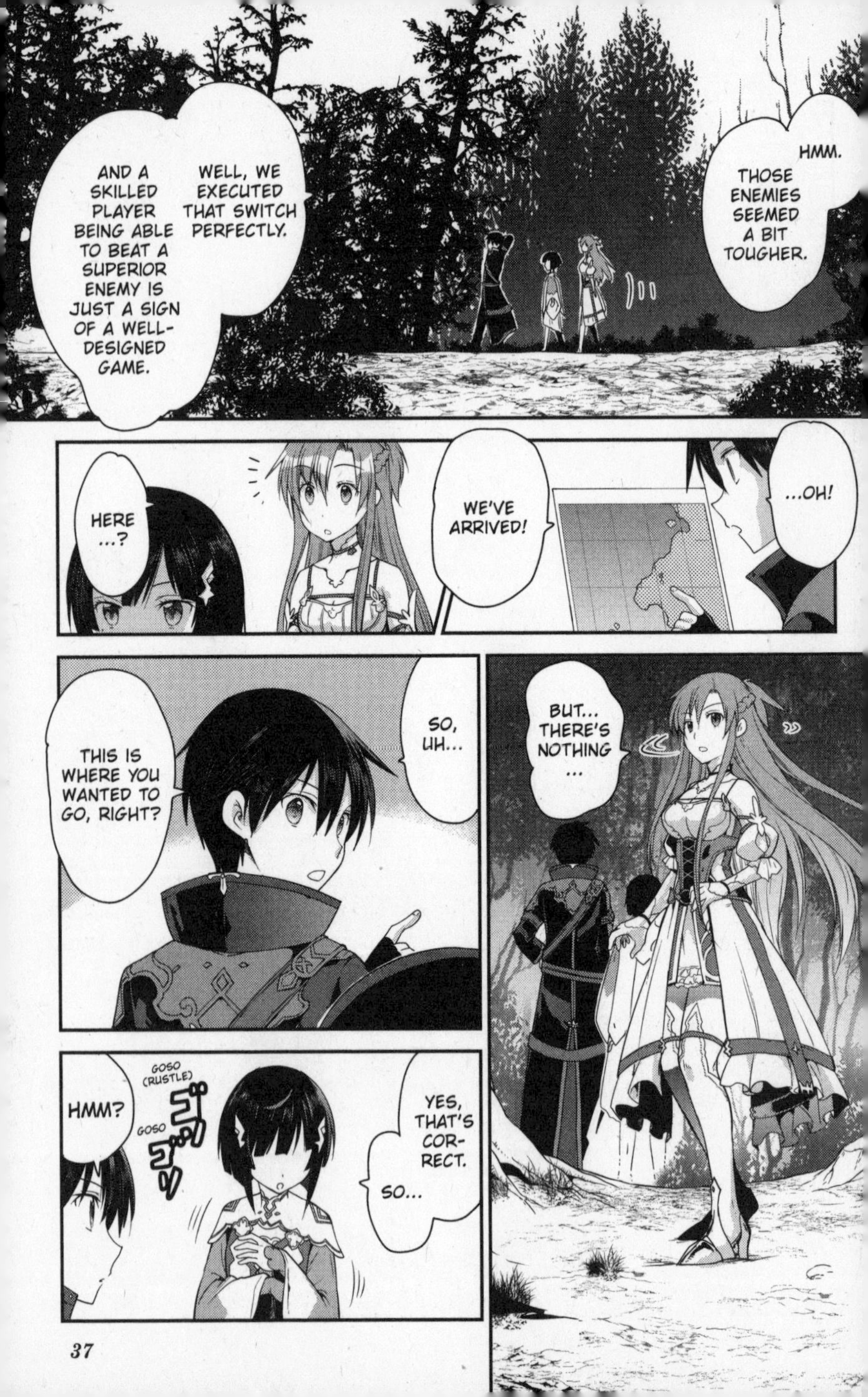

HMM. THOSE ENEMIES SEEMED A BIT TOUGHER.
WELL, WE EXECUTED THAT SWITCH PERFECTLY.
AND A SKILLED PLAYER BEING ABLE TO BEAT A SUPERIOR ENEMY IS JUST A SIGN OF A WELL-DESIGNED GAME.
...OH!
WE'VE ARRIVED!
HERE ...?
BUT... THERE'S NOTHING ...
SO, UH...
THIS IS WHERE YOU WANTED TO GO, RIGHT?
YES, THAT'S COR-RECT.
SO...
GOSO (RUSTLE)
GOSO
HMM?

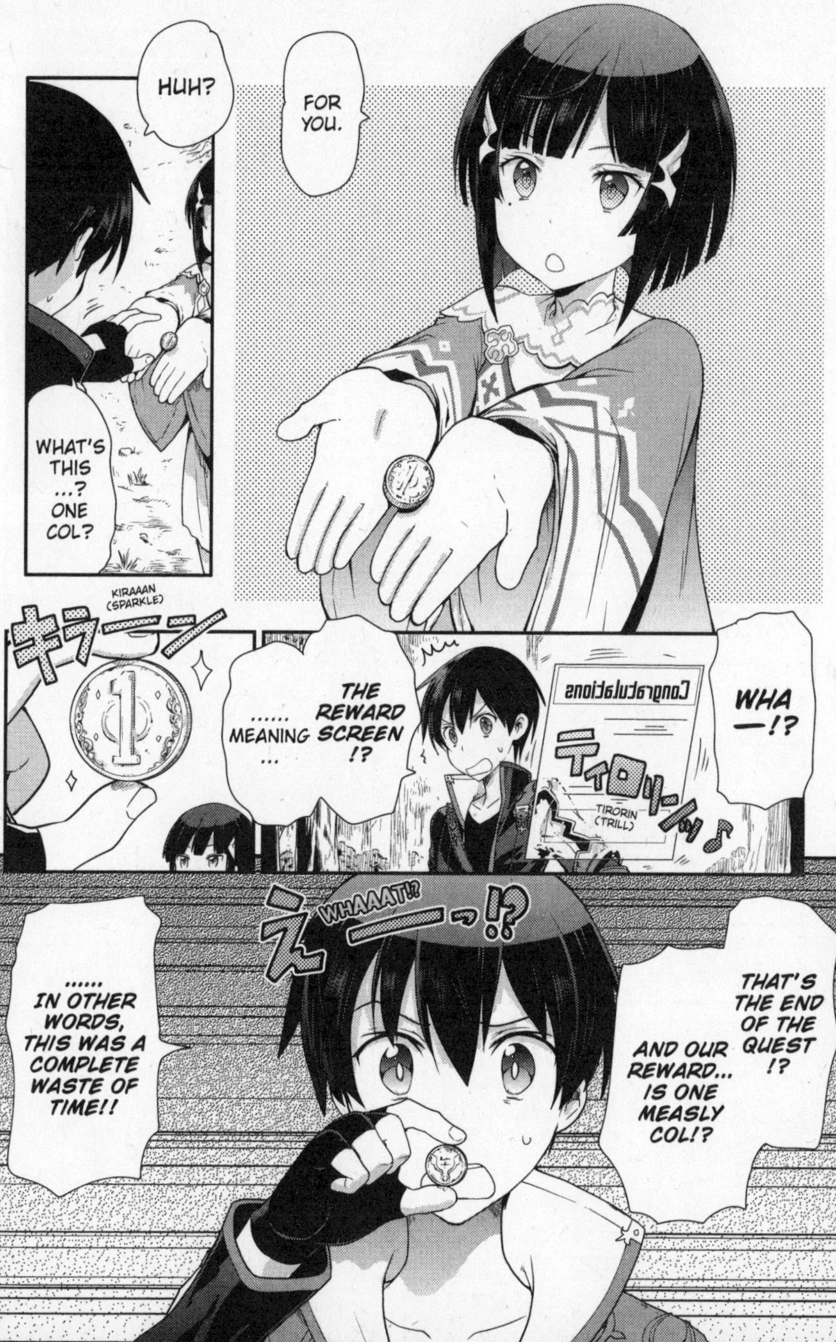
FOR YOU.
HUH?
WHAT'S THIS ...? ONE COL?
WHA—!?
TIRORIN (TRILL)
THE REWARD SCREEN !?
...... MEANING ...
KIRAAAN (SPARKLE)
WHAAAT!?
THAT'S THE END OF THE QUEST !?
AND OUR REWARD... IS ONE MEASLY COL!?
...... IN OTHER WORDS, THIS WAS A COMPLETE WASTE OF TIME!!

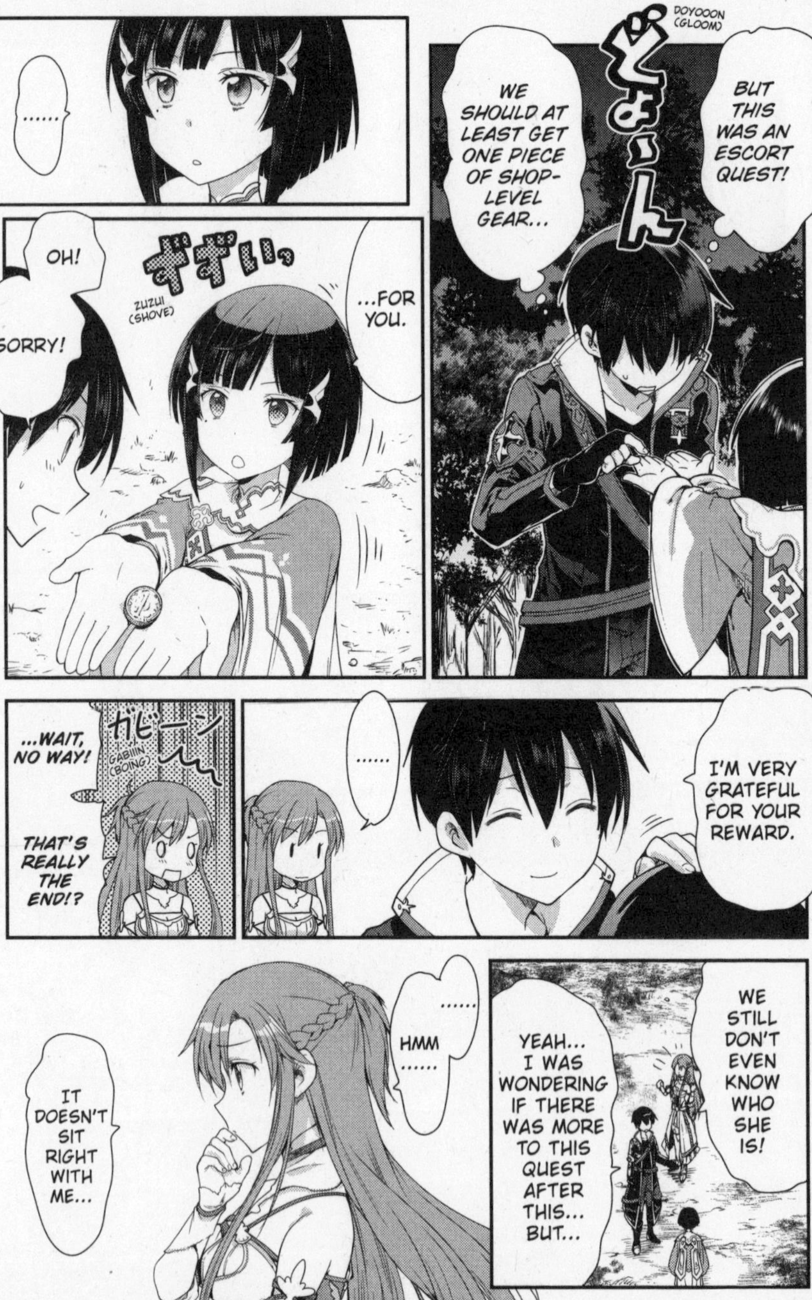
BUT THIS WAS AN ESCORT QUEST!
どよ〜ん
DOYOOON (GLOOM)
WE SHOULD AT LEAST GET ONE PIECE OF SHOP-LEVEL GEAR...
......
...FOR YOU.
ずずいっ
ZUZUI (SHOVE)
OH!
SORRY!
I'M VERY GRATEFUL FOR YOUR REWARD.
......
ガビーン
GABIIIN (BOING)
...WAIT, NO WAY!
THAT'S REALLY THE END!?
WE STILL DON'T EVEN KNOW WHO SHE IS!
YEAH... I WAS WONDERING IF THERE WAS MORE TO THIS QUEST AFTER THIS... BUT...
......
HMM ......
IT DOESN'T SIT RIGHT WITH ME...

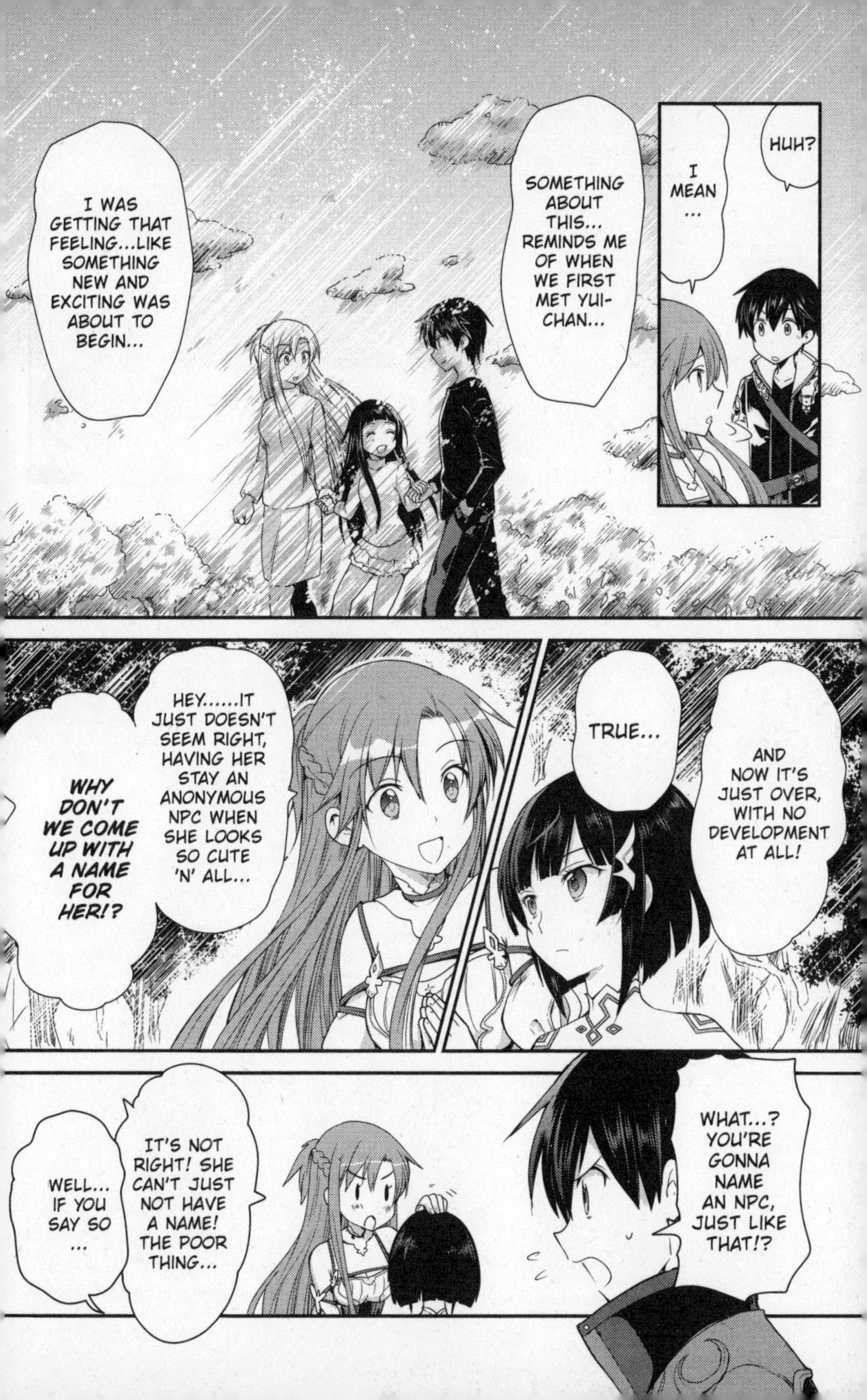
HUH?
I MEAN...
SOMETHING ABOUT THIS... REMINDS ME OF WHEN WE FIRST MET YUI-CHAN...
I WAS GETTING THAT FEELING...LIKE SOMETHING NEW AND EXCITING WAS ABOUT TO BEGIN...
AND NOW IT'S JUST OVER, WITH NO DEVELOPMENT AT ALL!
TRUE...
HEY......IT JUST DOESN'T SEEM RIGHT, HAVING HER STAY AN ANONYMOUS NPC WHEN SHE LOOKS SO CUTE 'N' ALL...
WHY DON'T WE COME UP WITH A NAME FOR HER!?
WHAT...? YOU'RE GONNA NAME AN NPC, JUST LIKE THAT!?
IT'S NOT RIGHT! SHE CAN'T JUST NOT HAVE A NAME! THE POOR THING...
WELL... IF YOU SAY SO ...

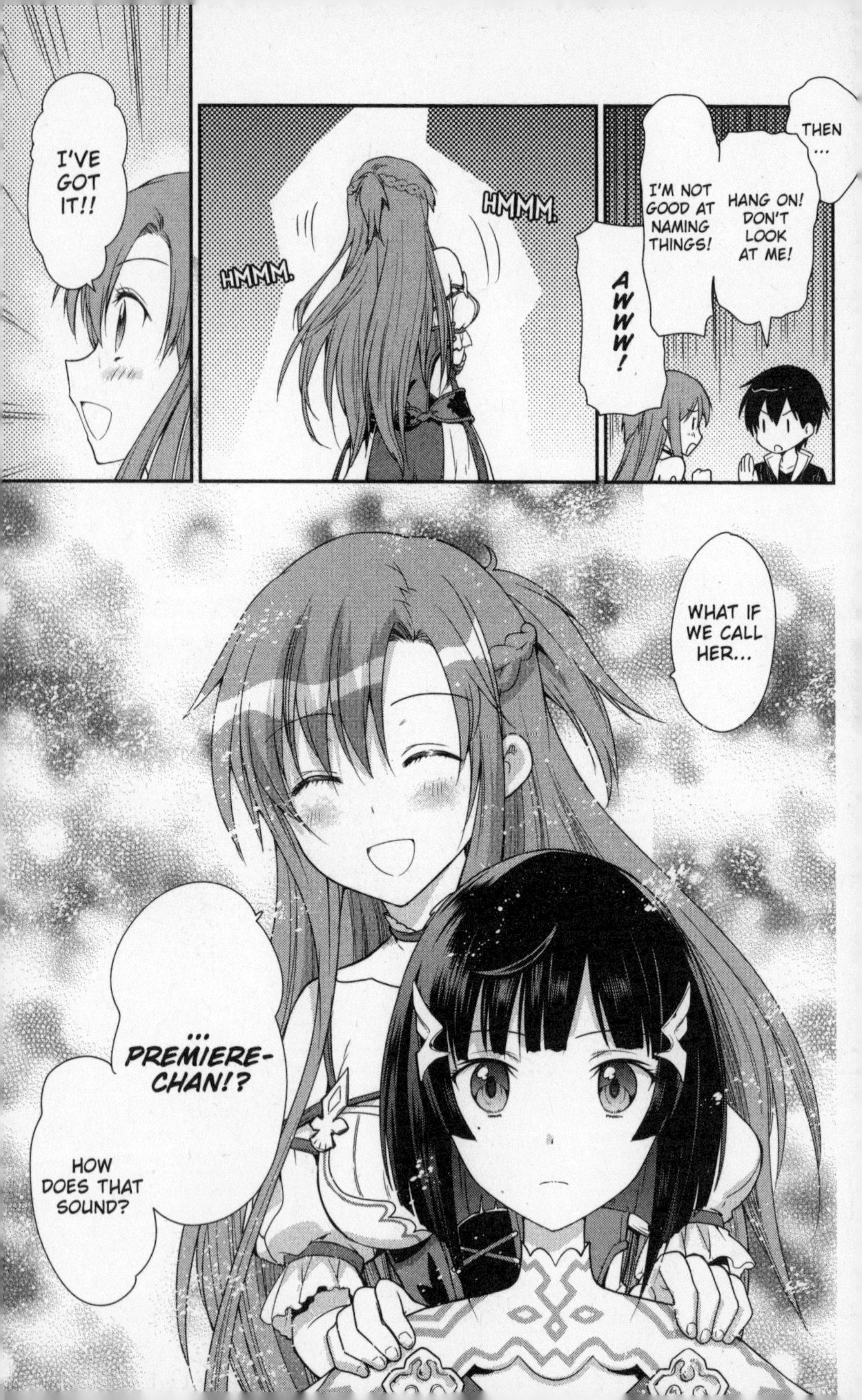
THEN ...
HANG ON! DON'T LOOK AT ME!
I'M NOT GOOD AT NAMING THINGS!
AWWW!
HMMM.
HMMM.
I'VE GOT IT!!
WHAT IF WE CALL HER...
... PREMIERE-CHAN!?
HOW DOES THAT SOUND?

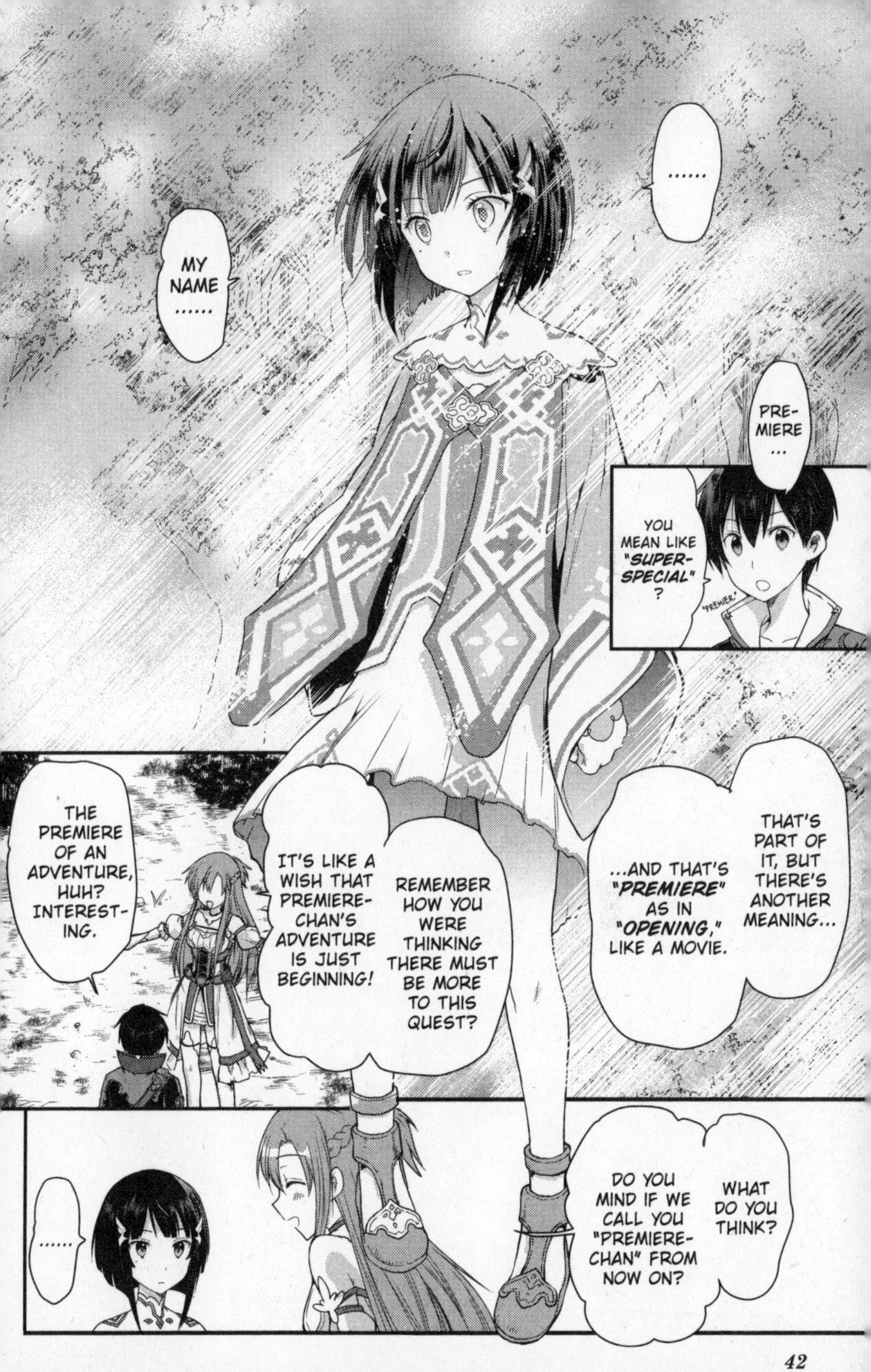
......
MY NAME ......
PRE-MIERE ...
YOU MEAN LIKE "*SUPER-SPECIAL*"?
"PREMIER."
THAT'S PART OF IT, BUT THERE'S ANOTHER MEANING...
...AND THAT'S "*PREMIERE*" AS IN "*OPENING*," LIKE A MOVIE.
REMEMBER HOW YOU WERE THINKING THERE MUST BE MORE TO THIS QUEST?
IT'S LIKE A WISH THAT PREMIERE-CHAN'S ADVENTURE IS JUST BEGINNING!
THE PREMIERE OF AN ADVENTURE, HUH? INTEREST-ING.
WHAT DO YOU THINK?
DO YOU MIND IF WE CALL YOU "PREMIERE-CHAN" FROM NOW ON?
......

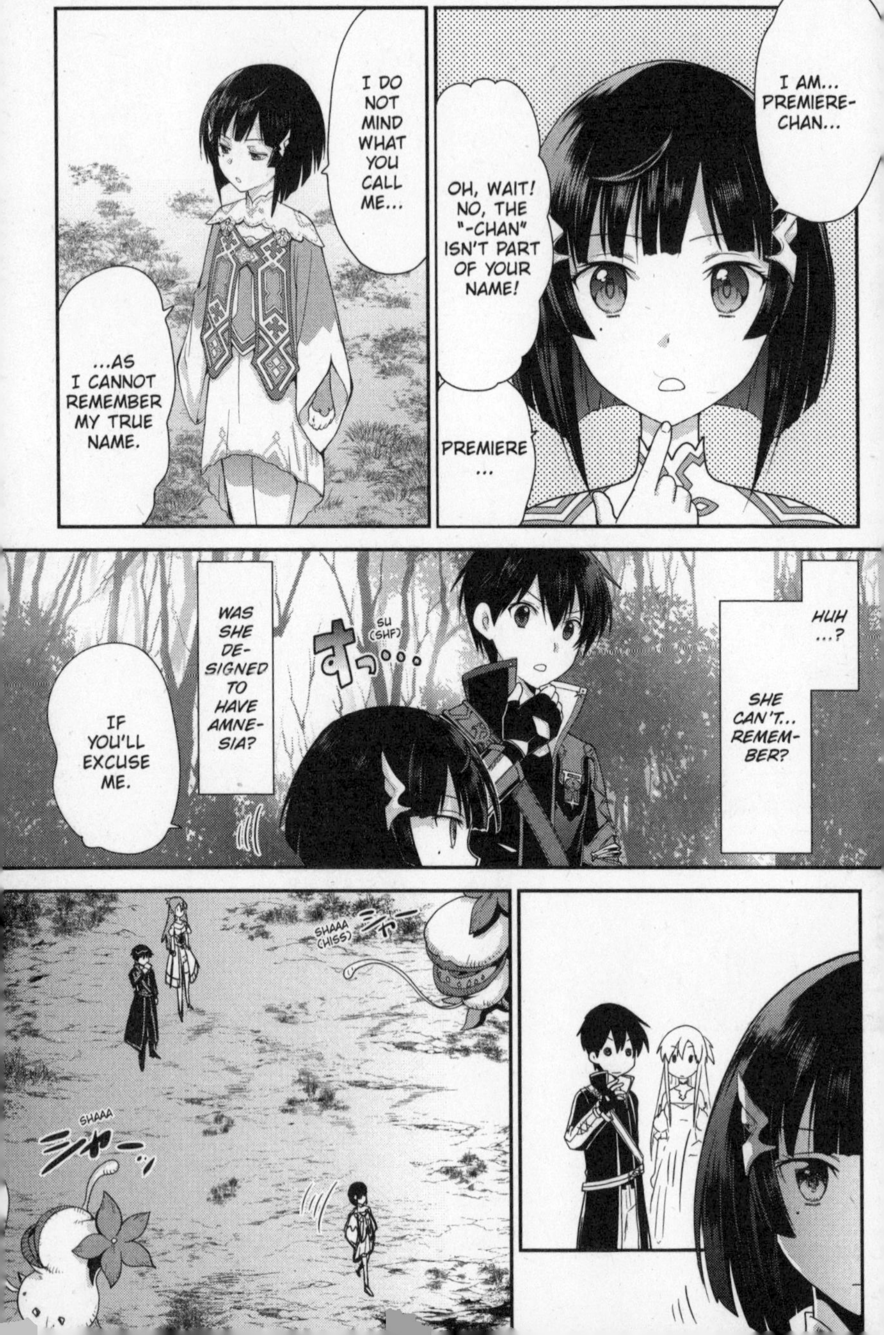
I AM... PREMIERE-CHAN...
OH, WAIT! NO, THE "-CHAN" ISN'T PART OF YOUR NAME!
PREMIERE ...
I DO NOT MIND WHAT YOU CALL ME...
...AS I CANNOT REMEMBER MY TRUE NAME.
HUH ...?
SHE CAN'T... REMEMBER?
すっ...
SU (SHF)
WAS SHE DE-SIGNED TO HAVE AMNE-SIA?
IF YOU'LL EXCUSE ME.
シャー
SHAAA (CHISS)
シャーッ
SHAAA

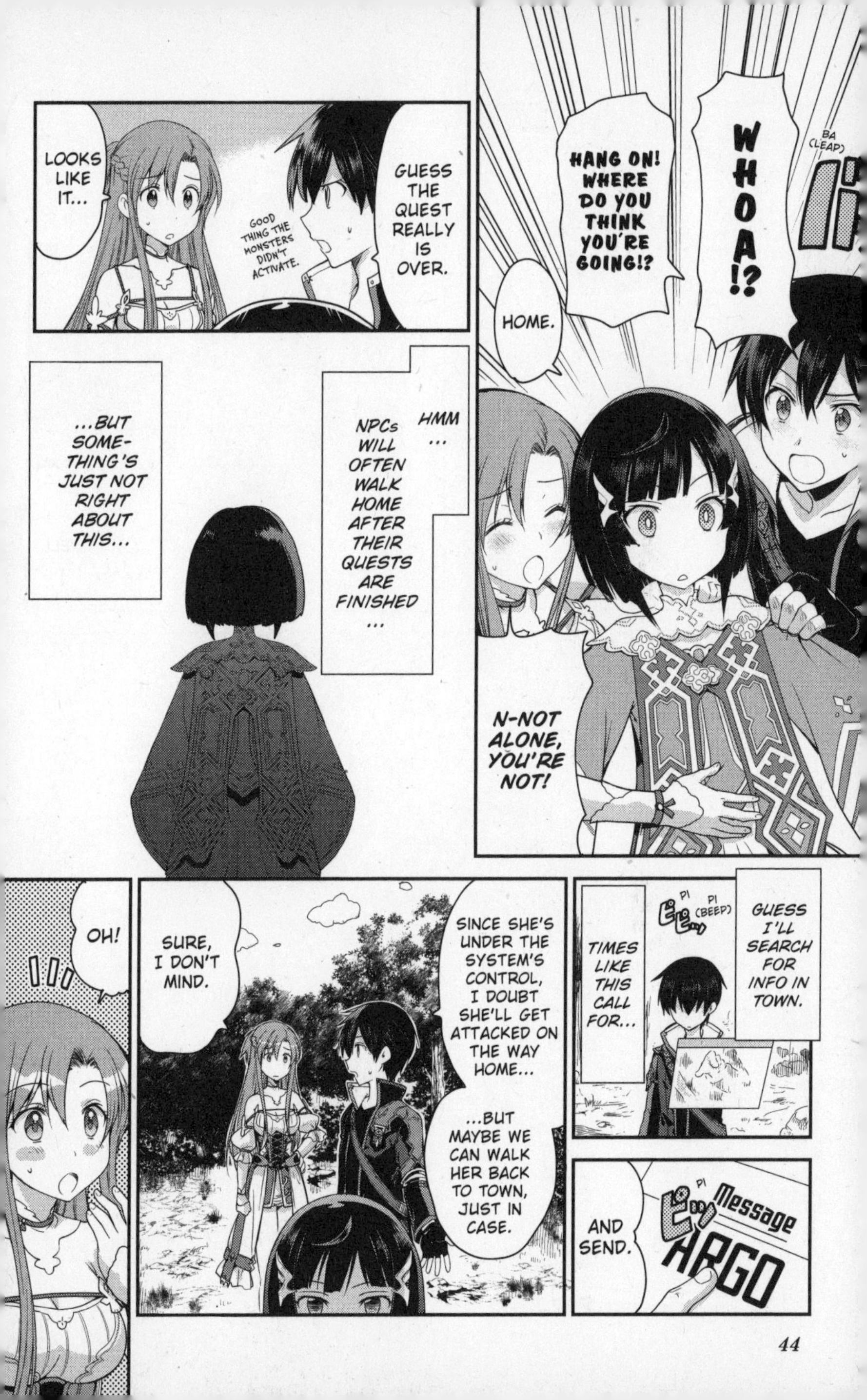
BA (LEAP)
WHOA!?
HANG ON! WHERE DO YOU THINK YOU'RE GOING!?
HOME.
N-NOT ALONE, YOU'RE NOT!
GUESS THE QUEST REALLY IS OVER.
GOOD THING THE MONSTERS DIDN'T ACTIVATE.
LOOKS LIKE IT...
HMM...
NPCs WILL OFTEN WALK HOME AFTER THEIR QUESTS ARE FINISHED...
...BUT SOMETHING'S JUST NOT RIGHT ABOUT THIS...
GUESS I'LL SEARCH FOR INFO IN TOWN.
PI PI (BEEP)
TIMES LIKE THIS CALL FOR...
PI
Message
ARGO
AND SEND.
SINCE SHE'S UNDER THE SYSTEM'S CONTROL, I DOUBT SHE'LL GET ATTACKED ON THE WAY HOME...
...BUT MAYBE WE CAN WALK HER BACK TO TOWN, JUST IN CASE.
SURE, I DON'T MIND.
OH!

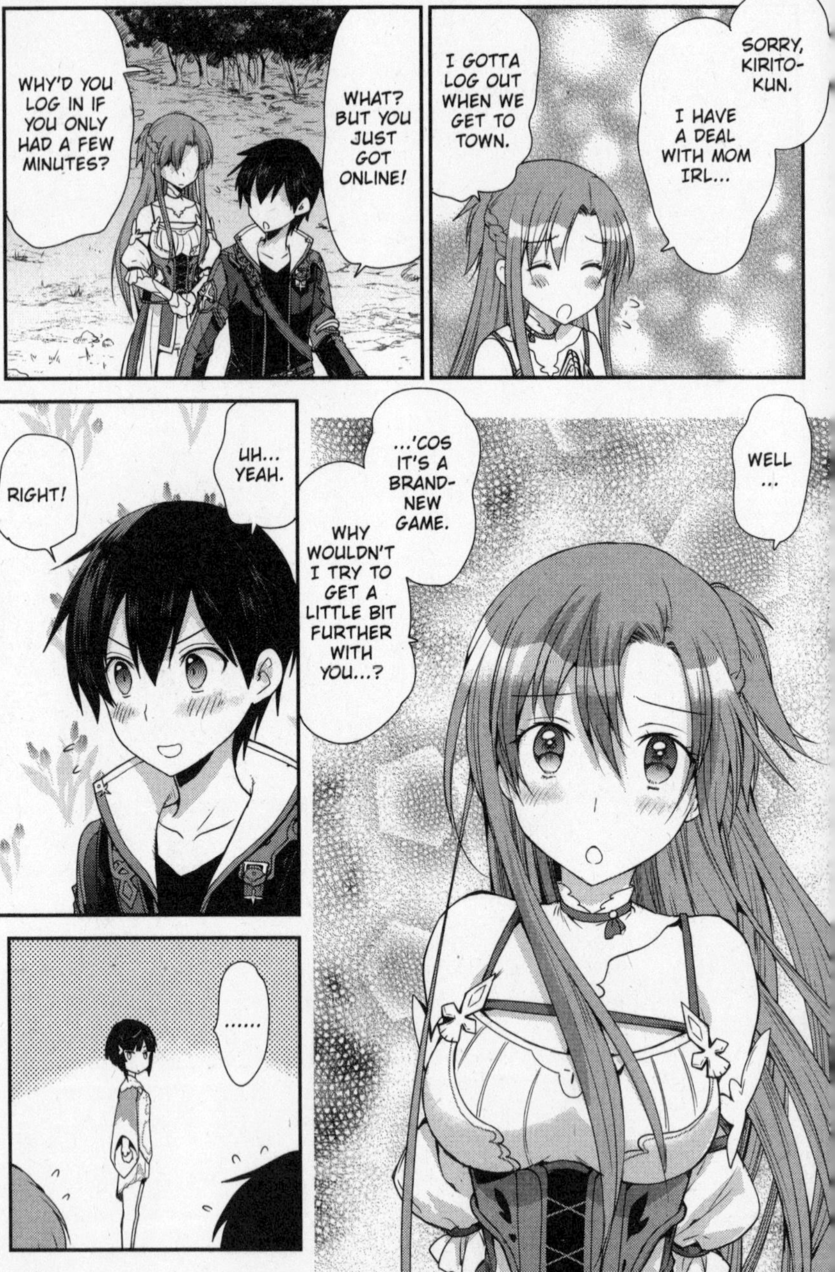
SORRY, KIRITO-KUN.
I HAVE A DEAL WITH MOM IRL...
I GOTTA LOG OUT WHEN WE GET TO TOWN.
WHAT? BUT YOU JUST GOT ONLINE!
WHY'D YOU LOG IN IF YOU ONLY HAD A FEW MINUTES?
WELL...
...'COS IT'S A BRAND-NEW GAME.
WHY WOULDN'T I TRY TO GET A LITTLE BIT FURTHER WITH YOU...?
UH... YEAH.
RIGHT!
......

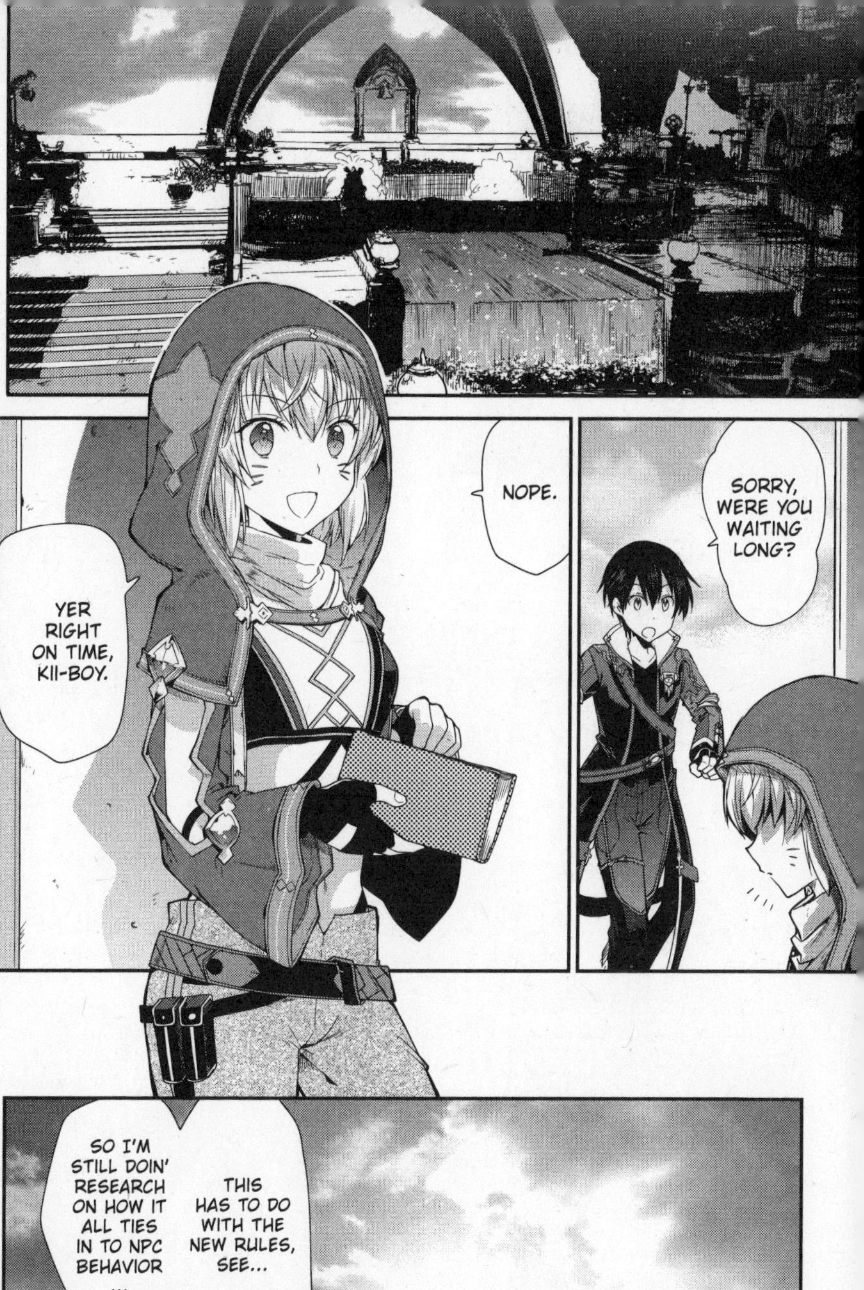

SORRY, WERE YOU WAITING LONG?
NOPE.
YER RIGHT ON TIME, KII-BOY.
THIS HAS TO DO WITH THE NEW RULES, SEE...
SO I'M STILL DOIN' RESEARCH ON HOW IT ALL TIES IN TO NPC BEHAVIOR ...

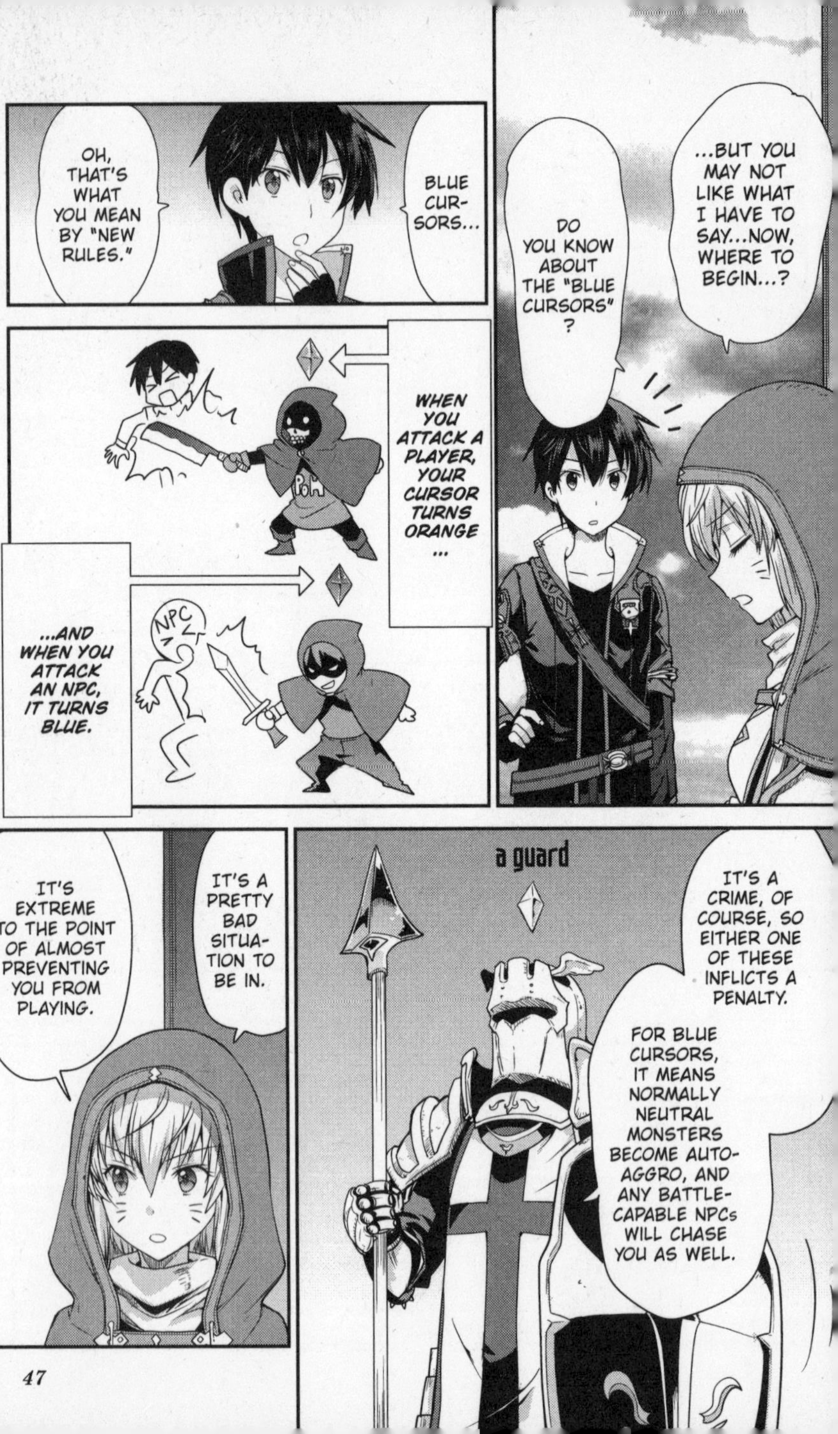
...BUT YOU MAY NOT LIKE WHAT I HAVE TO SAY...NOW, WHERE TO BEGIN...?
DO YOU KNOW ABOUT THE "BLUE CURSORS" ?
BLUE CURSORS...
OH, THAT'S WHAT YOU MEAN BY "NEW RULES."
PoH
WHEN YOU ATTACK A PLAYER, YOUR CURSOR TURNS ORANGE ...
NPC
...AND WHEN YOU ATTACK AN NPC, IT TURNS BLUE.
a guard
IT'S A CRIME, OF COURSE, SO EITHER ONE OF THESE INFLICTS A PENALTY.
FOR BLUE CURSORS, IT MEANS NORMALLY NEUTRAL MONSTERS BECOME AUTO-AGGRO, AND ANY BATTLE-CAPABLE NPCs WILL CHASE YOU AS WELL.
IT'S A PRETTY BAD SITUATION TO BE IN.
IT'S EXTREME TO THE POINT OF ALMOST PREVENTING YOU FROM PLAYING.

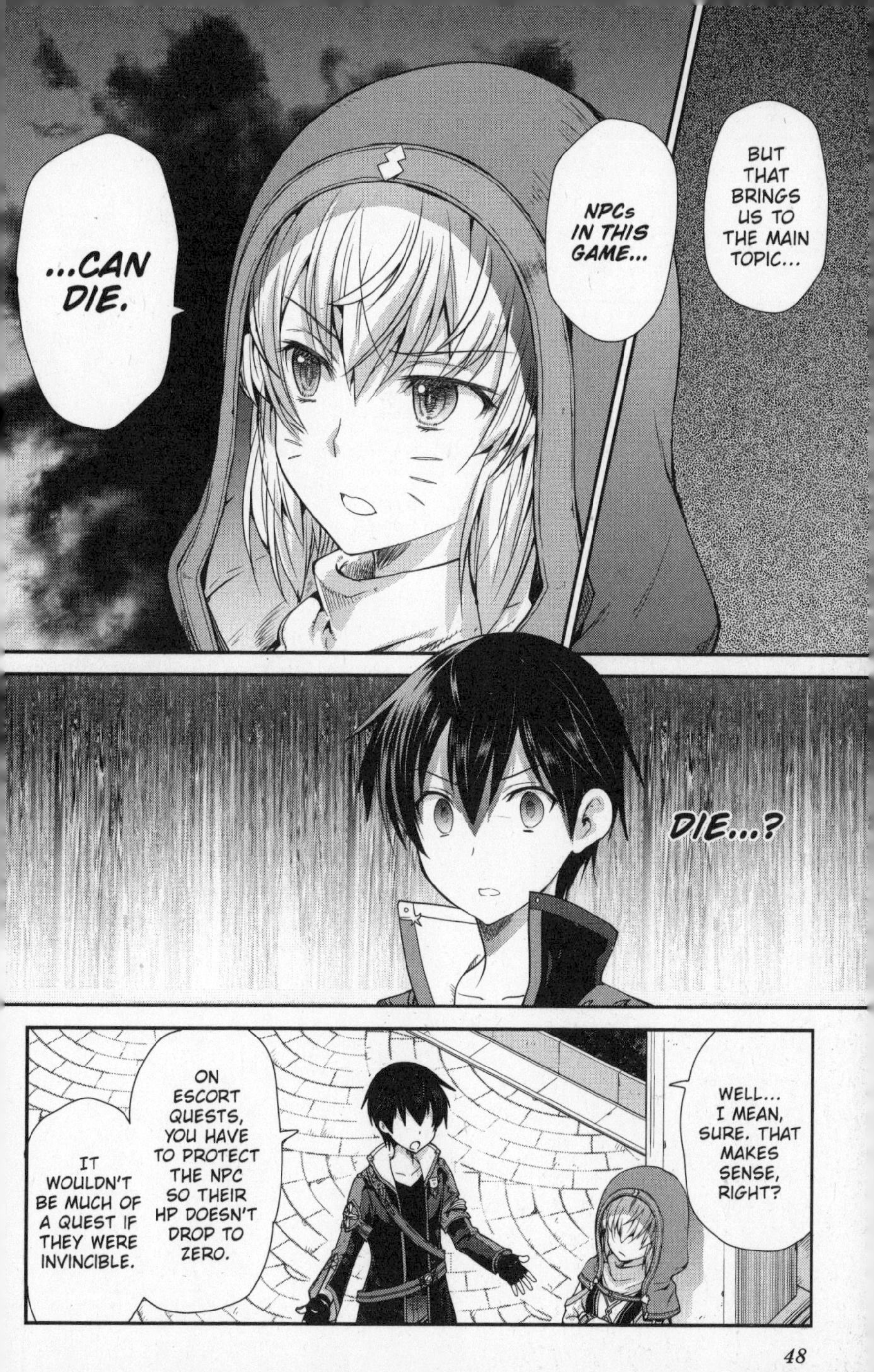
BUT THAT BRINGS US TO THE MAIN TOPIC...
NPCs IN THIS GAME...
...CAN DIE.
DIE...?
WELL... I MEAN, SURE. THAT MAKES SENSE, RIGHT?
ON ESCORT QUESTS, YOU HAVE TO PROTECT THE NPC SO THEIR HP DOESN'T DROP TO ZERO.
IT WOULDN'T BE MUCH OF A QUEST IF THEY WERE INVINCIBLE.

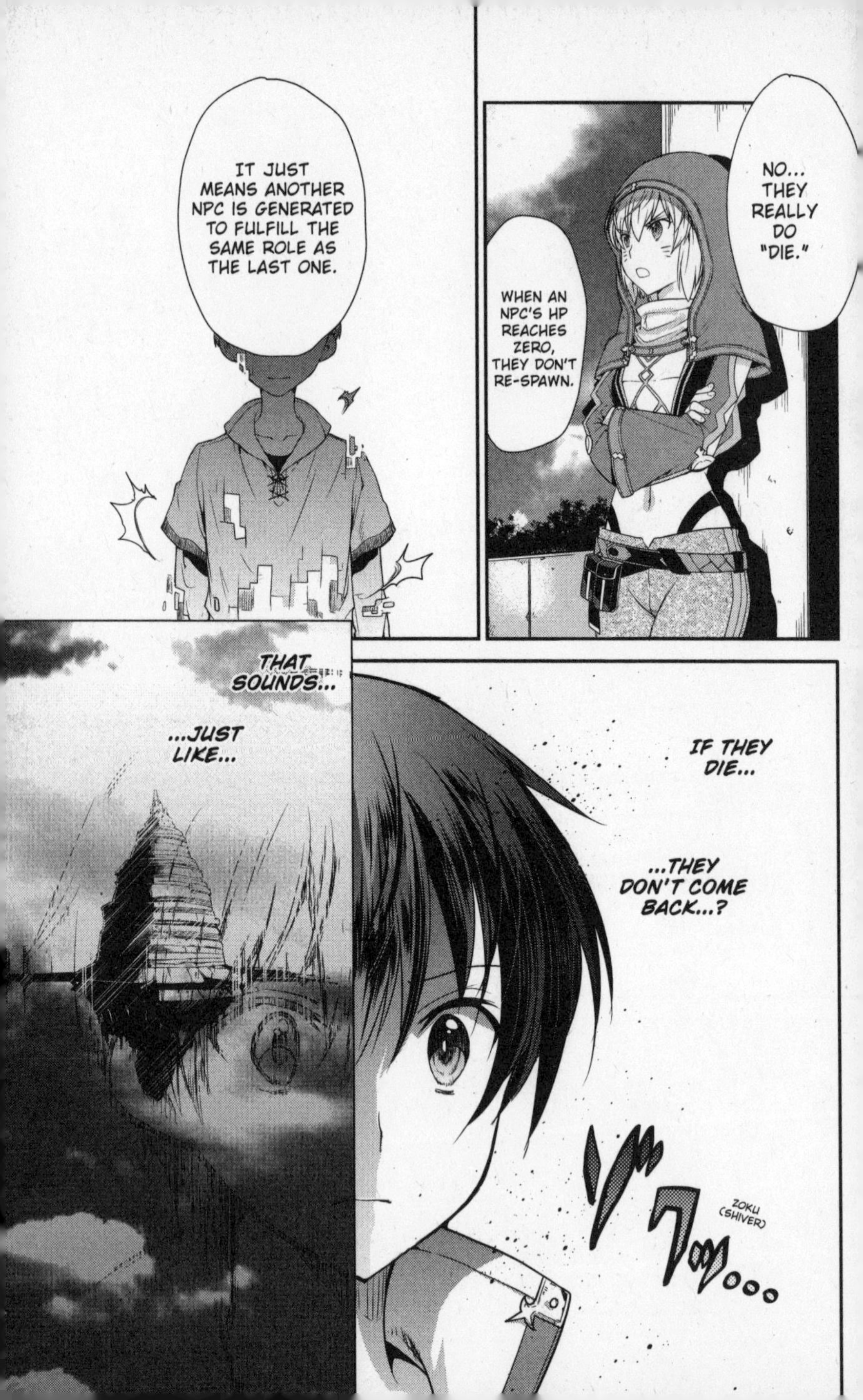
NO... THEY REALLY DO "DIE."
WHEN AN NPC'S HP REACHES ZERO, THEY DON'T RE-SPAWN.
IT JUST MEANS ANOTHER NPC IS GENERATED TO FULFILL THE SAME ROLE AS THE LAST ONE.
IF THEY DIE...
...THEY DON'T COME BACK...?
ZOKU (SHIVER)
THAT SOUNDS...
...JUST LIKE...

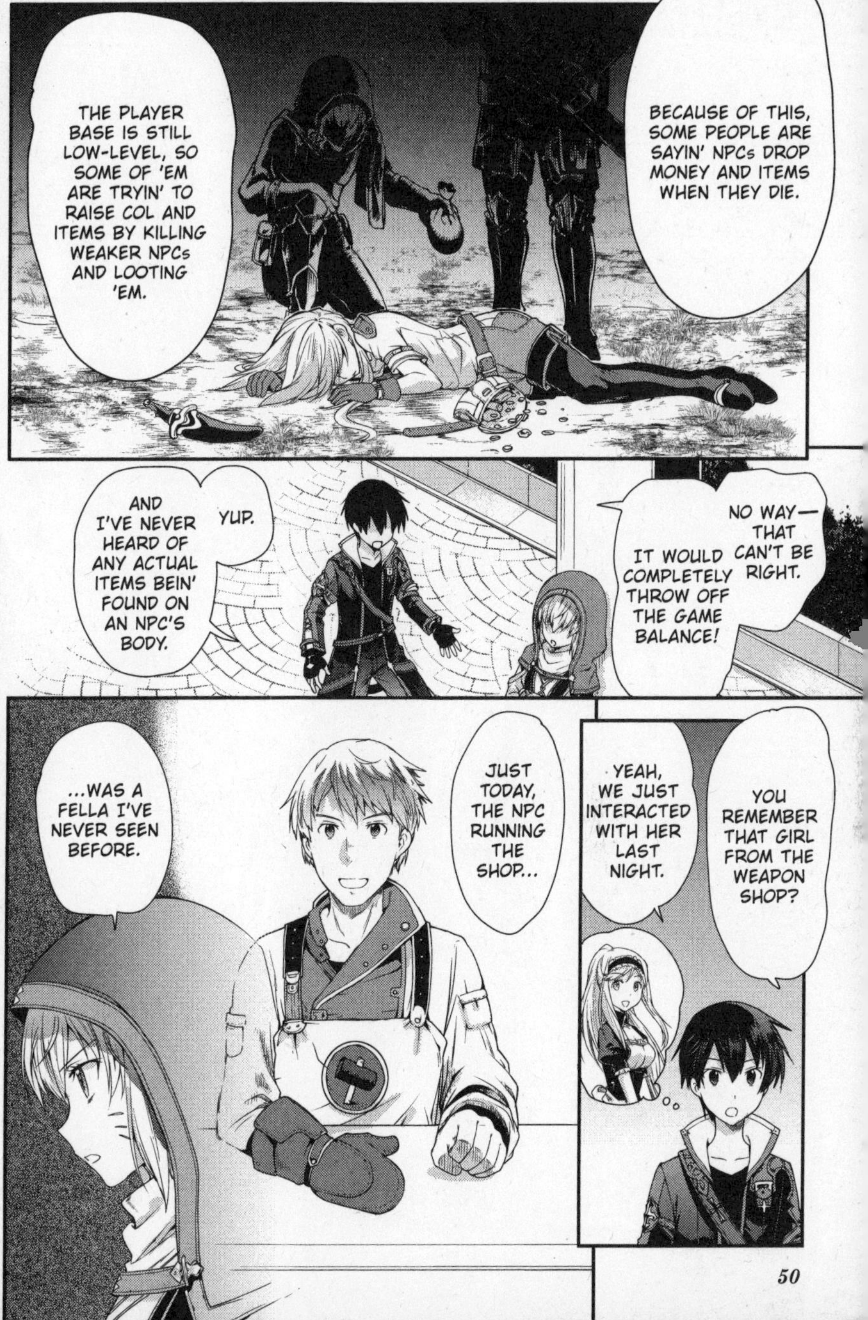
BECAUSE OF THIS, SOME PEOPLE ARE SAYIN' NPCs DROP MONEY AND ITEMS WHEN THEY DIE.
THE PLAYER BASE IS STILL LOW-LEVEL, SO SOME OF 'EM ARE TRYIN' TO RAISE COL AND ITEMS BY KILLING WEAKER NPCs AND LOOTING 'EM.
NO WAY— THAT CAN'T BE RIGHT.
IT WOULD COMPLETELY THROW OFF THE GAME BALANCE!
YUP.
AND I'VE NEVER HEARD OF ANY ACTUAL ITEMS BEIN' FOUND ON AN NPC'S BODY.
YOU REMEMBER THAT GIRL FROM THE WEAPON SHOP?
YEAH, WE JUST INTERACTED WITH HER LAST NIGHT.
JUST TODAY, THE NPC RUNNING THE SHOP...
...WAS A FELLA I'VE NEVER SEEN BEFORE.

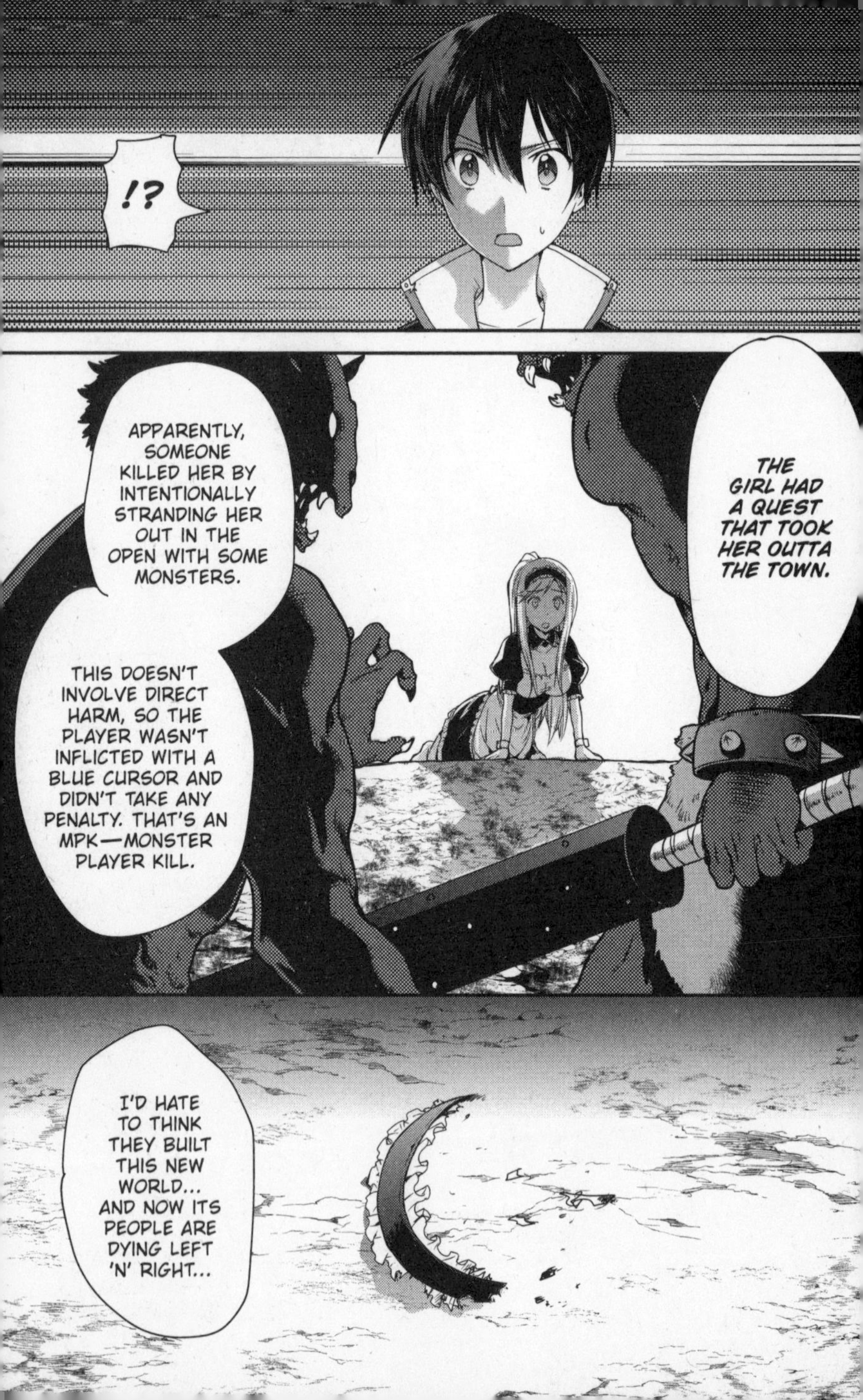
!?
THE GIRL HAD A QUEST THAT TOOK HER OUTTA THE TOWN.
APPARENTLY, SOMEONE KILLED HER BY INTENTIONALLY STRANDING HER OUT IN THE OPEN WITH SOME MONSTERS.
THIS DOESN'T INVOLVE DIRECT HARM, SO THE PLAYER WASN'T INFLICTED WITH A BLUE CURSOR AND DIDN'T TAKE ANY PENALTY. THAT'S AN MPK—MONSTER PLAYER KILL.
I'D HATE TO THINK THEY BUILT THIS NEW WORLD... AND NOW ITS PEOPLE ARE DYING LEFT 'N' RIGHT...

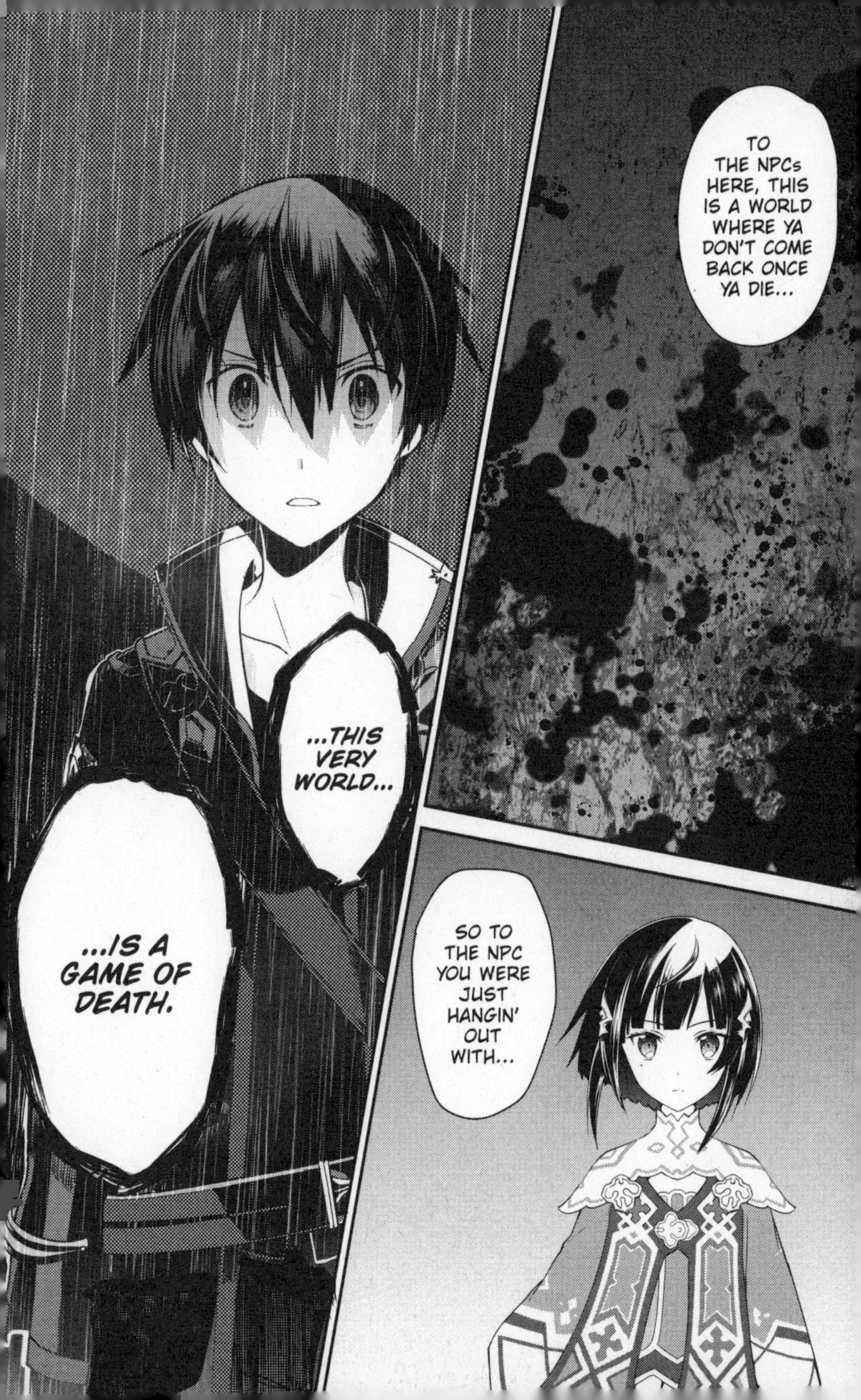
TO THE NPCs HERE, THIS IS A WORLD WHERE YA DON'T COME BACK ONCE YA DIE...
SO TO THE NPC YOU WERE JUST HANGIN' OUT WITH...
...THIS VERY WORLD...
...IS A GAME OF DEATH.

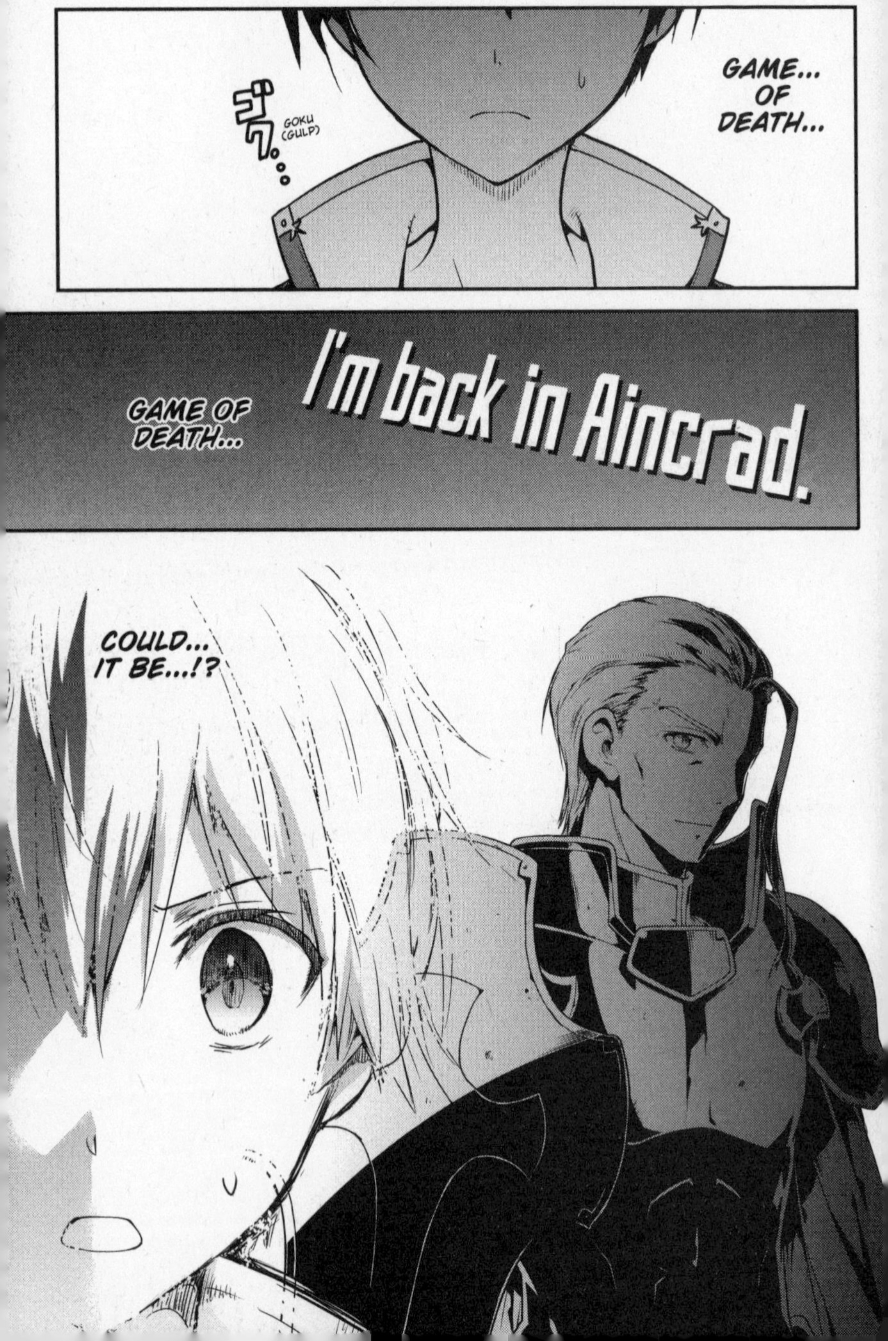
GAME... OF DEATH...
ゴク。。。
GOKU (GULP)
I'm back in Aincrad.
GAME OF DEATH...
COULD... IT BE...!?

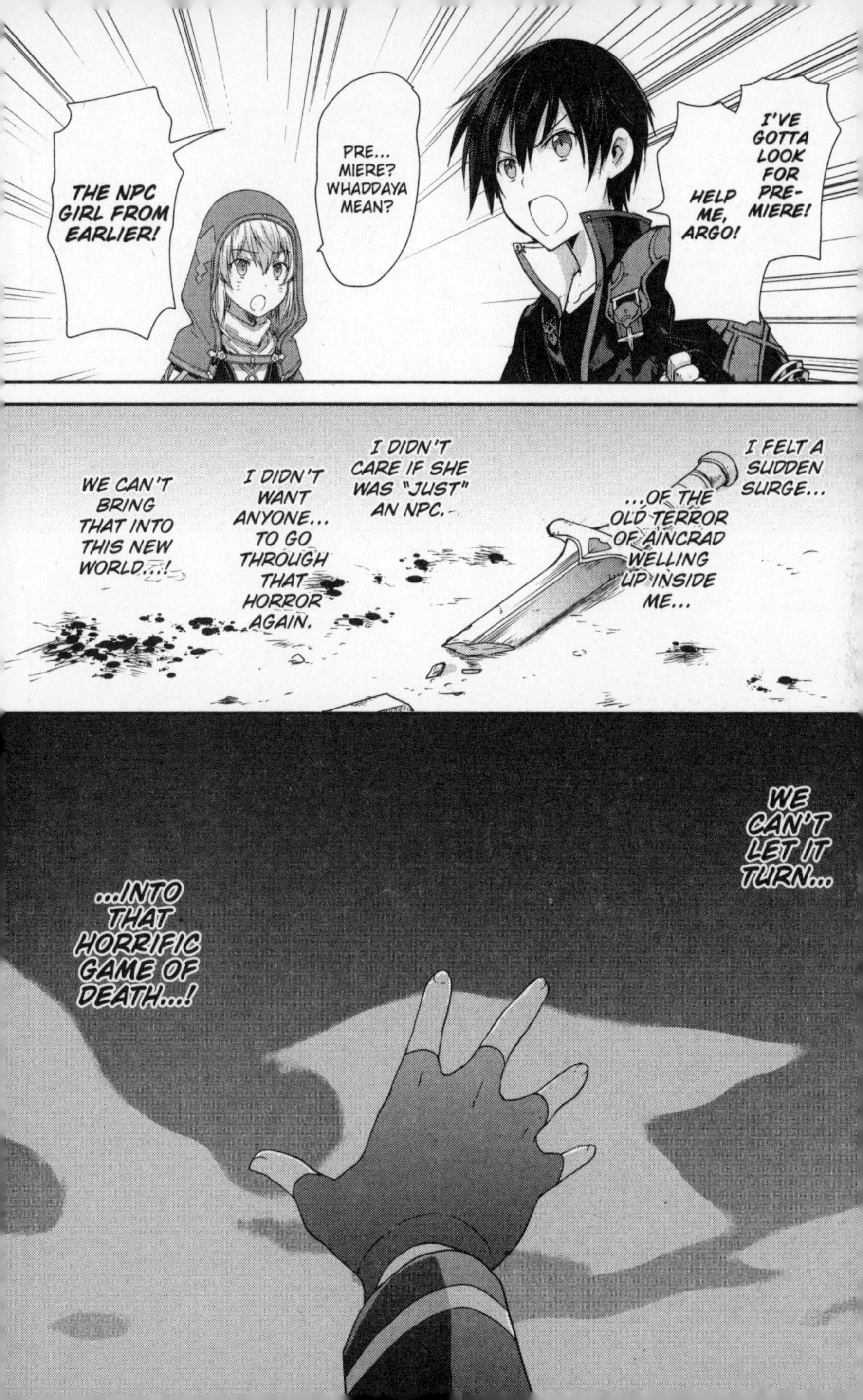
I'VE GOTTA LOOK FOR PRE-MIERE!
HELP ME, ARGO!
PRE... MIERE? WHADDAYA MEAN?
THE NPC GIRL FROM EARLIER!
I FELT A SUDDEN SURGE...
...OF THE OLD TERROR OF AINCRAD WELLING UP INSIDE ME...
I DIDN'T CARE IF SHE WAS "JUST" AN NPC.
I DIDN'T WANT ANYONE... TO GO THROUGH THAT HORROR AGAIN.
WE CAN'T BRING THAT INTO THIS NEW WORLD...!
WE CAN'T LET IT TURN...
...INTO THAT HORRIFIC GAME OF DEATH...!

#02

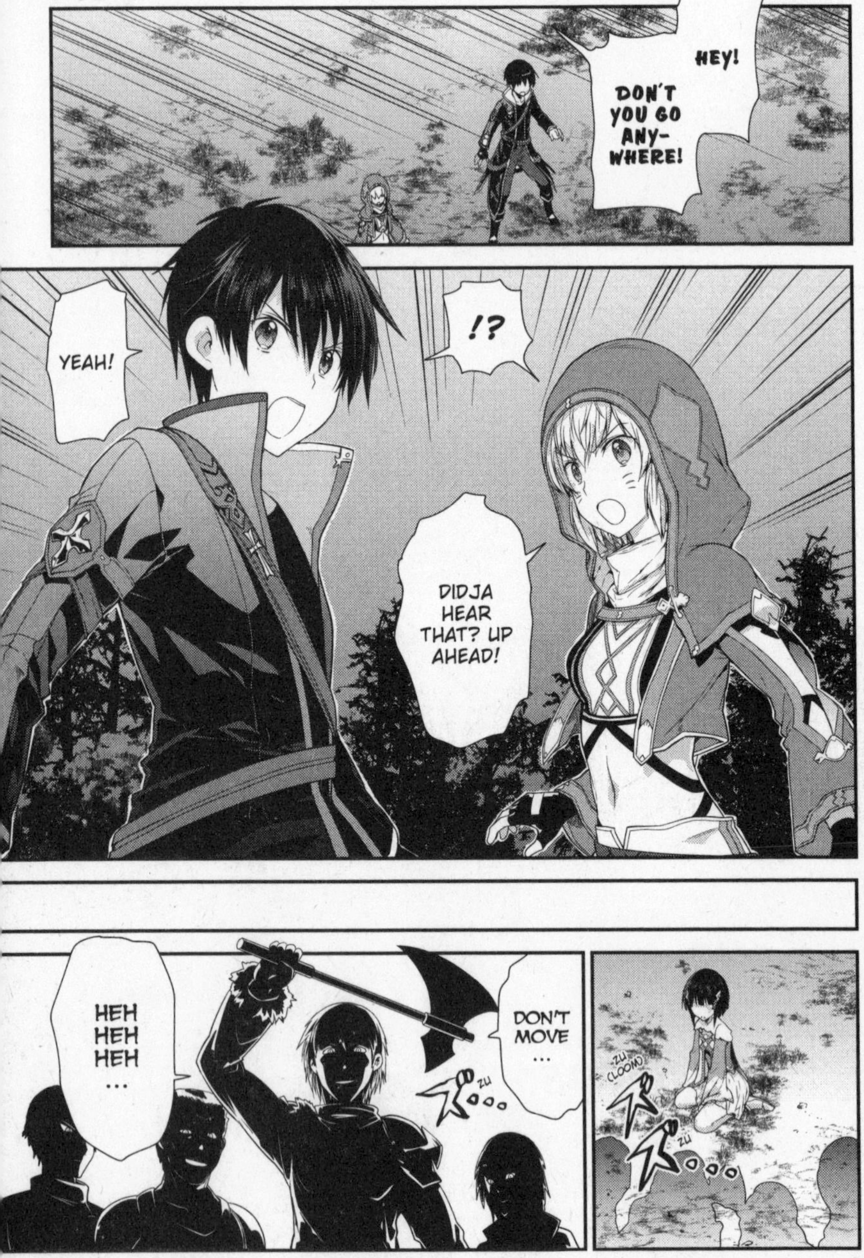
HEY!
DON'T YOU GO ANY-WHERE!
!?
DIDJA HEAR THAT? UP AHEAD!
YEAH!
ZU (LOOM)
ZU
DON'T MOVE ...
ZU
HEH HEH HEH ...

#02: Premiere

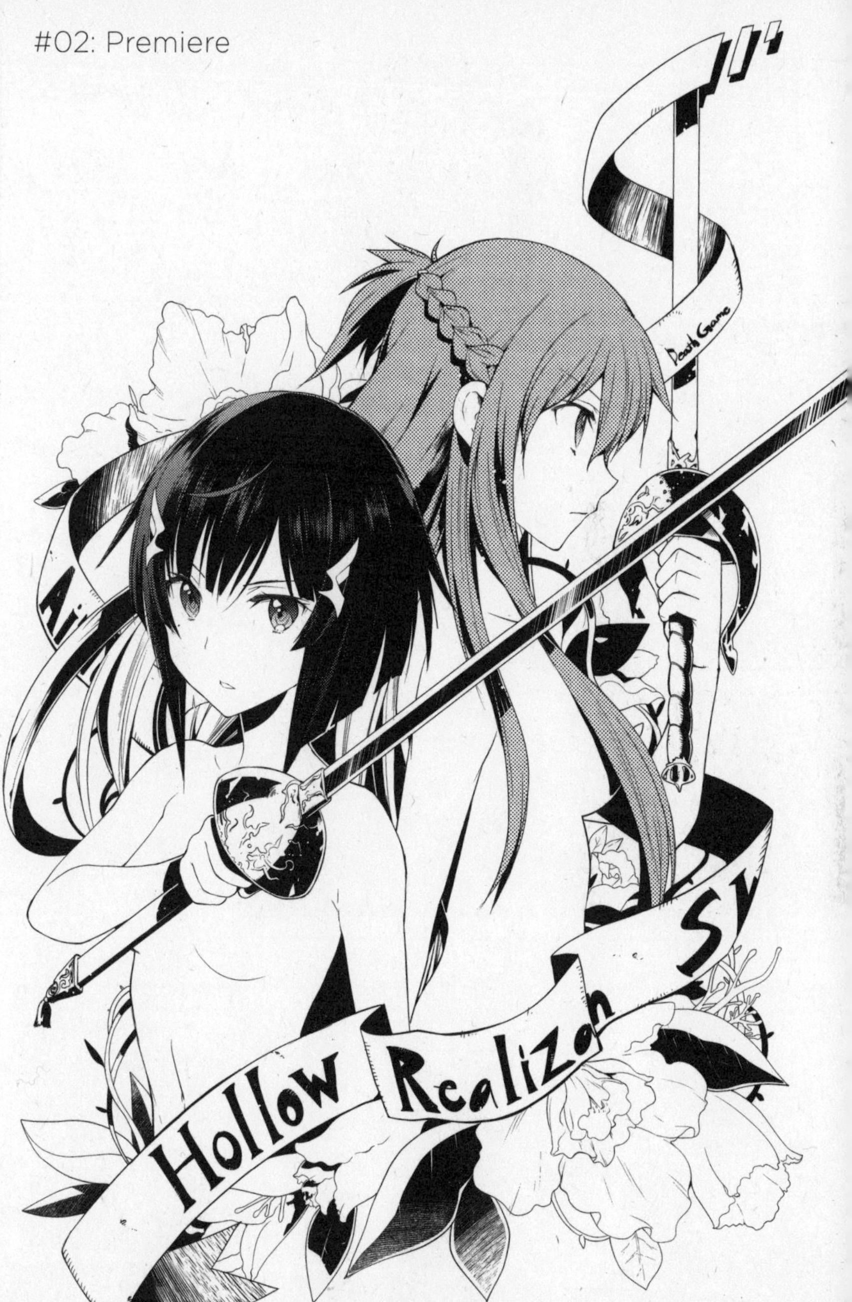
Death Game
Hollow Realizon

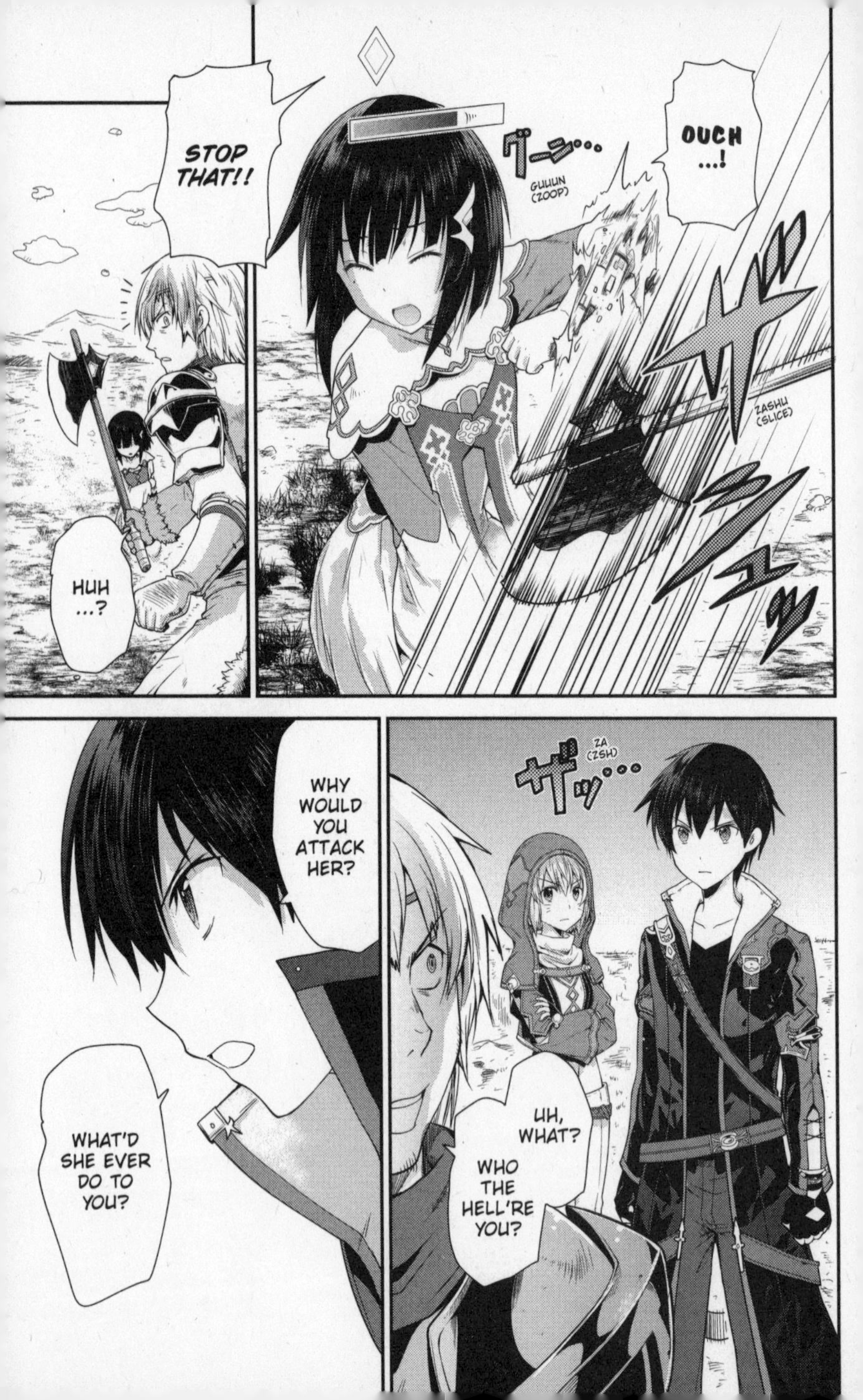
OUCH ...!
ザシュッ
ZASHU (SLICE)
グーン…
GUUUN (ZOOP)
STOP THAT!!
HUH ...?
ザッ…
ZA (ZSH)
UH, WHAT?
WHO THE HELL'RE YOU?
WHY WOULD YOU ATTACK HER?
WHAT'D SHE EVER DO TO YOU?

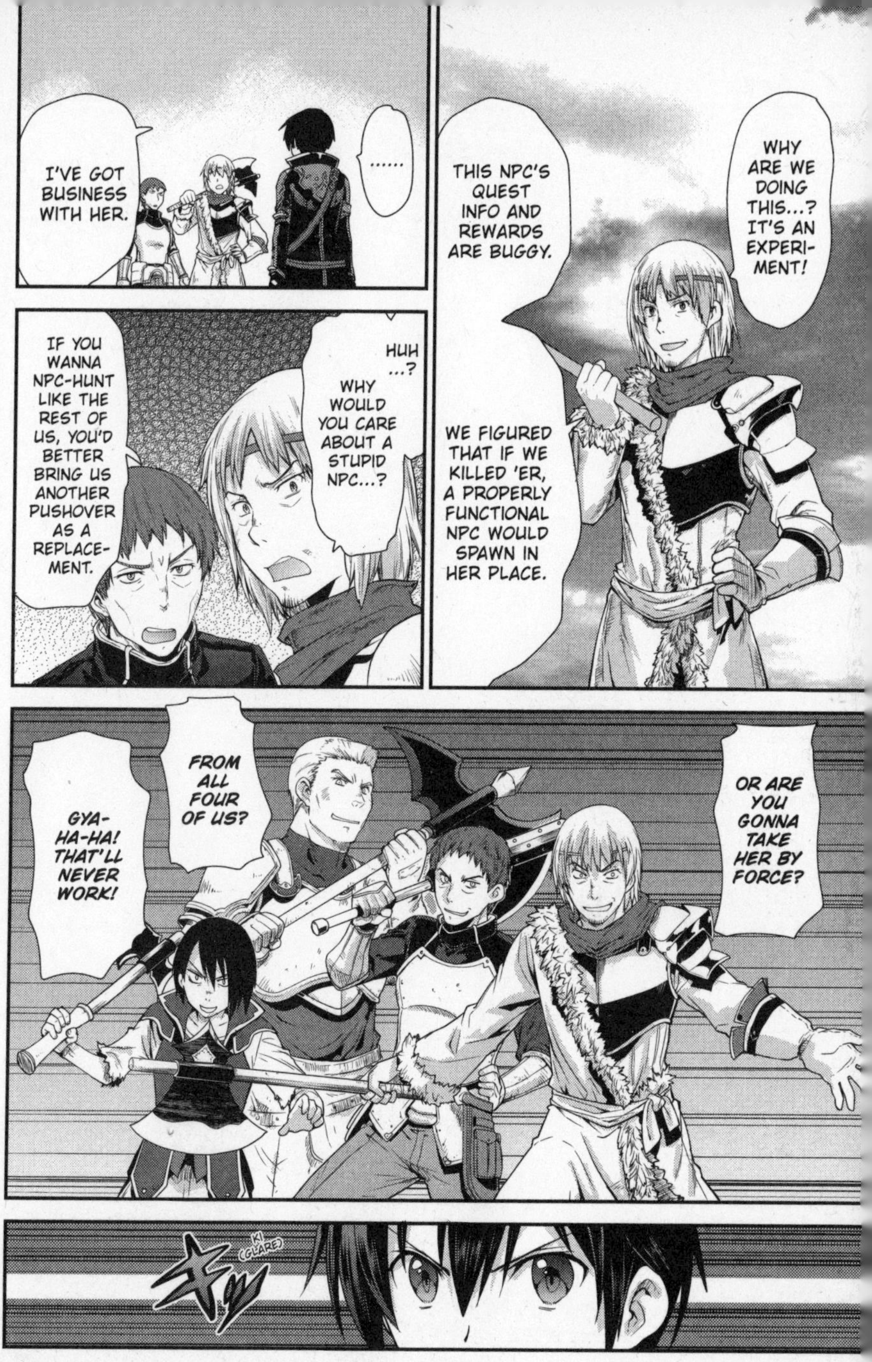
WHY ARE WE DOING THIS...? IT'S AN EXPERIMENT!
THIS NPC'S QUEST INFO AND REWARDS ARE BUGGY.
WE FIGURED THAT IF WE KILLED 'ER, A PROPERLY FUNCTIONAL NPC WOULD SPAWN IN HER PLACE.
......
I'VE GOT BUSINESS WITH HER.
HUH ...? WHY WOULD YOU CARE ABOUT A STUPID NPC...?
IF YOU WANNA NPC-HUNT LIKE THE REST OF US, YOU'D BETTER BRING US ANOTHER PUSHOVER AS A REPLACE-MENT.
OR ARE YOU GONNA TAKE HER BY FORCE?
FROM ALL FOUR OF US?
GYA-HA-HA! THAT'LL NEVER WORK!
KI (GLARE)

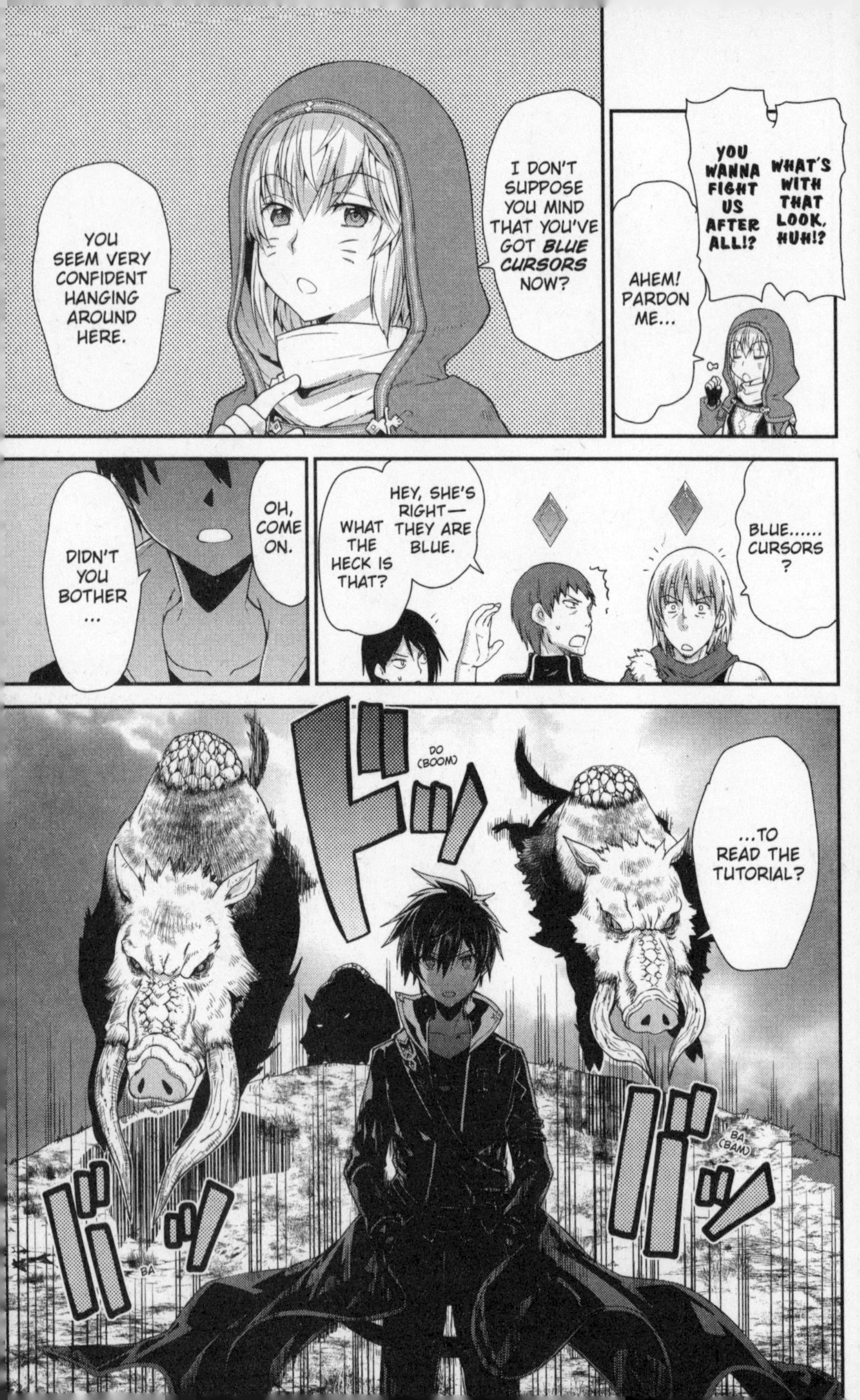
WHAT'S WITH THAT LOOK, HUH!?
YOU WANNA FIGHT US AFTER ALL!?
AHEM! PARDON ME...
I DON'T SUPPOSE YOU MIND THAT YOU'VE GOT *BLUE CURSORS* NOW?
YOU SEEM VERY CONFIDENT HANGING AROUND HERE.
BLUE...... CURSORS?
HEY, SHE'S RIGHT— THEY ARE BLUE.
WHAT THE HECK IS THAT?
OH, COME ON.
DIDN'T YOU BOTHER ...
...TO READ THE TUTORIAL?
ドッ
DO (BOOM)
バッ
BA (BAM)
バッ
BA

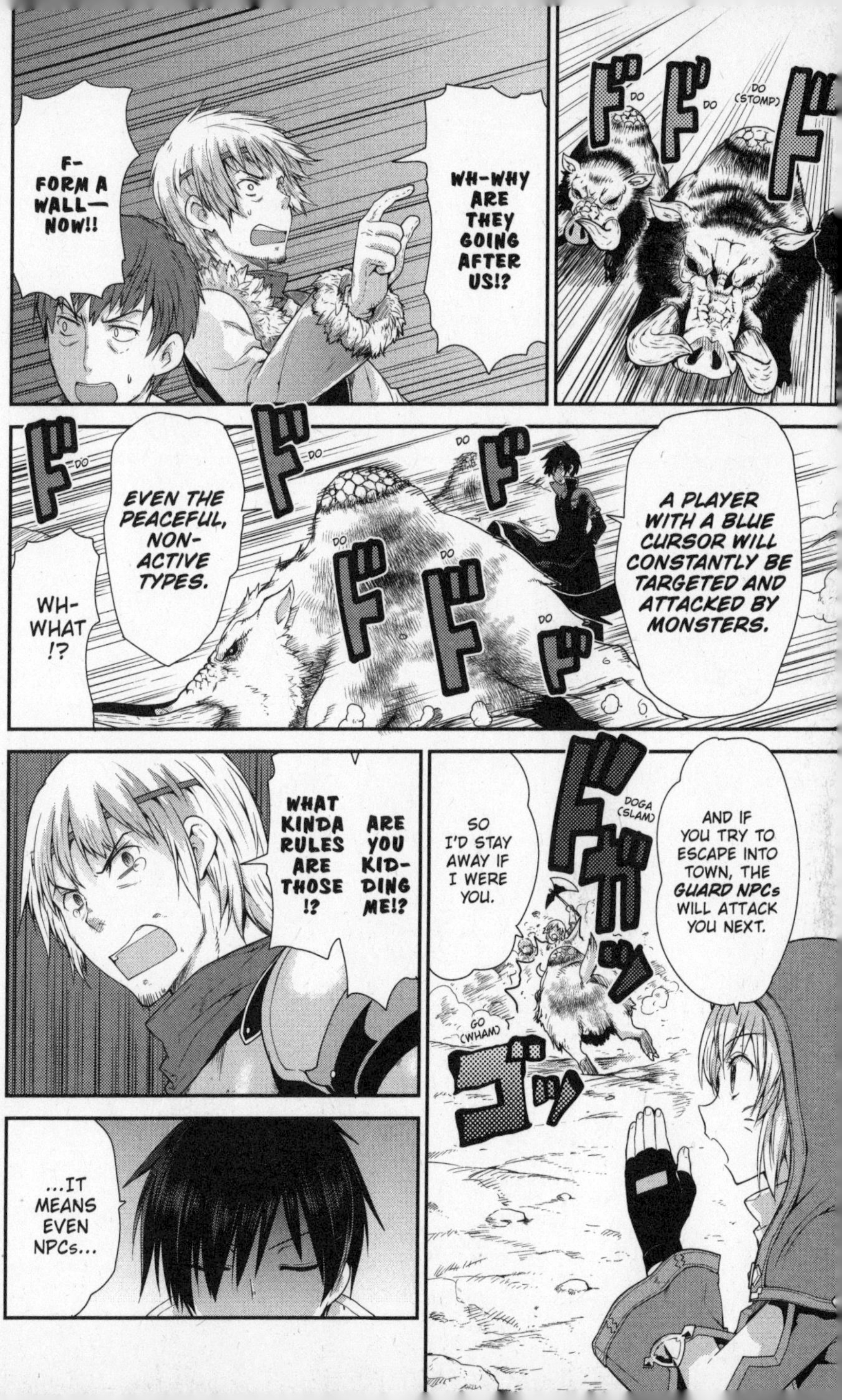
DO
DO
DO (STOMP)
WH-WHY ARE THEY GOING AFTER US!?
F-FORM A WALL—NOW!!
A PLAYER WITH A BLUE CURSOR WILL CONSTANTLY BE TARGETED AND ATTACKED BY MONSTERS.
DO
DO
DO
DO
DO
DO
EVEN THE PEACEFUL, NON-ACTIVE TYPES.
WH-WHAT!?
AND IF YOU TRY TO ESCAPE INTO TOWN, THE GUARD NPCs WILL ATTACK YOU NEXT.
DOGA (SLAM)
SO I'D STAY AWAY IF I WERE YOU.
GO (WHAM)
ARE YOU KID-DING ME!?
WHAT KINDA RULES ARE THOSE!?
...IT MEANS EVEN NPCs...

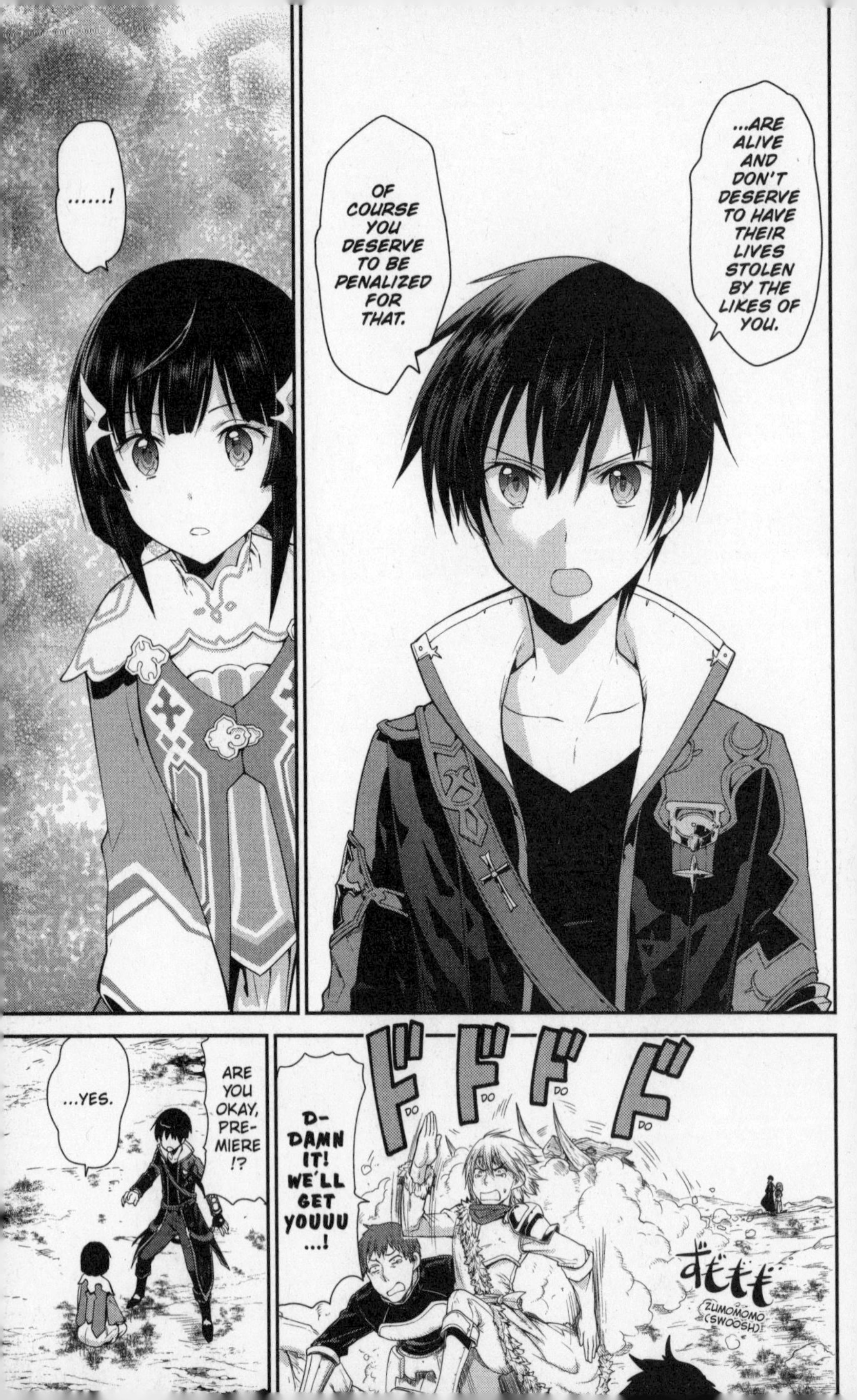
...ARE ALIVE AND DON'T DESERVE TO HAVE THEIR LIVES STOLEN BY THE LIKES OF YOU.
OF COURSE YOU DESERVE TO BE PENALIZED FOR THAT.
......!
ドドドド
DO DO DO DO
D-DAMN IT! WE'LL GET YOUUU ...!
ずももも
ZUMOMOMO (SWOOSH)
ARE YOU OKAY, PREMIERE!?
...YES.

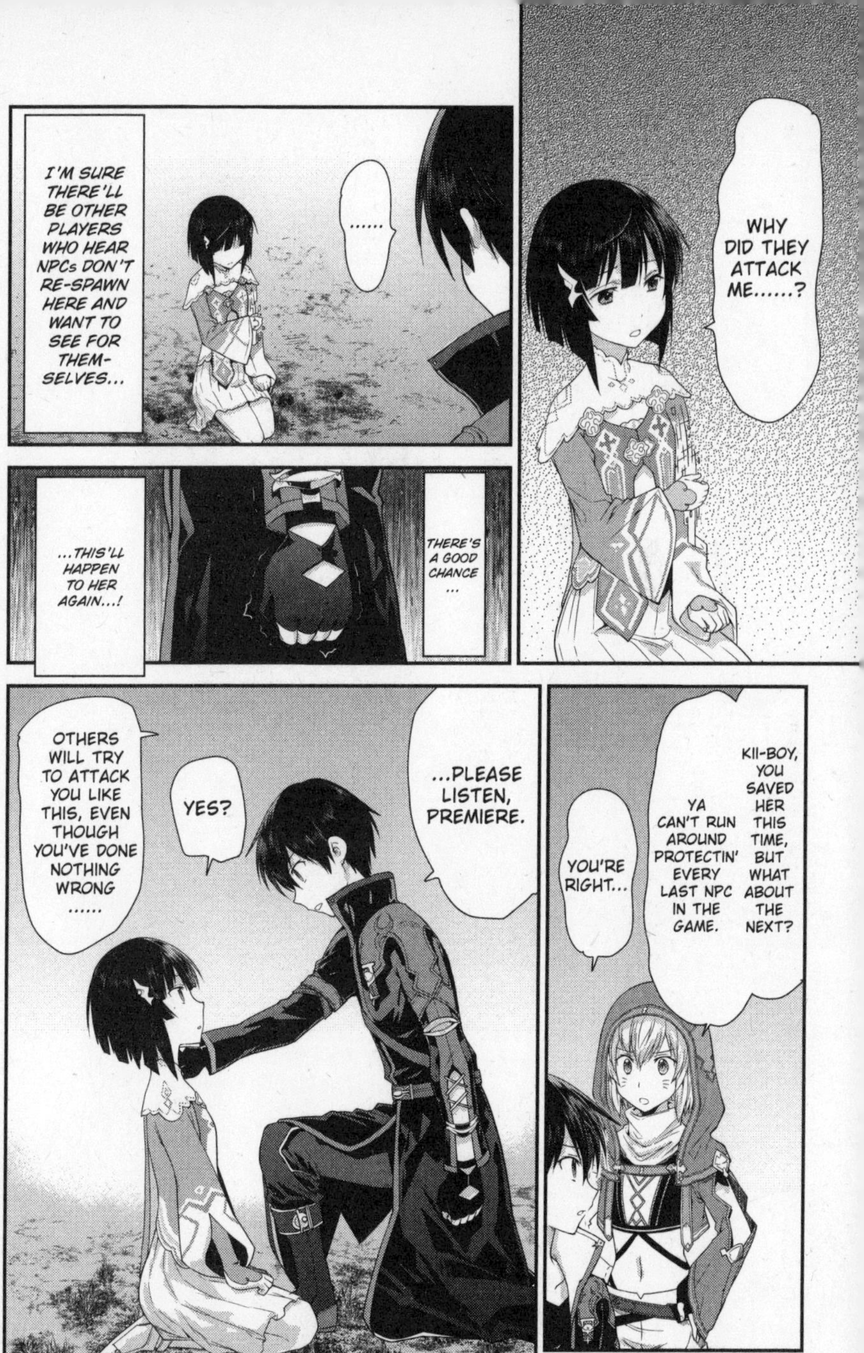
WHY DID THEY ATTACK ME......?
......
I'M SURE THERE'LL BE OTHER PLAYERS WHO HEAR NPCs DON'T RE-SPAWN HERE AND WANT TO SEE FOR THEM-SELVES...
THERE'S A GOOD CHANCE...
...THIS'LL HAPPEN TO HER AGAIN...!
KII-BOY, YOU SAVED HER THIS TIME, BUT WHAT ABOUT THE NEXT?
YA CAN'T RUN AROUND PROTECTIN' EVERY LAST NPC IN THE GAME.
YOU'RE RIGHT...
...PLEASE LISTEN, PREMIERE.
YES?
OTHERS WILL TRY TO ATTACK YOU LIKE THIS, EVEN THOUGH YOU'VE DONE NOTHING WRONG......

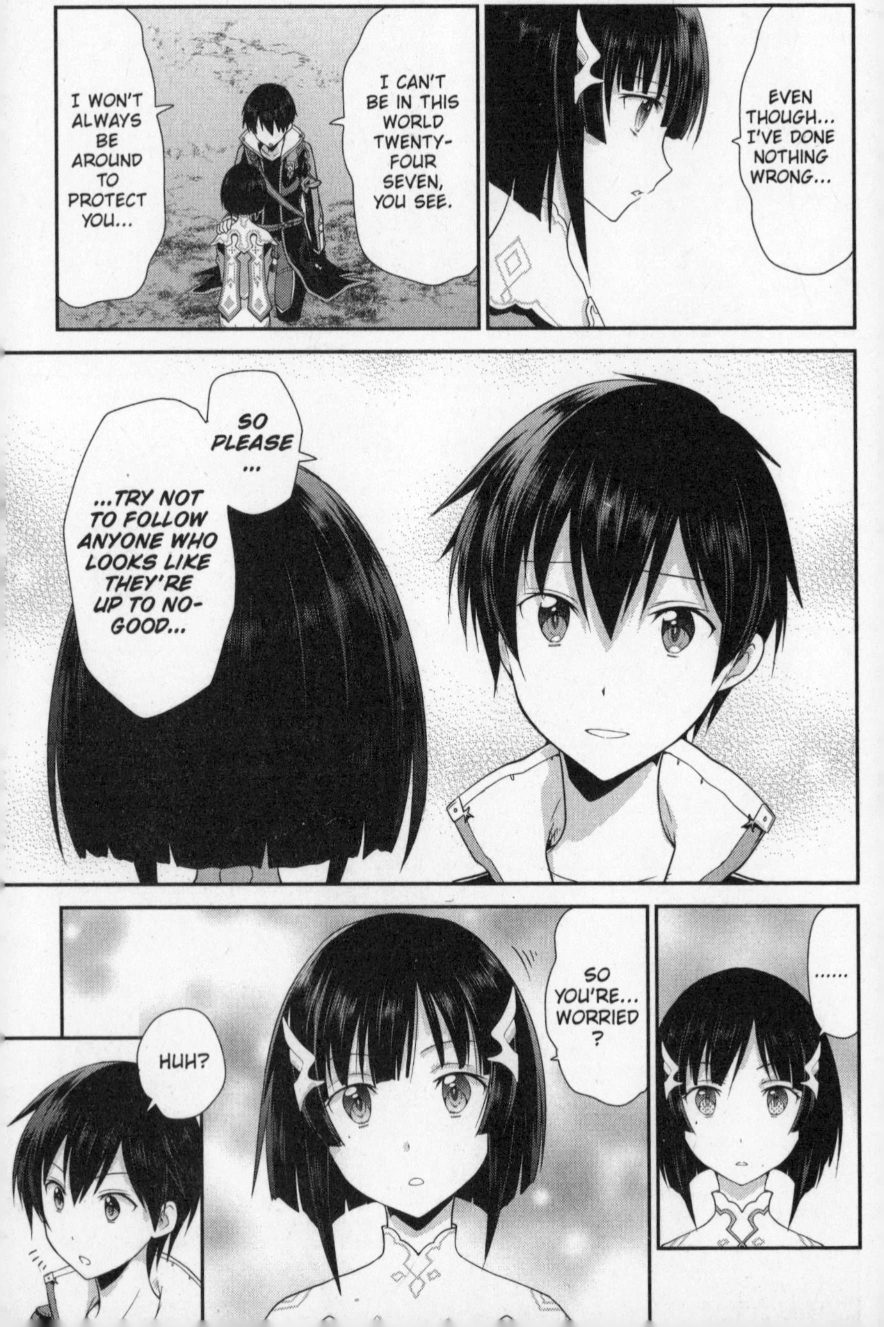
EVEN THOUGH... I'VE DONE NOTHING WRONG...
I CAN'T BE IN THIS WORLD TWENTY-FOUR SEVEN, YOU SEE.
I WON'T ALWAYS BE AROUND TO PROTECT YOU...
SO PLEASE ...
...TRY NOT TO FOLLOW ANYONE WHO LOOKS LIKE THEY'RE UP TO NO-GOOD...
......
SO YOU'RE... WORRIED ?
HUH?

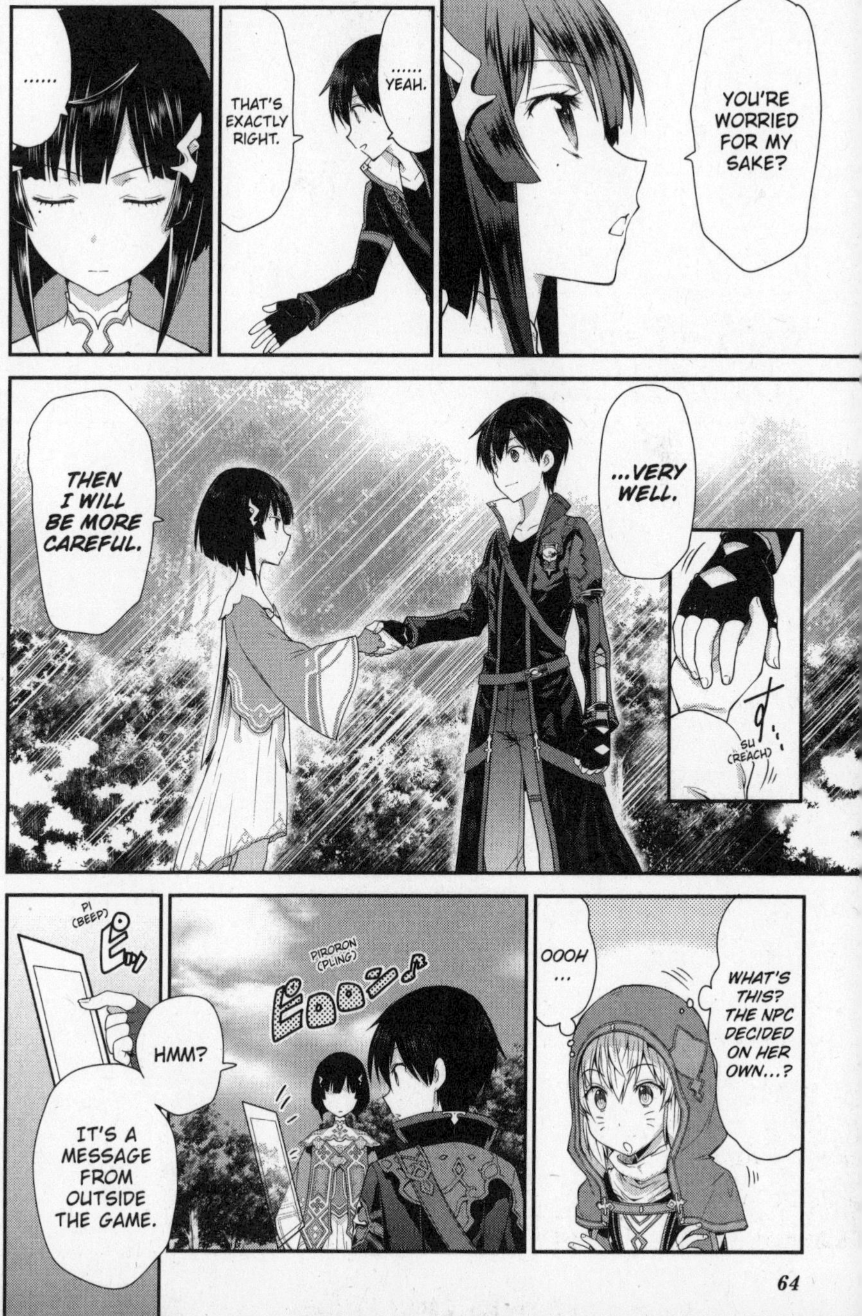
YOU'RE WORRIED FOR MY SAKE?
......YEAH.
THAT'S EXACTLY RIGHT.
......
...VERY WELL.
THEN I WILL BE MORE CAREFUL.
SU (REACH)
WHAT'S THIS? THE NPC DECIDED ON HER OWN...?
OOOH ...
PIRORON (PLING)
PI (BEEP)
HMM?
IT'S A MESSAGE FROM OUTSIDE THE GAME.

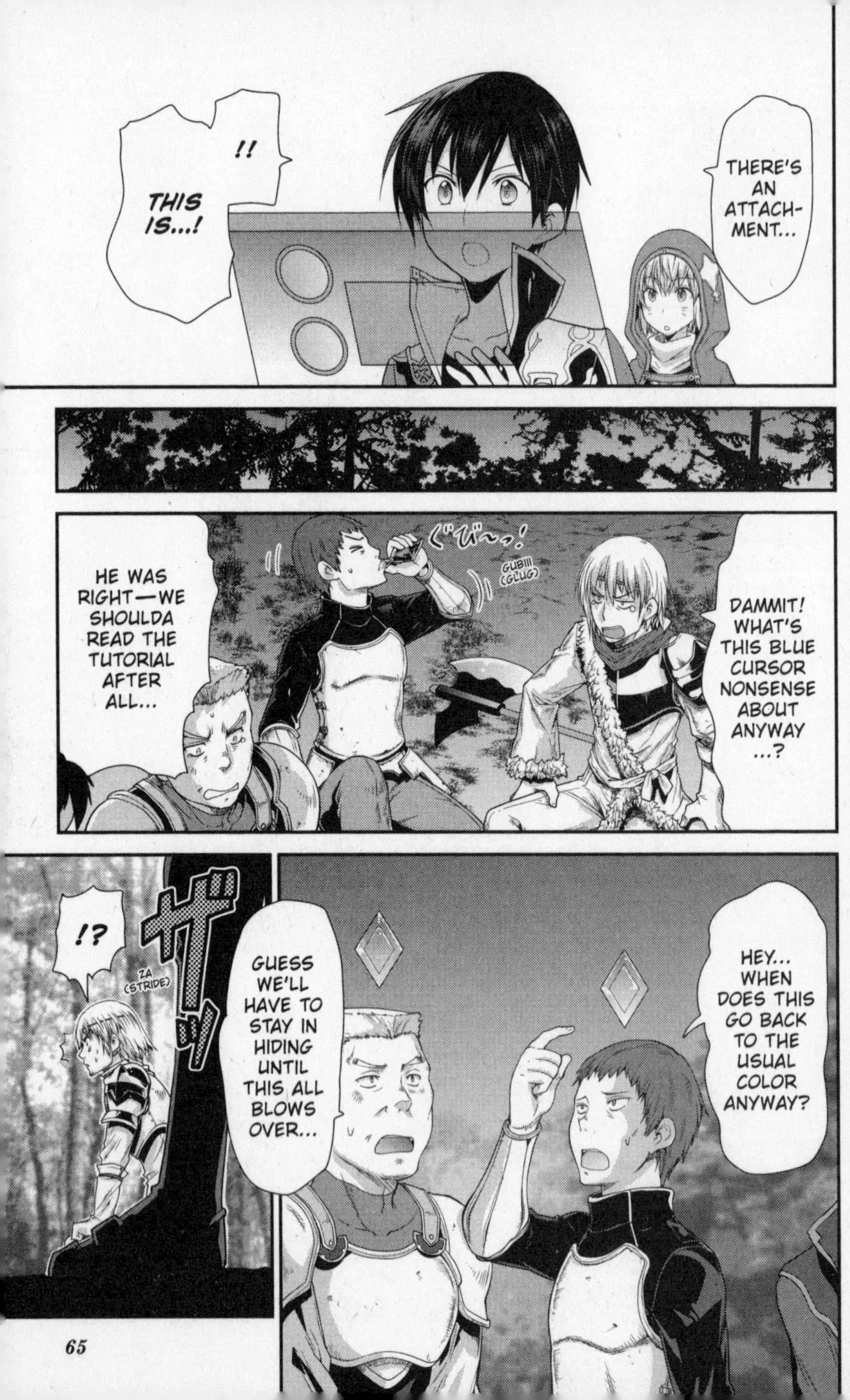
THERE'S AN ATTACHMENT...
!! THIS IS...!
DAMMIT! WHAT'S THIS BLUE CURSOR NONSENSE ABOUT ANYWAY ...?
ぐびーっ!
GUBIII (GLUG)
HE WAS RIGHT—WE SHOULDA READ THE TUTORIAL AFTER ALL...
HEY... WHEN DOES THIS GO BACK TO THE USUAL COLOR ANYWAY?
GUESS WE'LL HAVE TO STAY IN HIDING UNTIL THIS ALL BLOWS OVER...
ザッ
ZA (STRIDE)
!?

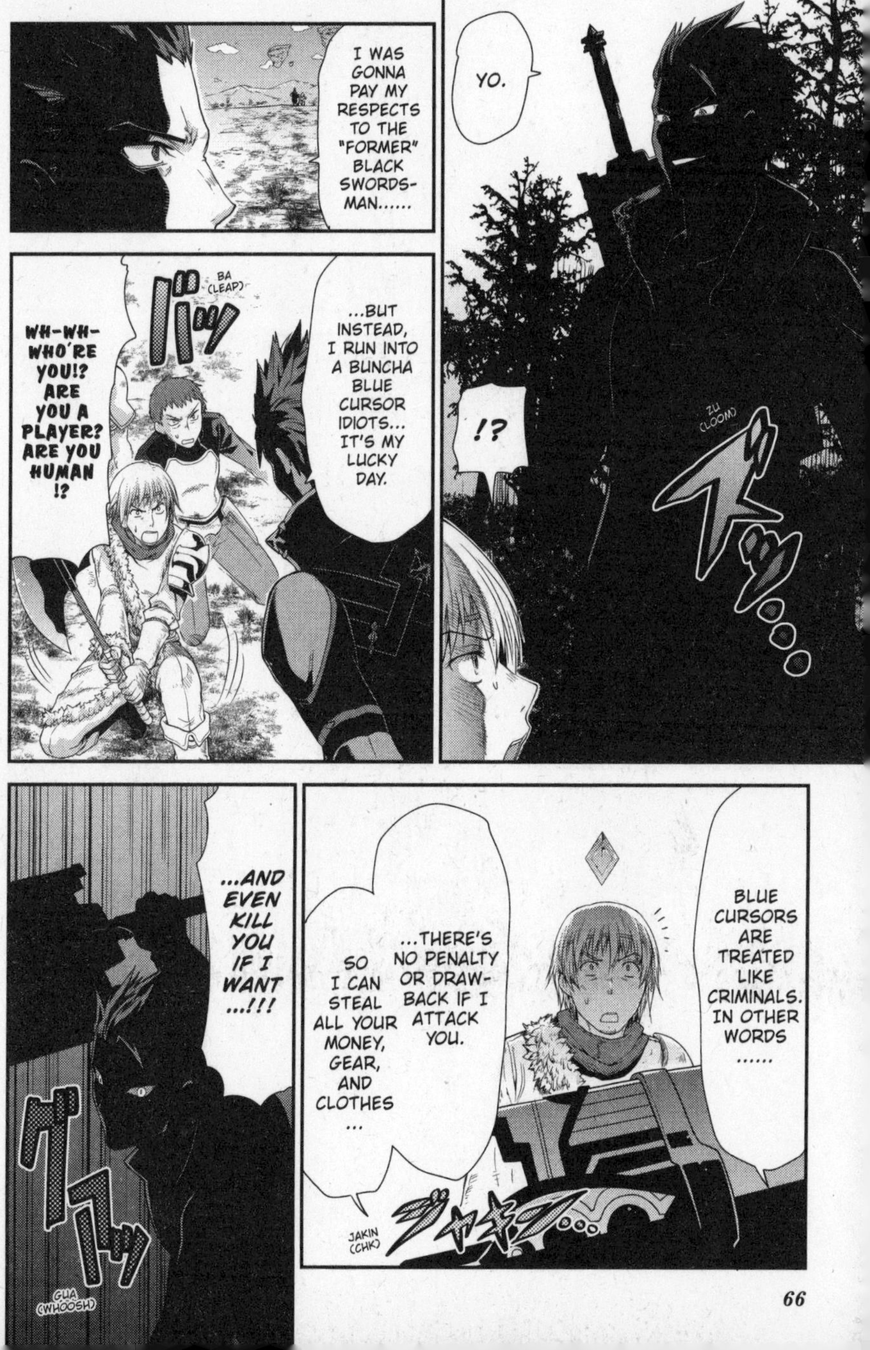
YO.
!?
ZU (LOOM)
I WAS GONNA PAY MY RESPECTS TO THE "FORMER" BLACK SWORDSMAN......
...BUT INSTEAD, I RUN INTO A BUNCHA BLUE CURSOR IDIOTS... IT'S MY LUCKY DAY.
BA (LEAP)
WH-WH-WHO'RE YOU!? ARE YOU A PLAYER? ARE YOU HUMAN!?
BLUE CURSORS ARE TREATED LIKE CRIMINALS. IN OTHER WORDS......
...THERE'S NO PENALTY OR DRAWBACK IF I ATTACK YOU.
SO I CAN STEAL ALL YOUR MONEY, GEAR, AND CLOTHES...
JAKIN (CHK)
...AND EVEN KILL YOU IF I WANT...!!!
GUA (WHOOSH)

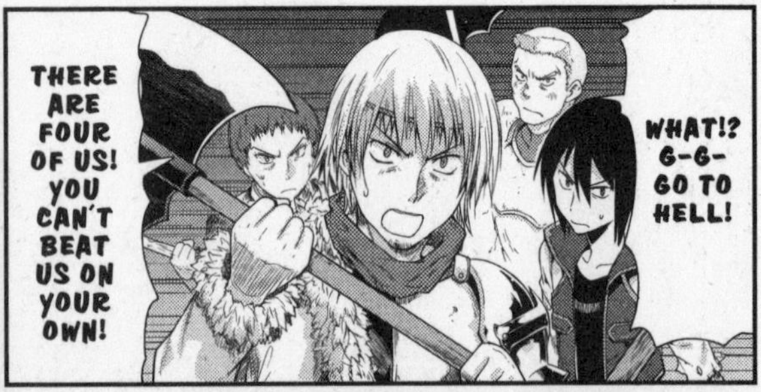
WHAT!? G-G-GO TO HELL!
THERE ARE FOUR OF US! YOU CAN'T BEAT US ON YOUR OWN!
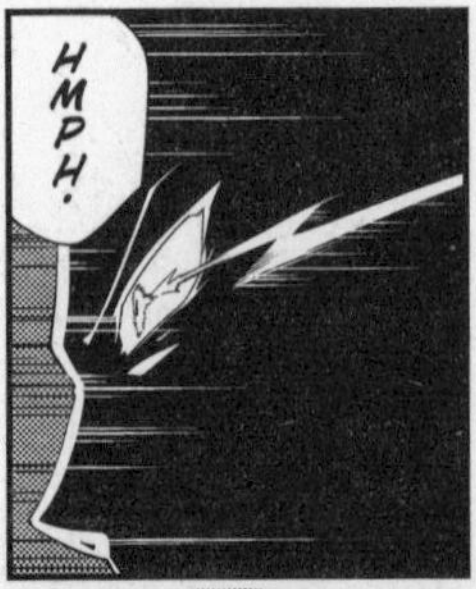
HMPH!
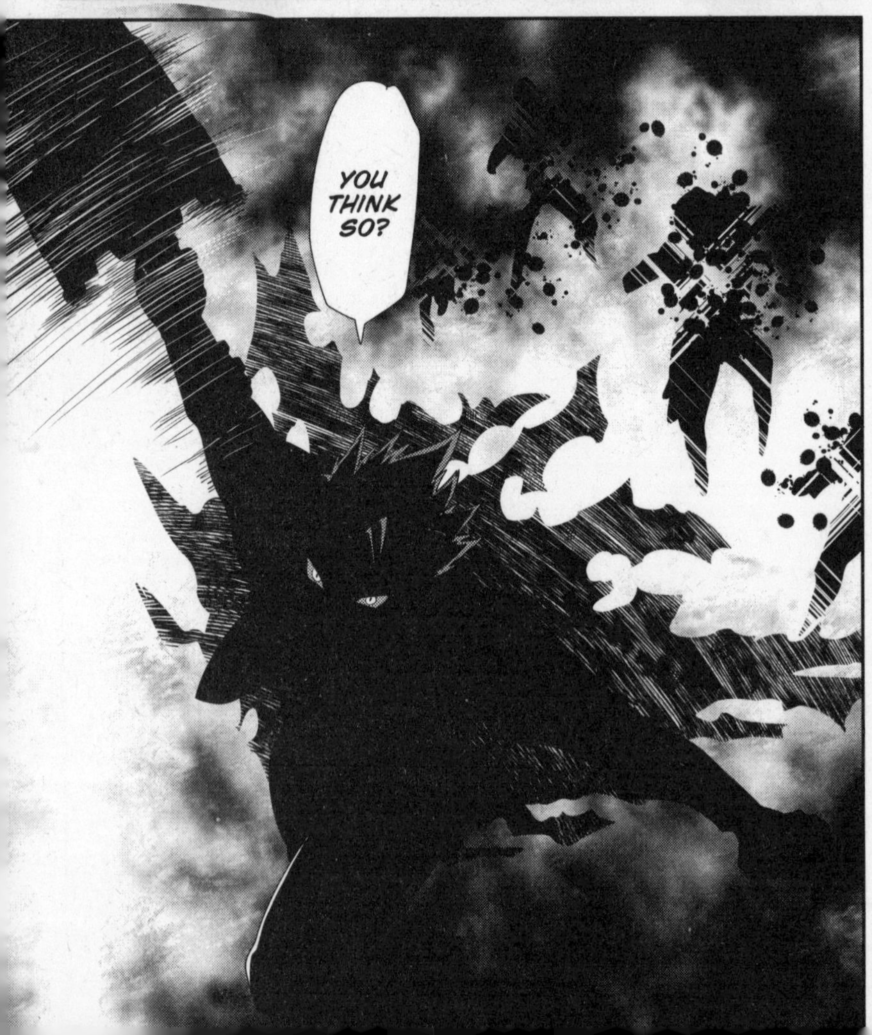
YOU THINK SO?

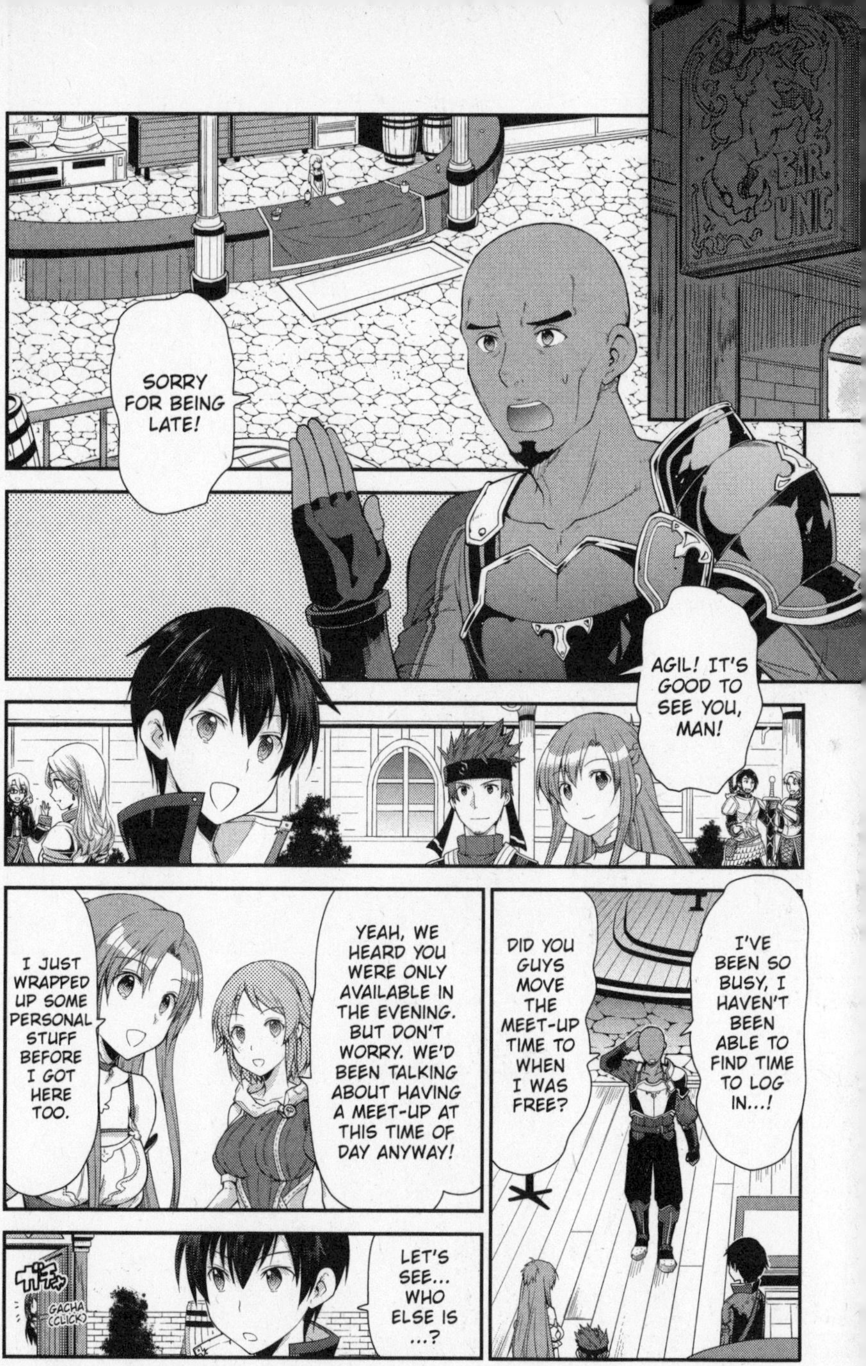
SORRY FOR BEING LATE!
AGIL! IT'S GOOD TO SEE YOU, MAN!
I'VE BEEN SO BUSY, I HAVEN'T BEEN ABLE TO FIND TIME TO LOG IN...!
DID YOU GUYS MOVE THE MEET-UP TIME TO WHEN I WAS FREE?
YEAH, WE HEARD YOU WERE ONLY AVAILABLE IN THE EVENING. BUT DON'T WORRY. WE'D BEEN TALKING ABOUT HAVING A MEET-UP AT THIS TIME OF DAY ANYWAY!
I JUST WRAPPED UP SOME PERSONAL STUFF BEFORE I GOT HERE TOO.
LET'S SEE... WHO ELSE IS ...?
GACHA (CLICK)

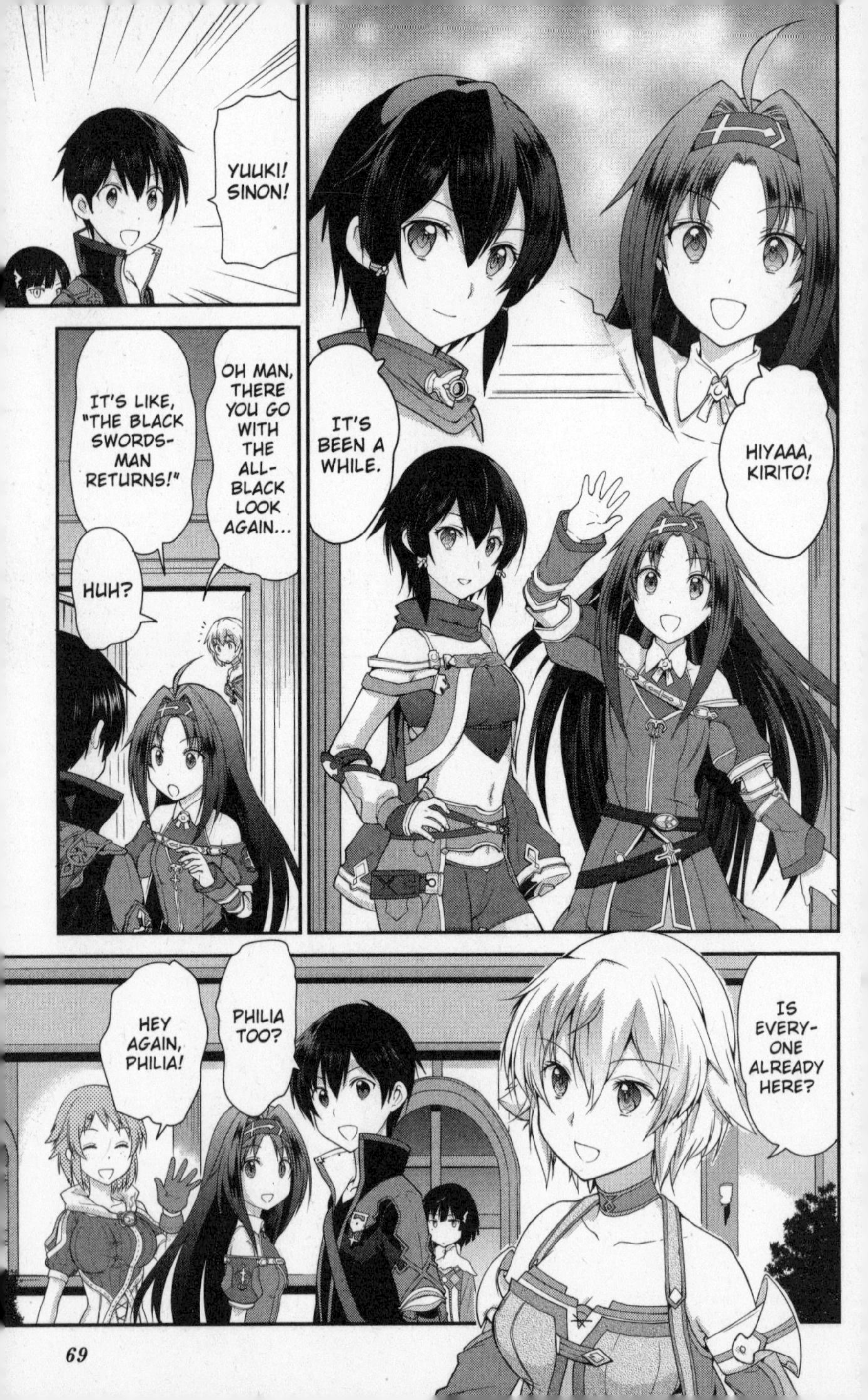
HIYAAA, KIRITO!
IT'S BEEN A WHILE.
YUUKI! SINON!
OH MAN, THERE YOU GO WITH THE ALL-BLACK LOOK AGAIN...
IT'S LIKE, "THE BLACK SWORDS-MAN RETURNS!"
HUH?
IS EVERY-ONE ALREADY HERE?
PHILIA TOO?
HEY AGAIN, PHILIA!

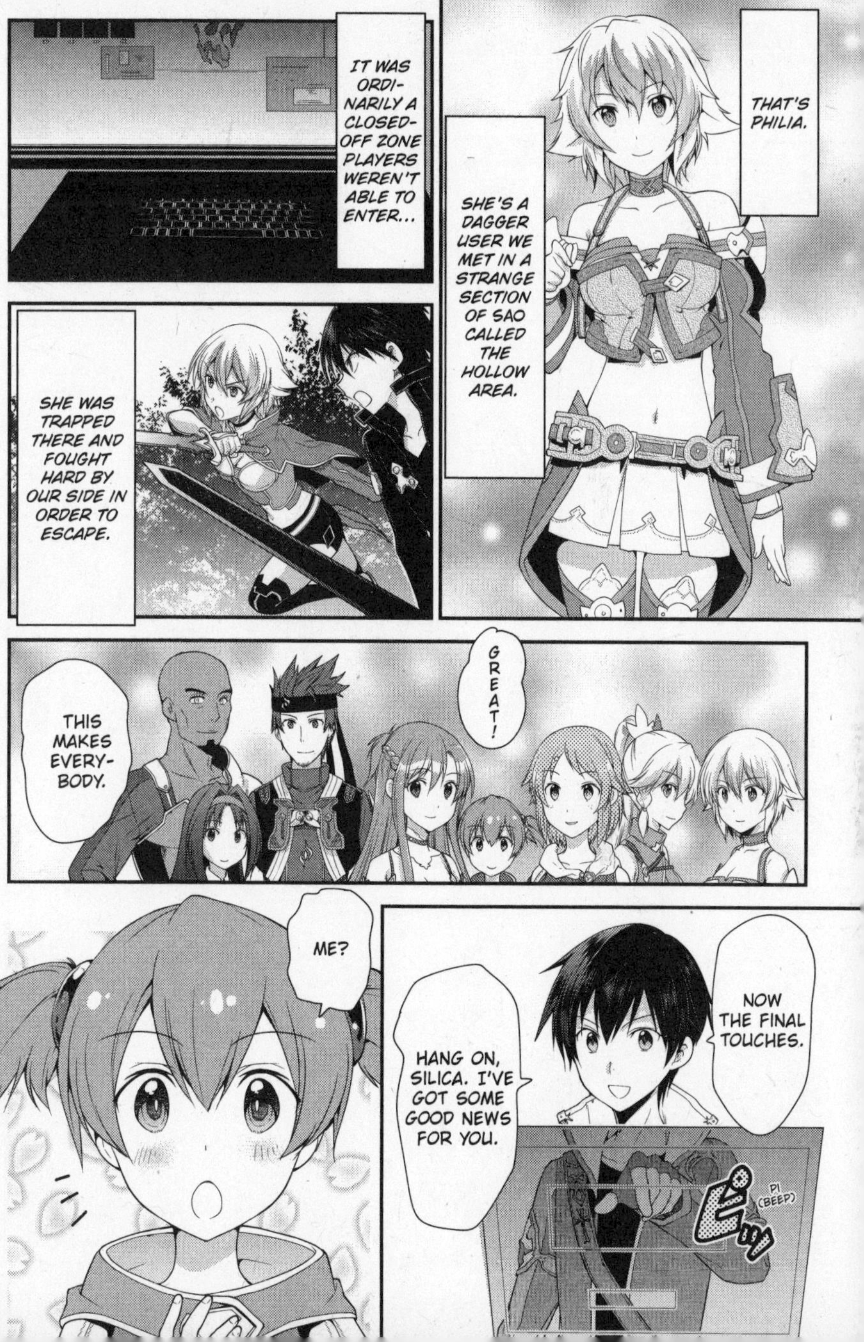
THAT'S PHILIA.
SHE'S A DAGGER USER WE MET IN A STRANGE SECTION OF SAO CALLED THE HOLLOW AREA.
IT WAS ORDINARILY A CLOSED-OFF ZONE PLAYERS WEREN'T ABLE TO ENTER...
SHE WAS TRAPPED THERE AND FOUGHT HARD BY OUR SIDE IN ORDER TO ESCAPE.
GREAT!
THIS MAKES EVERYBODY.
NOW THE FINAL TOUCHES.
HANG ON, SILICA. I'VE GOT SOME GOOD NEWS FOR YOU.
PI (BEEP)
ME?

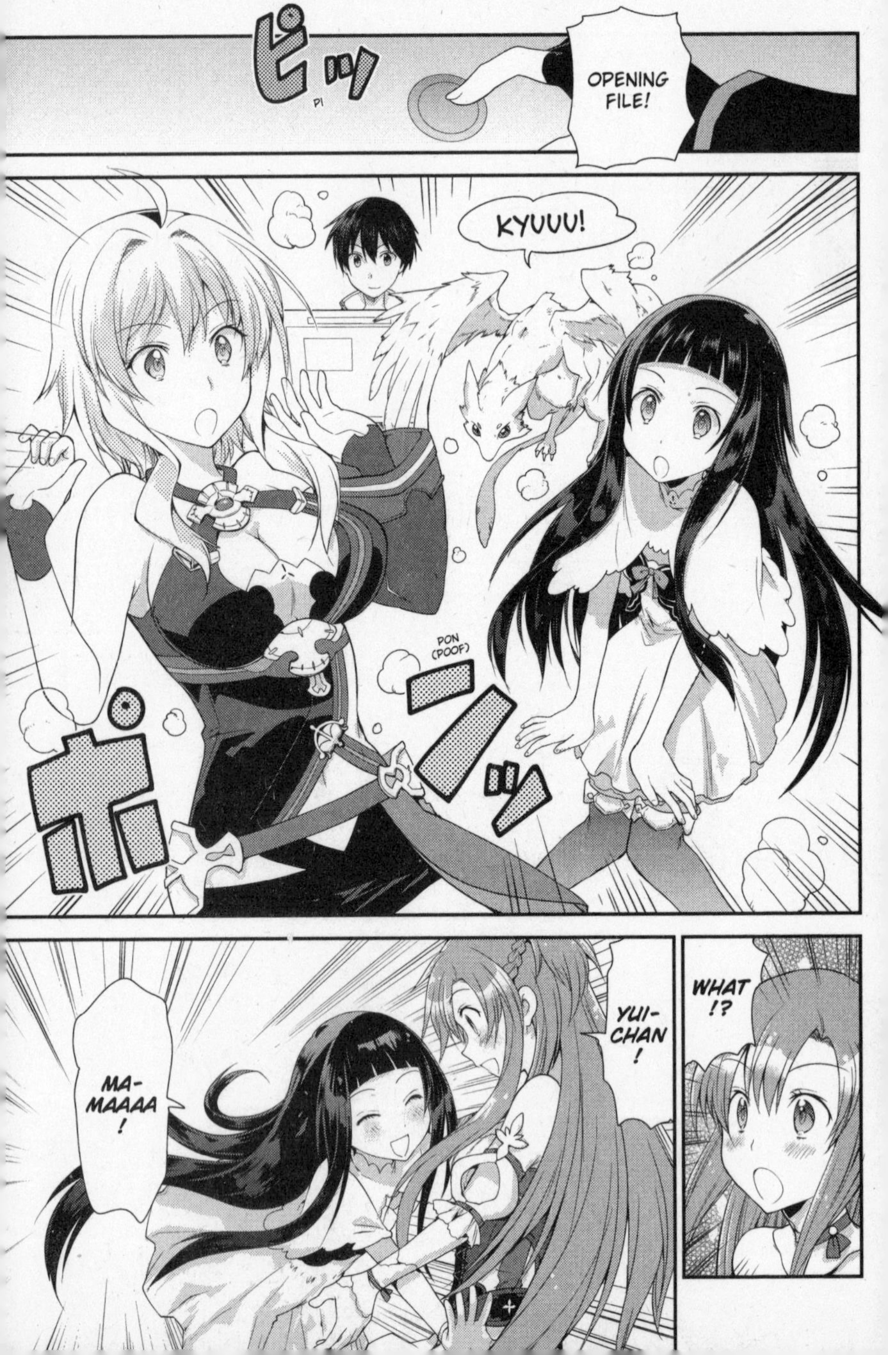
OPENING FILE!
ピッ
PI
KYUUU!
ポンッ
PON (POOF)
WHAT!?
YUI-CHAN!
MA-MAAAA!

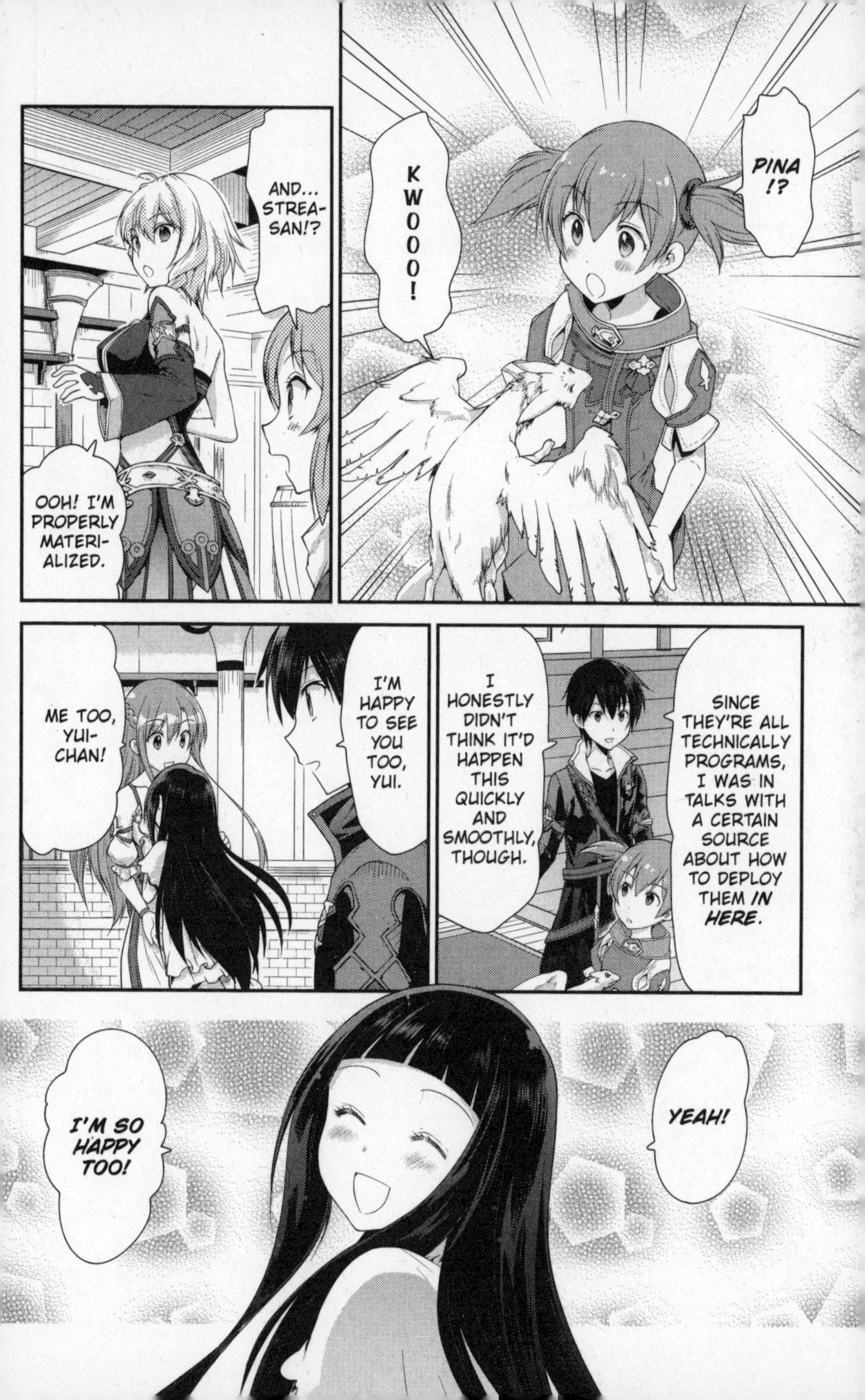
PINA !?
KWOOOO!
AND... STREA-SAN!?
OOH! I'M PROPERLY MATERI-ALIZED.
SINCE THEY'RE ALL TECHNICALLY PROGRAMS, I WAS IN TALKS WITH A CERTAIN SOURCE ABOUT HOW TO DEPLOY THEM *IN HERE*.
I HONESTLY DIDN'T THINK IT'D HAPPEN THIS QUICKLY AND SMOOTHLY, THOUGH.
I'M HAPPY TO SEE YOU TOO, YUI.
ME TOO, YUI-CHAN!
YEAH!
I'M SO HAPPY TOO!

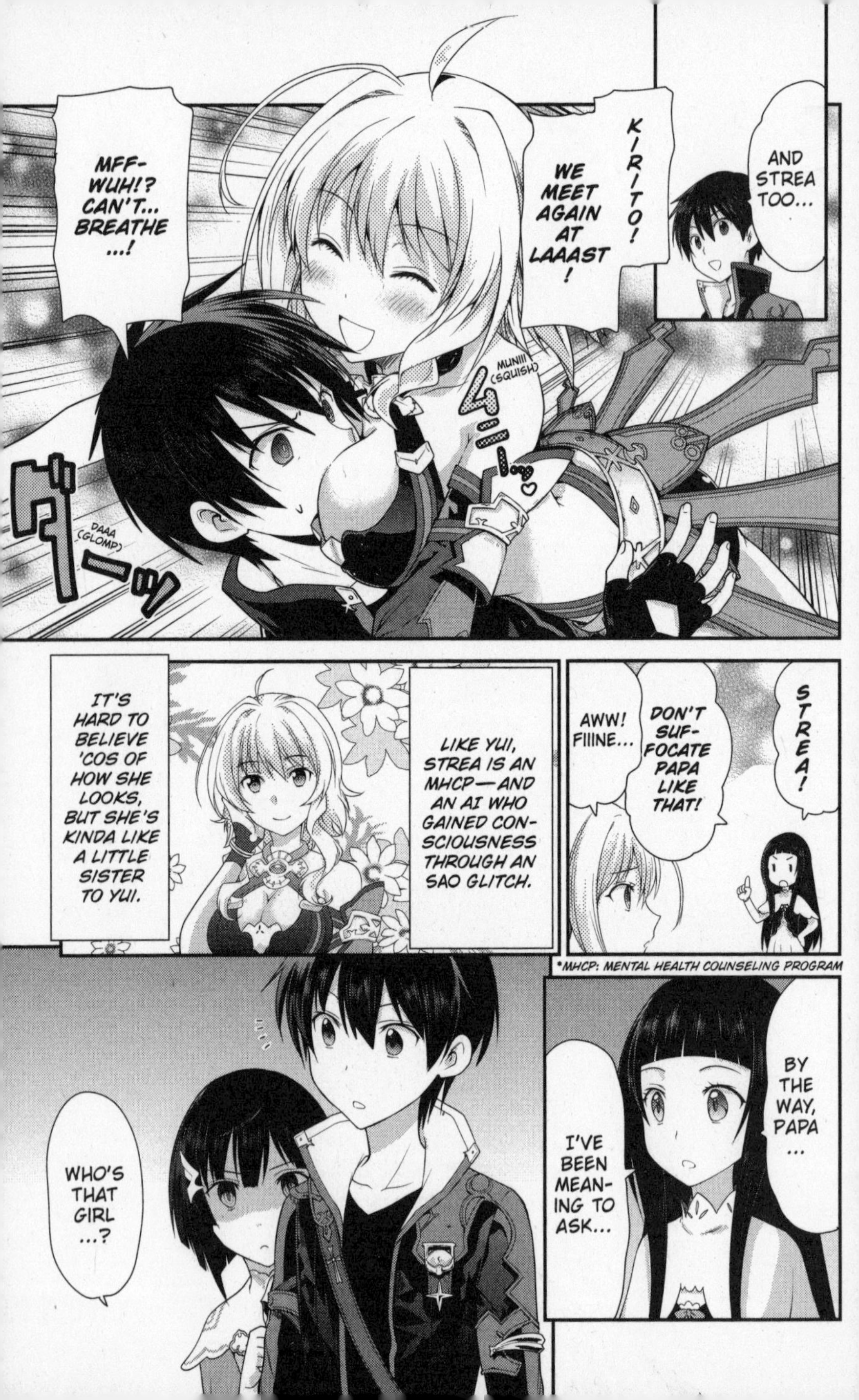
AND STREA TOO...
KIRITO! WE MEET AGAIN AT LAAAST!
MUNIII (SQUISH)
MFF-WUH!? CAN'T... BREATHE...!
DAAA (GLOMP)
STREA!
DON'T SUF-FOCATE PAPA LIKE THAT!
AWW! FIIINE...
LIKE YUI, STREA IS AN MHCP—AND AN AI WHO GAINED CON-SCIOUSNESS THROUGH AN SAO GLITCH.
IT'S HARD TO BELIEVE 'COS OF HOW SHE LOOKS, BUT SHE'S KINDA LIKE A LITTLE SISTER TO YUI.
*MHCP: MENTAL HEALTH COUNSELING PROGRAM
BY THE WAY, PAPA...
I'VE BEEN MEAN-ING TO ASK...
WHO'S THAT GIRL...?

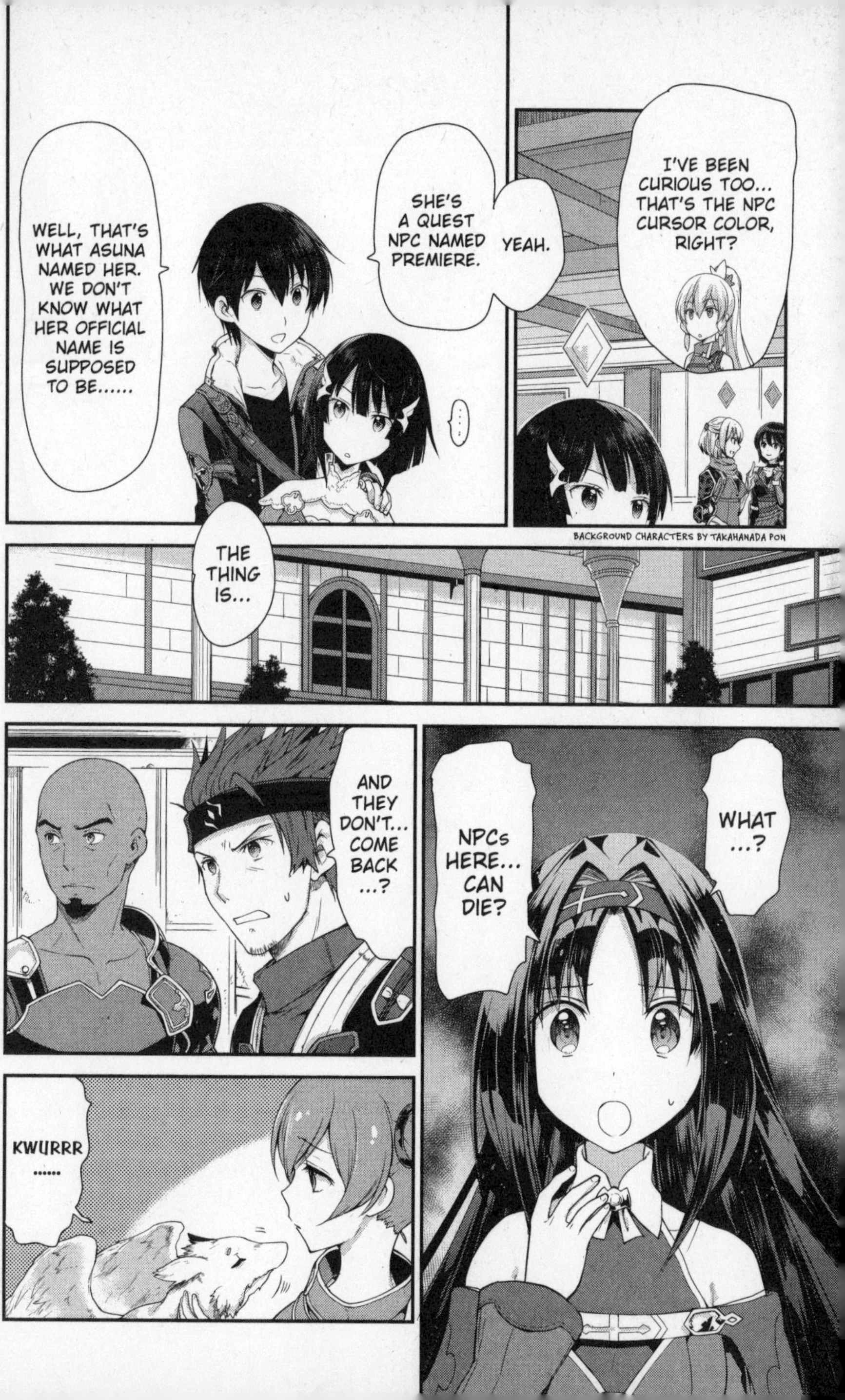
I'VE BEEN CURIOUS TOO... THAT'S THE NPC CURSOR COLOR, RIGHT?
YEAH.
SHE'S A QUEST NPC NAMED PREMIERE.
WELL, THAT'S WHAT ASUNA NAMED HER. WE DON'T KNOW WHAT HER OFFICIAL NAME IS SUPPOSED TO BE......
...
BACKGROUND CHARACTERS BY TAKAHANADA PON
THE THING IS...
WHAT ...?
NPCs HERE... CAN DIE?
AND THEY DON'T... COME BACK ...?
KWURRR ......

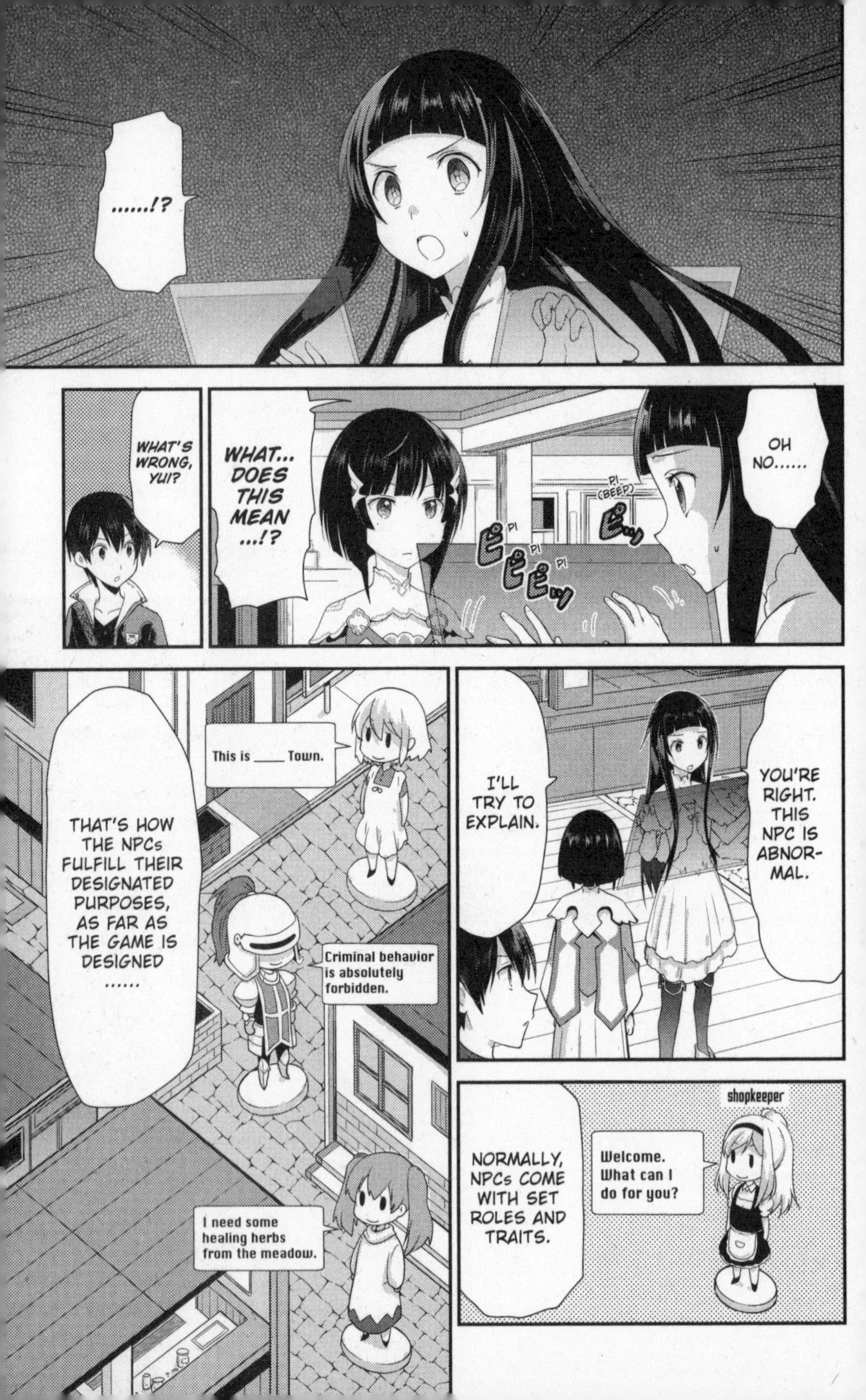
......!?
OH NO......
PI (BEEP)
PI PI PI
WHAT... DOES THIS MEAN ...!?
WHAT'S WRONG, YUI?
YOU'RE RIGHT. THIS NPC IS ABNORMAL.
I'LL TRY TO EXPLAIN.
shopkeeper
Welcome. What can I do for you?
NORMALLY, NPCs COME WITH SET ROLES AND TRAITS.
This is ____ Town.
THAT'S HOW THE NPCs FULFILL THEIR DESIGNATED PURPOSES, AS FAR AS THE GAME IS DESIGNED ......
Criminal behavior is absolutely forbidden.
I need some healing herbs from the meadow.

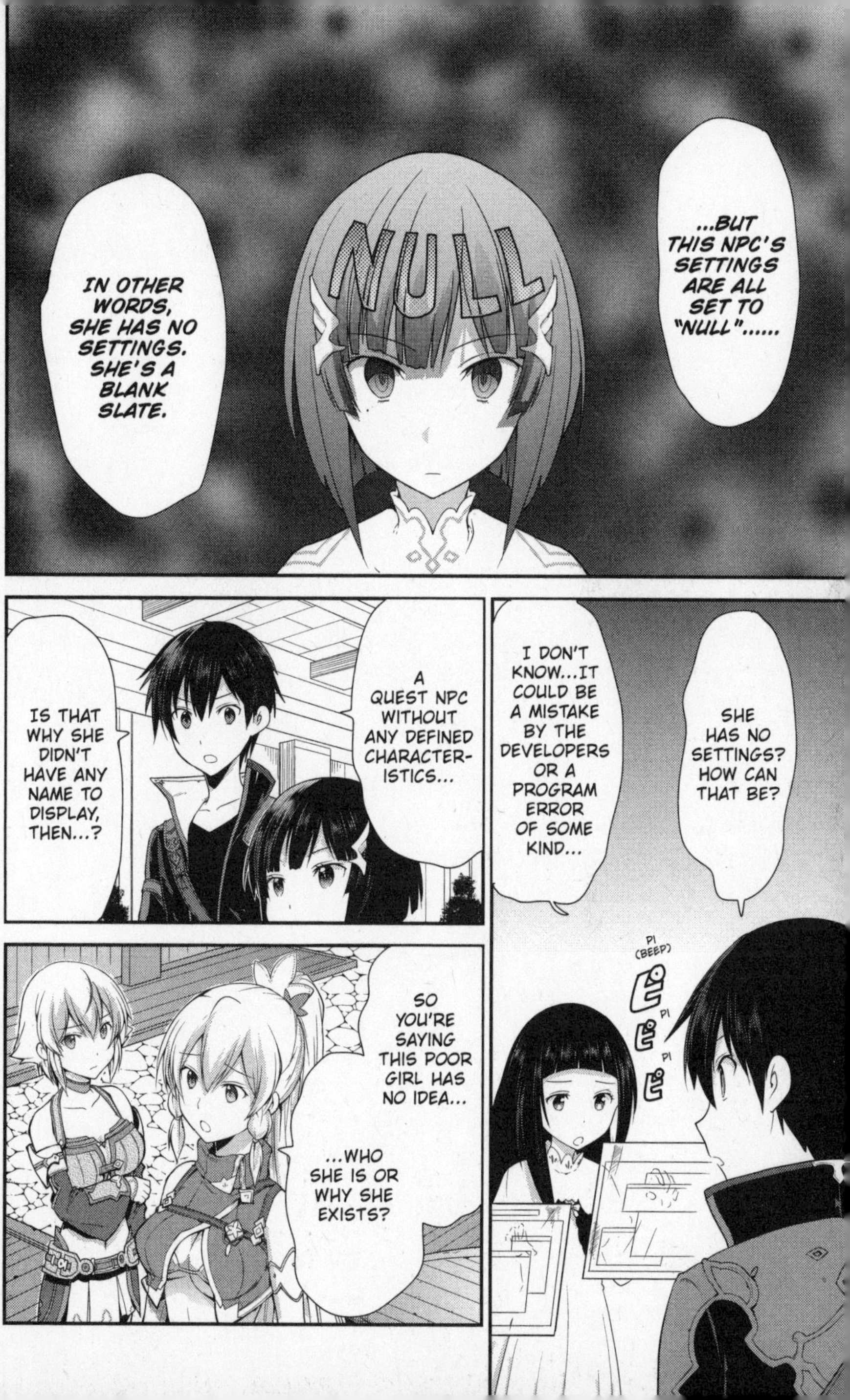
...BUT THIS NPC'S SETTINGS ARE ALL SET TO "NULL"......
NULL
IN OTHER WORDS, SHE HAS NO SETTINGS. SHE'S A BLANK SLATE.
SHE HAS NO SETTINGS? HOW CAN THAT BE?
I DON'T KNOW...IT COULD BE A MISTAKE BY THE DEVELOPERS OR A PROGRAM ERROR OF SOME KIND...
PI (BEEP)
PI
PI
A QUEST NPC WITHOUT ANY DEFINED CHARACTER-ISTICS...
IS THAT WHY SHE DIDN'T HAVE ANY NAME TO DISPLAY, THEN...?
SO YOU'RE SAYING THIS POOR GIRL HAS NO IDEA...
...WHO SHE IS OR WHY SHE EXISTS?

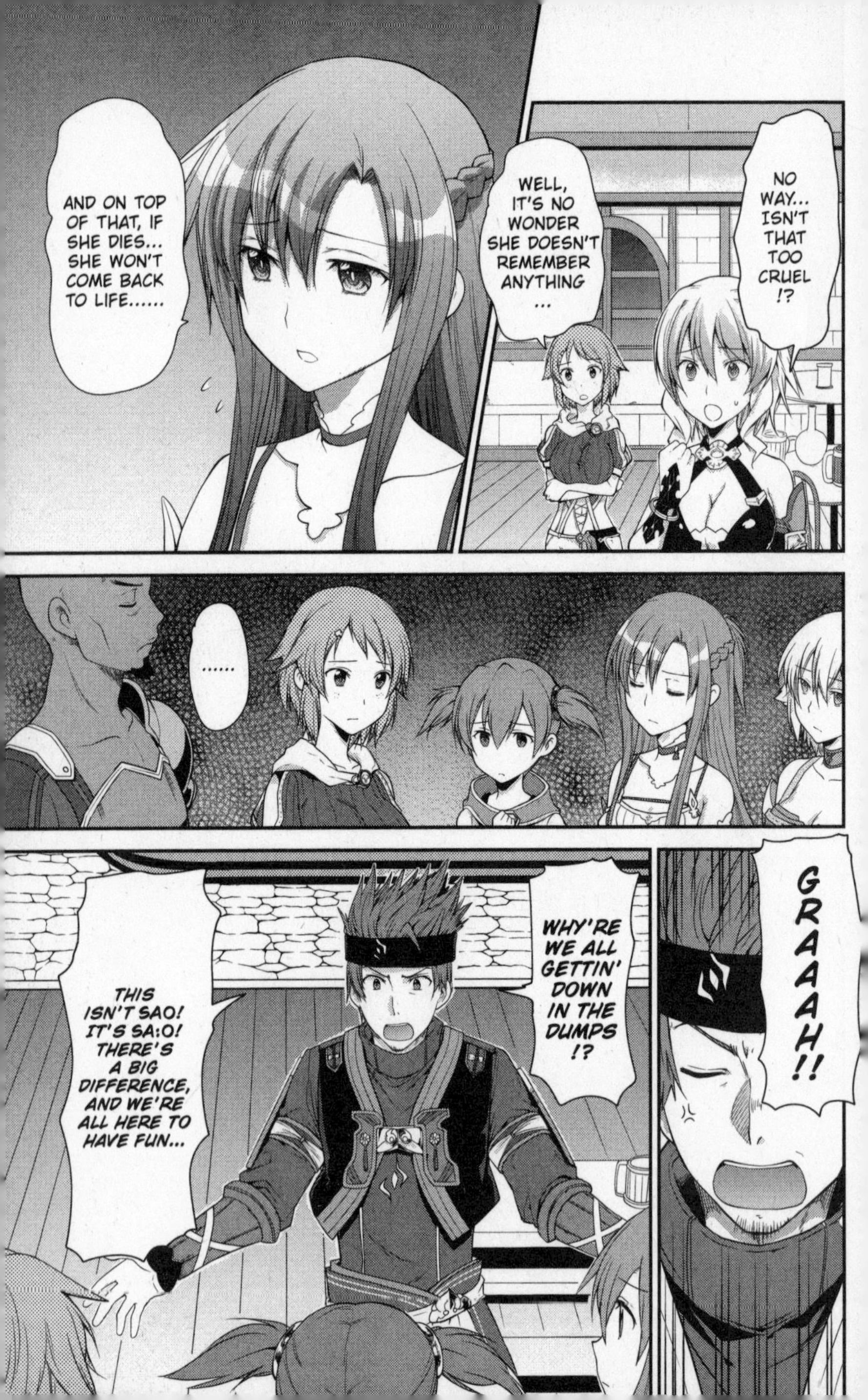
NO WAY... ISN'T THAT TOO CRUEL!?
WELL, IT'S NO WONDER SHE DOESN'T REMEMBER ANYTHING...
AND ON TOP OF THAT, IF SHE DIES... SHE WON'T COME BACK TO LIFE......
......
GRAAAAH!!
WHY'RE WE ALL GETTIN' DOWN IN THE DUMPS!?
THIS ISN'T SAO! IT'S SA:O! THERE'S A BIG DIFFERENCE, AND WE'RE ALL HERE TO HAVE FUN...

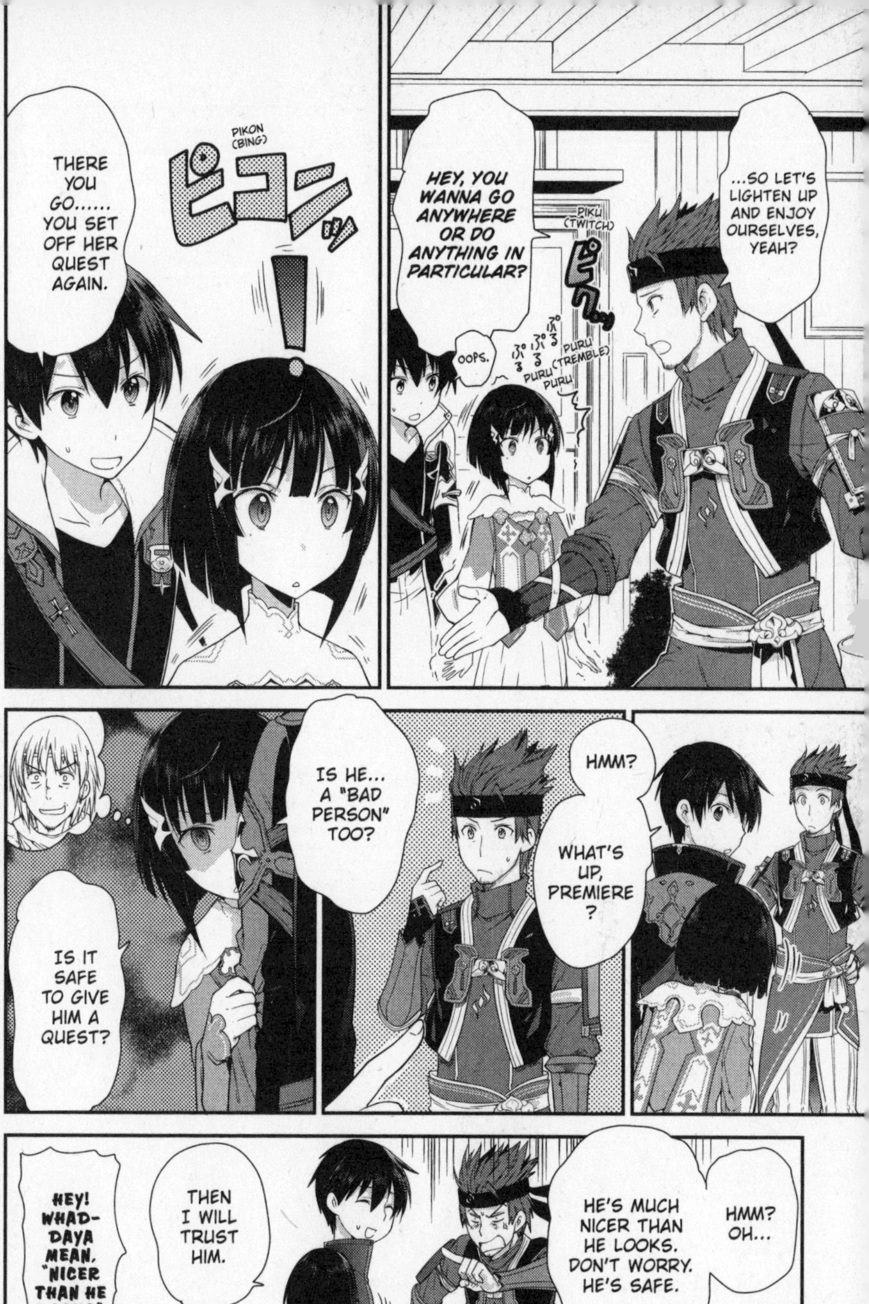
...SO LET'S LIGHTEN UP AND ENJOY OURSELVES, YEAH?
HEY, YOU WANNA GO ANYWHERE OR DO ANYTHING IN PARTICULAR?
PIKU (TWITCH)
OOPS.
PURU PURU (TREMBLE)
PURU
PIKON (BING)
THERE YOU GO...... YOU SET OFF HER QUEST AGAIN.
HMM?
WHAT'S UP, PREMIERE?
IS HE... A "BAD PERSON" TOO?
IS IT SAFE TO GIVE HIM A QUEST?
HMM? OH...
HE'S MUCH NICER THAN HE LOOKS. DON'T WORRY. HE'S SAFE.
THEN I WILL TRUST HIM.
HEY! WHAD-DAYA MEAN, "NICER THAN HE LOOKS" !?

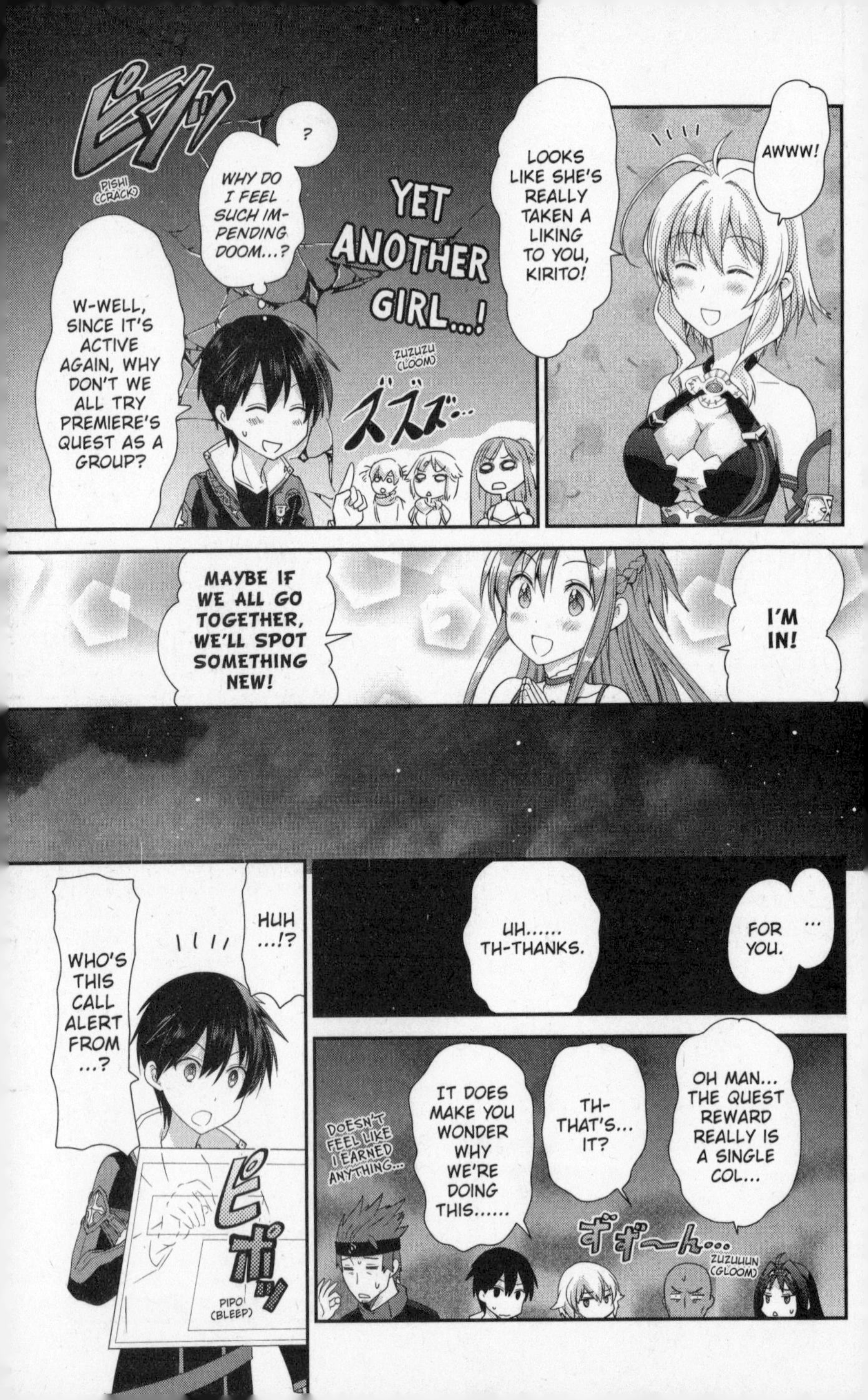
AWWW!
LOOKS LIKE SHE'S REALLY TAKEN A LIKING TO YOU, KIRITO!
YET ANOTHER GIRL...!
ZUZUZU (GLOOM)
?
WHY DO I FEEL SUCH IM-PENDING DOOM...?
PISHI (CRACK)
W-WELL, SINCE IT'S ACTIVE AGAIN, WHY DON'T WE ALL TRY PREMIERE'S QUEST AS A GROUP?
I'M IN!
MAYBE IF WE ALL GO TOGETHER, WE'LL SPOT SOMETHING NEW!
...
FOR YOU.
UH...... TH-THANKS.
OH MAN... THE QUEST REWARD REALLY IS A SINGLE COL...
TH-THAT'S... IT?
IT DOES MAKE YOU WONDER WHY WE'RE DOING THIS......
DOESN'T FEEL LIKE I EARNED ANYTHING...
ZUZUUUN (GLOOM)
HUH...!?
WHO'S THIS CALL ALERT FROM...?
PIPO (BLEEP)

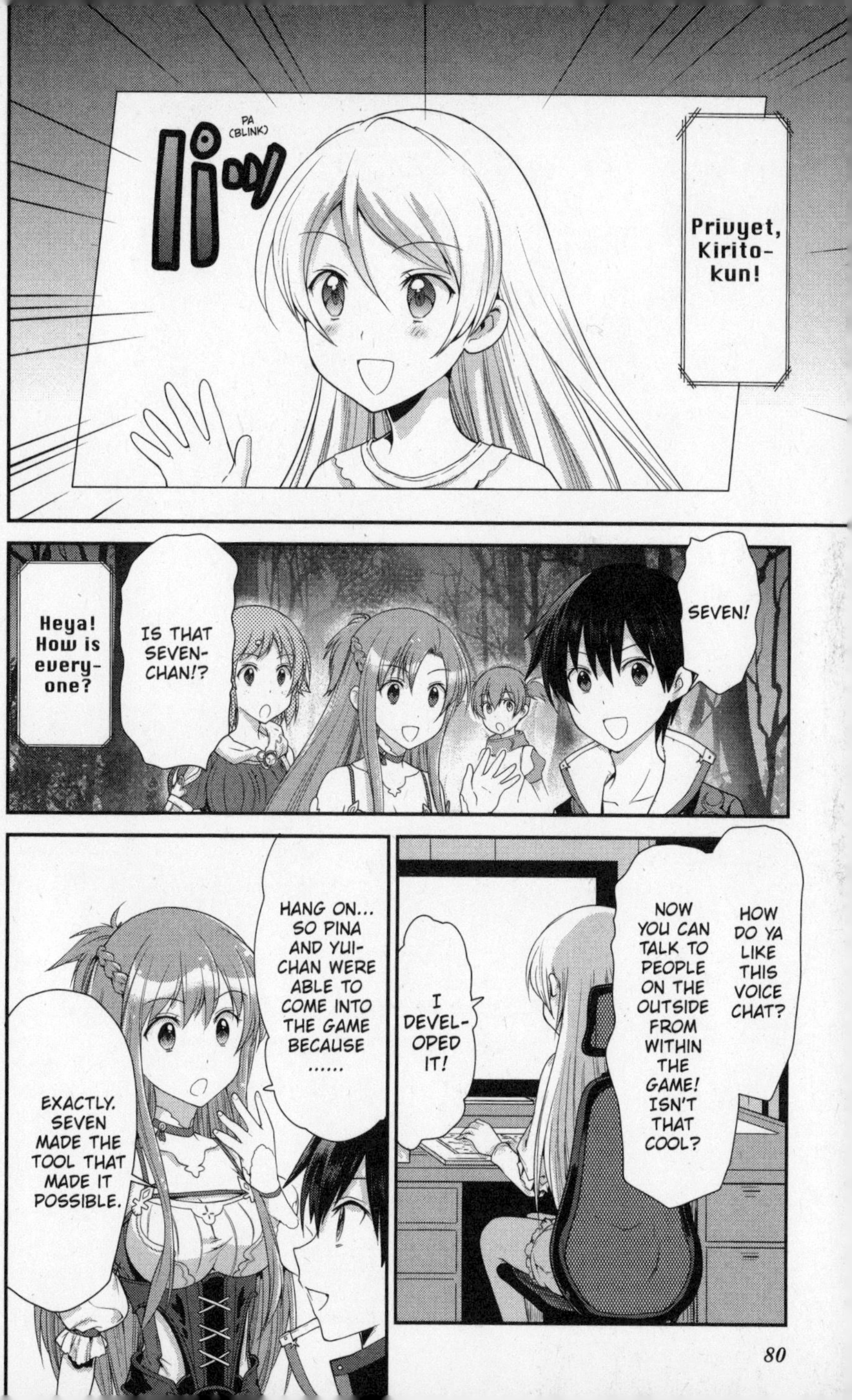
PA (BLINK)
Privyet, Kirito-kun!
SEVEN!
IS THAT SEVEN-CHAN!?
Heya! How is every-one?
HOW DO YA LIKE THIS VOICE CHAT?
NOW YOU CAN TALK TO PEOPLE ON THE OUTSIDE FROM WITHIN THE GAME! ISN'T THAT COOL?
I DEVEL-OPED IT!
HANG ON... SO PINA AND YUI-CHAN WERE ABLE TO COME INTO THE GAME BECAUSE ......
EXACTLY. SEVEN MADE THE TOOL THAT MADE IT POSSIBLE.

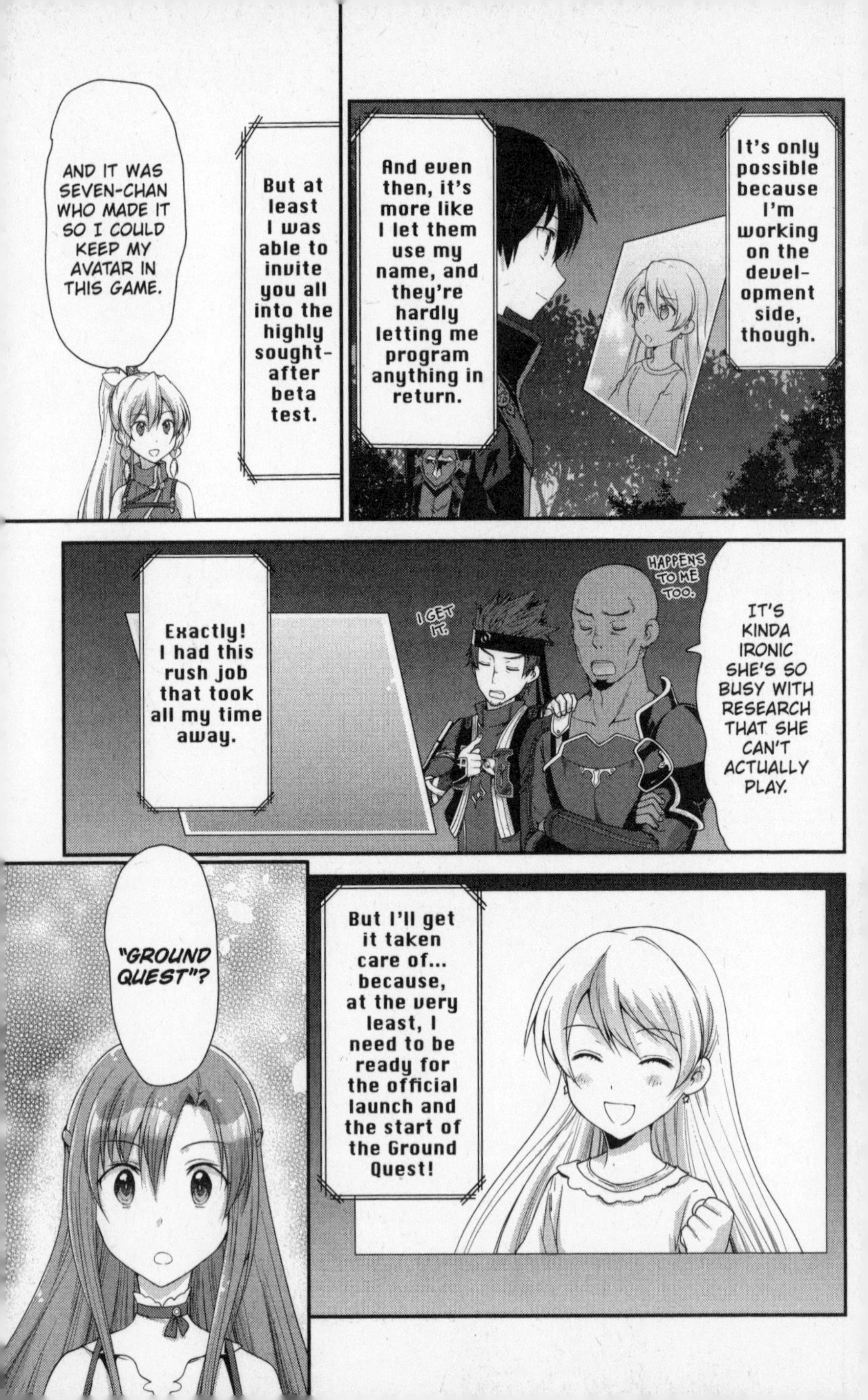

It's only possible because I'm working on the devel-opment side, though.
And even then, it's more like I let them use my name, and they're hardly letting me program anything in return.
But at least I was able to invite you all into the highly sought-after beta test.
AND IT WAS SEVEN-CHAN WHO MADE IT SO I COULD KEEP MY AVATAR IN THIS GAME.
IT'S KINDA IRONIC SHE'S SO BUSY WITH RESEARCH THAT SHE CAN'T ACTUALLY PLAY.
HAPPENS TO ME TOO.
I GET IT.
Exactly! I had this rush job that took all my time away.
But I'll get it taken care of... because, at the very least, I need to be ready for the official launch and the start of the Ground Quest!
"GROUND QUEST"?

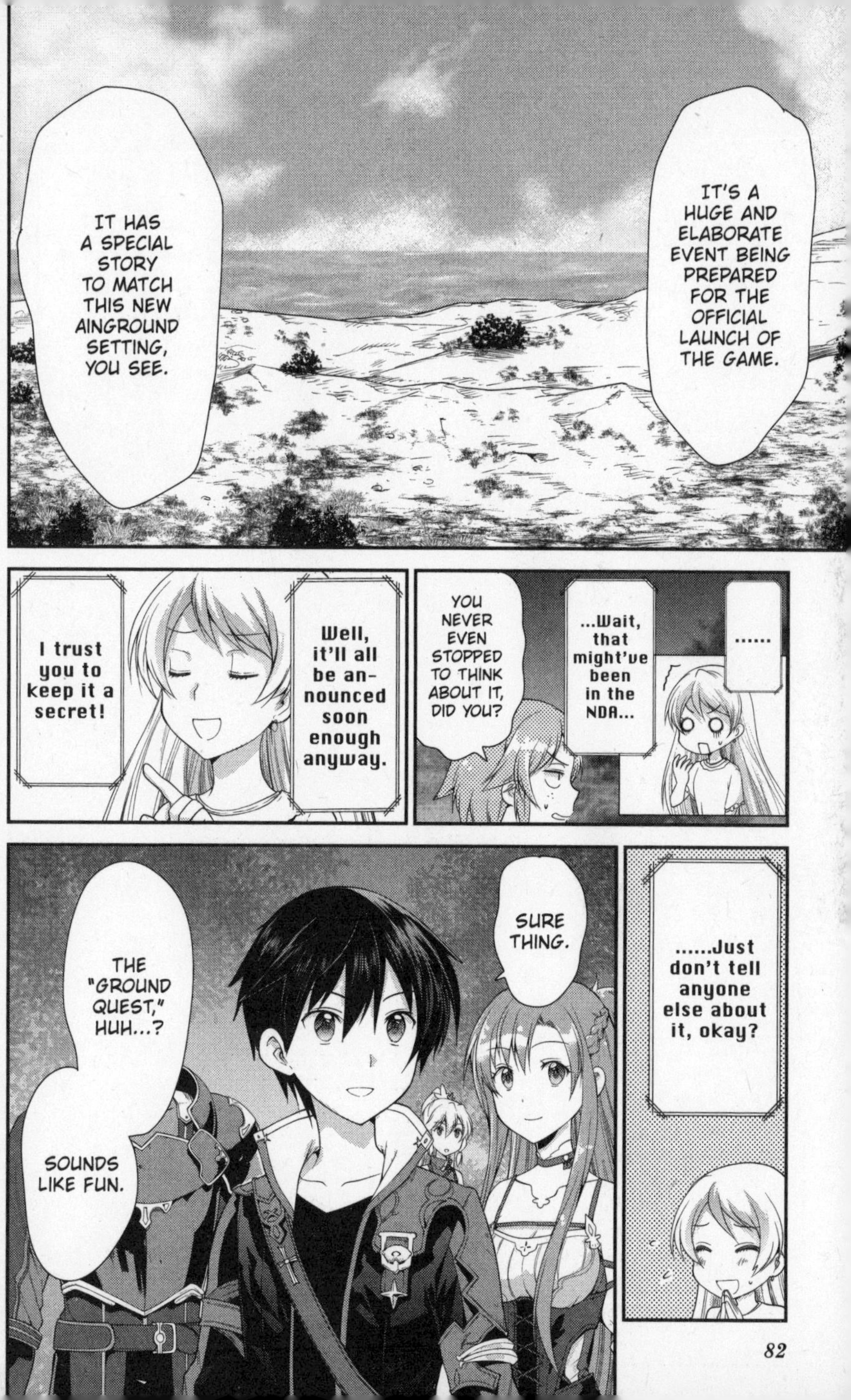
IT'S A HUGE AND ELABORATE EVENT BEING PREPARED FOR THE OFFICIAL LAUNCH OF THE GAME.
IT HAS A SPECIAL STORY TO MATCH THIS NEW AINGROUND SETTING, YOU SEE.
......
...Wait, that might've been in the NDA...
YOU NEVER EVEN STOPPED TO THINK ABOUT IT, DID YOU?
Well, it'll all be an-nounced soon enough anyway.
I trust you to keep it a secret!
......Just don't tell anyone else about it, okay?
SURE THING.
THE "GROUND QUEST," HUH...?
SOUNDS LIKE FUN.

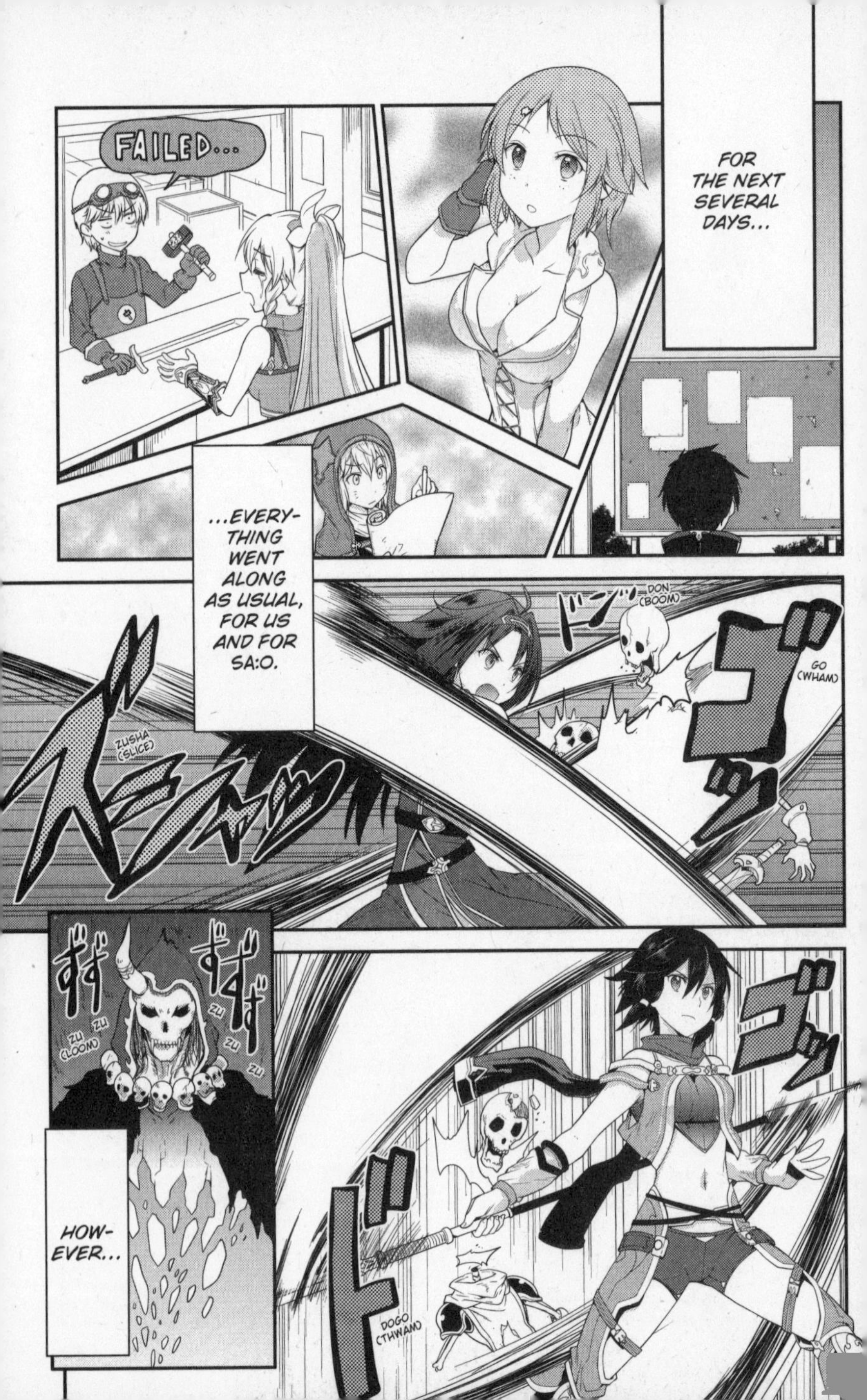
FOR THE NEXT SEVERAL DAYS...
FAILED...
...EVERYTHING WENT ALONG AS USUAL, FOR US AND FOR SA:O.
DON (BOOM)
GO (WHAM)
ZUSHA (SLICE)
DOGO (THWAM)
ZU ZU ZU ZU ZU (LOOM)
HOWEVER...

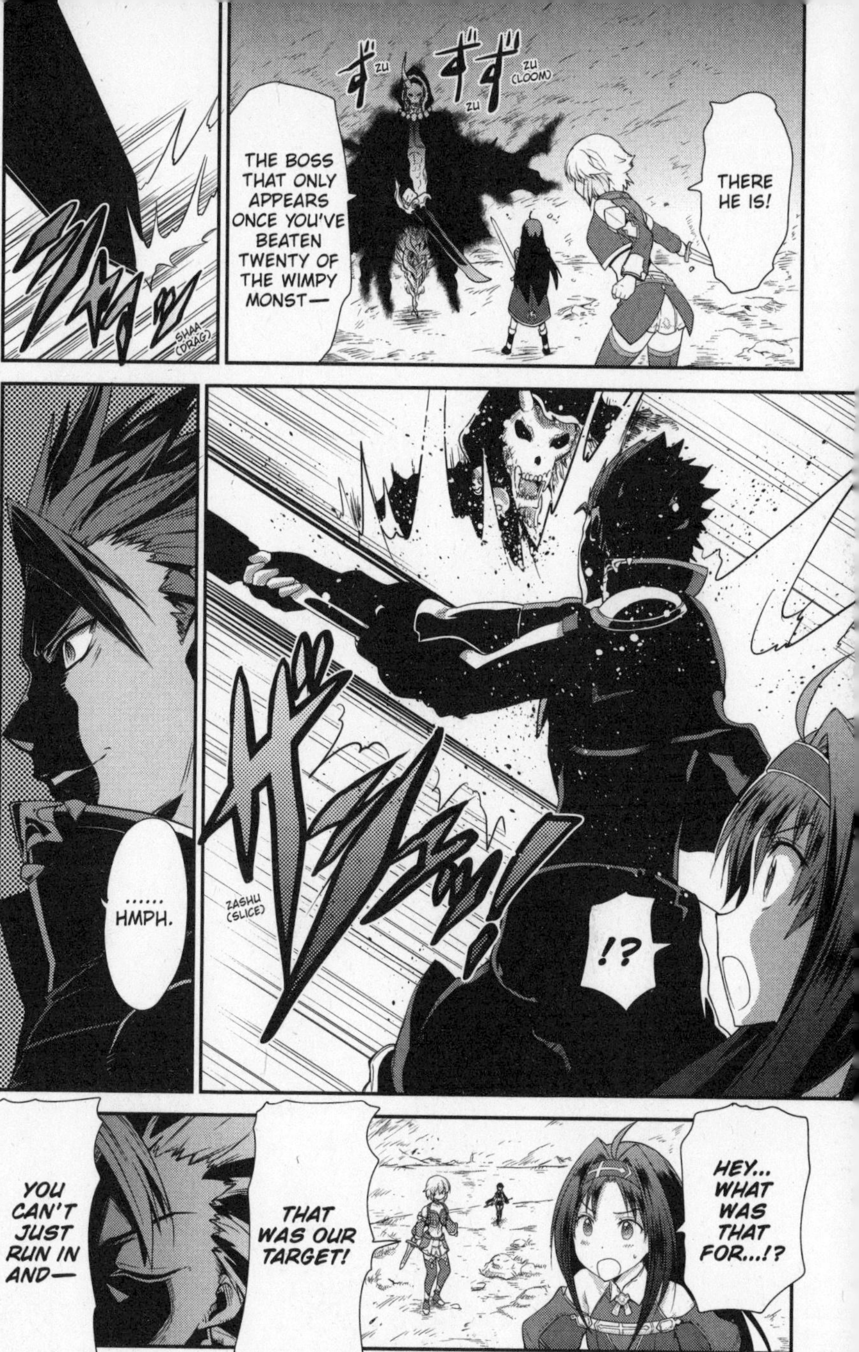
ZU ZU ZU (LOOM)
THERE HE IS!
THE BOSS THAT ONLY APPEARS ONCE YOU'VE BEATEN TWENTY OF THE WIMPY MONST—
SHAA (DRAG)
!?
ZASHU (SLICE)
...... HMPH.
HEY... WHAT WAS THAT FOR...!?
THAT WAS OUR TARGET!
YOU CAN'T JUST RUN IN AND—

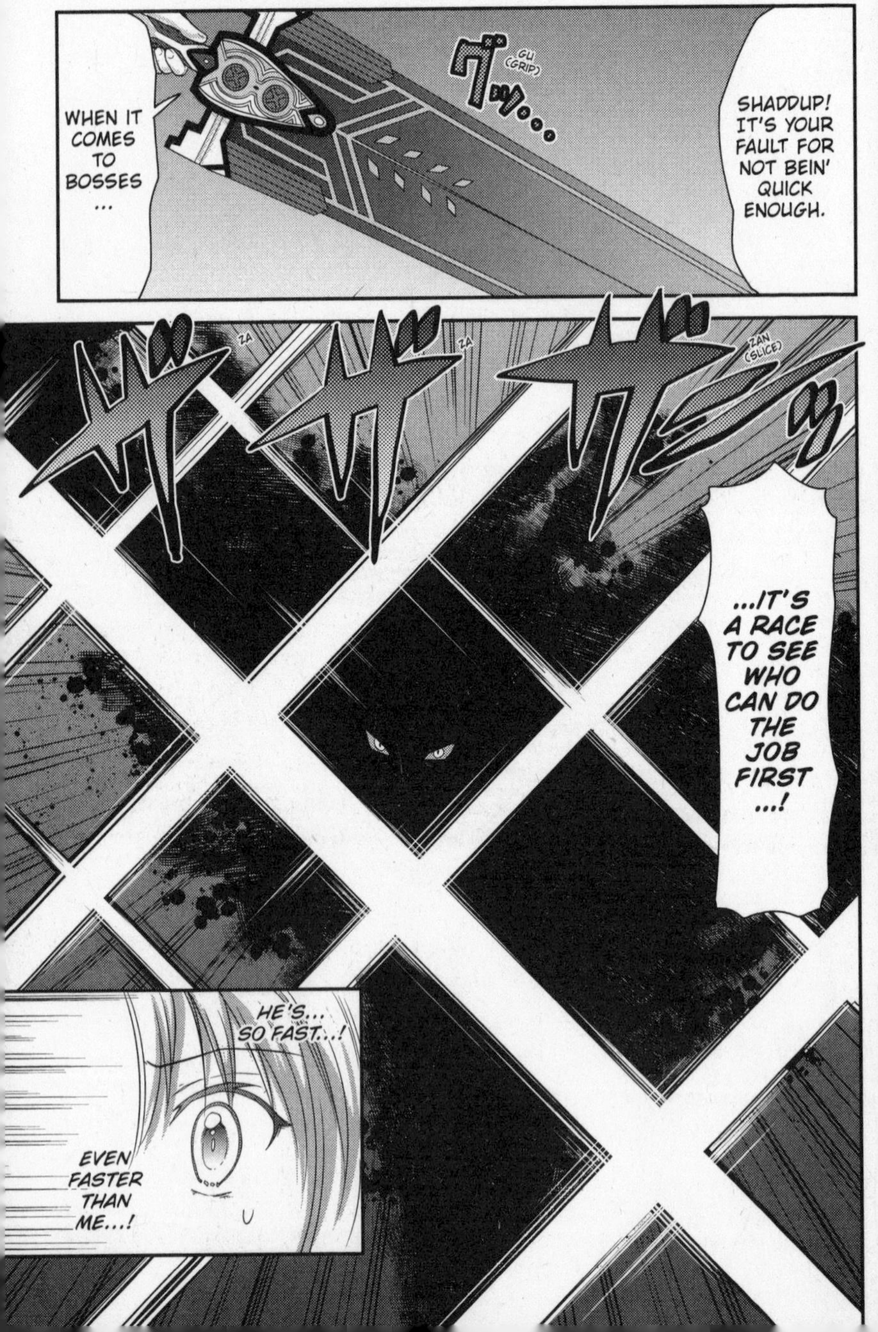
SHADDUP! IT'S YOUR FAULT FOR NOT BEIN' QUICK ENOUGH.
GU (GRIP)
WHEN IT COMES TO BOSSES...
ZAN (SLICE)
ZA
ZA
...IT'S A RACE TO SEE WHO CAN DO THE JOB FIRST...!
HE'S... SO FAST...!
EVEN FASTER THAN ME...!

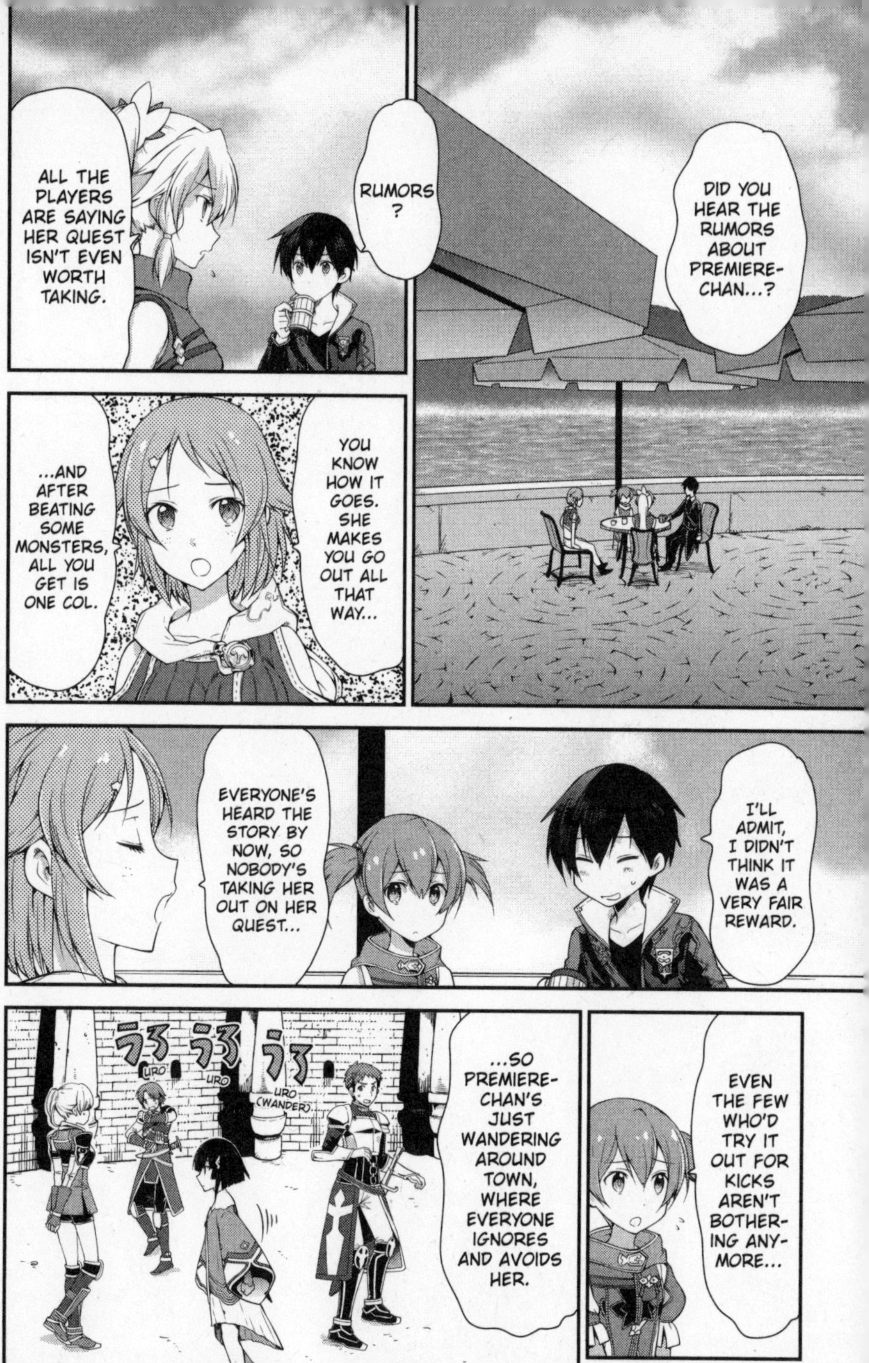

DID YOU HEAR THE RUMORS ABOUT PREMIERE-CHAN...?
RUMORS?
ALL THE PLAYERS ARE SAYING HER QUEST ISN'T EVEN WORTH TAKING.
YOU KNOW HOW IT GOES. SHE MAKES YOU GO OUT ALL THAT WAY...
...AND AFTER BEATING SOME MONSTERS, ALL YOU GET IS ONE COL.
I'LL ADMIT, I DIDN'T THINK IT WAS A VERY FAIR REWARD.
EVERYONE'S HEARD THE STORY BY NOW, SO NOBODY'S TAKING HER OUT ON HER QUEST...
EVEN THE FEW WHO'D TRY IT OUT FOR KICKS AREN'T BOTHERING ANYMORE...
...SO PREMIERE-CHAN'S JUST WANDERING AROUND TOWN, WHERE EVERYONE IGNORES AND AVOIDS HER.
うろ
URO
うろ
URO
うろ
URO (WANDER)

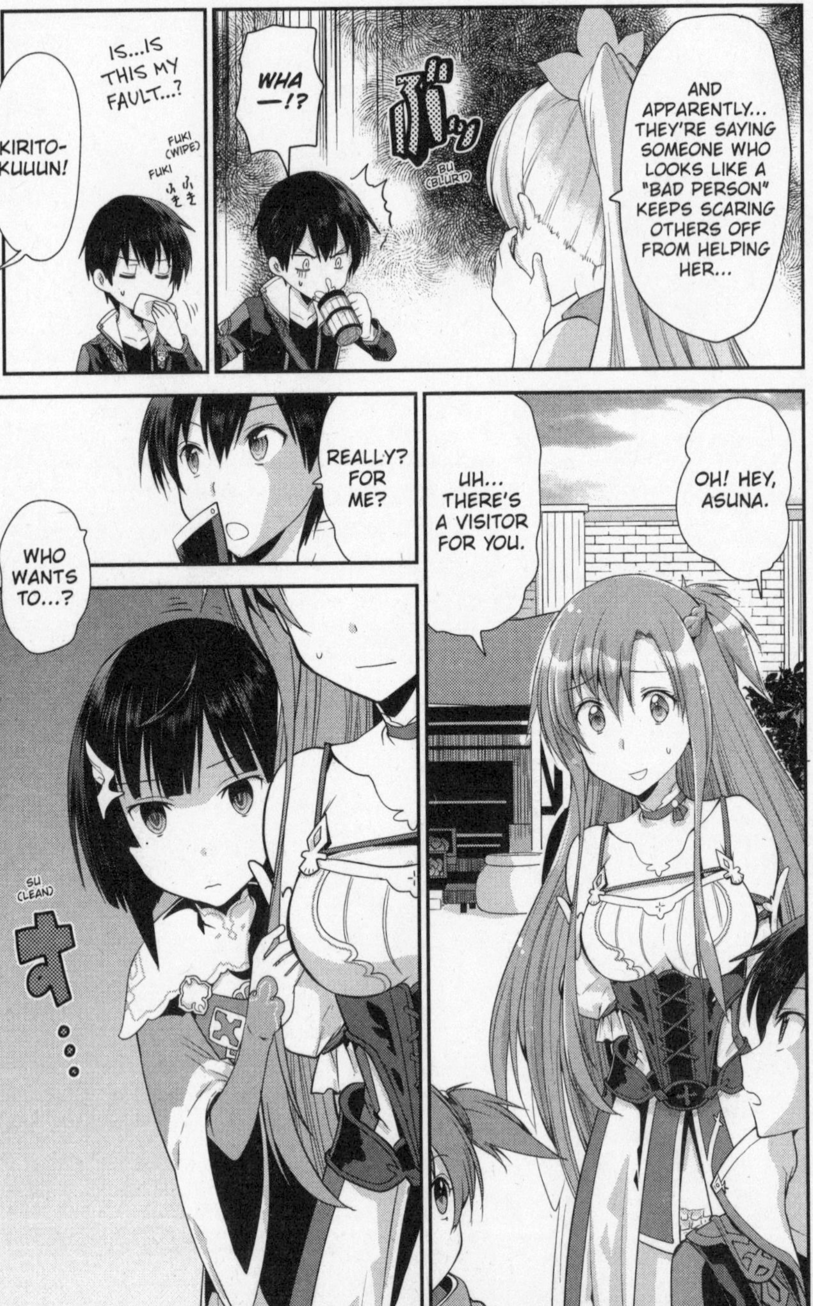
AND APPARENTLY... THEY'RE SAYING SOMEONE WHO LOOKS LIKE A "BAD PERSON" KEEPS SCARING OTHERS OFF FROM HELPING HER...
ぶっ
BU (BLURT)
WHA—!?
IS...IS THIS MY FAULT...?
FUKI (WIPE)
FUKI
ふきふき
KIRITO-KUUUN!
OH! HEY, ASUNA.
UH... THERE'S A VISITOR FOR YOU.
REALLY? FOR ME?
WHO WANTS TO...?
SU (LEAN)
さ...

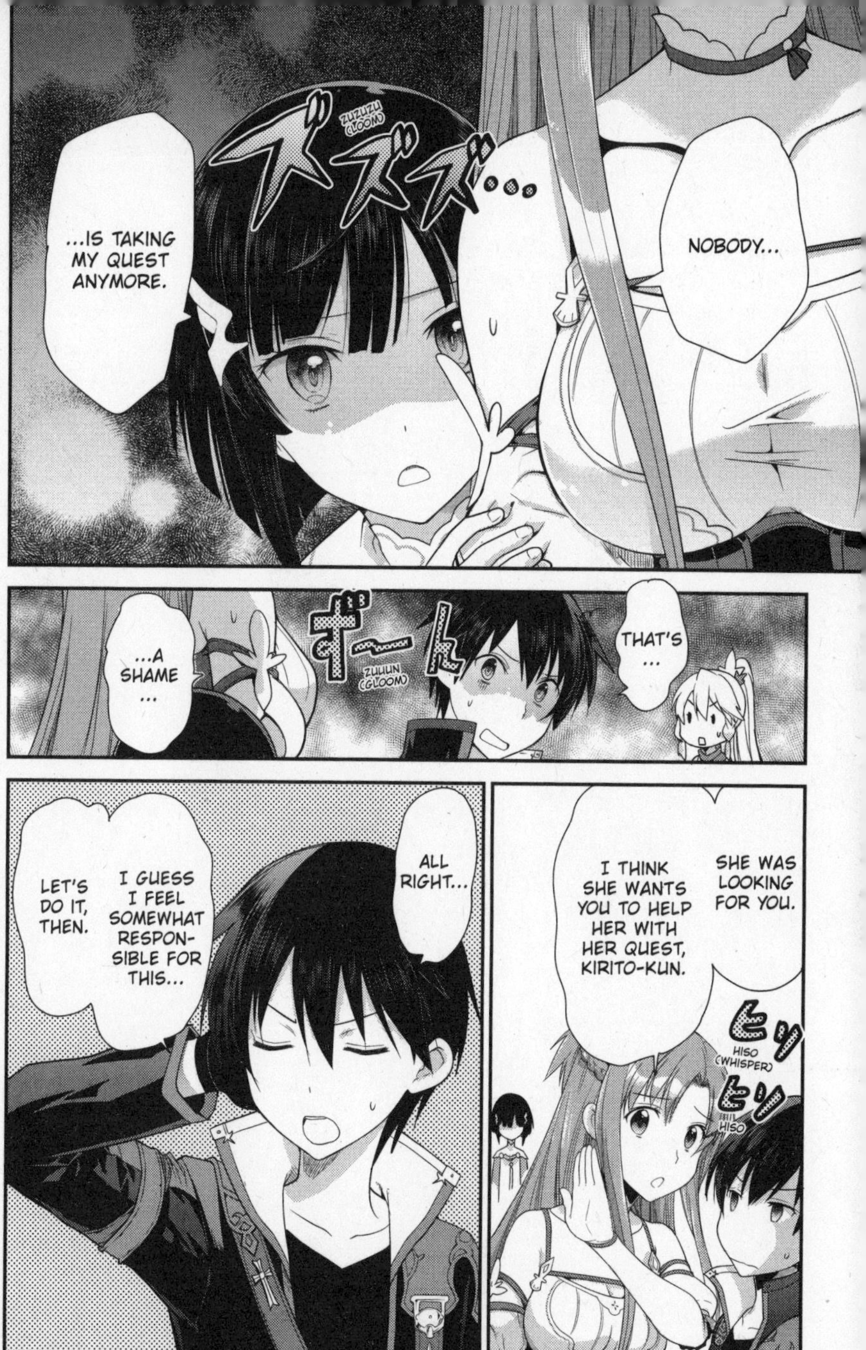
ZUZUZU (GLOOM)
NOBODY...
...IS TAKING MY QUEST ANYMORE.
THAT'S ...
ZUUUN (GLOOM)
...A SHAME ...
SHE WAS LOOKING FOR YOU.
I THINK SHE WANTS YOU TO HELP HER WITH HER QUEST, KIRITO-KUN.
HISO (WHISPER)
HISO
ALL RIGHT...
I GUESS I FEEL SOMEWHAT RESPON-SIBLE FOR THIS...
LET'S DO IT, THEN.

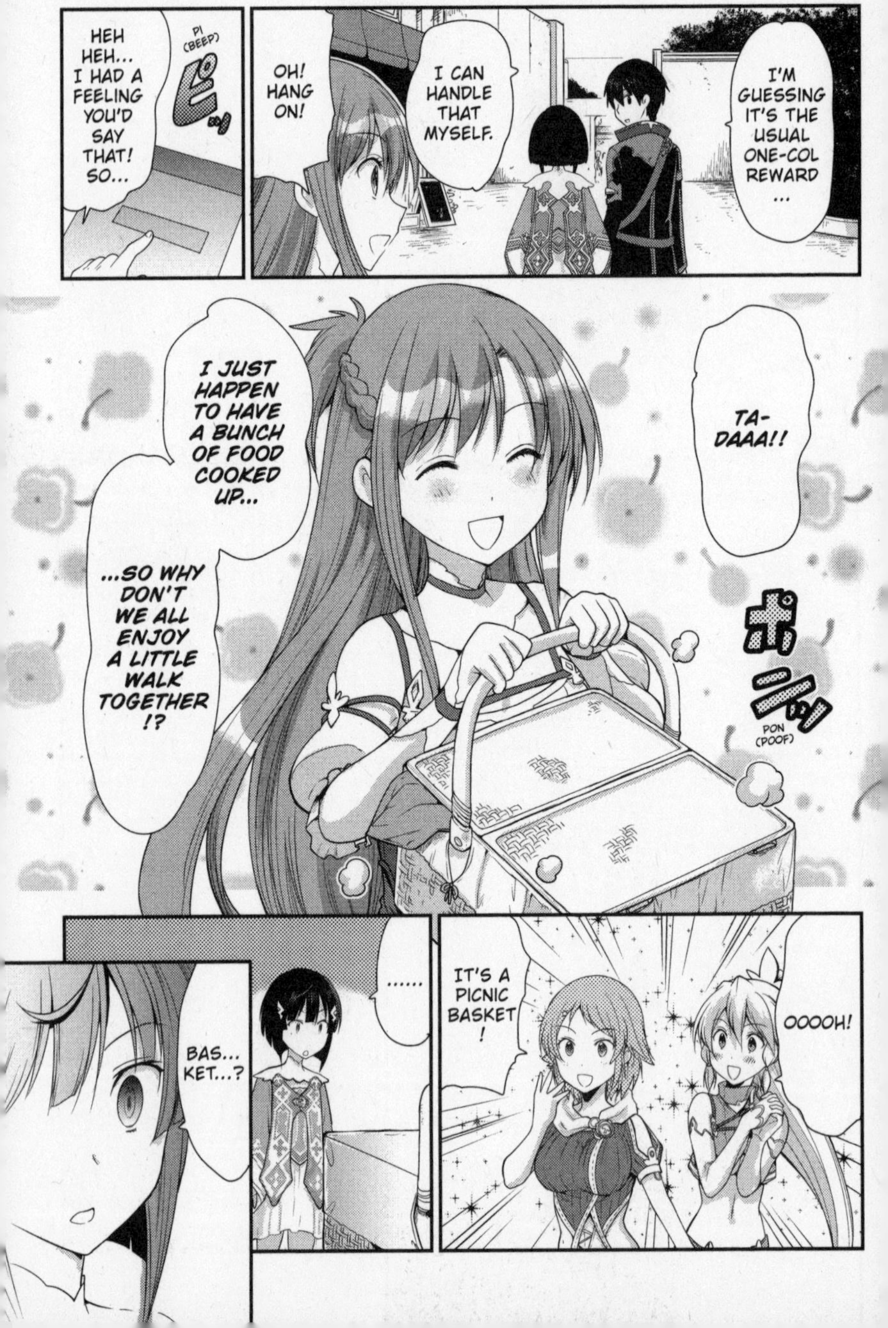
I'M GUESSING IT'S THE USUAL ONE-COL REWARD...
I CAN HANDLE THAT MYSELF.
OH! HANG ON!
PI (BEEP)
HEH HEH... I HAD A FEELING YOU'D SAY THAT! SO...
TA-DAAA!!
PON (POOF)
I JUST HAPPEN TO HAVE A BUNCH OF FOOD COOKED UP...
...SO WHY DON'T WE ALL ENJOY A LITTLE WALK TOGETHER!?
OOOOH!
IT'S A PICNIC BASKET!
......
BAS... KET...?

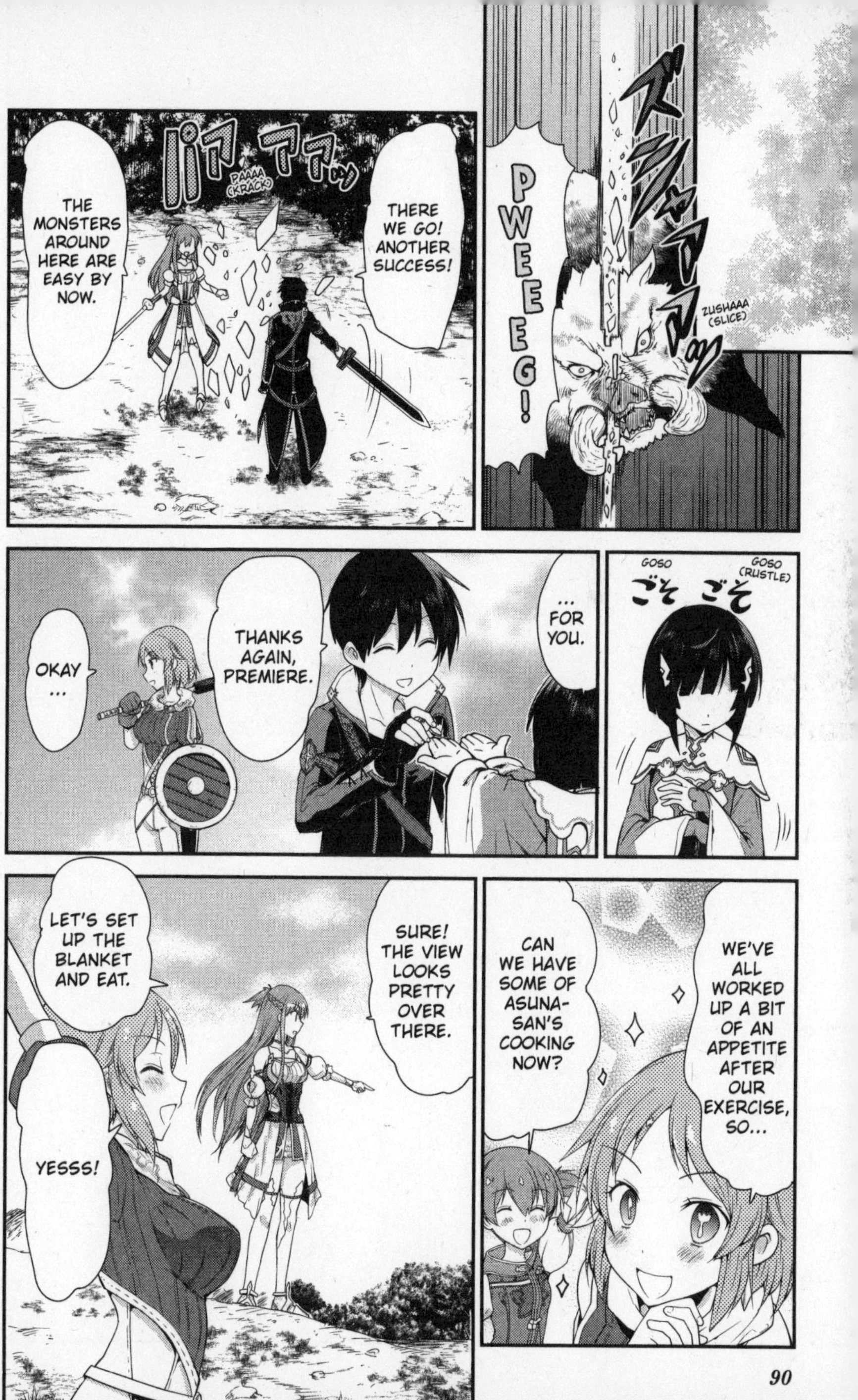

ズシャアアアッ
ZUSHAAA (SLICE)
PWEEG!
THERE WE GO! ANOTHER SUCCESS!
パァアアッ
PAAAA (KRACK)
THE MONSTERS AROUND HERE ARE EASY BY NOW.
GOSO GOSO (RUSTLE)
ごそ ごそ
... FOR YOU.
THANKS AGAIN, PREMIERE.
OKAY ...
WE'VE ALL WORKED UP A BIT OF AN APPETITE AFTER OUR EXERCISE, SO...
CAN WE HAVE SOME OF ASUNA-SAN'S COOKING NOW?
SURE! THE VIEW LOOKS PRETTY OVER THERE.
LET'S SET UP THE BLANKET AND EAT.
YESSS!

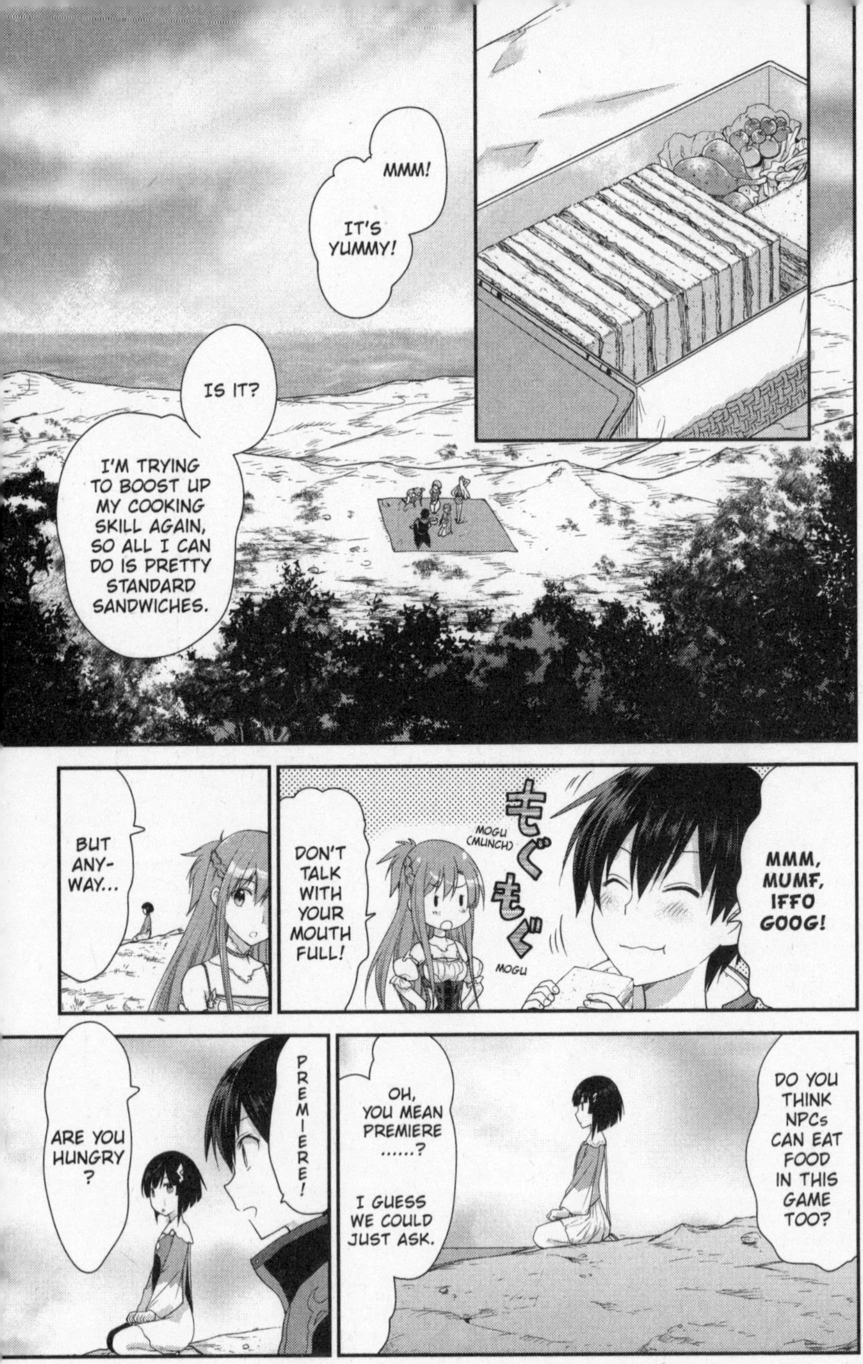
MMM!
IT'S YUMMY!
IS IT?
I'M TRYING TO BOOST UP MY COOKING SKILL AGAIN, SO ALL I CAN DO IS PRETTY STANDARD SANDWICHES.
MMM, MUMF, IFFO GOOG!
もぐもぐ
MOGU (MUNCH)
MOGU
DON'T TALK WITH YOUR MOUTH FULL!
BUT ANY-WAY...
DO YOU THINK NPCs CAN EAT FOOD IN THIS GAME TOO?
OH, YOU MEAN PREMIERE ......?
I GUESS WE COULD JUST ASK.
PREMIERE!
ARE YOU HUNGRY?

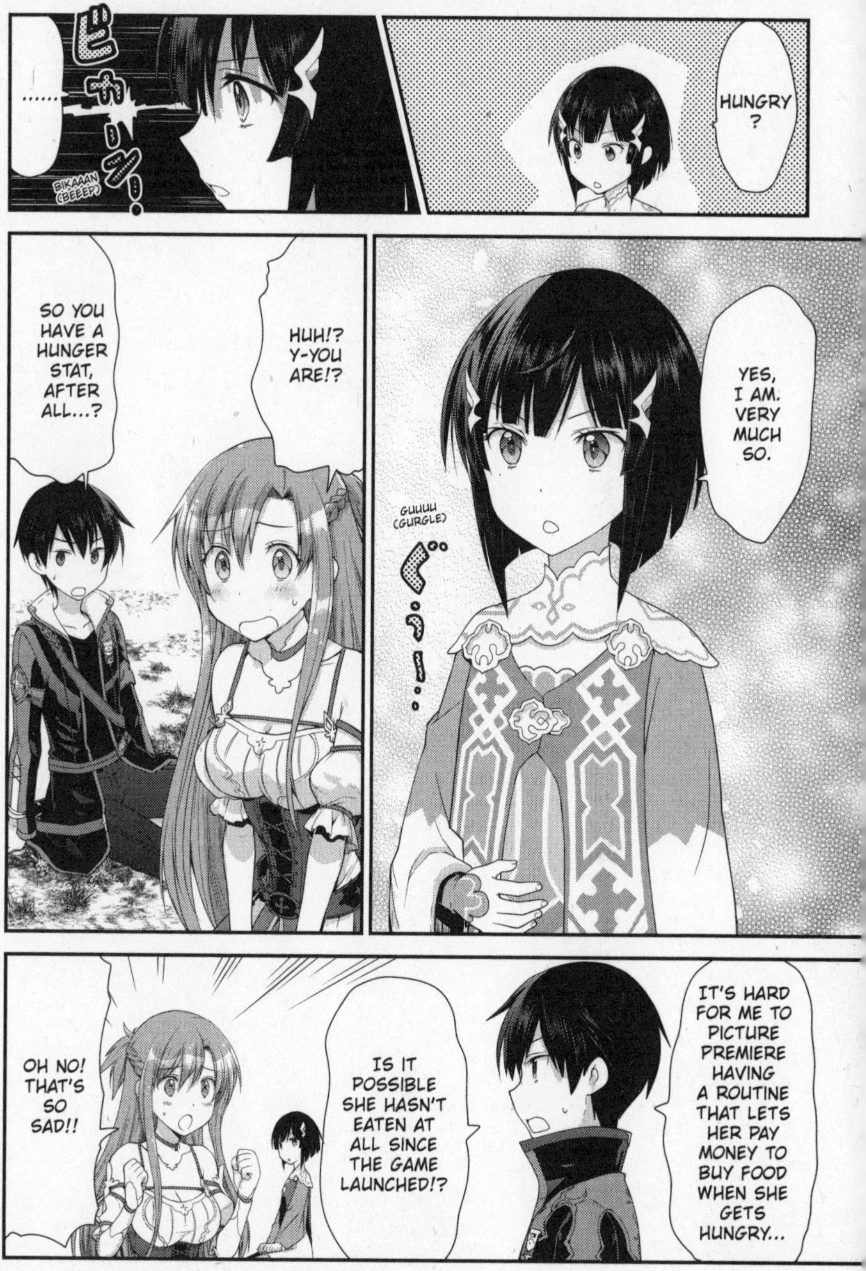
HUNGRY?
......
BIKAAAN (BEEEP)
YES, I AM. VERY MUCH SO.
GUUUU (GURGLE)
HUH!? Y-YOU ARE!?
SO YOU HAVE A HUNGER STAT, AFTER ALL...?
IT'S HARD FOR ME TO PICTURE PREMIERE HAVING A ROUTINE THAT LETS HER PAY MONEY TO BUY FOOD WHEN SHE GETS HUNGRY...
IS IT POSSIBLE SHE HASN'T EATEN AT ALL SINCE THE GAME LAUNCHED!?
OH NO! THAT'S SO SAD!!

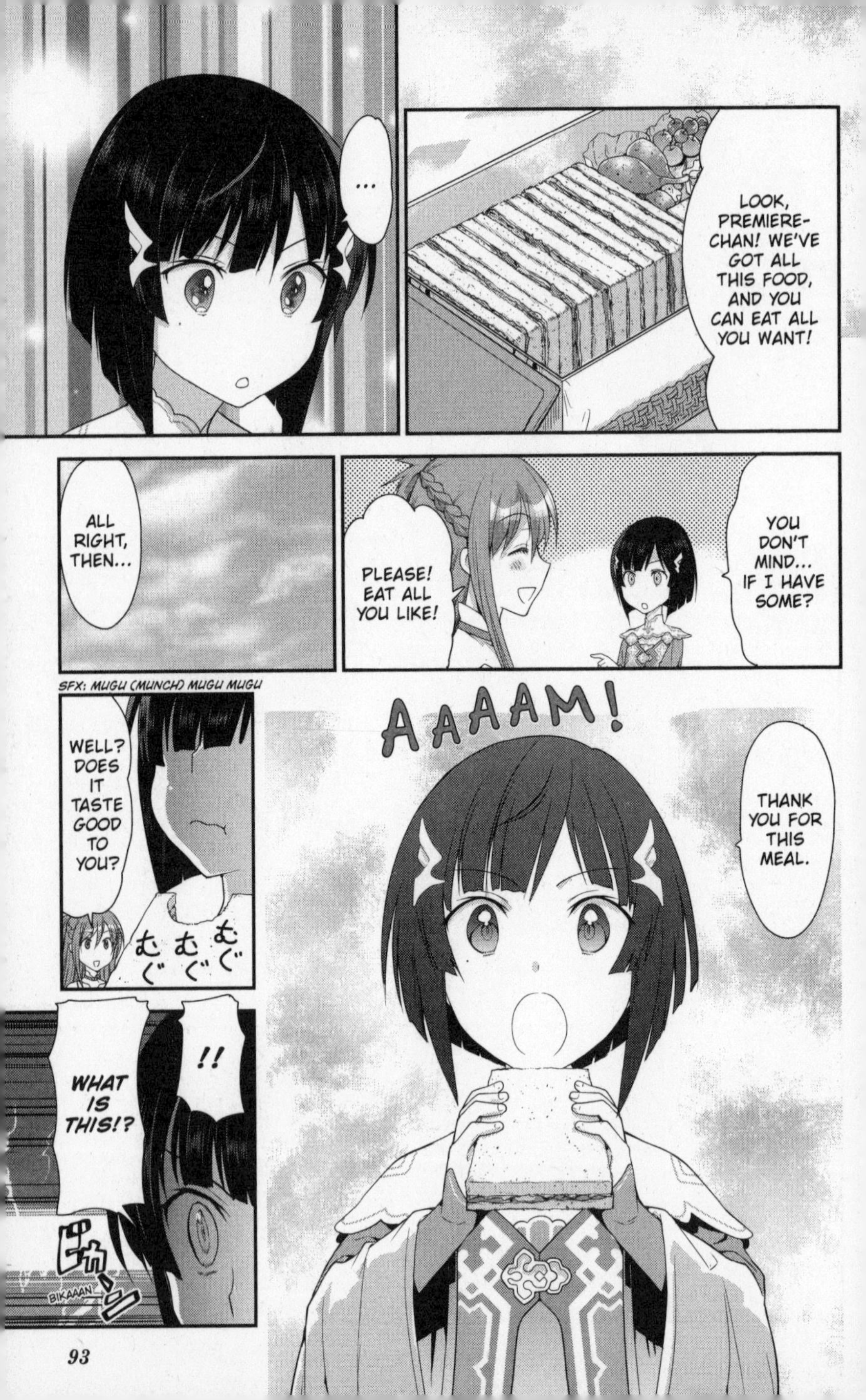
LOOK, PREMIERE-CHAN! WE'VE GOT ALL THIS FOOD, AND YOU CAN EAT ALL YOU WANT!
...
YOU DON'T MIND... IF I HAVE SOME?
PLEASE! EAT ALL YOU LIKE!
ALL RIGHT, THEN...
THANK YOU FOR THIS MEAL.
AAAAM!
SFX: MUGU (MUNCH) MUGU MUGU
WELL? DOES IT TASTE GOOD TO YOU?
むぐむぐむぐ
!!
WHAT IS THIS!?
BIKAAAN

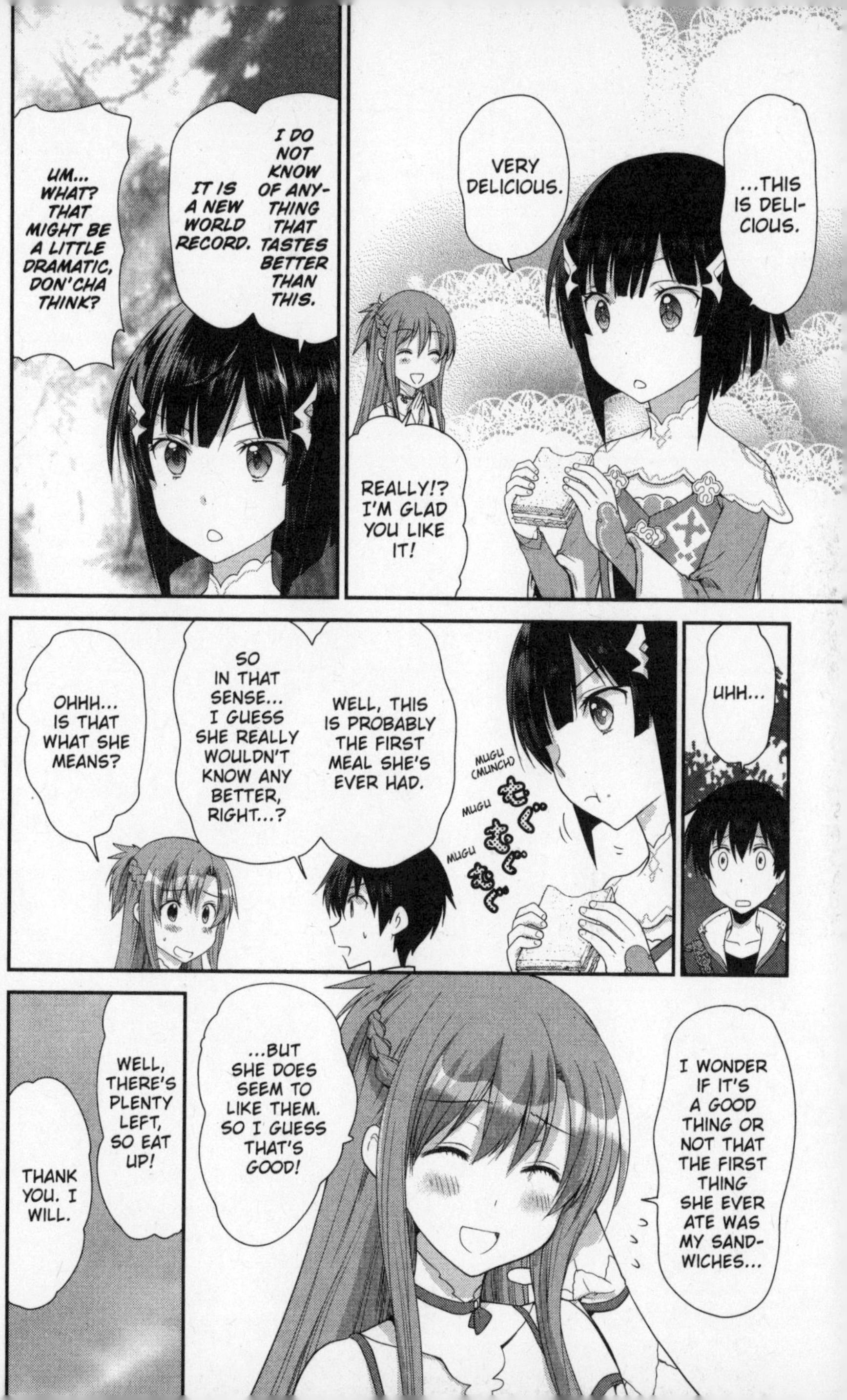
...THIS IS DELICIOUS.
VERY DELICIOUS.
REALLY!? I'M GLAD YOU LIKE IT!
I DO NOT KNOW OF ANYTHING THAT TASTES BETTER THAN THIS.
IT IS A NEW WORLD RECORD.
UM... WHAT? THAT MIGHT BE A LITTLE DRAMATIC, DON'CHA THINK?
UHH...
MUGU (MUNCH)
MUGU
MUGU
WELL, THIS IS PROBABLY THE FIRST MEAL SHE'S EVER HAD.
SO IN THAT SENSE... I GUESS SHE REALLY WOULDN'T KNOW ANY BETTER, RIGHT...?
OHHH... IS THAT WHAT SHE MEANS?
I WONDER IF IT'S A GOOD THING OR NOT THAT THE FIRST THING SHE EVER ATE WAS MY SANDWICHES...
...BUT SHE DOES SEEM TO LIKE THEM. SO I GUESS THAT'S GOOD!
WELL, THERE'S PLENTY LEFT, SO EAT UP!
THANK YOU. I WILL.

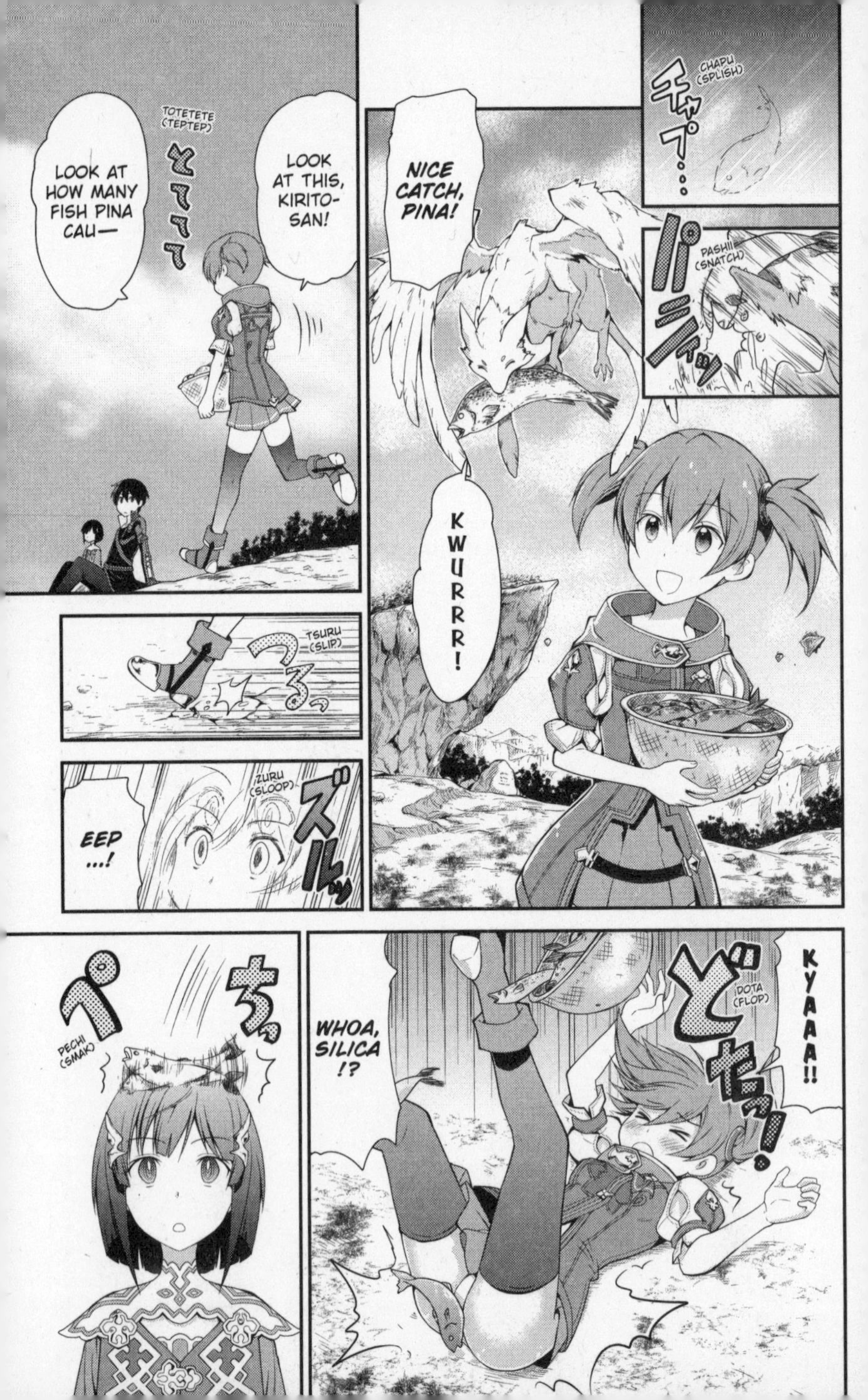

CHAPU (SPLISH)
PASHII (SNATCH)
NICE CATCH, PINA!
KWURRRR!
LOOK AT THIS, KIRITO-SAN!
TOTETETE (TEPTEP)
LOOK AT HOW MANY FISH PINA CAU—
TSURU (SLIP)
ZURU (SLOOP)
EEP ...!
KYAAAA!!
DOTA (FLOP)
WHOA, SILICA!?
PECHI (SMAK)

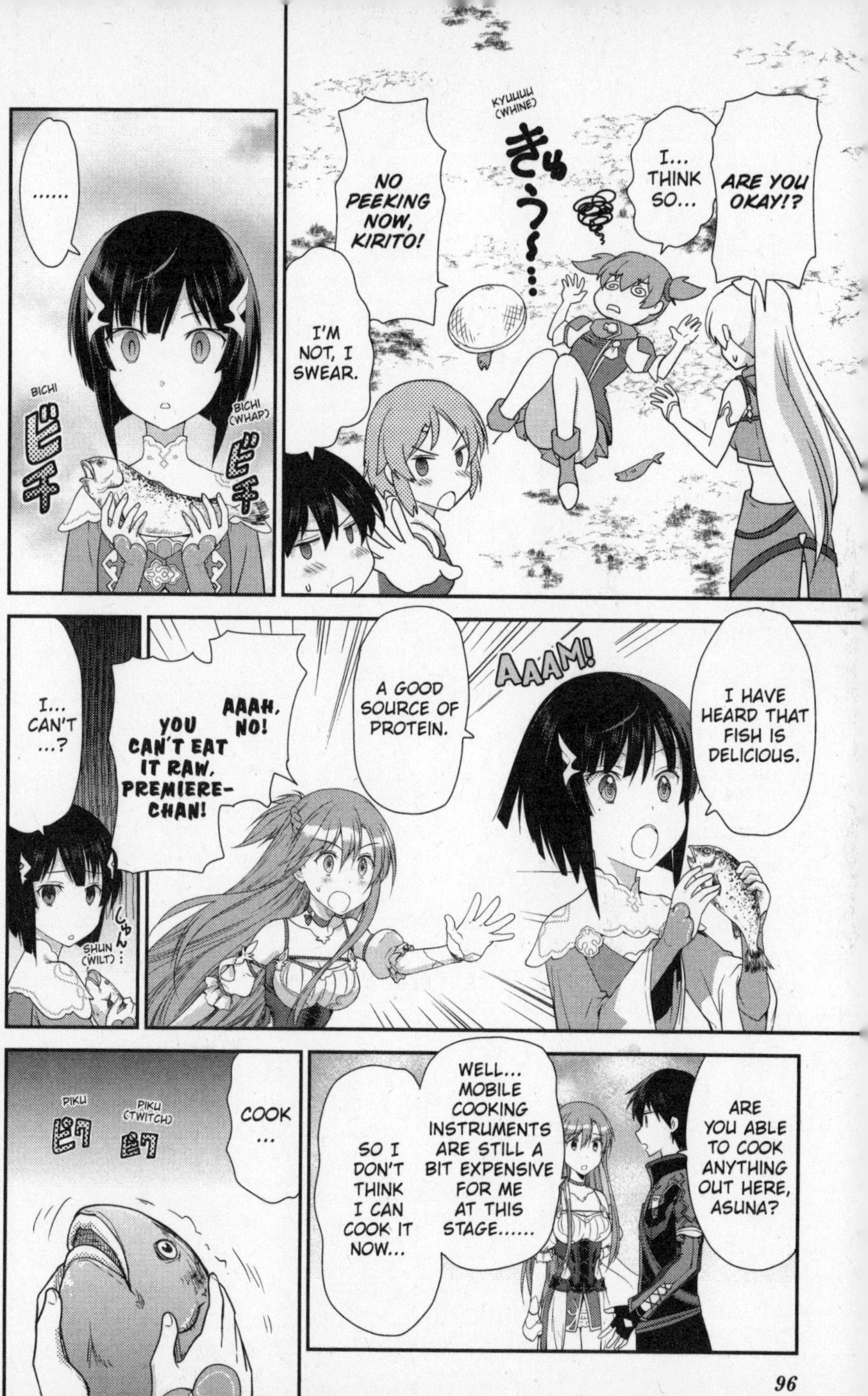
ARE YOU OKAY!?
I... THINK SO...
KYUUUU (WHINE)
きゅう~…
NO PEEKING NOW, KIRITO!
I'M NOT, I SWEAR.
......
BICHI (WHAP)
ビチ
BICHI
ビチ
AAAM!
I HAVE HEARD THAT FISH IS DELICIOUS.
A GOOD SOURCE OF PROTEIN.
AAAH, NO! YOU CAN'T EAT IT RAW, PREMIERE-CHAN!
I... CAN'T ...?
SHUN (WILT)
しゅん…
ARE YOU ABLE TO COOK ANYTHING OUT HERE, ASUNA?
WELL... MOBILE COOKING INSTRUMENTS ARE STILL A BIT EXPENSIVE FOR ME AT THIS STAGE......
SO I DON'T THINK I CAN COOK IT NOW...
COOK ...
PIKU (TWITCH)
ピク
PIKU
ピク

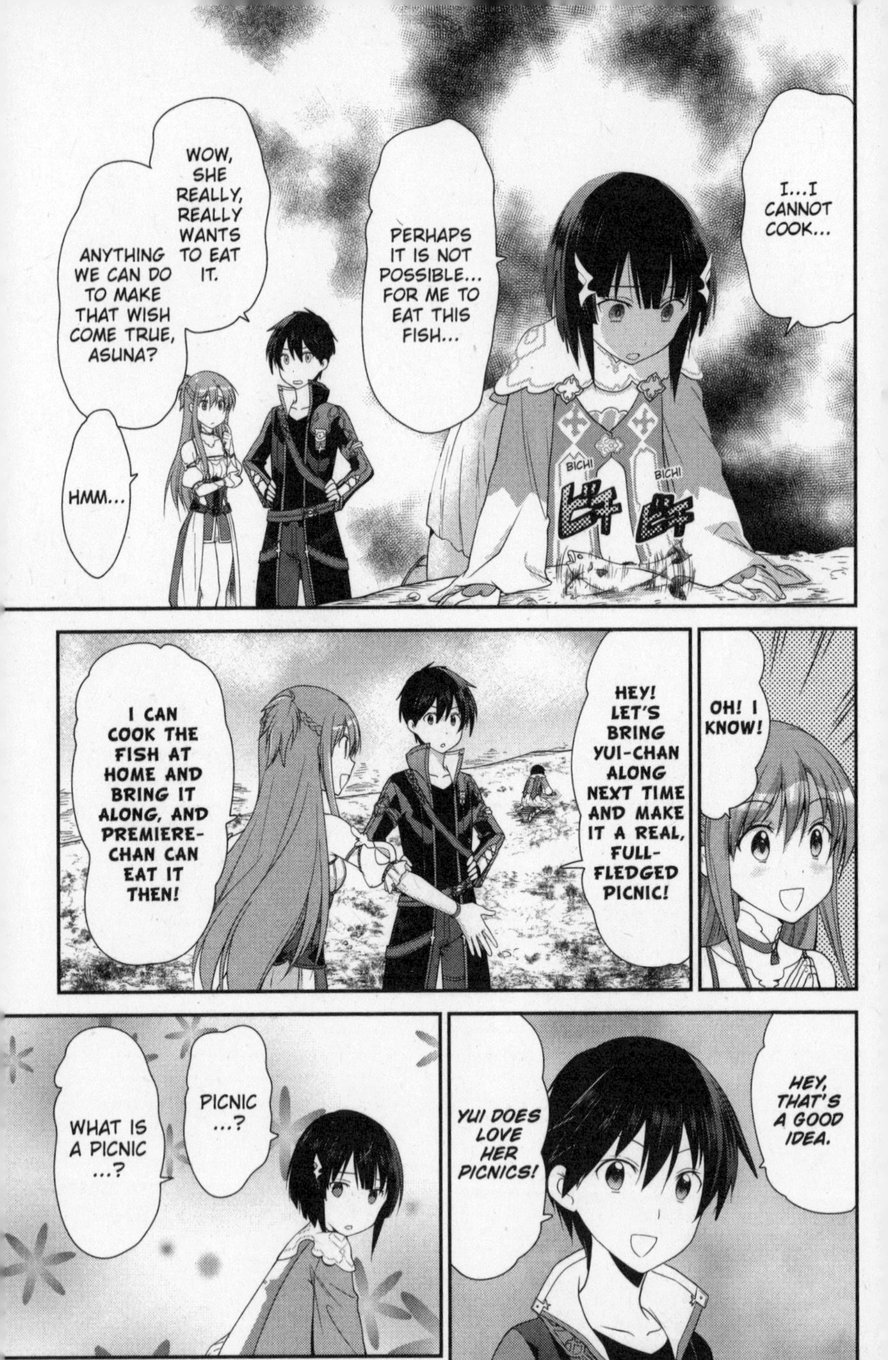
I...I CANNOT COOK...
PERHAPS IT IS NOT POSSIBLE... FOR ME TO EAT THIS FISH...
BICHI
BICHI
WOW, SHE REALLY, REALLY WANTS TO EAT IT.
ANYTHING WE CAN DO TO MAKE THAT WISH COME TRUE, ASUNA?
HMM...
OH! I KNOW!
HEY! LET'S BRING YUI-CHAN ALONG NEXT TIME AND MAKE IT A REAL, FULL-FLEDGED PICNIC!
I CAN COOK THE FISH AT HOME AND BRING IT ALONG, AND PREMIERE-CHAN CAN EAT IT THEN!
HEY, THAT'S A GOOD IDEA.
YUI DOES LOVE HER PICNICS!
PICNIC ...?
WHAT IS A PICNIC ...?

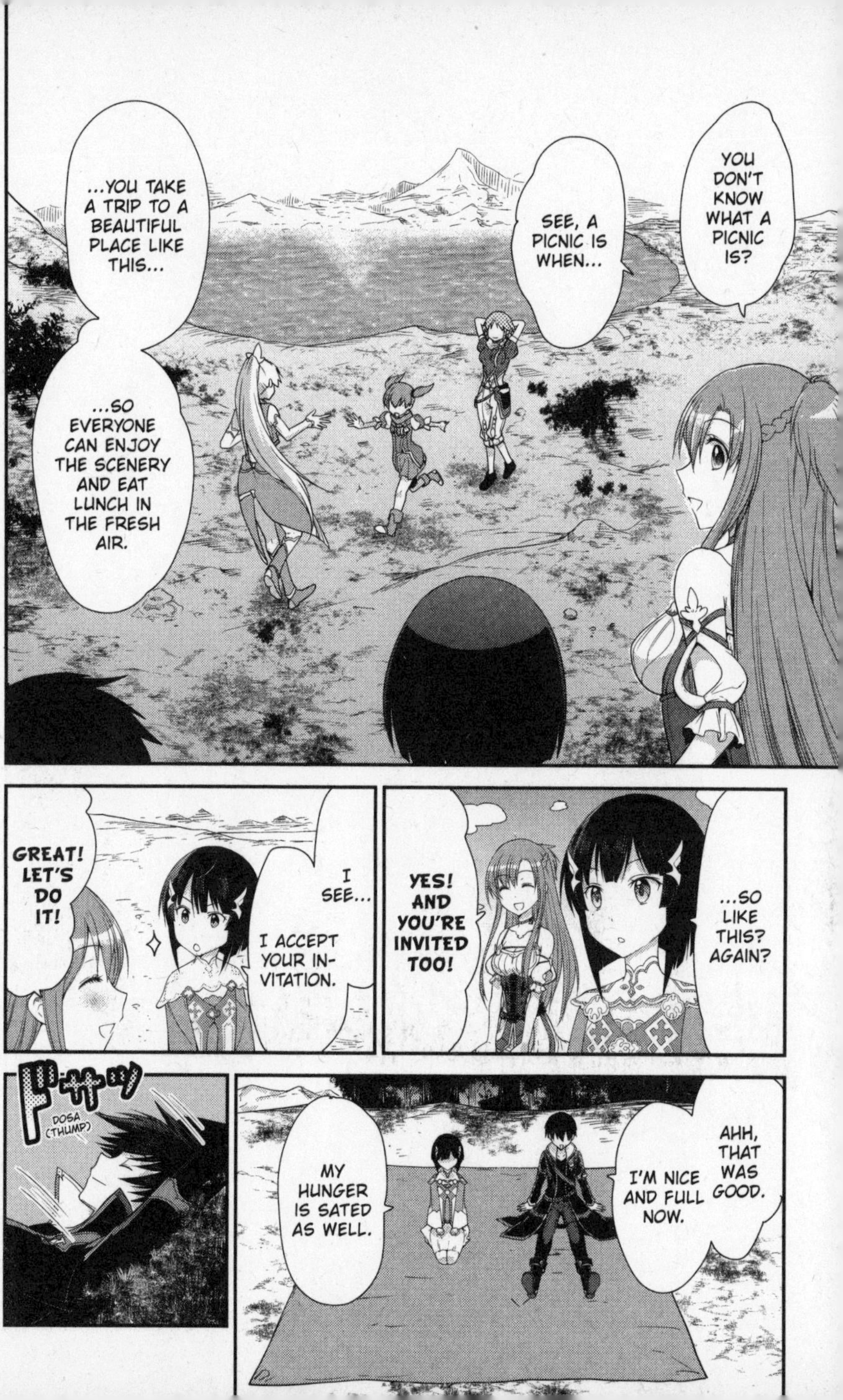
YOU DON'T KNOW WHAT A PICNIC IS?
SEE, A PICNIC IS WHEN...
...YOU TAKE A TRIP TO A BEAUTIFUL PLACE LIKE THIS...
...SO EVERYONE CAN ENJOY THE SCENERY AND EAT LUNCH IN THE FRESH AIR.
...SO LIKE THIS? AGAIN?
YES! AND YOU'RE INVITED TOO!
I SEE...
I ACCEPT YOUR INVITATION.
GREAT! LET'S DO IT!
AHH, THAT WAS GOOD.
I'M NICE AND FULL NOW.
MY HUNGER IS SATED AS WELL.
DOSA (THUMP)

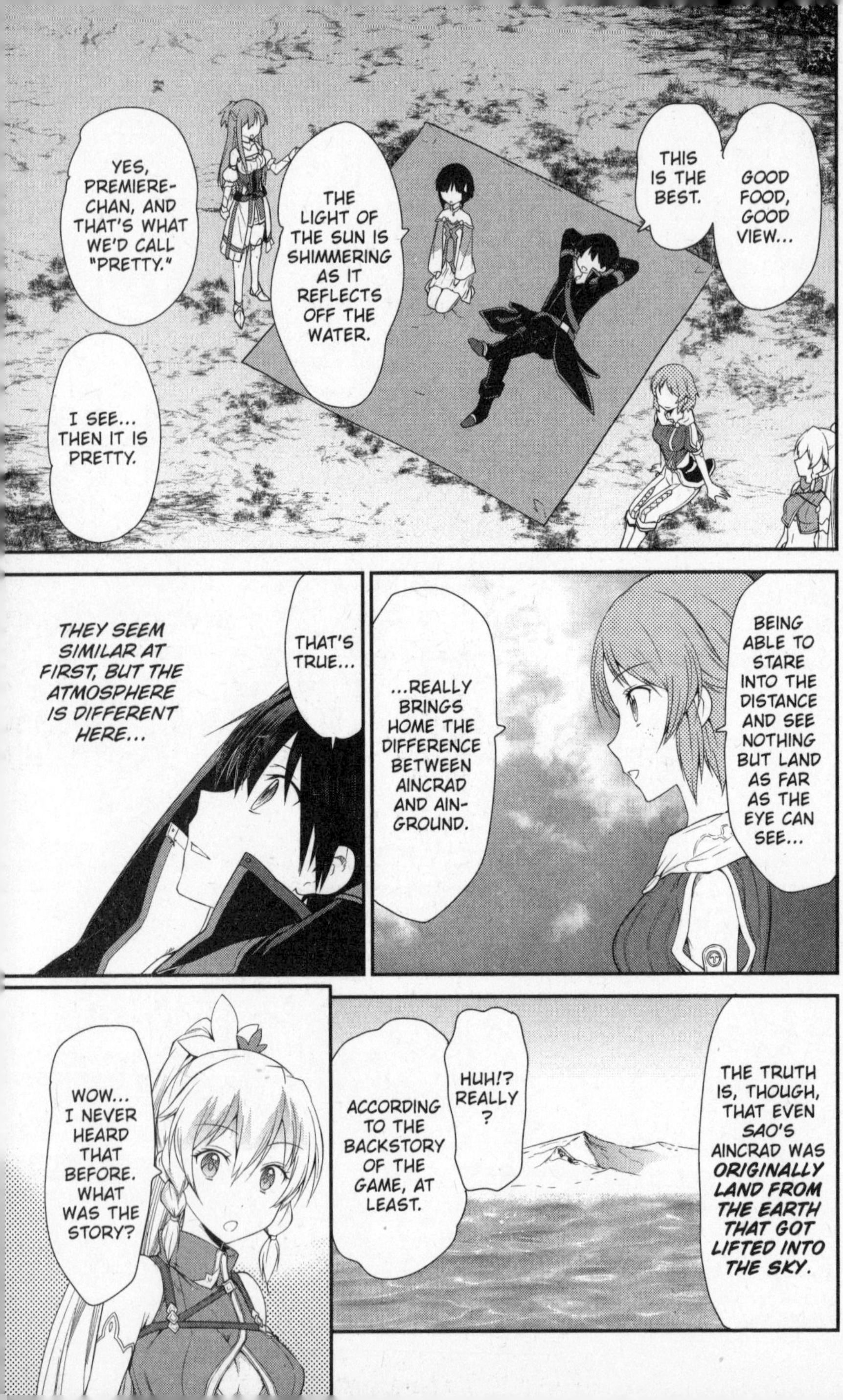
GOOD FOOD, GOOD VIEW...
THIS IS THE BEST.
THE LIGHT OF THE SUN IS SHIMMERING AS IT REFLECTS OFF THE WATER.
YES, PREMIERE-CHAN, AND THAT'S WHAT WE'D CALL "PRETTY."
I SEE... THEN IT IS PRETTY.
BEING ABLE TO STARE INTO THE DISTANCE AND SEE NOTHING BUT LAND AS FAR AS THE EYE CAN SEE...
...REALLY BRINGS HOME THE DIFFERENCE BETWEEN AINCRAD AND AIN-GROUND.
THAT'S TRUE...
THEY SEEM SIMILAR AT FIRST, BUT THE ATMOSPHERE IS DIFFERENT HERE...
THE TRUTH IS, THOUGH, THAT EVEN SAO'S AINCRAD WAS ORIGINALLY LAND FROM THE EARTH THAT GOT LIFTED INTO THE SKY.
HUH!? REALLY?
ACCORDING TO THE BACKSTORY OF THE GAME, AT LEAST.
WOW... I NEVER HEARD THAT BEFORE. WHAT WAS THE STORY?

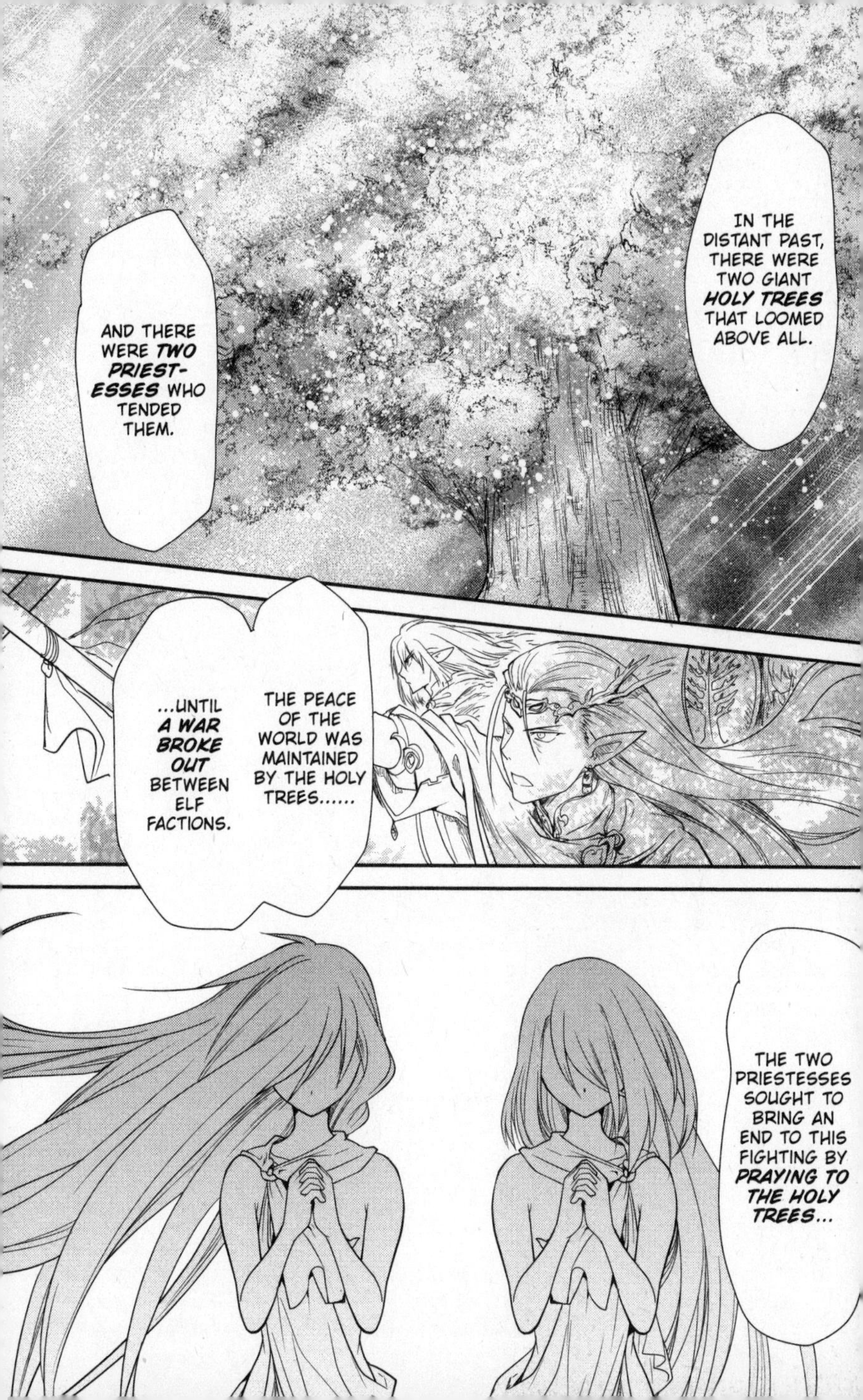
IN THE DISTANT PAST, THERE WERE TWO GIANT **HOLY TREES** THAT LOOMED ABOVE ALL.
AND THERE WERE **TWO PRIEST-ESSES** WHO TENDED THEM.
THE PEACE OF THE WORLD WAS MAINTAINED BY THE HOLY TREES......
...UNTIL **A WAR BROKE OUT** BETWEEN ELF FACTIONS.
THE TWO PRIESTESSES SOUGHT TO BRING AN END TO THIS FIGHTING BY **PRAYING TO THE HOLY TREES**...

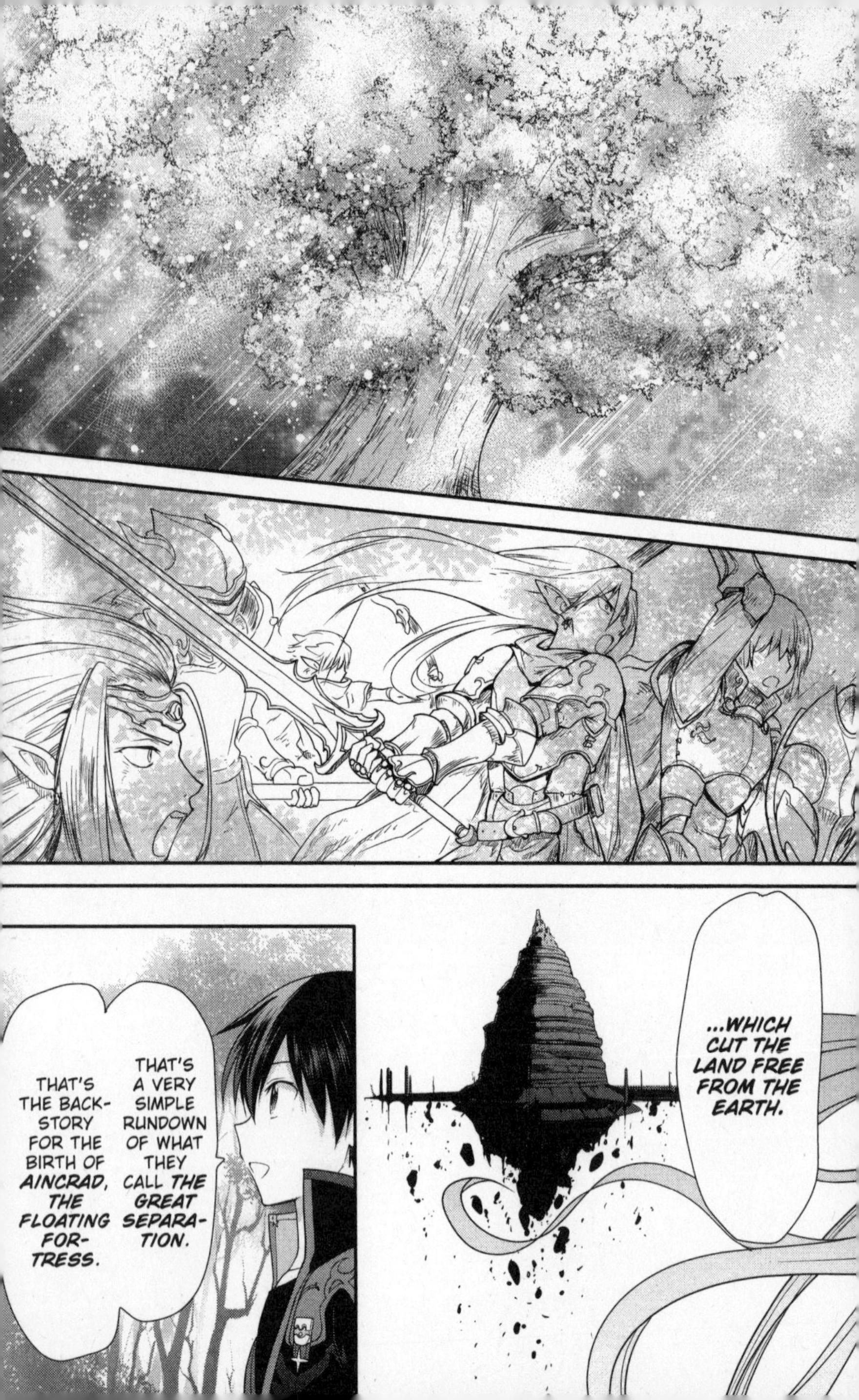
...WHICH CUT THE LAND FREE FROM THE EARTH.
THAT'S A VERY SIMPLE RUNDOWN OF WHAT THEY CALL *THE GREAT SEPARATION*.
THAT'S THE BACKSTORY FOR THE BIRTH OF *AINCRAD, THE FLOATING FORTRESS*.

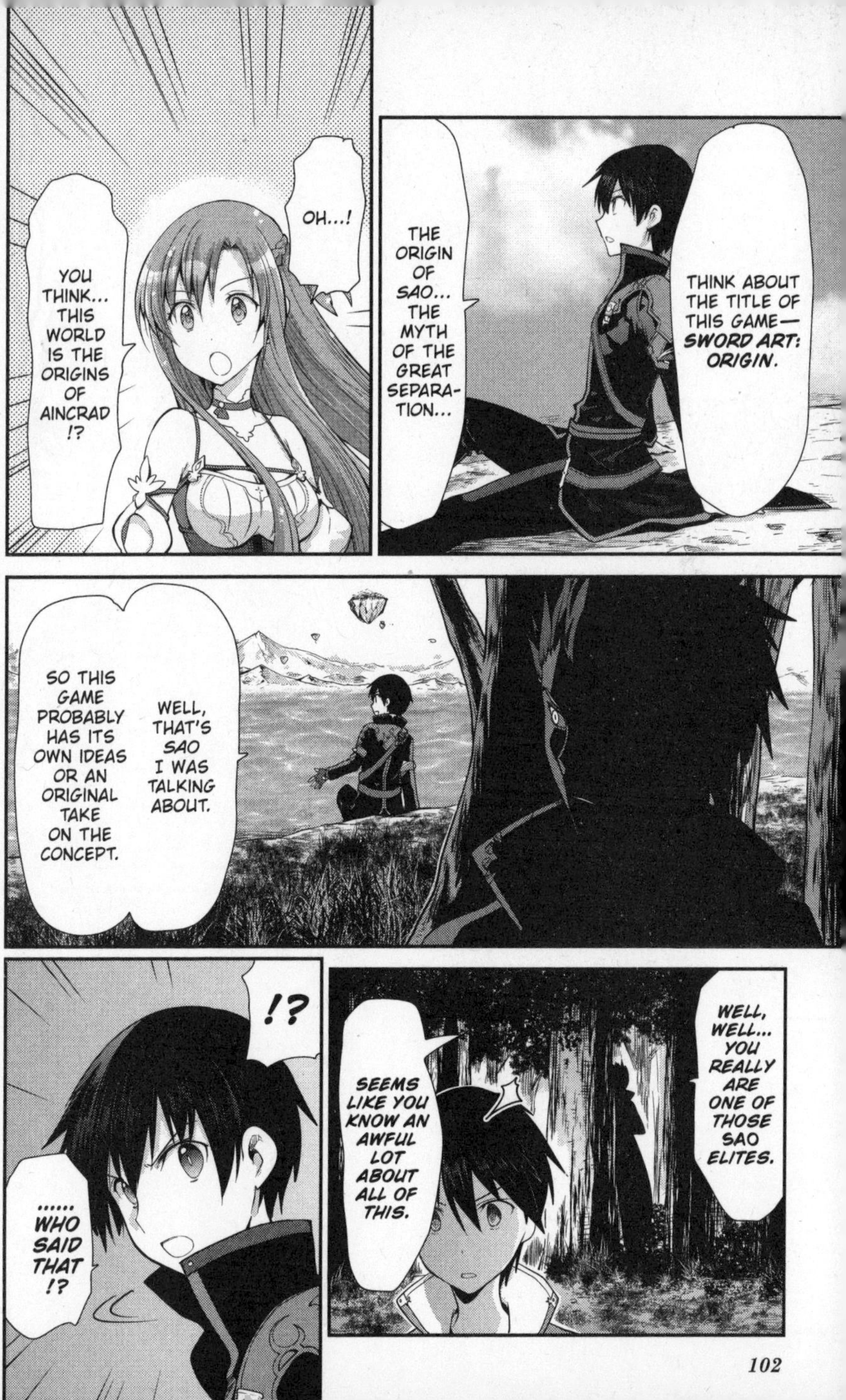
THINK ABOUT THE TITLE OF THIS GAME—*SWORD ART: ORIGIN*.
THE ORIGIN OF SAO... THE MYTH OF THE GREAT SEPARA-TION...
OH...!
YOU THINK... THIS WORLD IS THE ORIGINS OF AINCRAD!?
WELL, THAT'S SAO I WAS TALKING ABOUT.
SO THIS GAME PROBABLY HAS ITS OWN IDEAS OR AN ORIGINAL TAKE ON THE CONCEPT.
WELL, WELL... YOU REALLY ARE ONE OF THOSE SAO ELITES.
SEEMS LIKE YOU KNOW AN AWFUL LOT ABOUT ALL OF THIS.
!?
......WHO SAID THAT!?

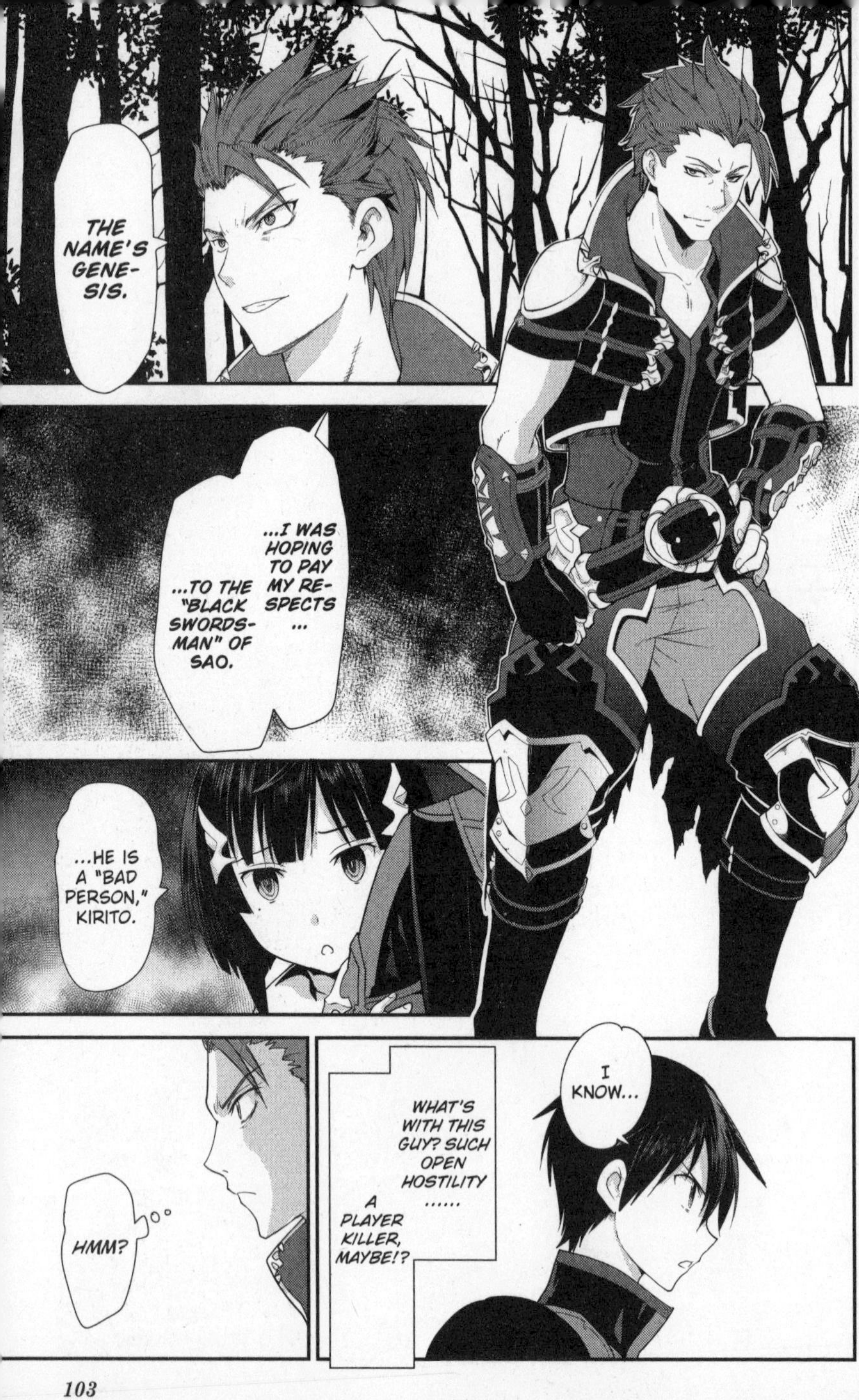
THE NAME'S GENESIS.
...I WAS HOPING TO PAY MY RESPECTS...
...TO THE "BLACK SWORDSMAN" OF SAO.
...HE IS A "BAD PERSON," KIRITO.
I KNOW...
WHAT'S WITH THIS GUY? SUCH OPEN HOSTILITY......
A PLAYER KILLER, MAYBE!?
HMM?

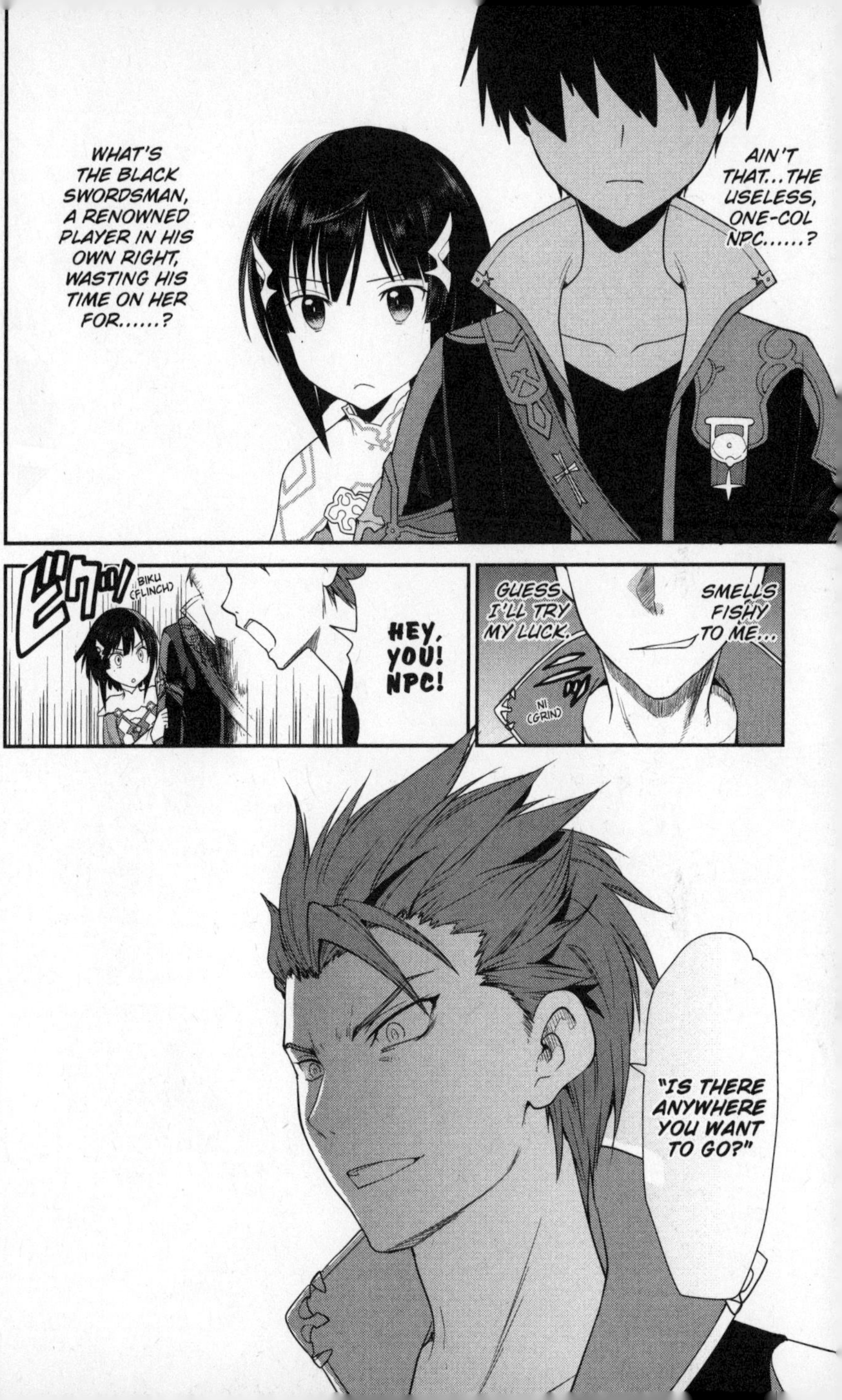
AIN'T THAT...THE USELESS, ONE-COL NPC......?
WHAT'S THE BLACK SWORDSMAN, A RENOWNED PLAYER IN HIS OWN RIGHT, WASTING HIS TIME ON HER FOR......?
SMELLS FISHY TO ME...
GUESS I'LL TRY MY LUCK.
NI (GRIN)
HEY, YOU! NPC!
BIKU (FLINCH)
"IS THERE ANYWHERE YOU WANT TO GO?"

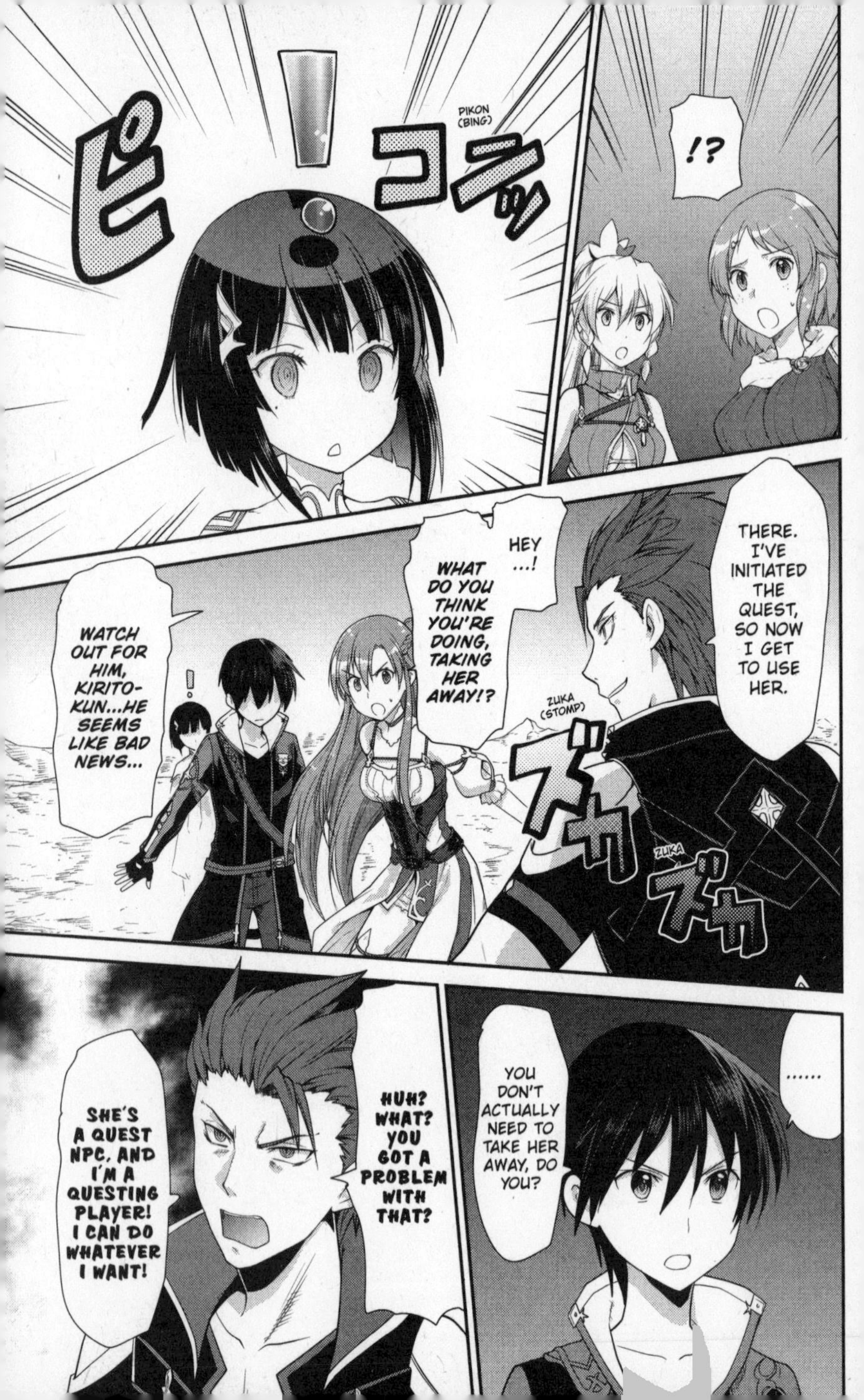
!?
PIKON (BING)
THERE. I'VE INITIATED THE QUEST, SO NOW I GET TO USE HER.
ZUKA (STOMP)
ZUKA
HEY ...!
WHAT DO YOU THINK YOU'RE DOING, TAKING HER AWAY!?
!
WATCH OUT FOR HIM, KIRITO-KUN...HE SEEMS LIKE BAD NEWS...
......
YOU DON'T ACTUALLY NEED TO TAKE HER AWAY, DO YOU?
HUH? WHAT? YOU GOT A PROBLEM WITH THAT?
SHE'S A QUEST NPC, AND I'M A QUESTING PLAYER! I CAN DO WHATEVER I WANT!

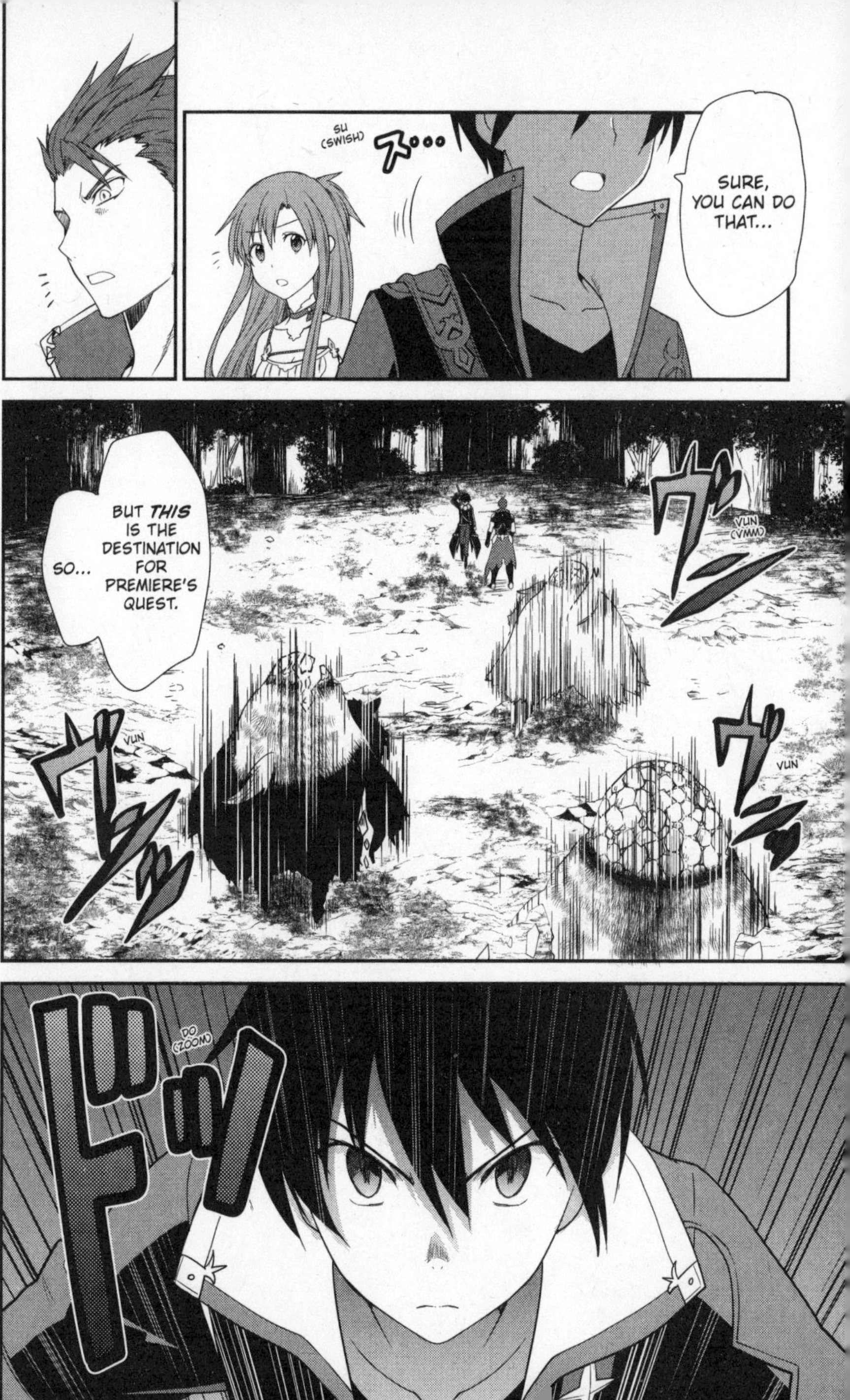
SURE, YOU CAN DO THAT...
SU (SWISH)
BUT THIS IS THE DESTINATION FOR PREMIERE'S QUEST.
SO...
VUN (VMM)
VUN
VUN
DO (ZOOM)

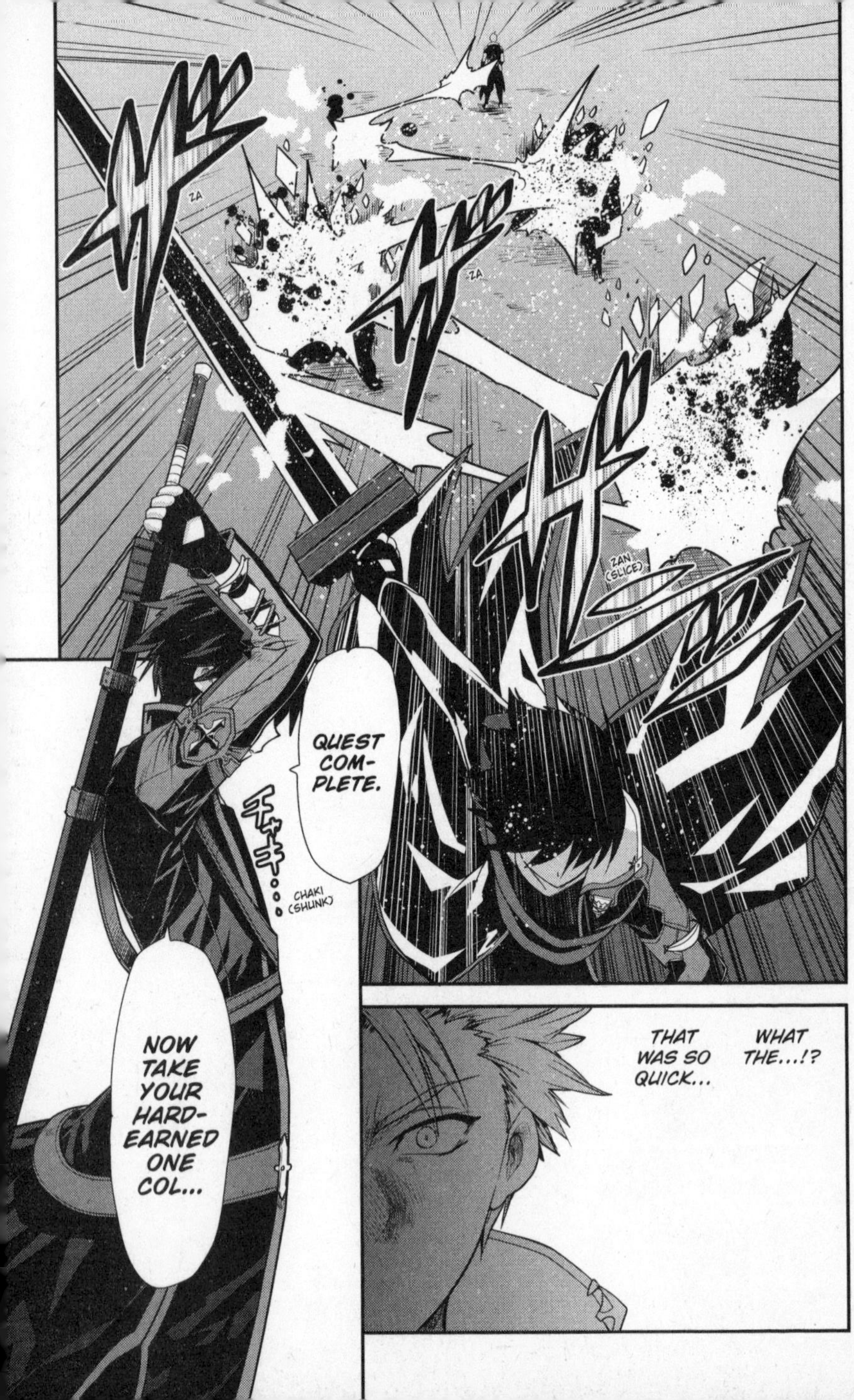
ZA
ZA
ZAN (SLICE)
QUEST COM-PLETE.
CHAKI (SHUNK)
NOW TAKE YOUR HARD-EARNED ONE COL...
WHAT THE...!?
THAT WAS SO QUICK...

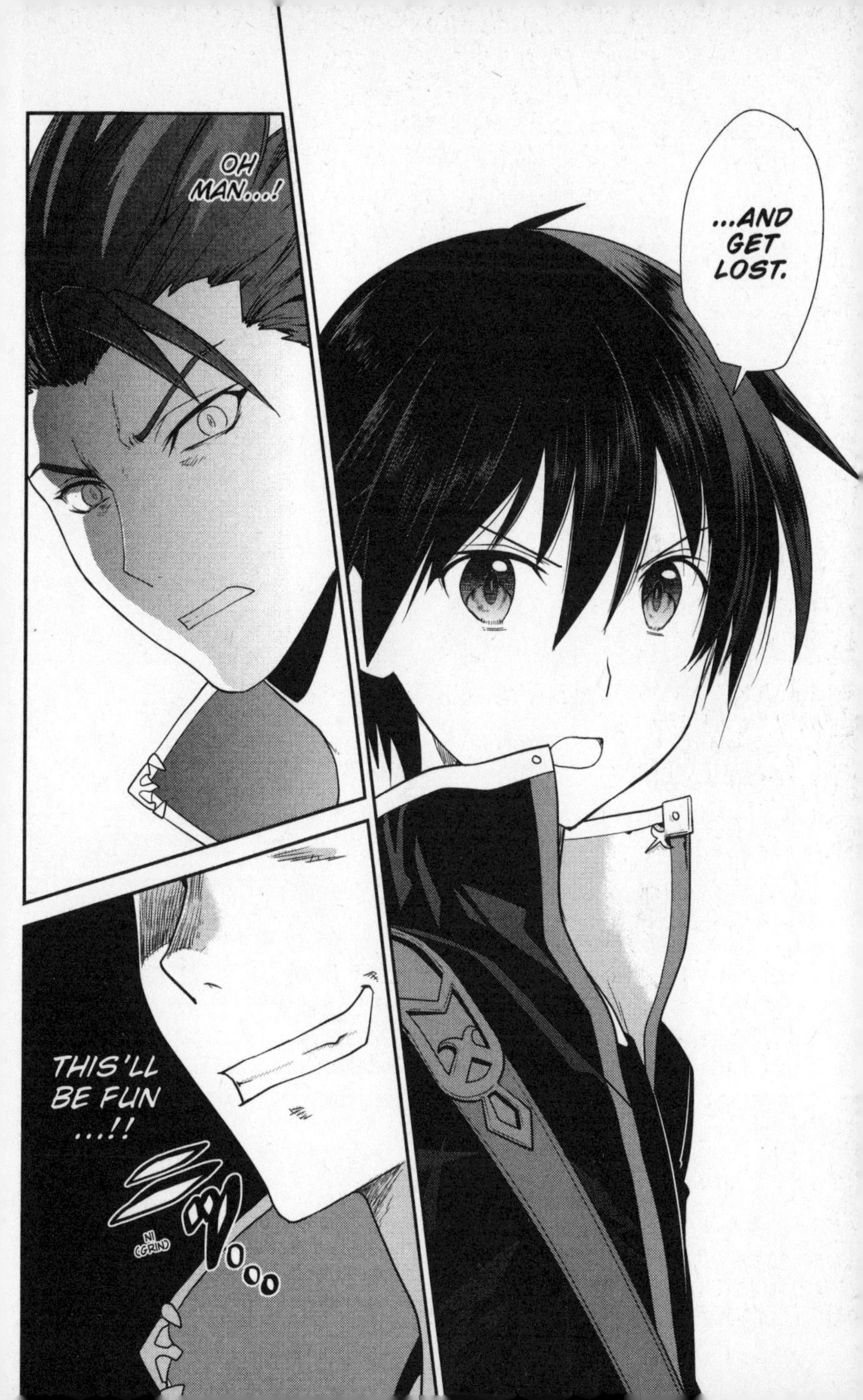
...AND GET LOST.
OH MAN...!
THIS'LL BE FUN ...!!
NI (GRIN)

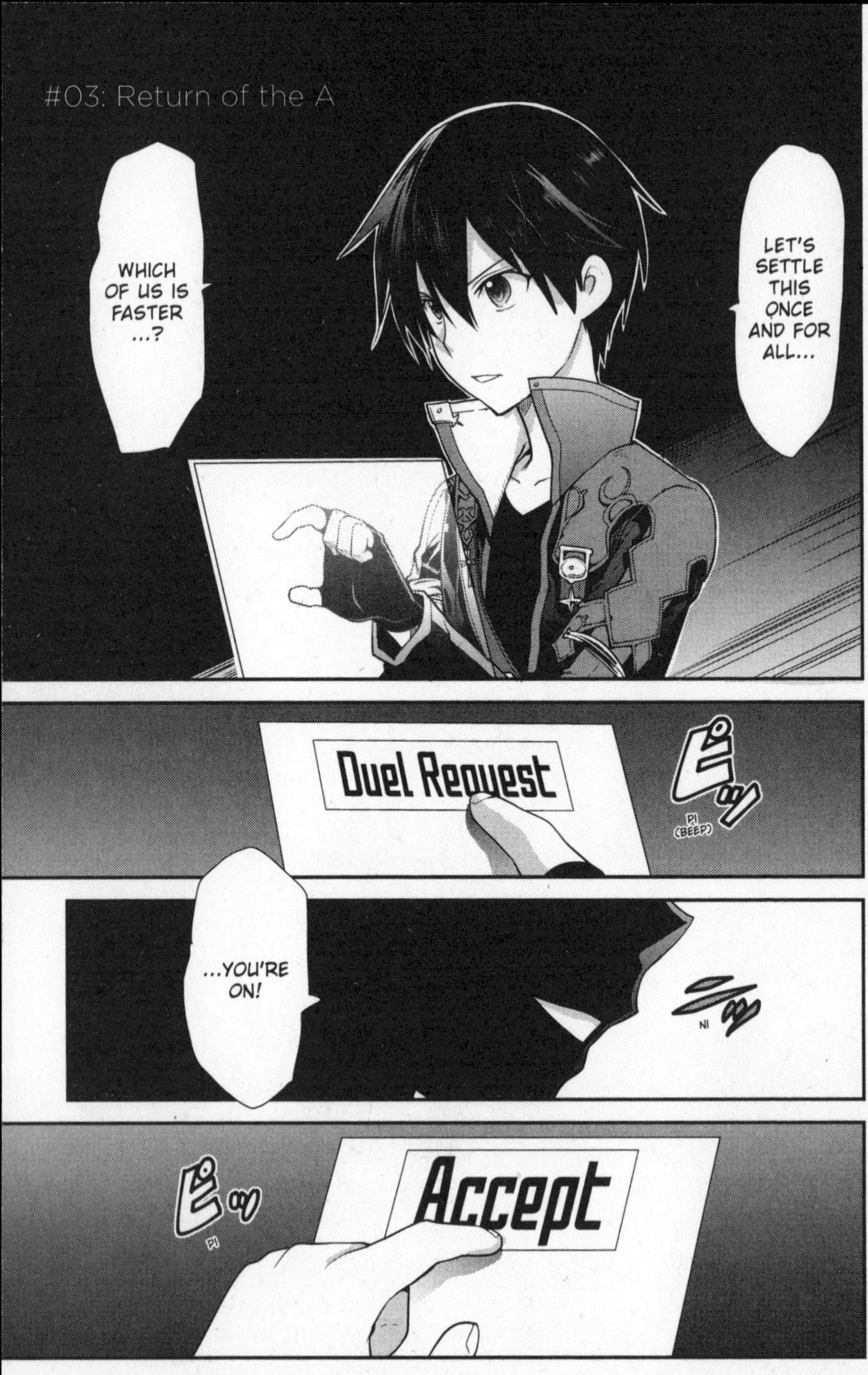
#03: Return of the A
LET'S SETTLE THIS ONCE AND FOR ALL...
WHICH OF US IS FASTER ...?
Duel Request
PI (BEEP)
...YOU'RE ON!
NI
Accept
PI

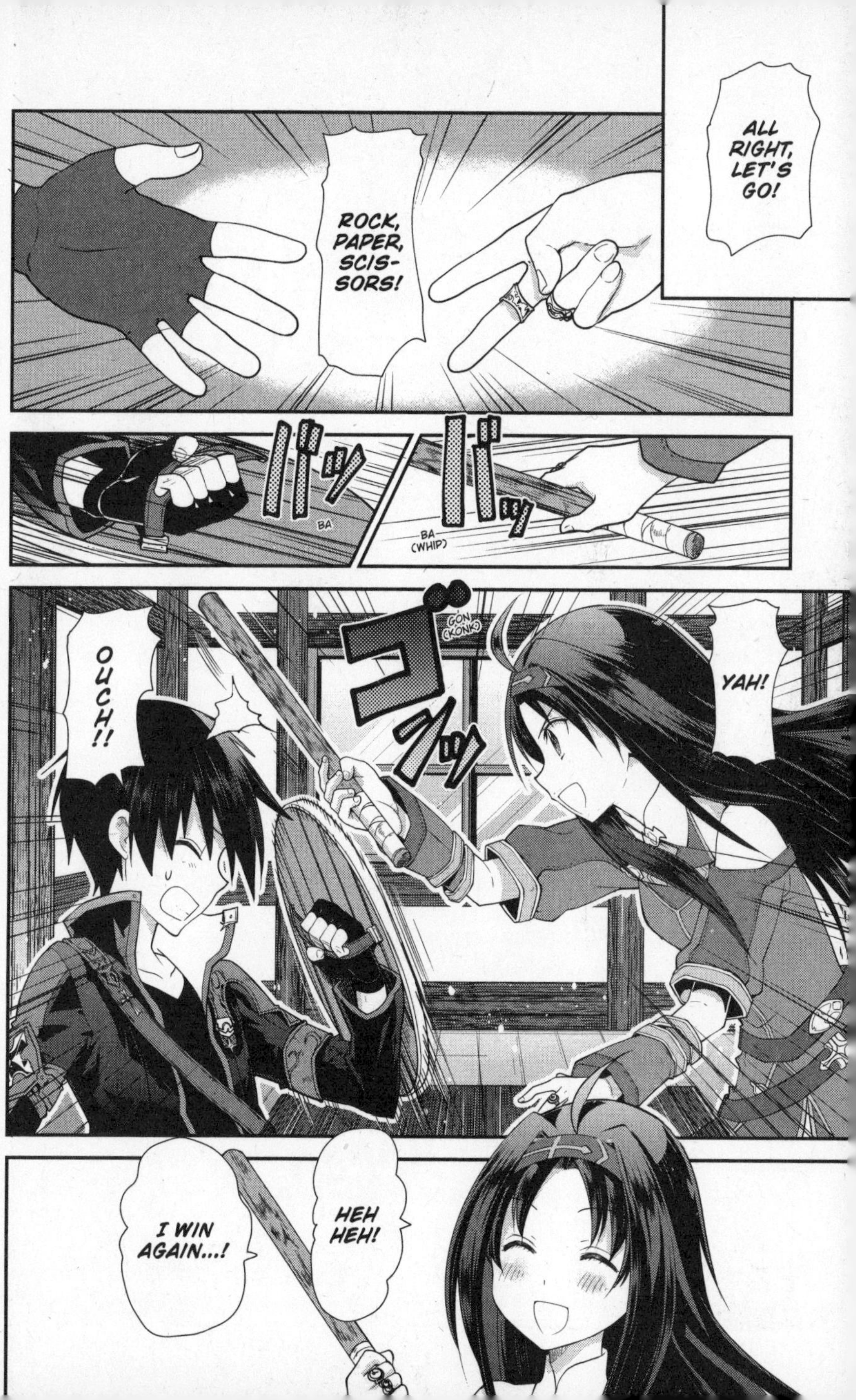
ALL RIGHT, LET'S GO!
ROCK, PAPER, SCIS-SORS!
バッ
BA (WHIP)
バッ
BA
YAH!
ゴッ
GON (KONK)
OUCH!!
HEH HEH!
I WIN AGAIN...!

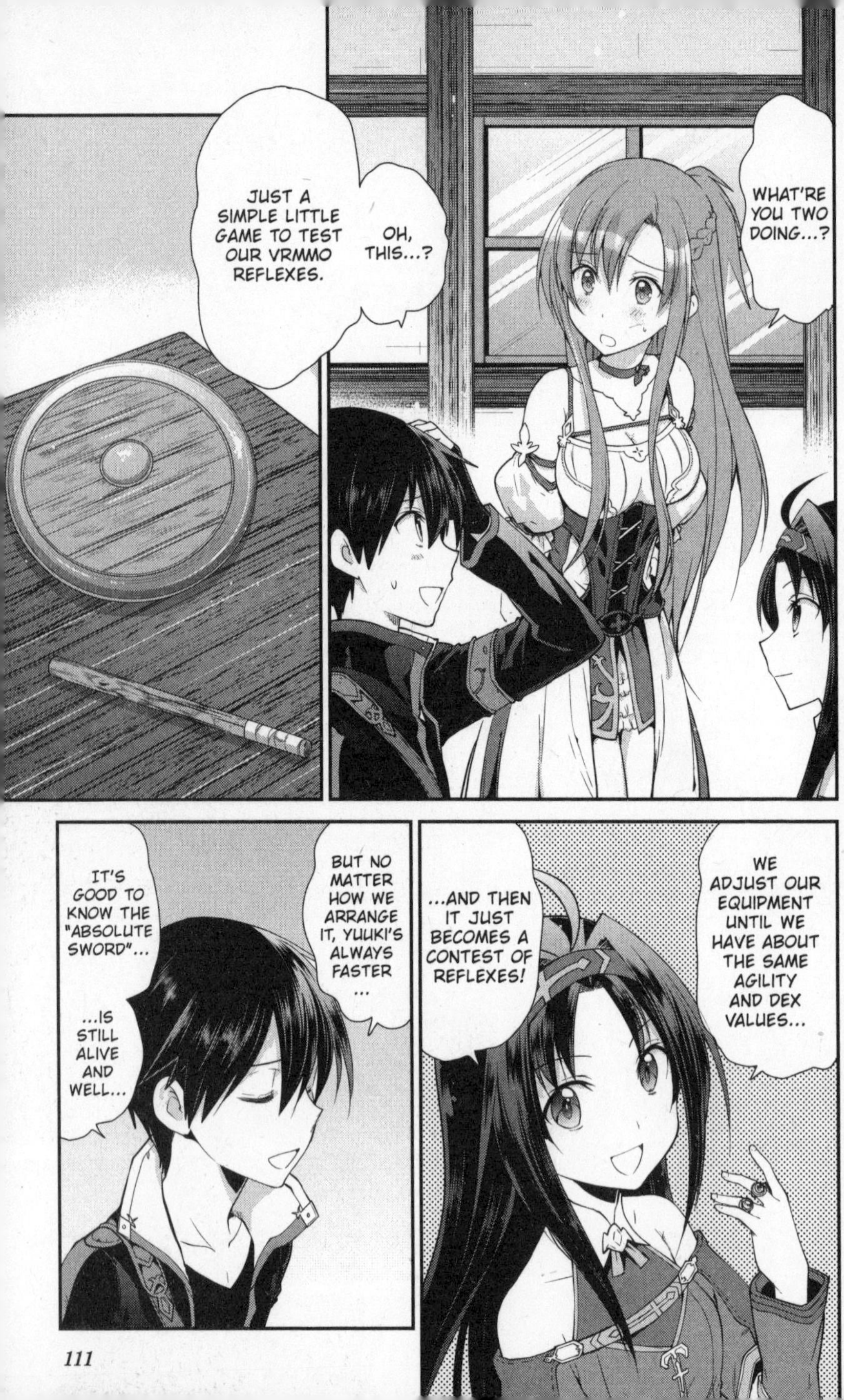
WHAT'RE YOU TWO DOING...?
OH, THIS...?
JUST A SIMPLE LITTLE GAME TO TEST OUR VRMMO REFLEXES.
WE ADJUST OUR EQUIPMENT UNTIL WE HAVE ABOUT THE SAME AGILITY AND DEX VALUES...
...AND THEN IT JUST BECOMES A CONTEST OF REFLEXES!
BUT NO MATTER HOW WE ARRANGE IT, YUUKI'S ALWAYS FASTER...
IT'S GOOD TO KNOW THE "ABSOLUTE SWORD"...
...IS STILL ALIVE AND WELL...

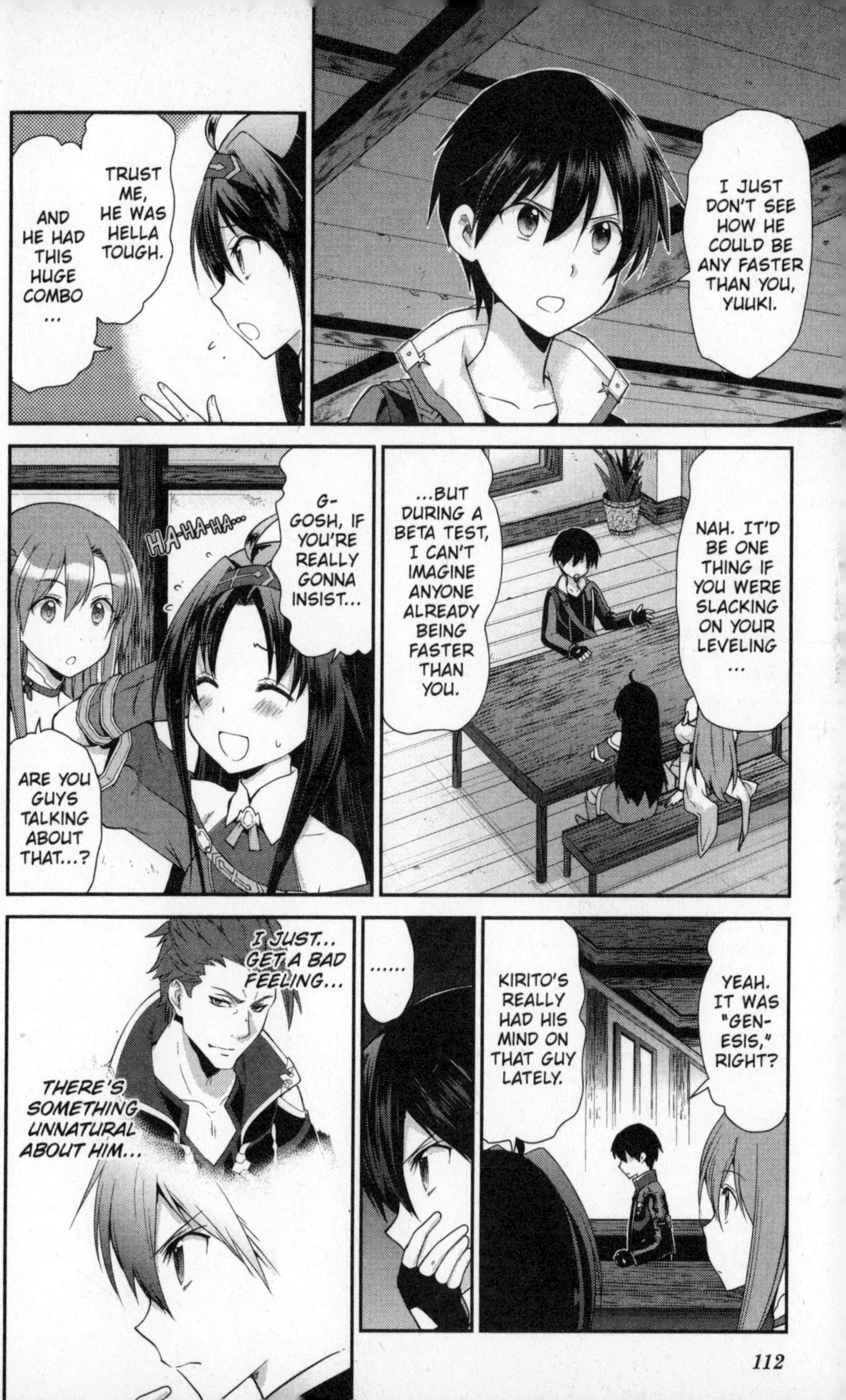

I JUST DON'T SEE HOW HE COULD BE ANY FASTER THAN YOU, YUUKI.
TRUST ME, HE WAS HELLA TOUGH.
AND HE HAD THIS HUGE COMBO...
NAH. IT'D BE ONE THING IF YOU WERE SLACKING ON YOUR LEVELING...
...BUT DURING A BETA TEST, I CAN'T IMAGINE ANYONE ALREADY BEING FASTER THAN YOU.
G-GOSH, IF YOU'RE REALLY GONNA INSIST...
HA-HA-HA...
ARE YOU GUYS TALKING ABOUT THAT...?
YEAH. IT WAS "GEN-ESIS," RIGHT?
KIRITO'S REALLY HAD HIS MIND ON THAT GUY LATELY.
......
I JUST... GET A BAD FEELING...
THERE'S SOMETHING UNNATURAL ABOUT HIM...

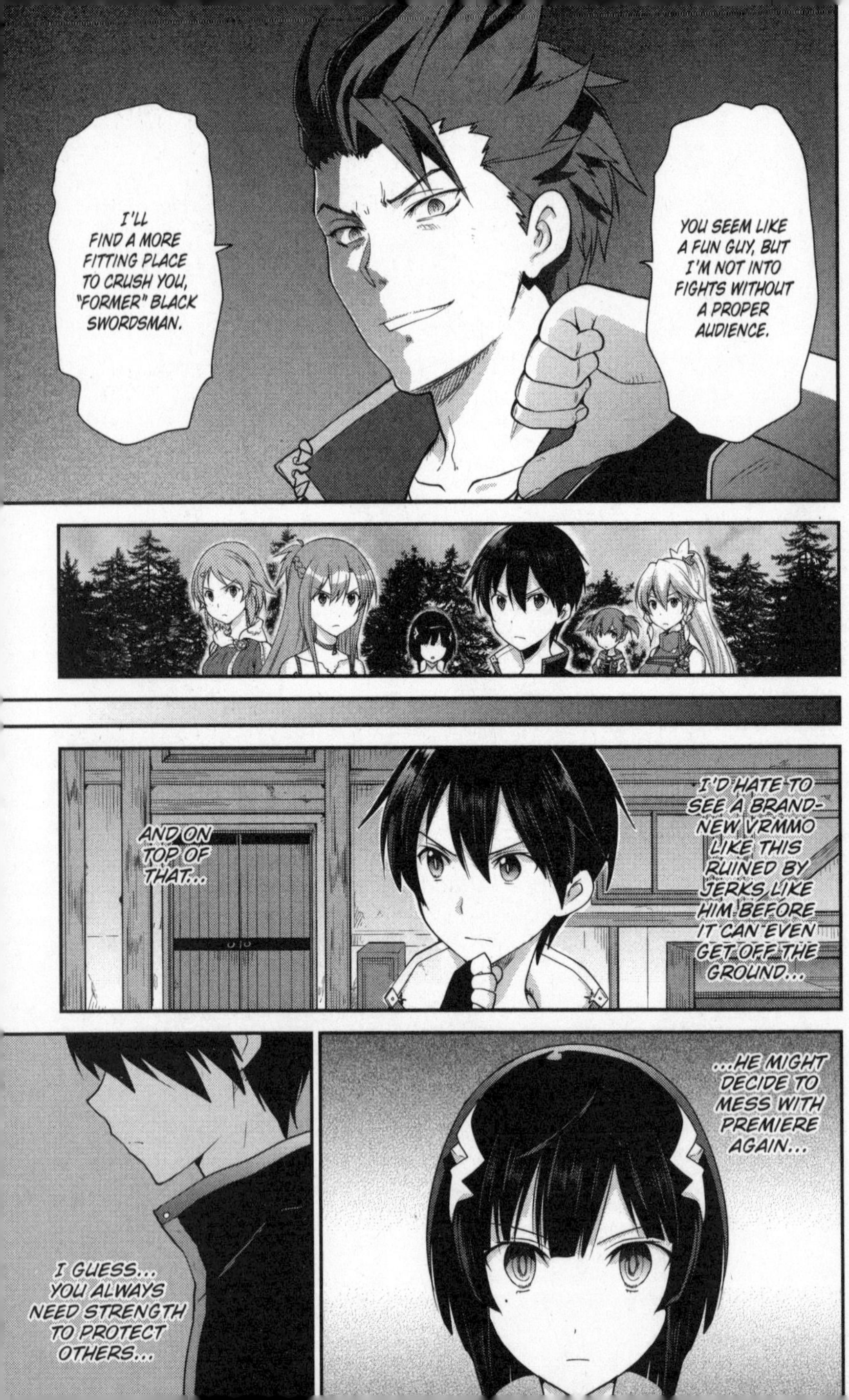
YOU SEEM LIKE A FUN GUY, BUT I'M NOT INTO FIGHTS WITHOUT A PROPER AUDIENCE.
I'LL FIND A MORE FITTING PLACE TO CRUSH YOU, "FORMER" BLACK SWORDSMAN.
I'D HATE TO SEE A BRAND-NEW VRMMO LIKE THIS RUINED BY JERKS LIKE HIM BEFORE IT CAN EVEN GET OFF THE GROUND...
AND ON TOP OF THAT...
...HE MIGHT DECIDE TO MESS WITH PREMIERE AGAIN...
I GUESS... YOU ALWAYS NEED STRENGTH TO PROTECT OTHERS...

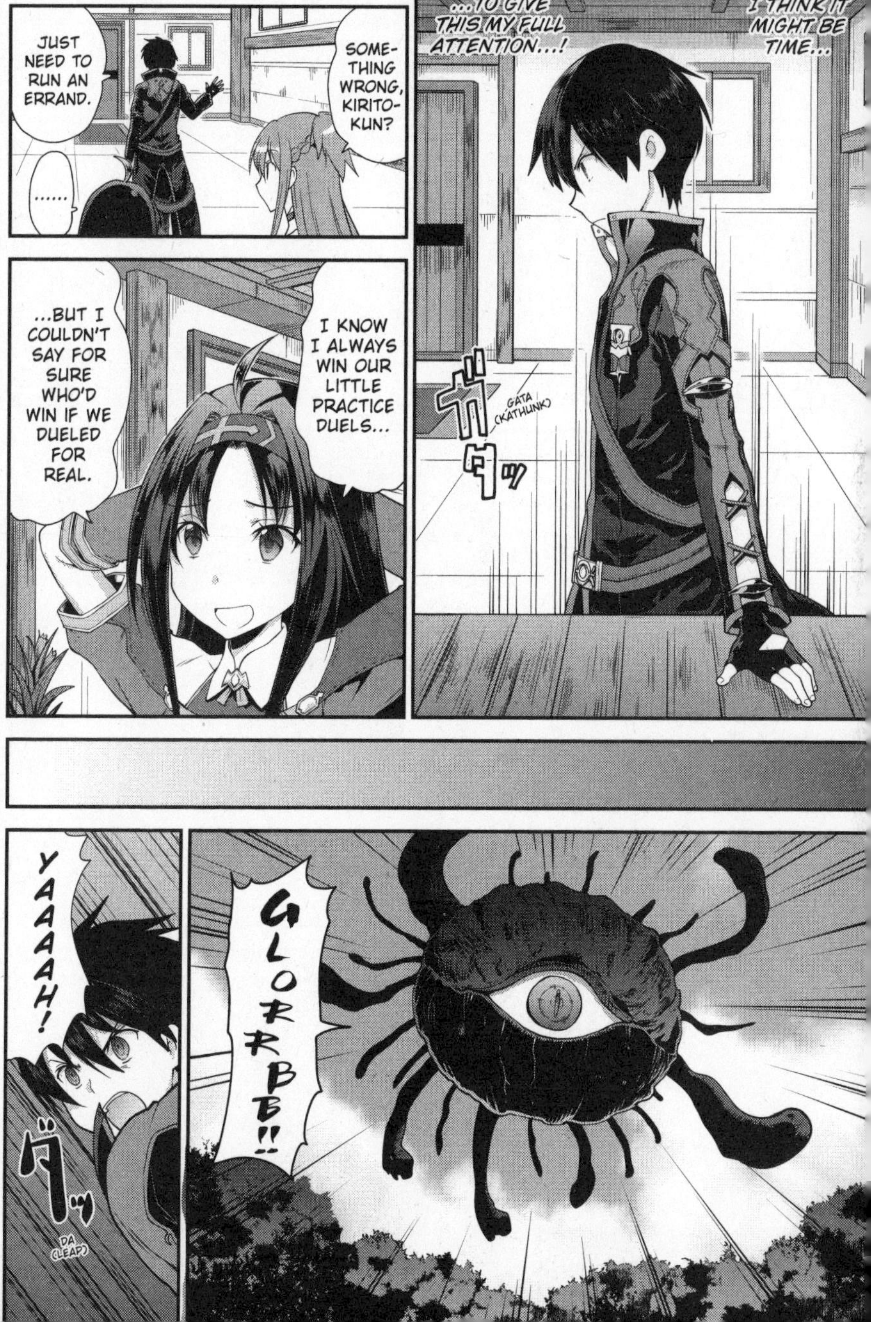
I THINK IT MIGHT BE TIME...
...TO GIVE THIS MY FULL ATTENTION...!
GATA (KATHUNK)
SOME-THING WRONG, KIRITO-KUN?
JUST NEED TO RUN AN ERRAND.
......
I KNOW I ALWAYS WIN OUR LITTLE PRACTICE DUELS...
...BUT I COULDN'T SAY FOR SURE WHO'D WIN IF WE DUELED FOR REAL.
GLORRBB!!
YAAAAH!
DA (LEAP)

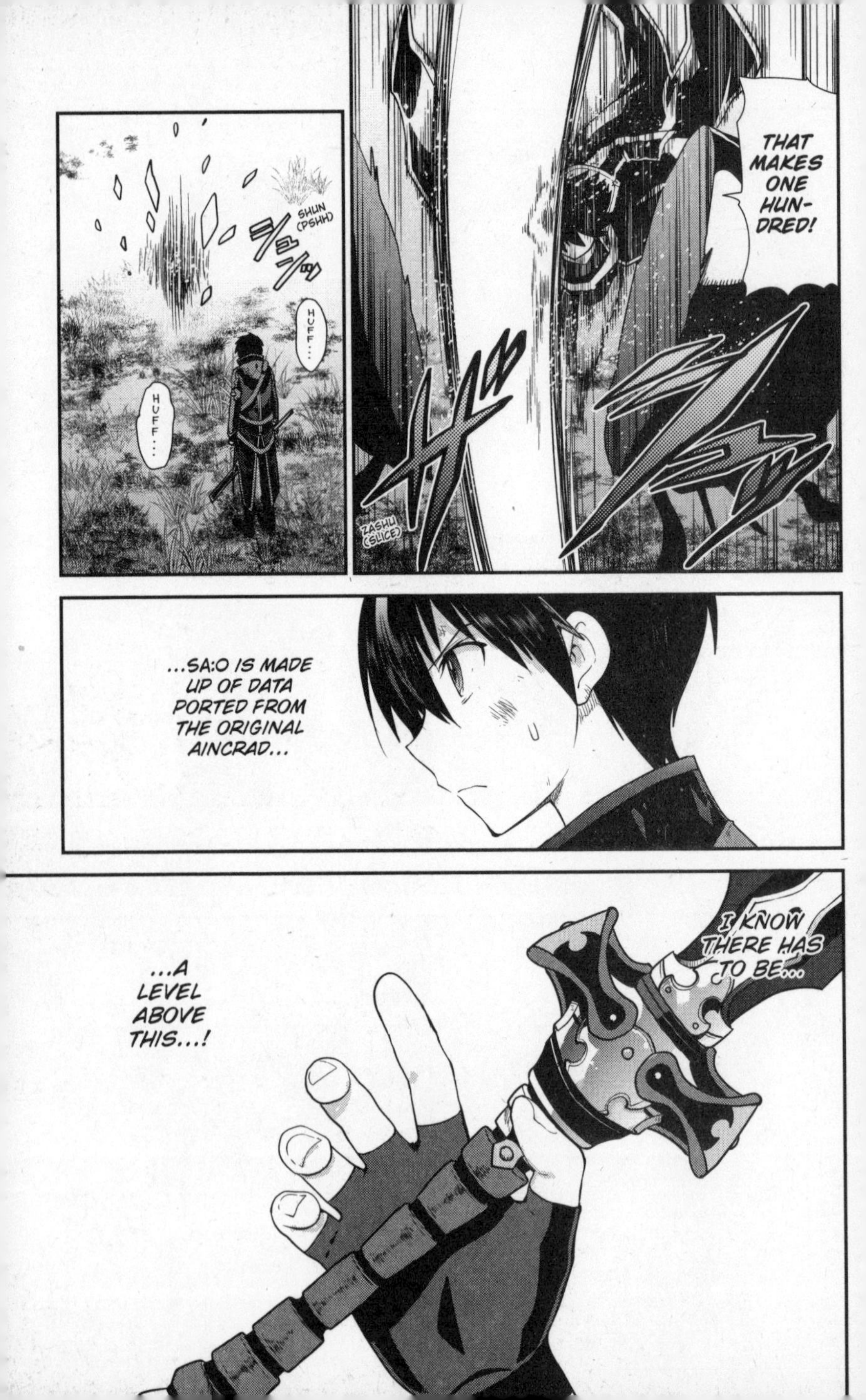
THAT MAKES ONE HUNDRED!
ZASHU (SLICE)
SHUN (PSHH)
HUFF...
HUFF...
...SA:O IS MADE UP OF DATA PORTED FROM THE ORIGINAL AINCRAD...
I KNOW THERE HAS TO BE...
...A LEVEL ABOVE THIS...!

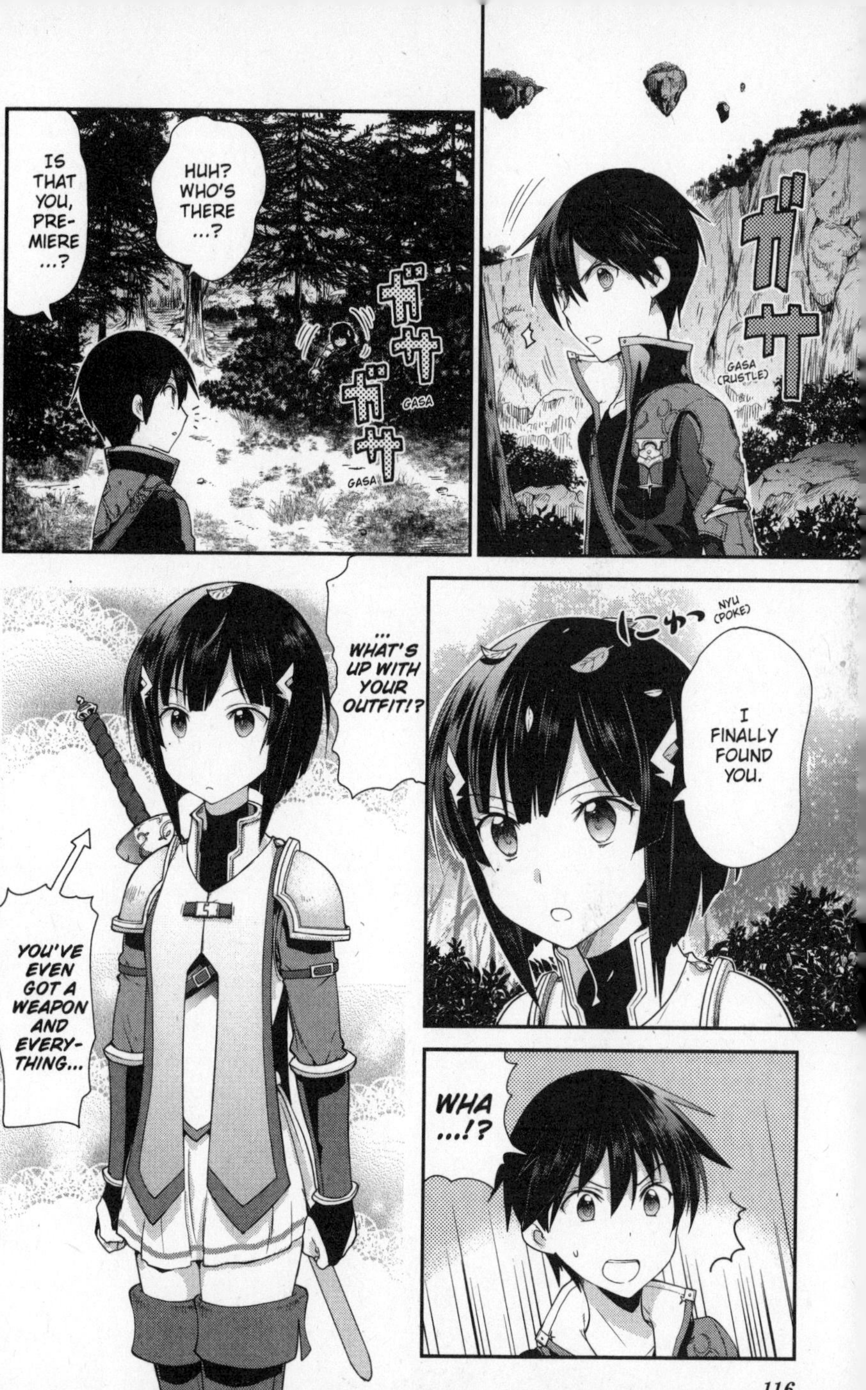
ガサ
GASA (RUSTLE)
HUH? WHO'S THERE ...?
IS THAT YOU, PRE-MIERE ...?
ガサ
GASA
ガサ
GASA
にゅっ
NYU (POKE)
I FINALLY FOUND YOU.
WHA ...!?
... WHAT'S UP WITH YOUR OUTFIT!?
YOU'VE EVEN GOT A WEAPON AND EVERY-THING...

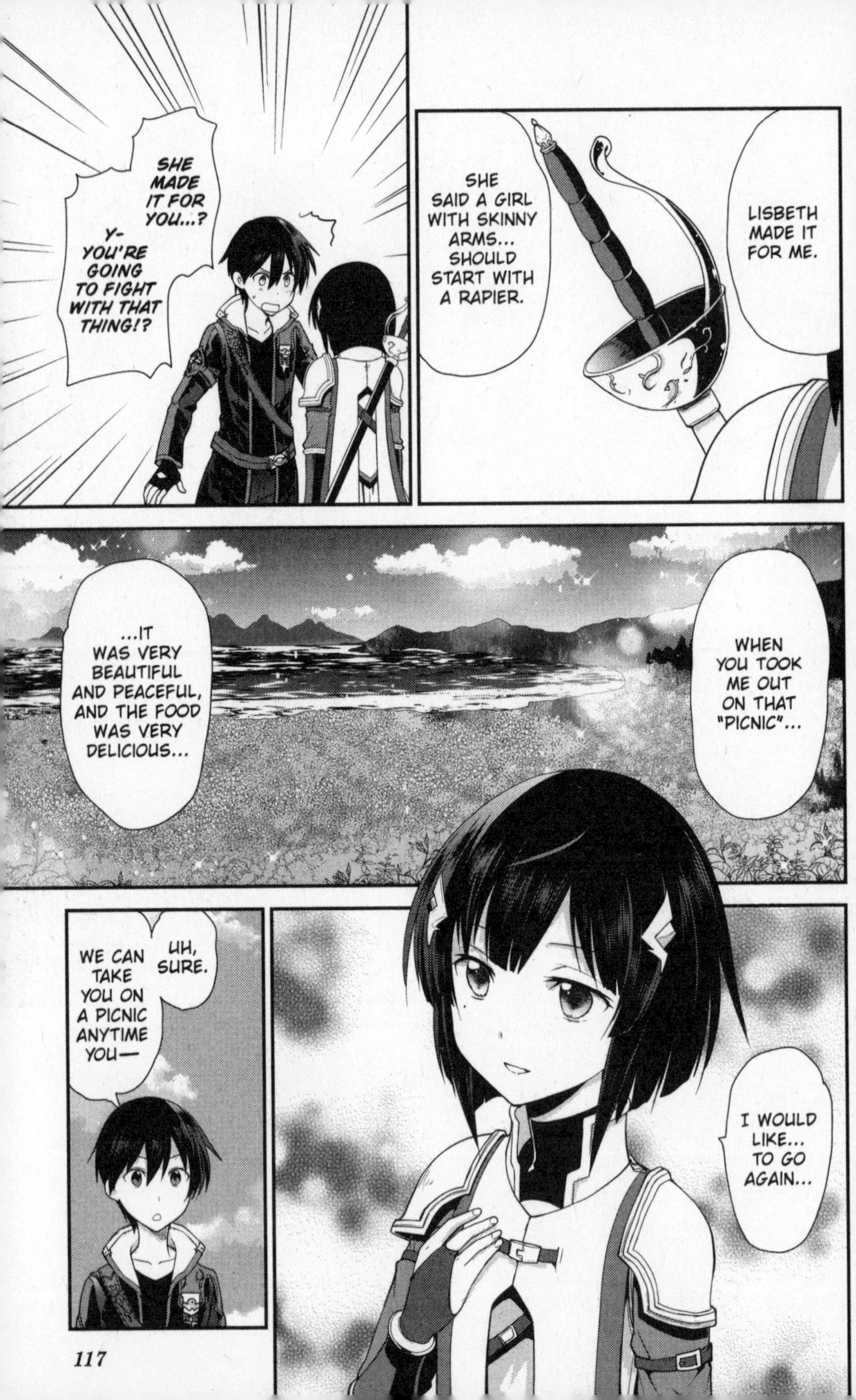
LISBETH MADE IT FOR ME.
SHE SAID A GIRL WITH SKINNY ARMS... SHOULD START WITH A RAPIER.
SHE MADE IT FOR YOU...?
Y-YOU'RE GOING TO FIGHT WITH THAT THING!?
WHEN YOU TOOK ME OUT ON THAT "PICNIC"...
...IT WAS VERY BEAUTIFUL AND PEACEFUL, AND THE FOOD WAS VERY DELICIOUS...
I WOULD LIKE... TO GO AGAIN...
UH, SURE.
WE CAN TAKE YOU ON A PICNIC ANYTIME YOU—

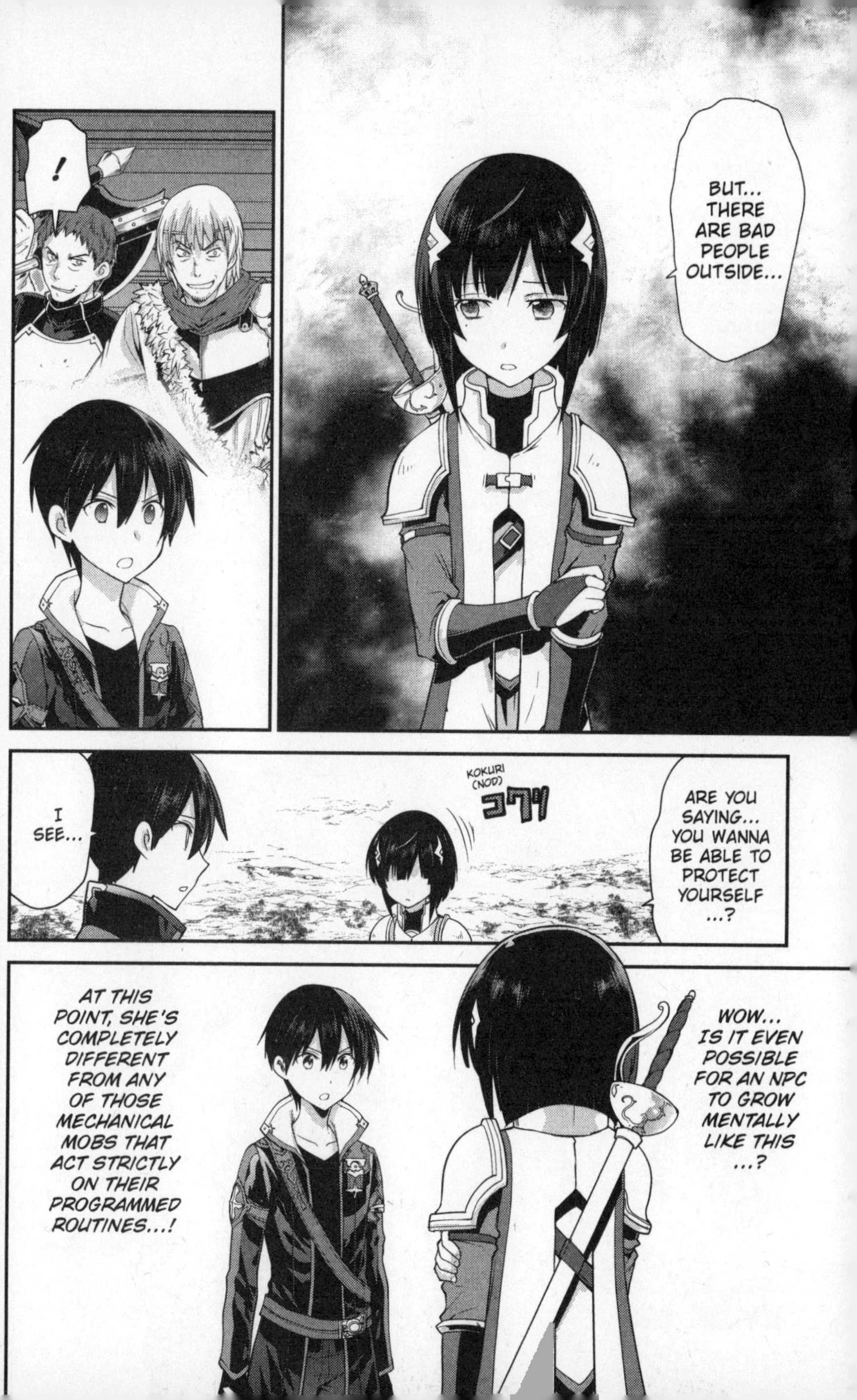
BUT... THERE ARE BAD PEOPLE OUTSIDE...
!
ARE YOU SAYING... YOU WANNA BE ABLE TO PROTECT YOURSELF ...?
KOKURI (NOD)
コクリ
I SEE...
WOW... IS IT EVEN POSSIBLE FOR AN NPC TO GROW MENTALLY LIKE THIS ...?
AT THIS POINT, SHE'S COMPLETELY DIFFERENT FROM ANY OF THOSE MECHANICAL MOBS THAT ACT STRICTLY ON THEIR PROGRAMMED ROUTINES...!

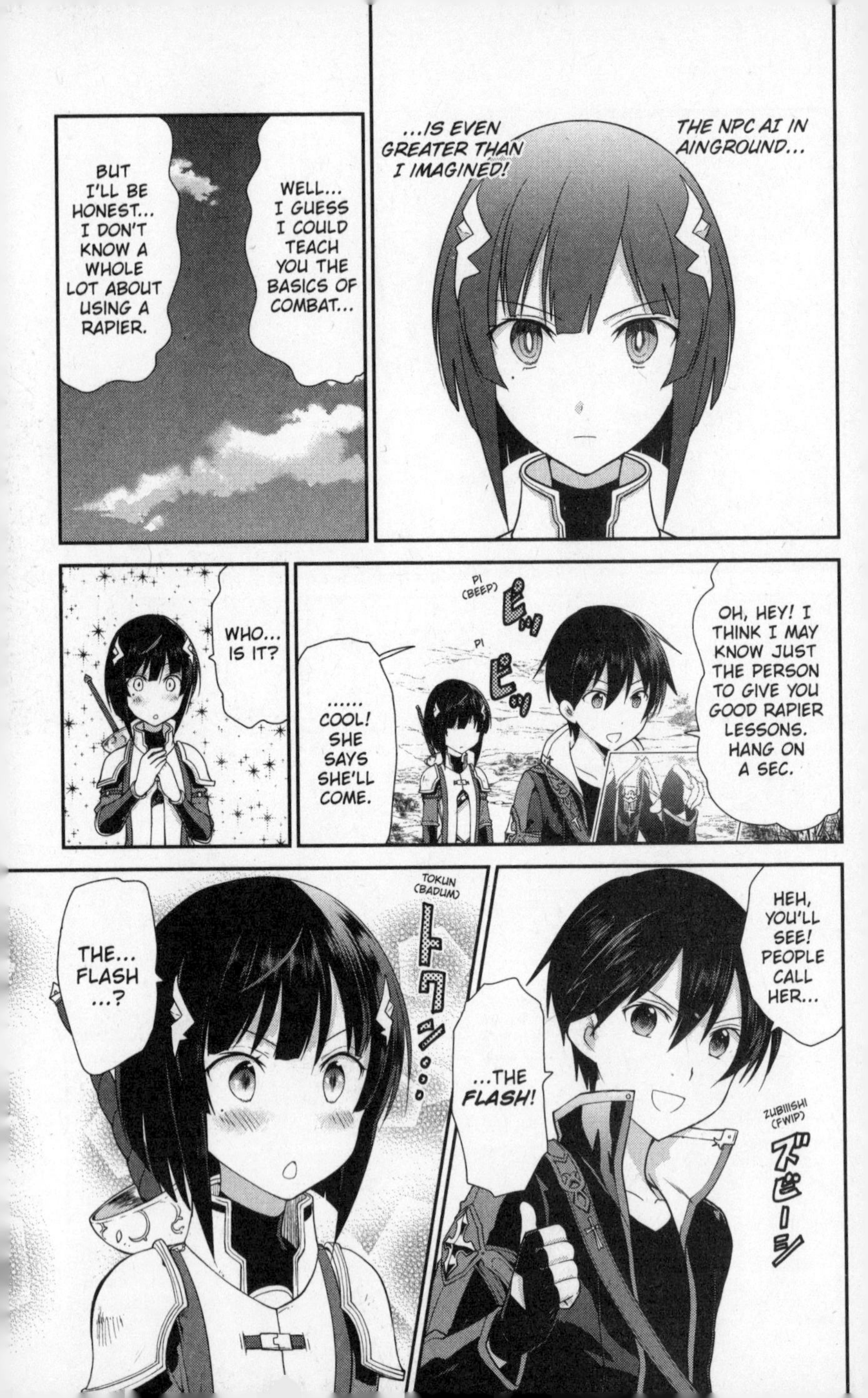
THE NPC AI IN AINGROUND...
...IS EVEN GREATER THAN I IMAGINED!
WELL... I GUESS I COULD TEACH YOU THE BASICS OF COMBAT...
BUT I'LL BE HONEST... I DON'T KNOW A WHOLE LOT ABOUT USING A RAPIER.
OH, HEY! I THINK I MAY KNOW JUST THE PERSON TO GIVE YOU GOOD RAPIER LESSONS. HANG ON A SEC.
PI (BEEP)
PI
...... COOL! SHE SAYS SHE'LL COME.
WHO... IS IT?
HEH, YOU'LL SEE! PEOPLE CALL HER...
...THE *FLASH*!
ZUBIIISHI (FWIP)
TOKUN (BADUM)
THE... FLASH ...?

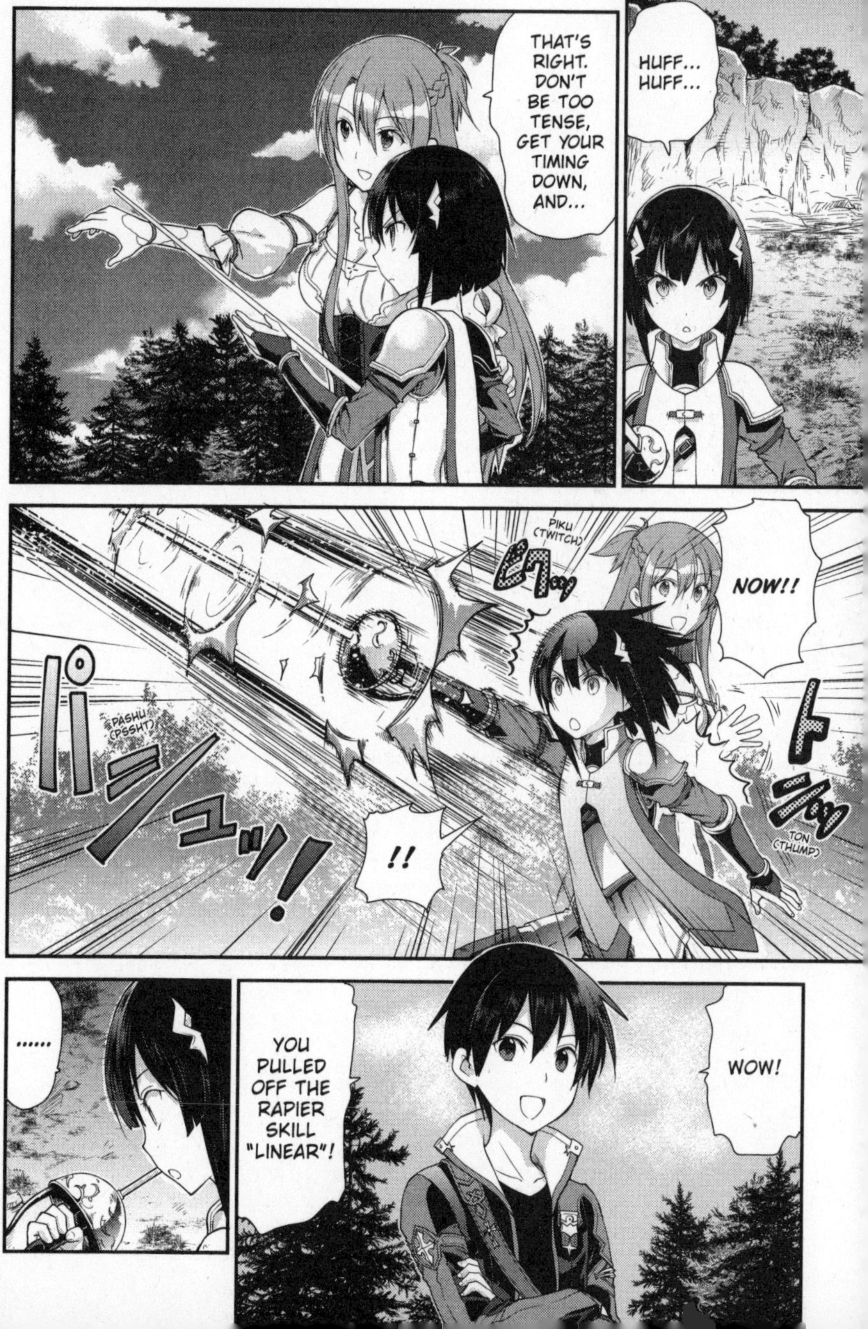
HUFF... HUFF...
THAT'S RIGHT. DON'T BE TOO TENSE, GET YOUR TIMING DOWN, AND...
NOW!!
PIKU (TWITCH)
TON (THUMP)
!!
PASHU (PSSHT)
WOW!
YOU PULLED OFF THE RAPIER SKILL "LINEAR"!
......

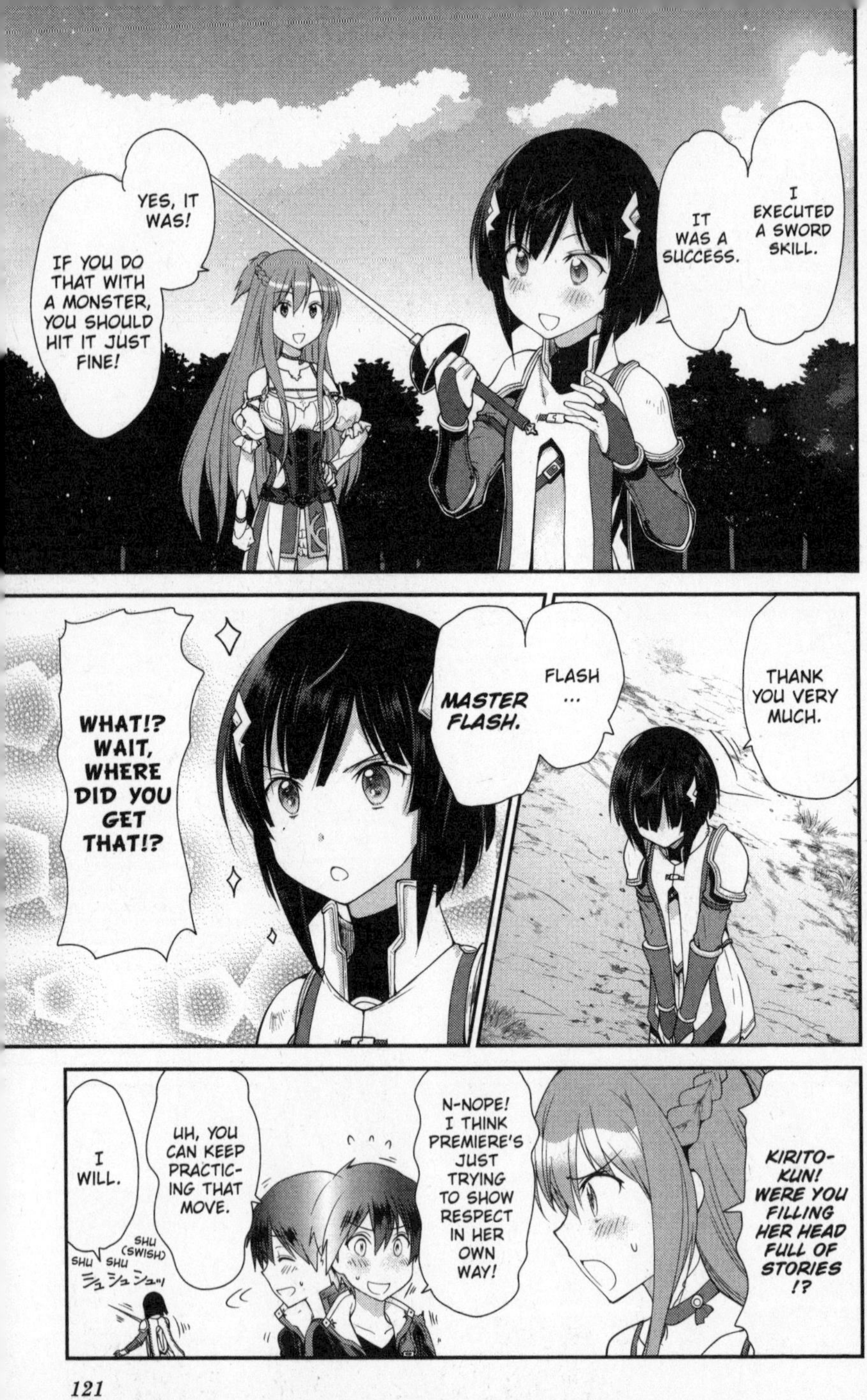
I EXECUTED A SWORD SKILL.
IT WAS A SUCCESS.
YES, IT WAS!
IF YOU DO THAT WITH A MONSTER, YOU SHOULD HIT IT JUST FINE!
THANK YOU VERY MUCH.
FLASH ...
MASTER FLASH.
WHAT!? WAIT, WHERE DID YOU GET THAT!?
KIRITO-KUN! WERE YOU FILLING HER HEAD FULL OF STORIES!?
N-NOPE! I THINK PREMIERE'S JUST TRYING TO SHOW RESPECT IN HER OWN WAY!
UH, YOU CAN KEEP PRACTIC-ING THAT MOVE.
I WILL.
SHU SHU SHU (SWISH)
シュシュシュッ

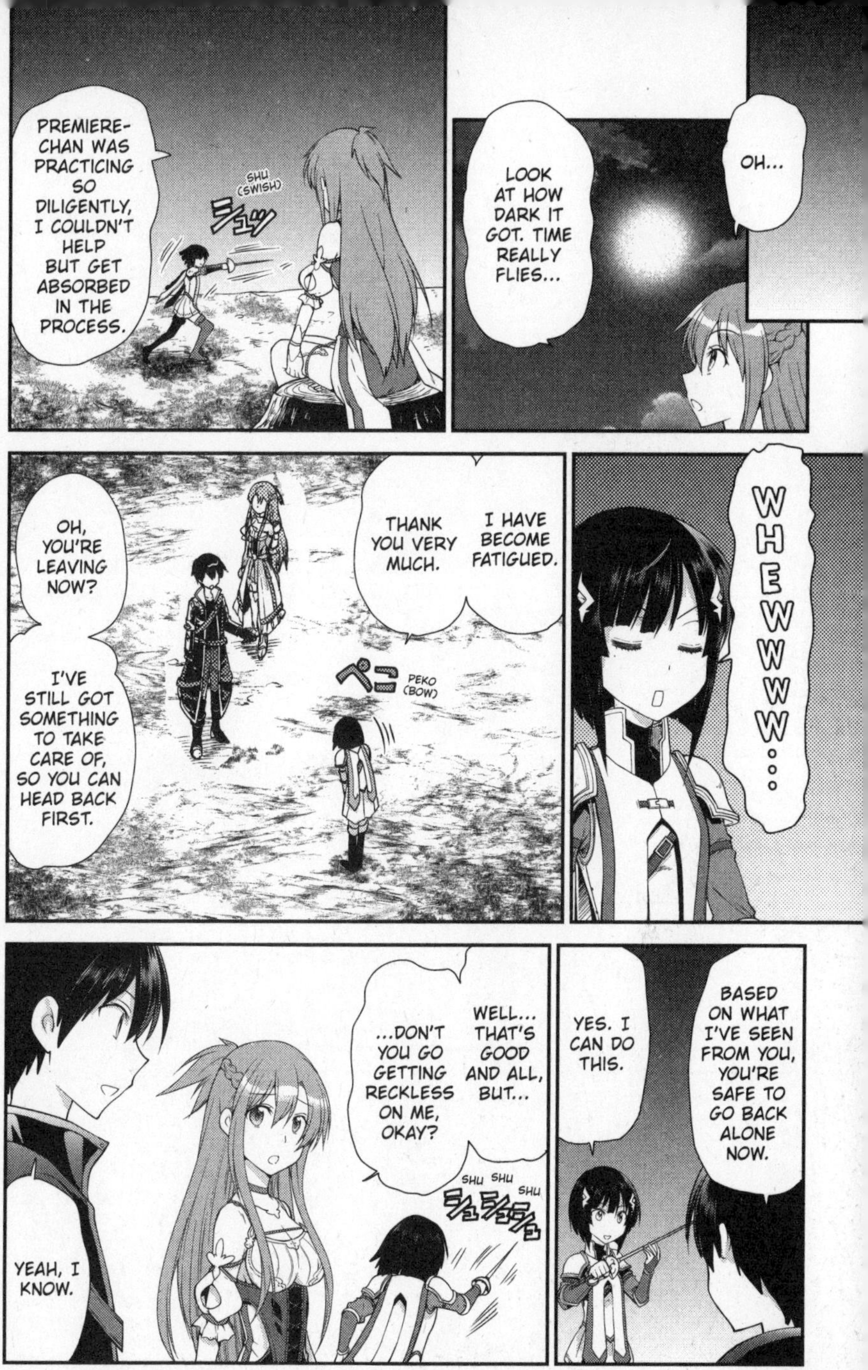
OH...
LOOK AT HOW DARK IT GOT. TIME REALLY FLIES...
PREMIERE-CHAN WAS PRACTICING SO DILIGENTLY, I COULDN'T HELP BUT GET ABSORBED IN THE PROCESS.
シュッ
SHU (SWISH)
WHEWWWW...
I HAVE BECOME FATIGUED.
THANK YOU VERY MUCH.
ペコ
PEKO (BOW)
OH, YOU'RE LEAVING NOW?
I'VE STILL GOT SOMETHING TO TAKE CARE OF, SO YOU CAN HEAD BACK FIRST.
BASED ON WHAT I'VE SEEN FROM YOU, YOU'RE SAFE TO GO BACK ALONE NOW.
YES. I CAN DO THIS.
WELL... THAT'S GOOD AND ALL, BUT...
...DON'T YOU GO GETTING RECKLESS ON ME, OKAY?
シュシュシュ
SHU SHU SHU
YEAH, I KNOW.

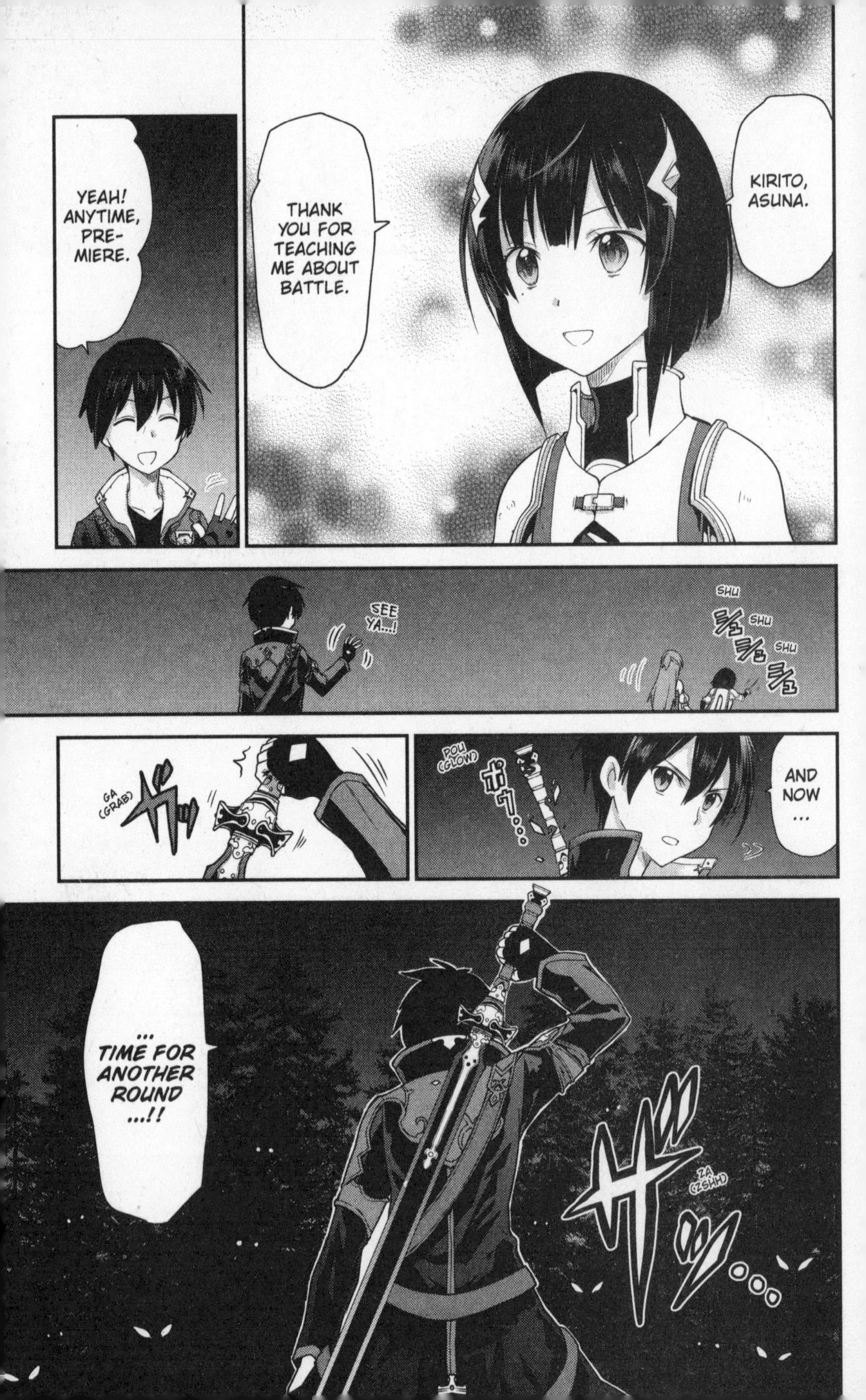
KIRITO, ASUNA.
THANK YOU FOR TEACHING ME ABOUT BATTLE.
YEAH! ANYTIME, PRE-MIERE.
SHU
SHU
SHU
SEE YA...!
AND NOW ...
POU (GLOW)
GA (GRAB)
... TIME FOR ANOTHER ROUND ...!!
ZA (ZSHH)

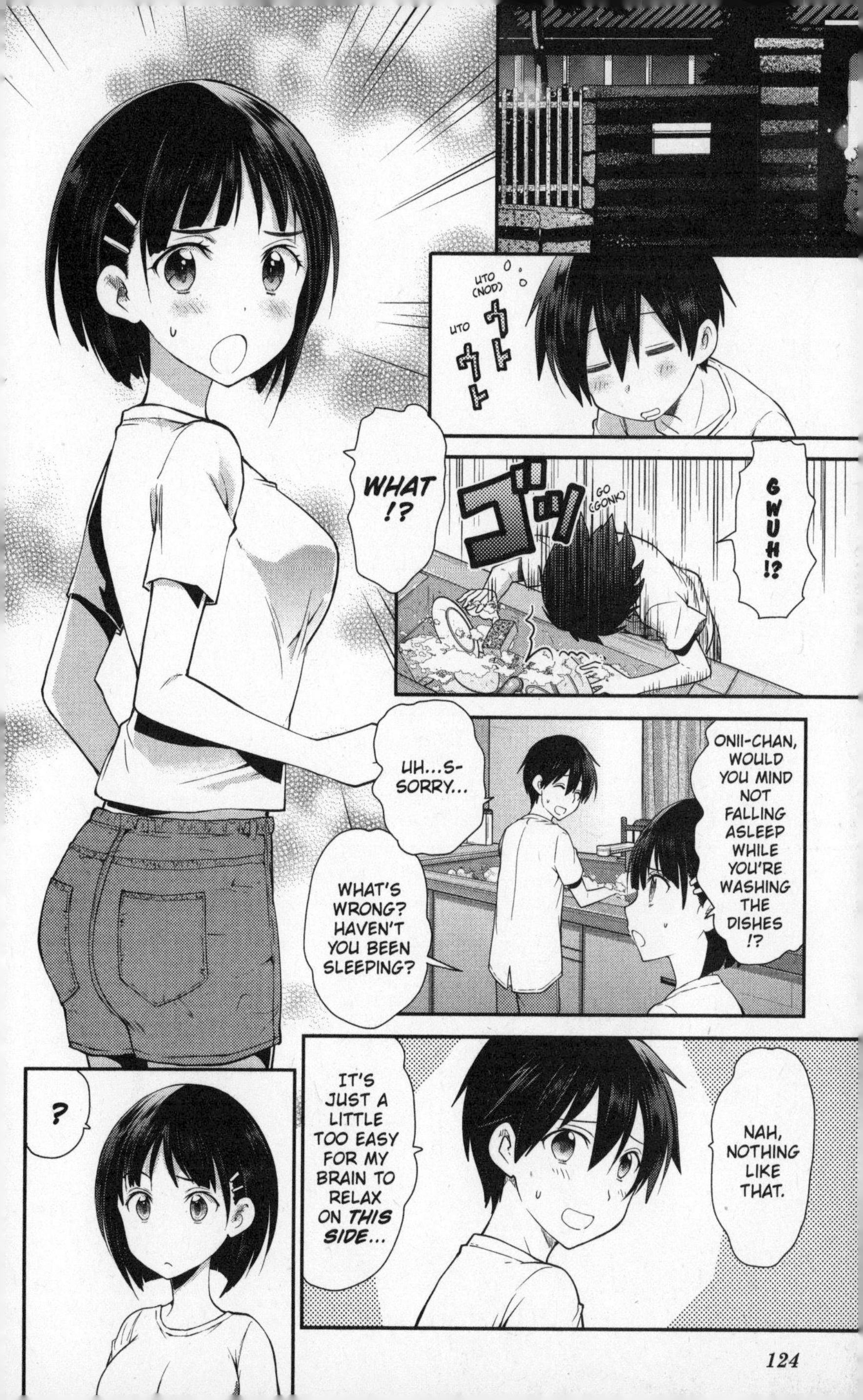
UTO (NOD)
UTO
GO (GONK)
GWUH!?
ONII-CHAN, WOULD YOU MIND NOT FALLING ASLEEP WHILE YOU'RE WASHING THE DISHES!?
WHAT!?
UH...S-SORRY...
WHAT'S WRONG? HAVEN'T YOU BEEN SLEEPING?
NAH, NOTHING LIKE THAT.
IT'S JUST A LITTLE TOO EASY FOR MY BRAIN TO RELAX ON THIS SIDE...
?

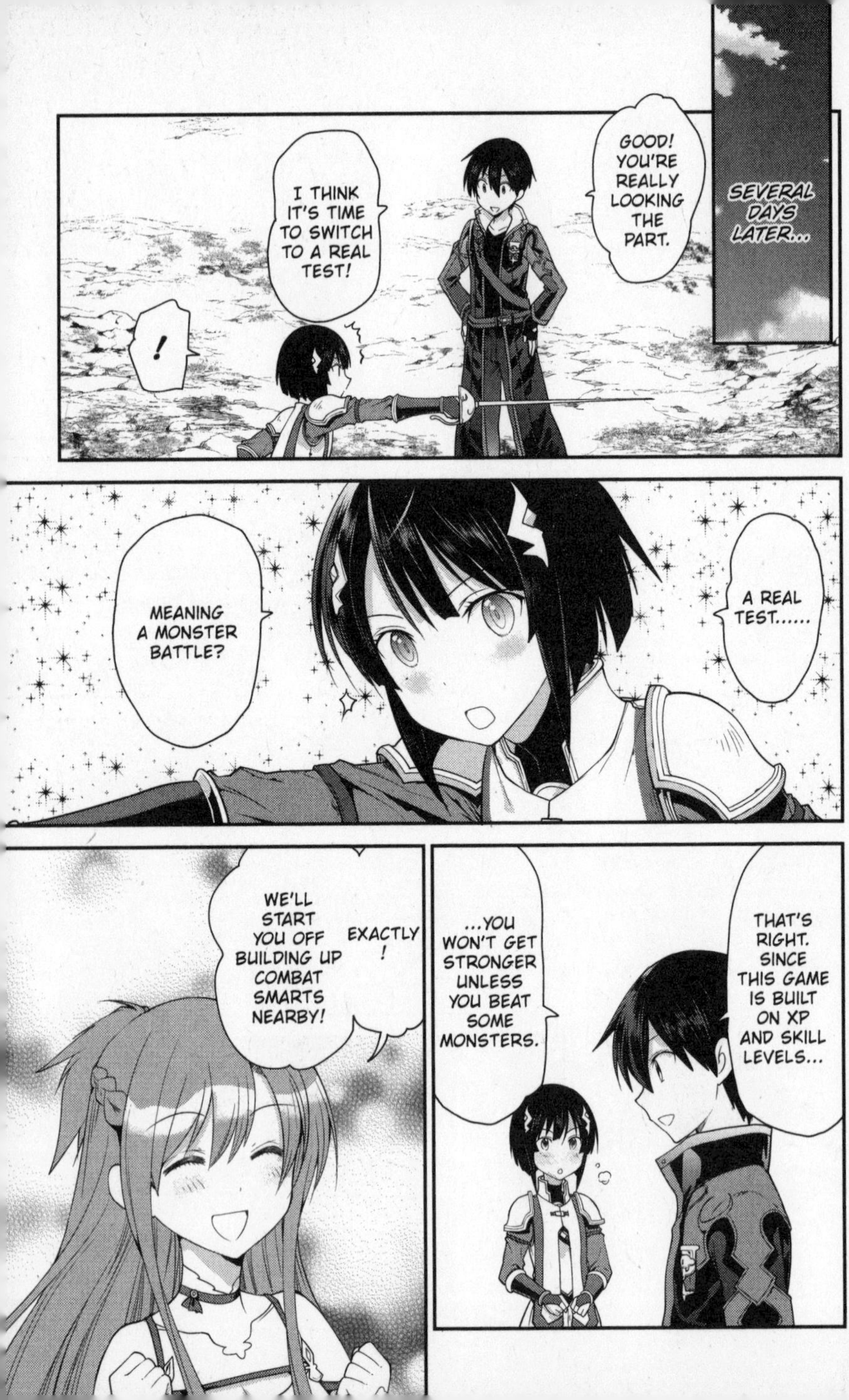
SEVERAL DAYS LATER...
GOOD! YOU'RE REALLY LOOKING THE PART.
I THINK IT'S TIME TO SWITCH TO A REAL TEST!
!
A REAL TEST......
MEANING A MONSTER BATTLE?
THAT'S RIGHT. SINCE THIS GAME IS BUILT ON XP AND SKILL LEVELS...
...YOU WON'T GET STRONGER UNLESS YOU BEAT SOME MONSTERS.
EXACTLY!
WE'LL START YOU OFF BUILDING UP COMBAT SMARTS NEARBY!

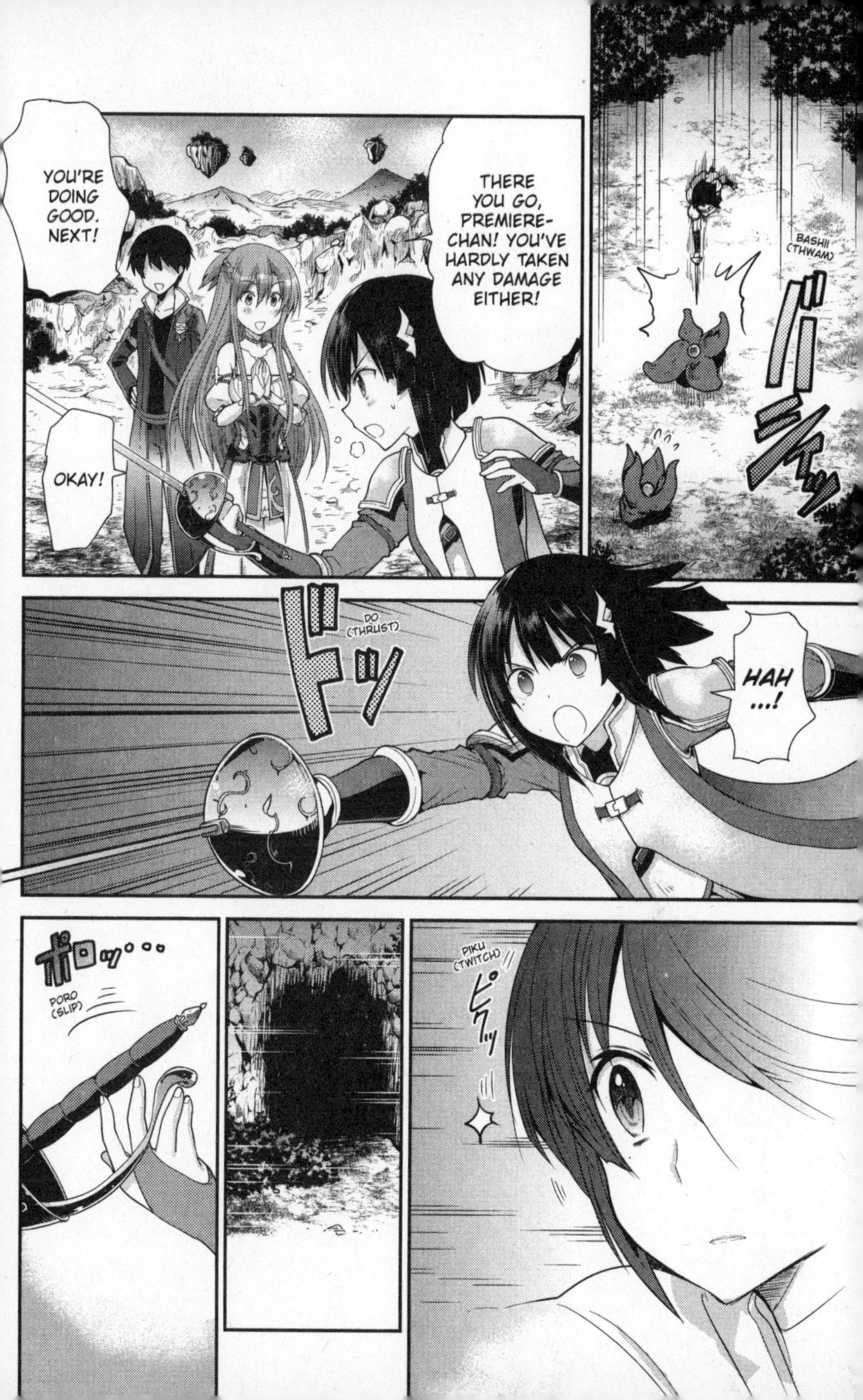
BASHII (THWAM)
THERE YOU GO, PREMIERE-CHAN! YOU'VE HARDLY TAKEN ANY DAMAGE EITHER!
YOU'RE DOING GOOD. NEXT!
OKAY!
HAH ...!
ドッ
DO (THRUST)
ピクッ
PIKU (TWITCH)
ポロッ・・・
PORO (SLIP)

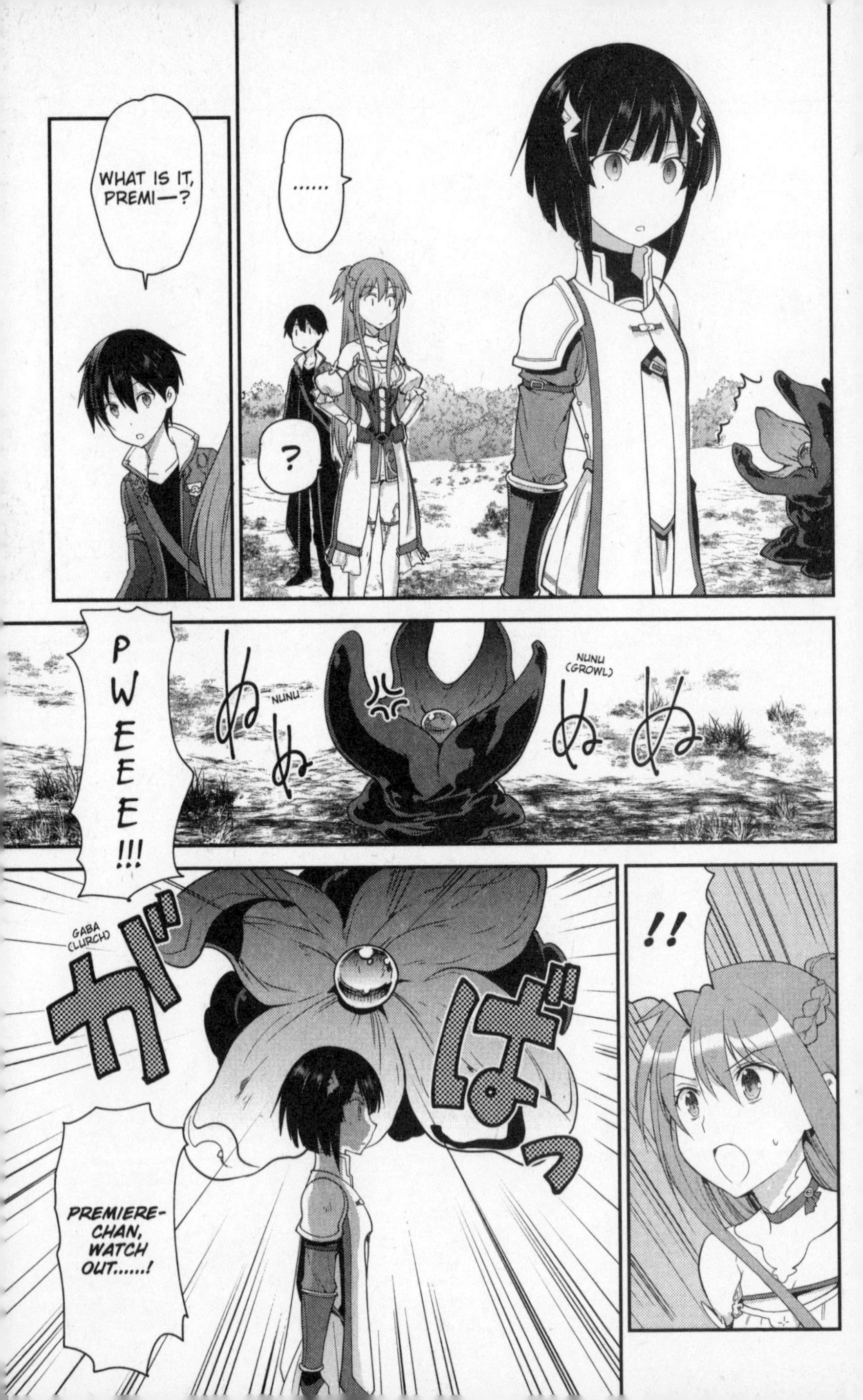

......
?
WHAT IS IT, PREMI—?
ぬぬ
NUNU (GROWL)
ぬぬ
NUNU
PWEEE!!!
!!
ガばっ
GABA (LURCH)
PREMIERE-CHAN, WATCH OUT......!

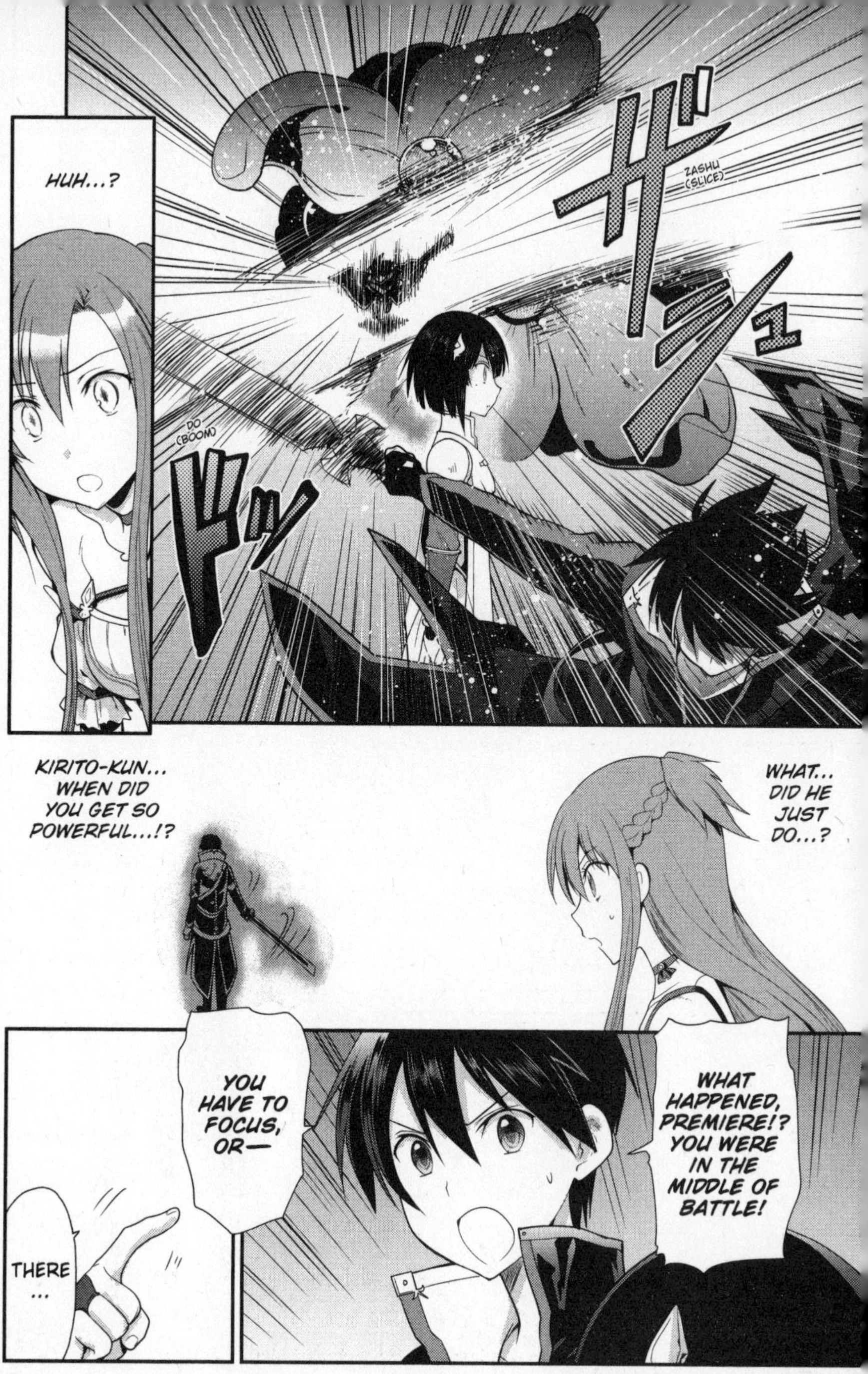
ZASHU (SLICE)
DO (BOOM)
HUH...?
WHAT... DID HE JUST DO...?
KIRITO-KUN... WHEN DID YOU GET SO POWERFUL...!?
WHAT HAPPENED, PREMIERE!? YOU WERE IN THE MIDDLE OF BATTLE!
YOU HAVE TO FOCUS, OR—
THERE ...

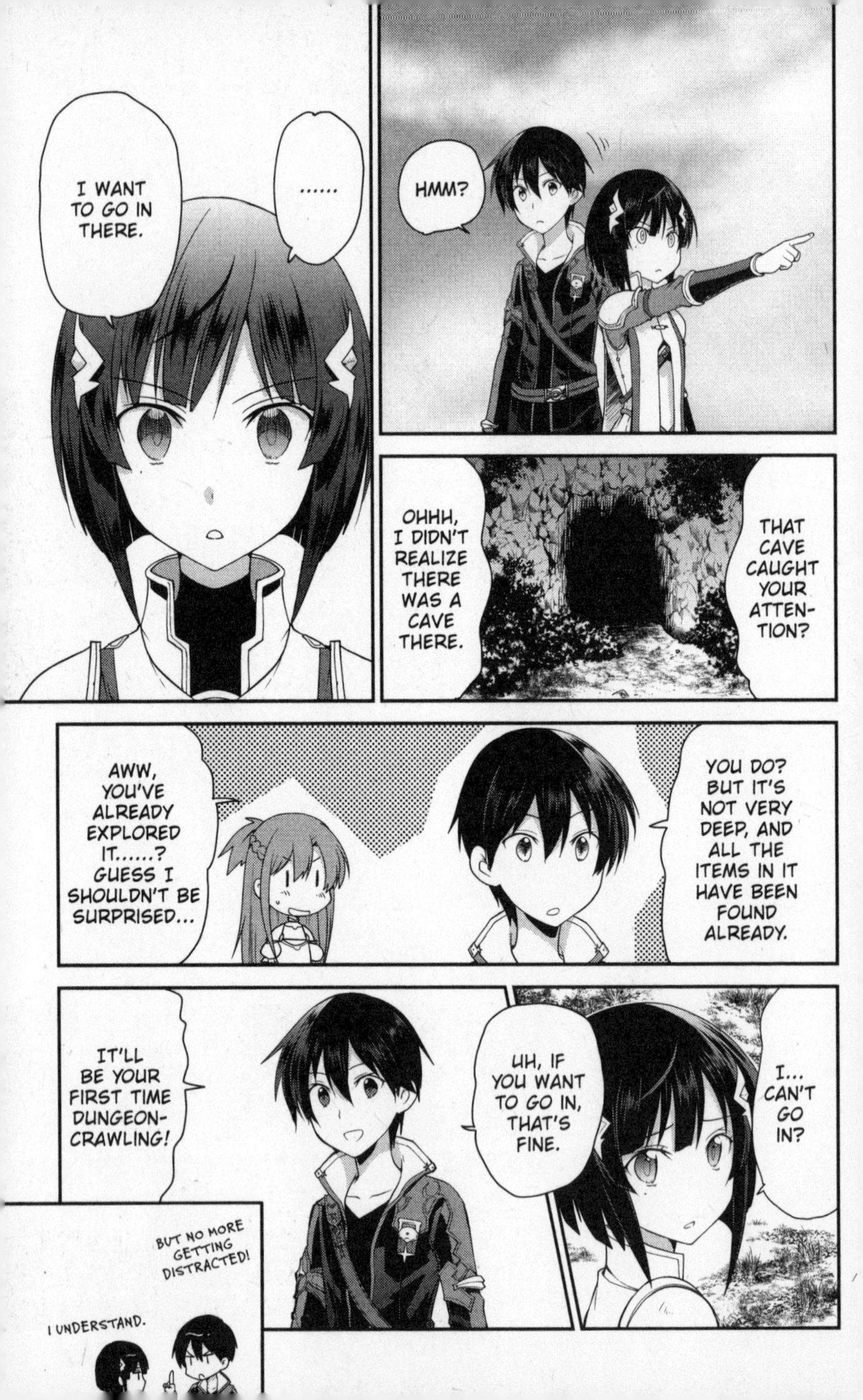
HMM?
THAT CAVE CAUGHT YOUR ATTENTION?
OHHH, I DIDN'T REALIZE THERE WAS A CAVE THERE.
......
I WANT TO GO IN THERE.
YOU DO? BUT IT'S NOT VERY DEEP, AND ALL THE ITEMS IN IT HAVE BEEN FOUND ALREADY.
AWW, YOU'VE ALREADY EXPLORED IT......? GUESS I SHOULDN'T BE SURPRISED...
I... CAN'T GO IN?
UH, IF YOU WANT TO GO IN, THAT'S FINE.
IT'LL BE YOUR FIRST TIME DUNGEON-CRAWLING!
BUT NO MORE GETTING DISTRACTED!
I UNDERSTAND.

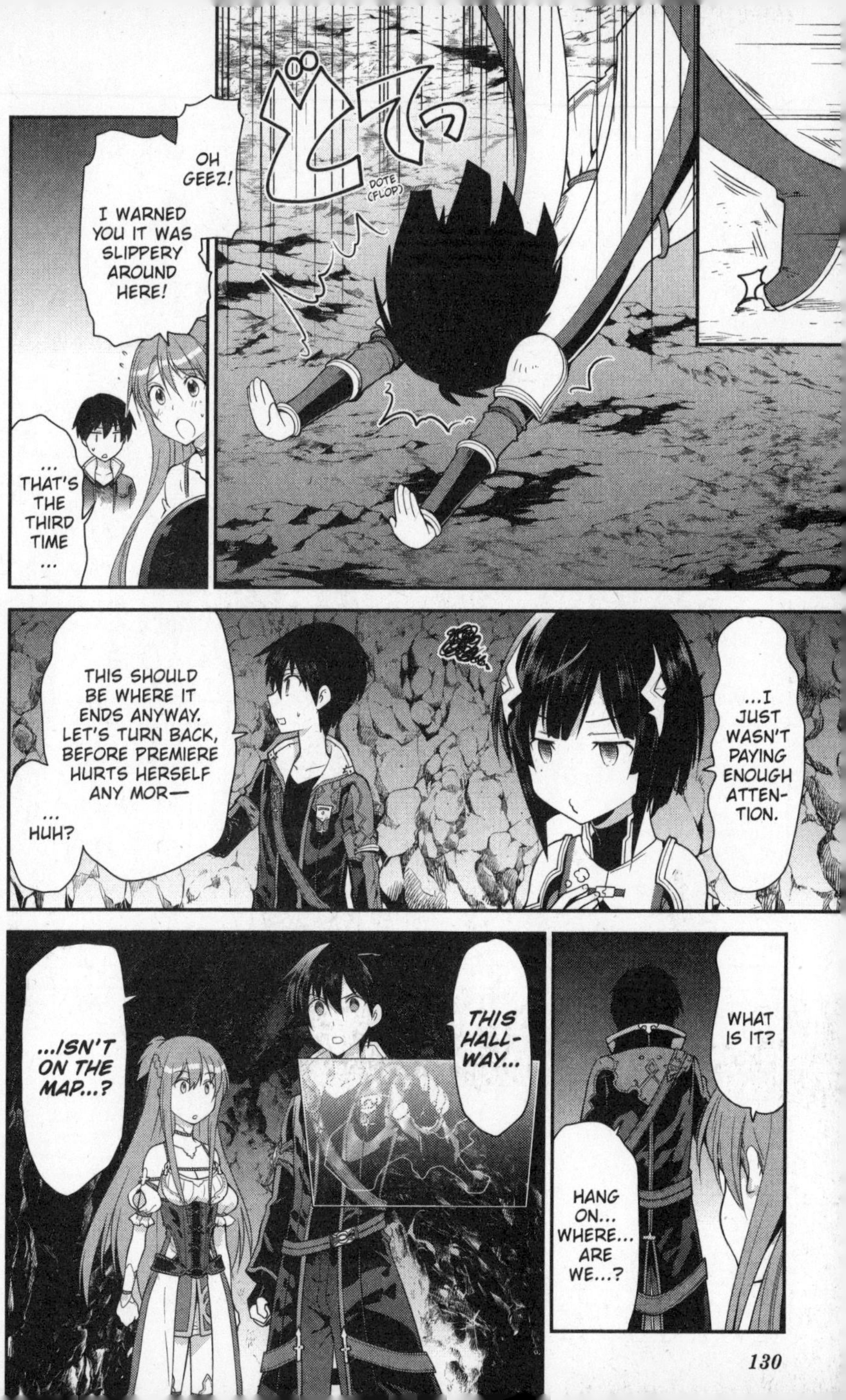
どてっ
DOTE (FLOP)
OH GEEZ!
I WARNED YOU IT WAS SLIPPERY AROUND HERE!
...THAT'S THE THIRD TIME...
...I JUST WASN'T PAYING ENOUGH ATTENTION.
THIS SHOULD BE WHERE IT ENDS ANYWAY. LET'S TURN BACK, BEFORE PREMIERE HURTS HERSELF ANY MOR—
...HUH?
WHAT IS IT?
HANG ON... WHERE... ARE WE...?
THIS HALLWAY...
...ISN'T ON THE MAP...?

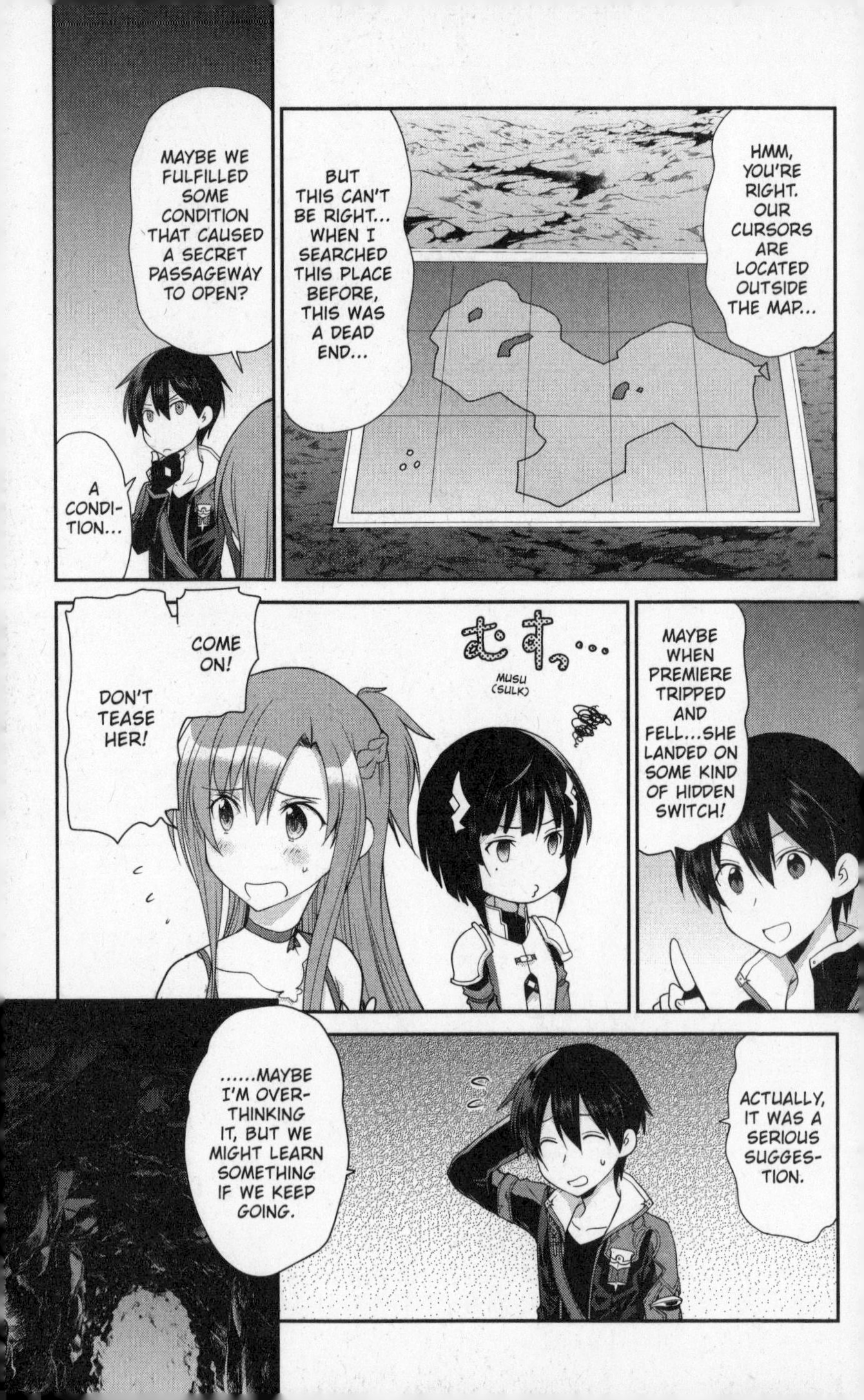
HMM, YOU'RE RIGHT. OUR CURSORS ARE LOCATED OUTSIDE THE MAP...
BUT THIS CAN'T BE RIGHT... WHEN I SEARCHED THIS PLACE BEFORE, THIS WAS A DEAD END...
MAYBE WE FULFILLED SOME CONDITION THAT CAUSED A SECRET PASSAGEWAY TO OPEN?
A CONDITION...
MAYBE WHEN PREMIERE TRIPPED AND FELL...SHE LANDED ON SOME KIND OF HIDDEN SWITCH!
むすっ...
MUSU (SULK)
COME ON!
DON'T TEASE HER!
ACTUALLY, IT WAS A SERIOUS SUGGESTION.
......MAYBE I'M OVERTHINKING IT, BUT WE MIGHT LEARN SOMETHING IF WE KEEP GOING.

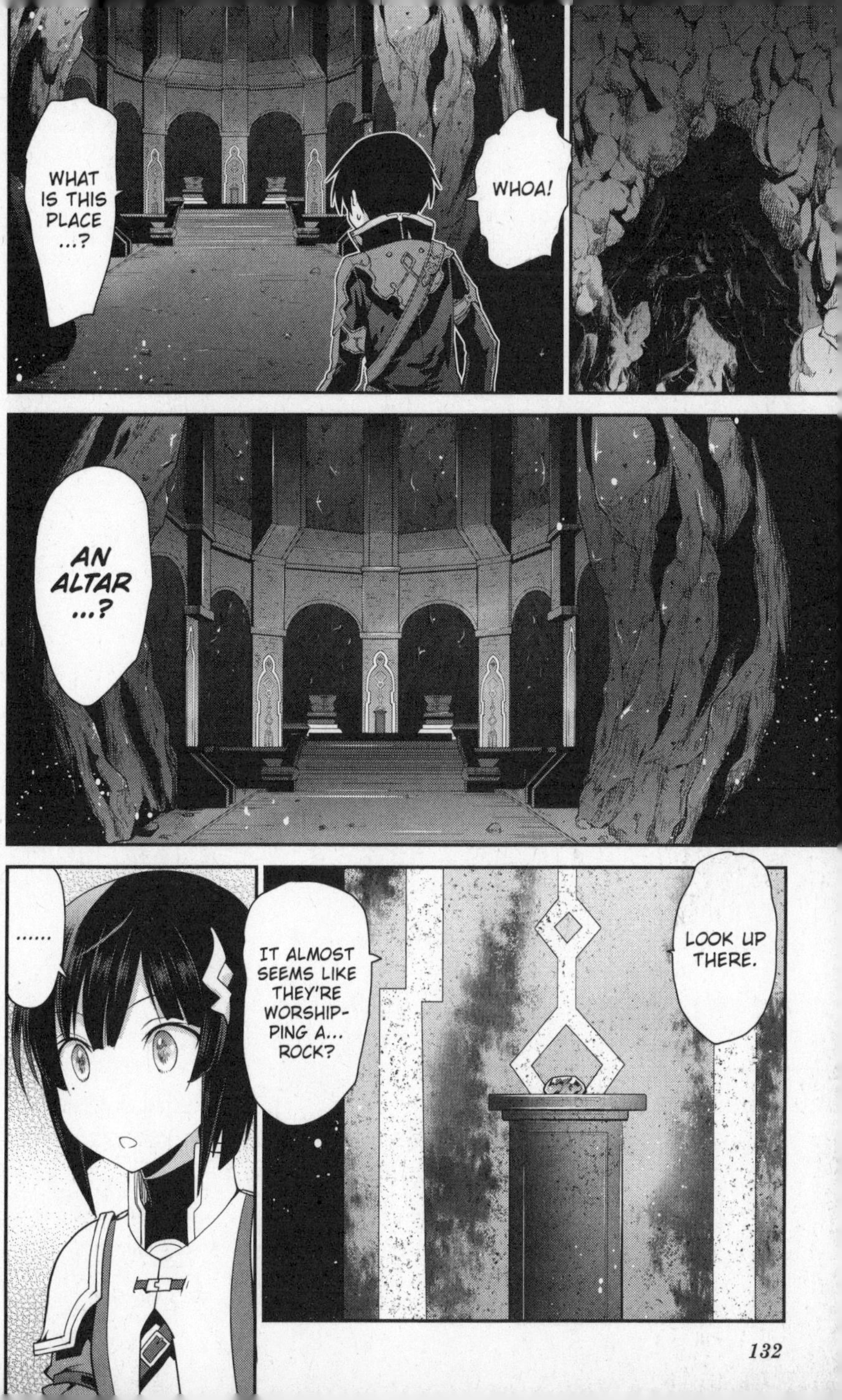
WHOA!
WHAT IS THIS PLACE ...?
AN ALTAR ...?
LOOK UP THERE.
IT ALMOST SEEMS LIKE THEY'RE WORSHIP-PING A... ROCK?
......

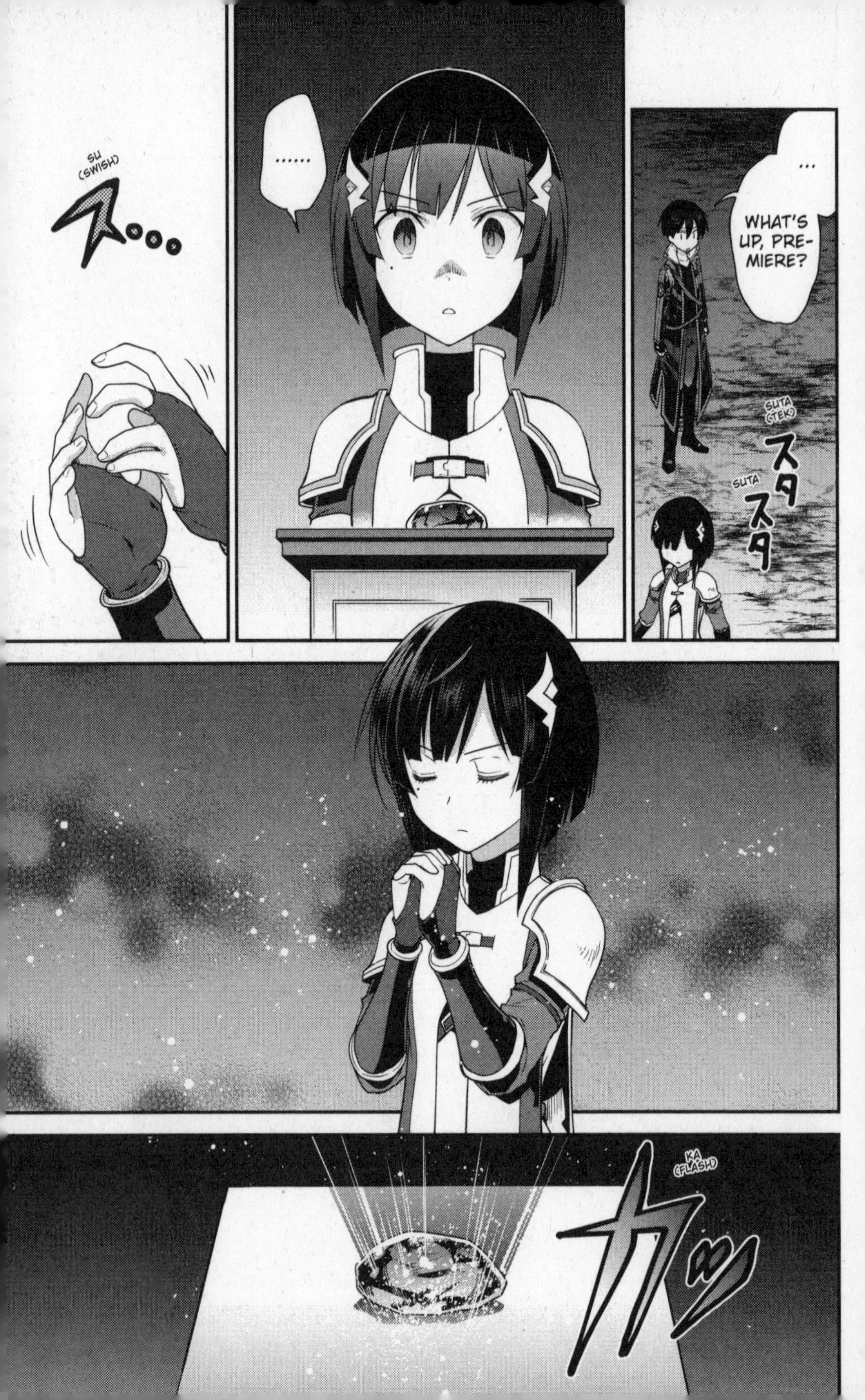
...
WHAT'S UP, PRE-MIERE?
SUTA (TEK)
スタ
SUTA
スタ
......
SU (SWISH)
ス...
KA (FLASH)
カッ

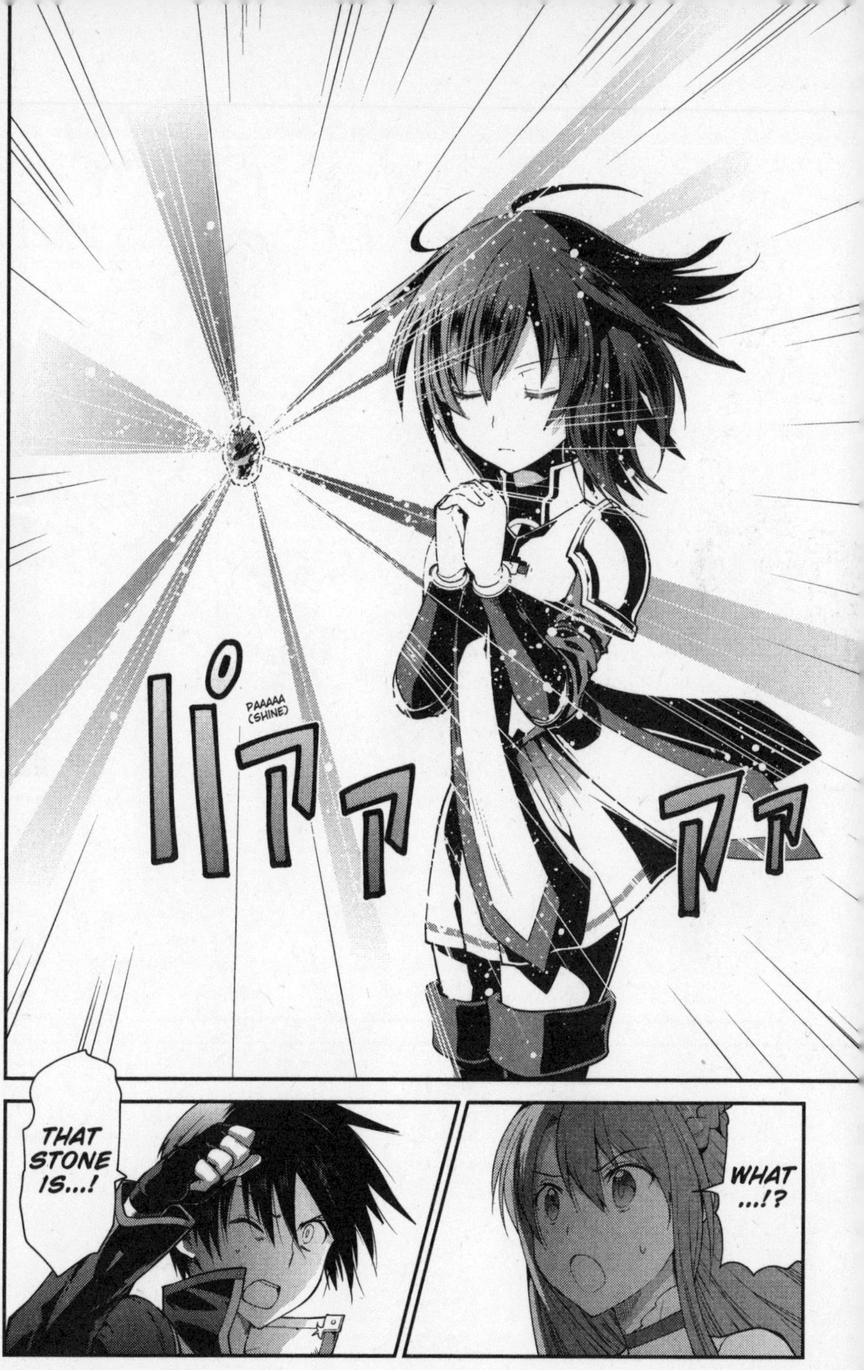
パァァァァ
PAAAAA (SHINE)
WHAT ...!?
THAT STONE IS...!

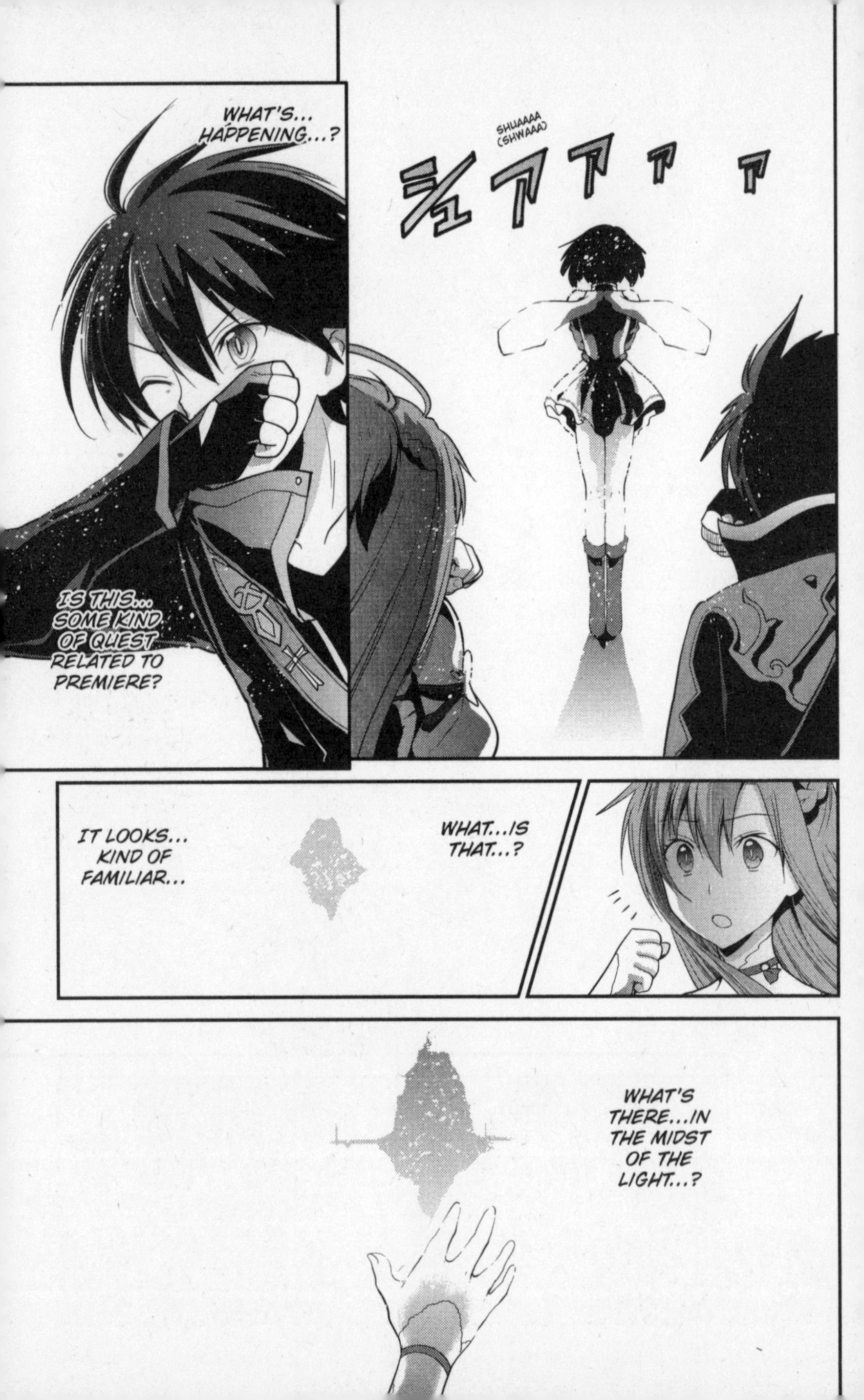
シュアアァァ
SHUAAAA (SHWAAA)
WHAT'S... HAPPENING...?
IS THIS... SOME KIND OF QUEST RELATED TO PREMIERE?
WHAT...IS THAT...?
IT LOOKS... KIND OF FAMILIAR...
WHAT'S THERE...IN THE MIDST OF THE LIGHT...?

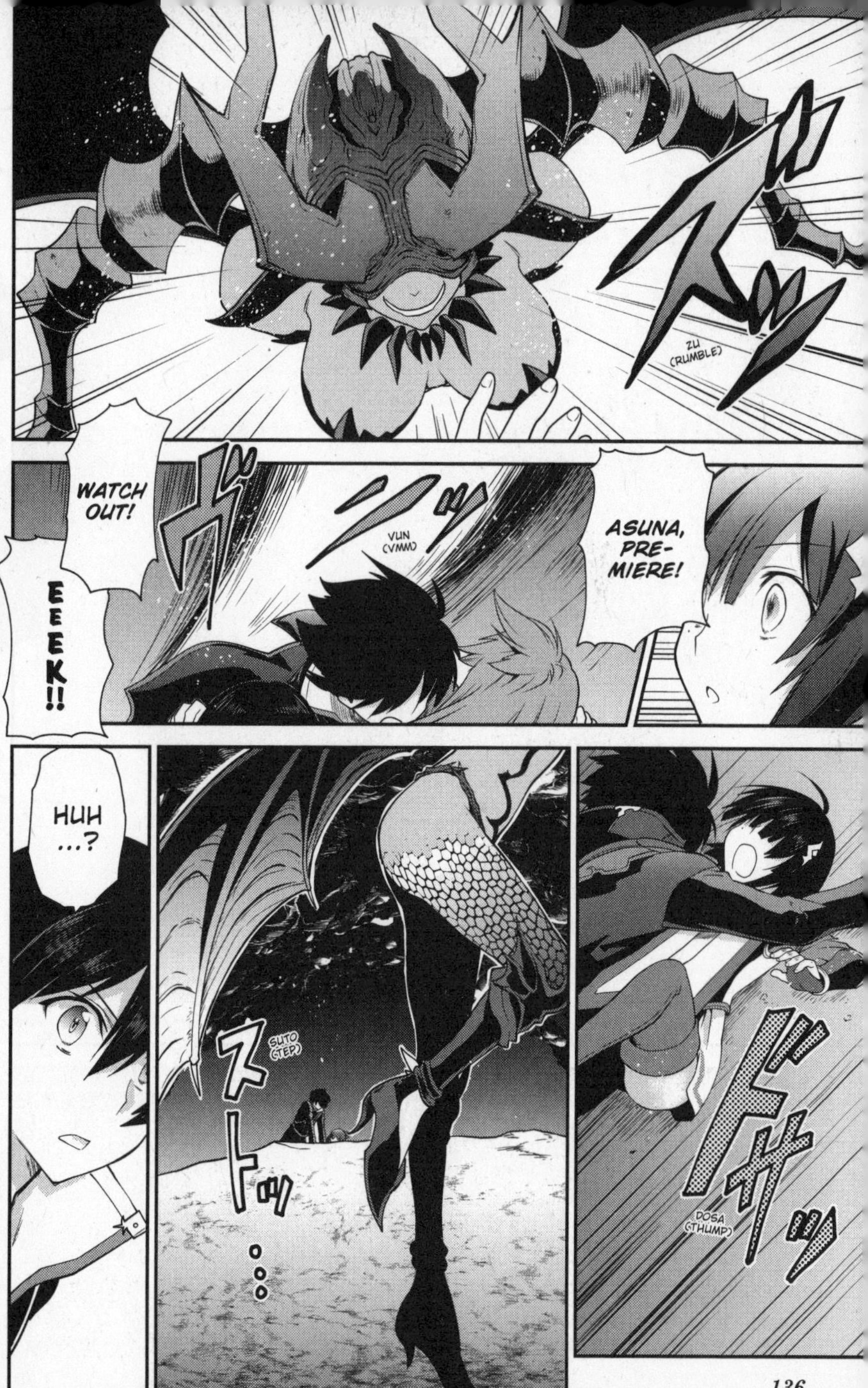
ZU
(RUMBLE)
ASUNA, PREMIERE!
VUN
(VMM)
WATCH OUT!
EEEEK!!
DOSA
(THUMP)
SUTO
(TEP)
...
HUH ...?

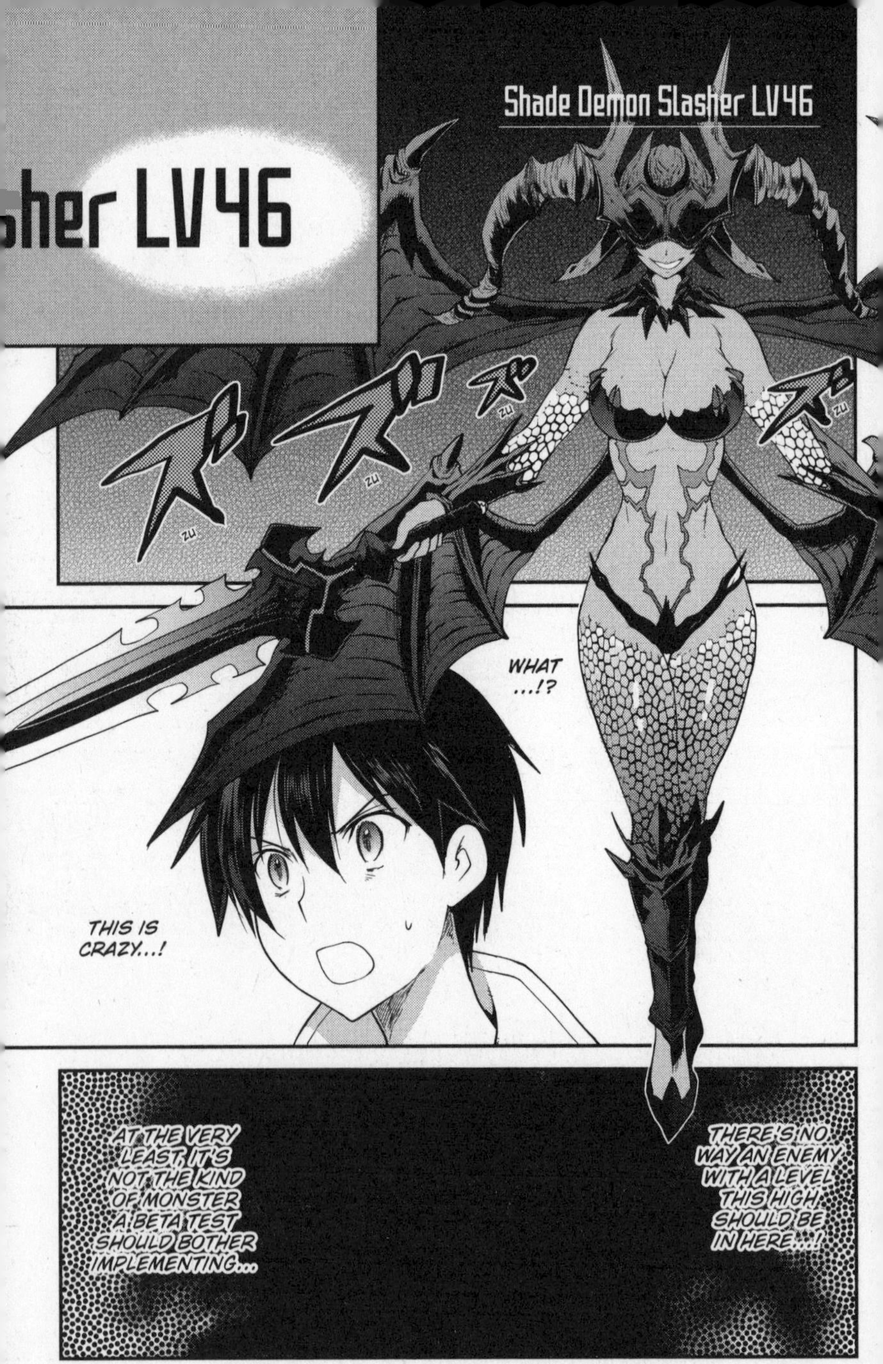
Shade Demon Slasher LV46
sher LV46
ZU
ZU
ZU
ZU
WHAT ...!?
THIS IS CRAZY...!
THERE'S NO WAY AN ENEMY WITH A LEVEL THIS HIGH SHOULD BE IN HERE...!
AT THE VERY LEAST, IT'S NOT THE KIND OF MONSTER A BETA TEST SHOULD BOTHER IMPLEMENTING...

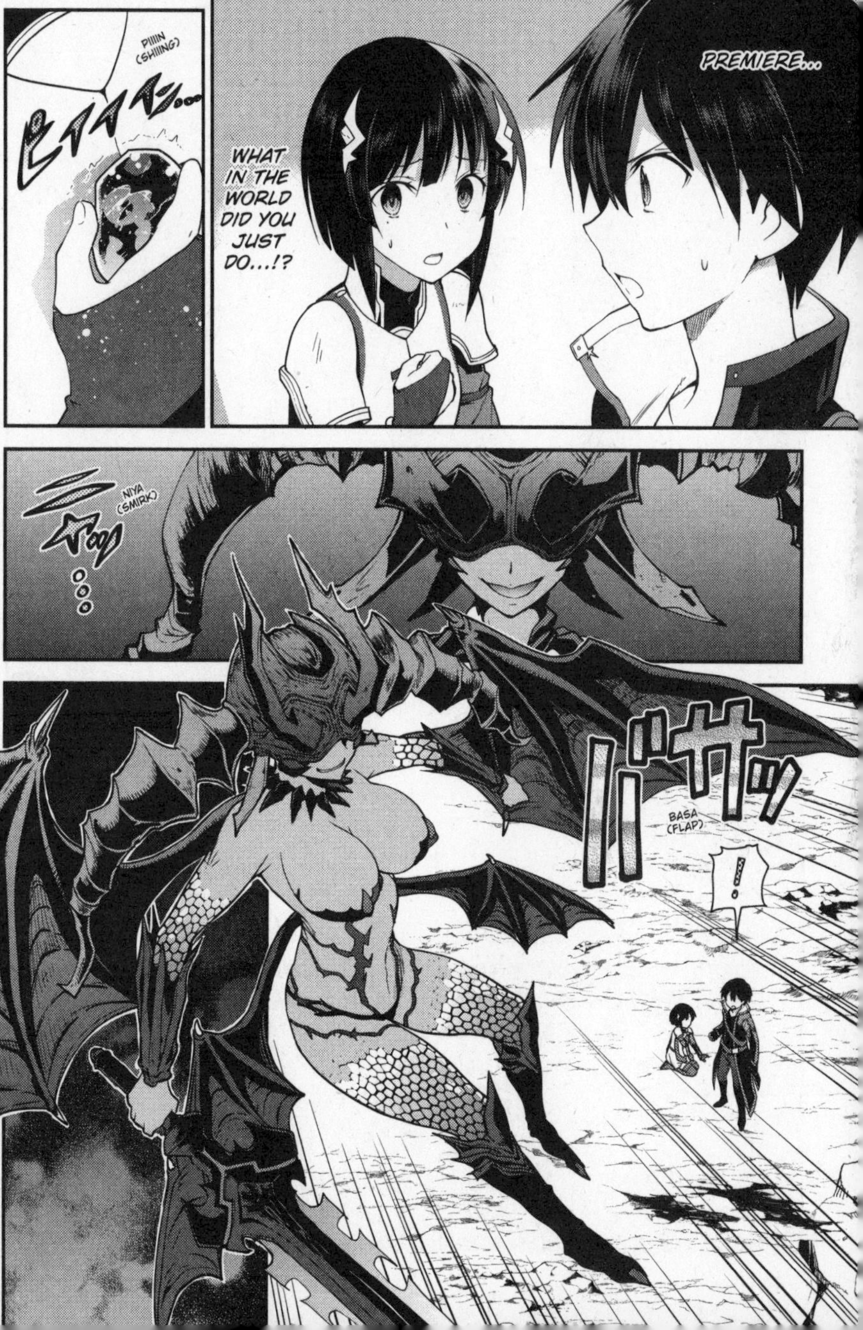
PREMIERE...
WHAT IN THE WORLD DID YOU JUST DO...!?
PIIIN (SHIIING)
NIYA (SMIRK)
ニヤッ...
バサッ
BASA (FLAP)
!

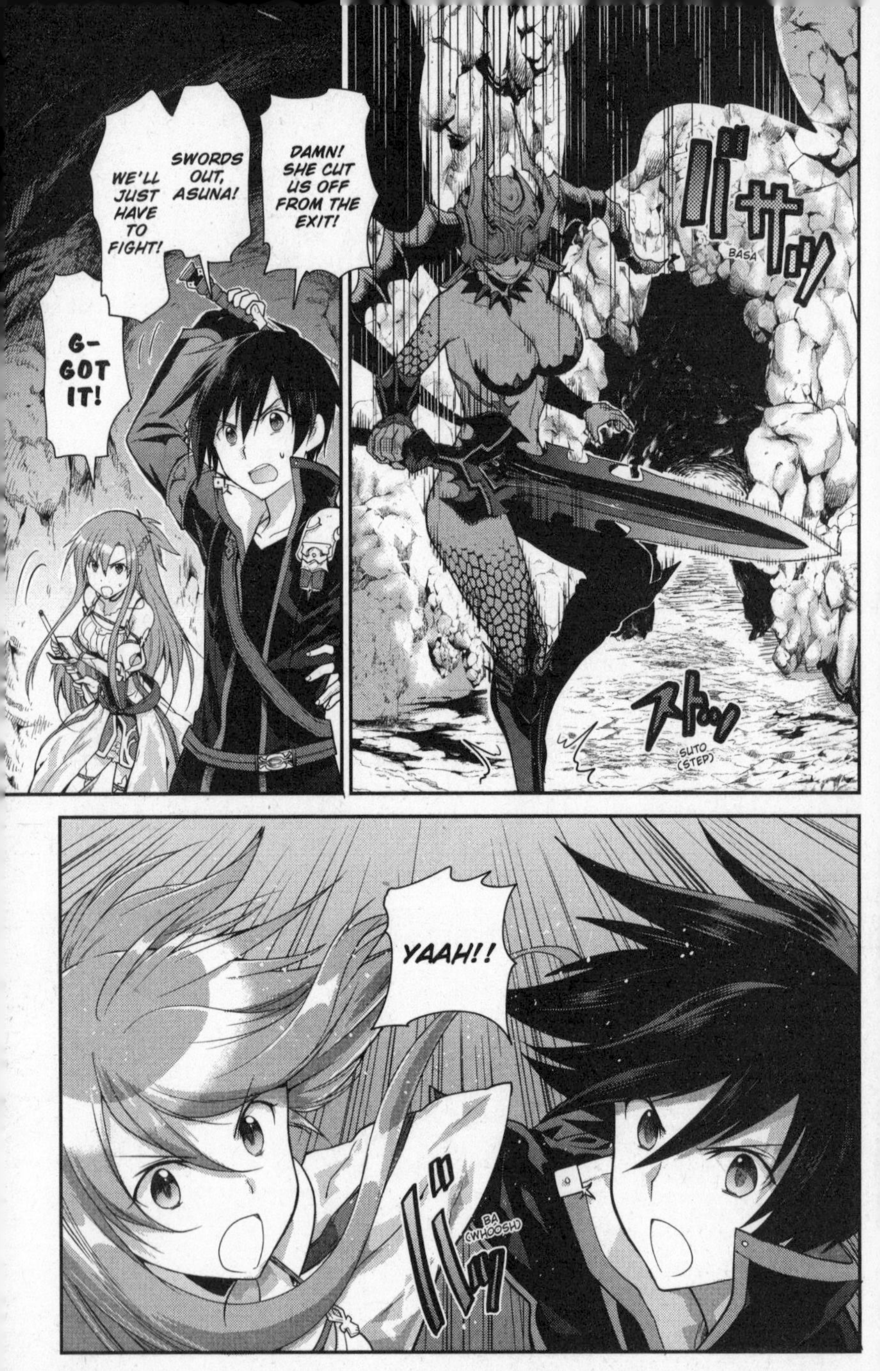
BASA
SUTO (STEP)
DAMN! SHE CUT US OFF FROM THE EXIT!
SWORDS OUT, ASUNA!
WE'LL JUST HAVE TO FIGHT!
G-GOT IT!
YAAH!!
BA (WHOOSH)

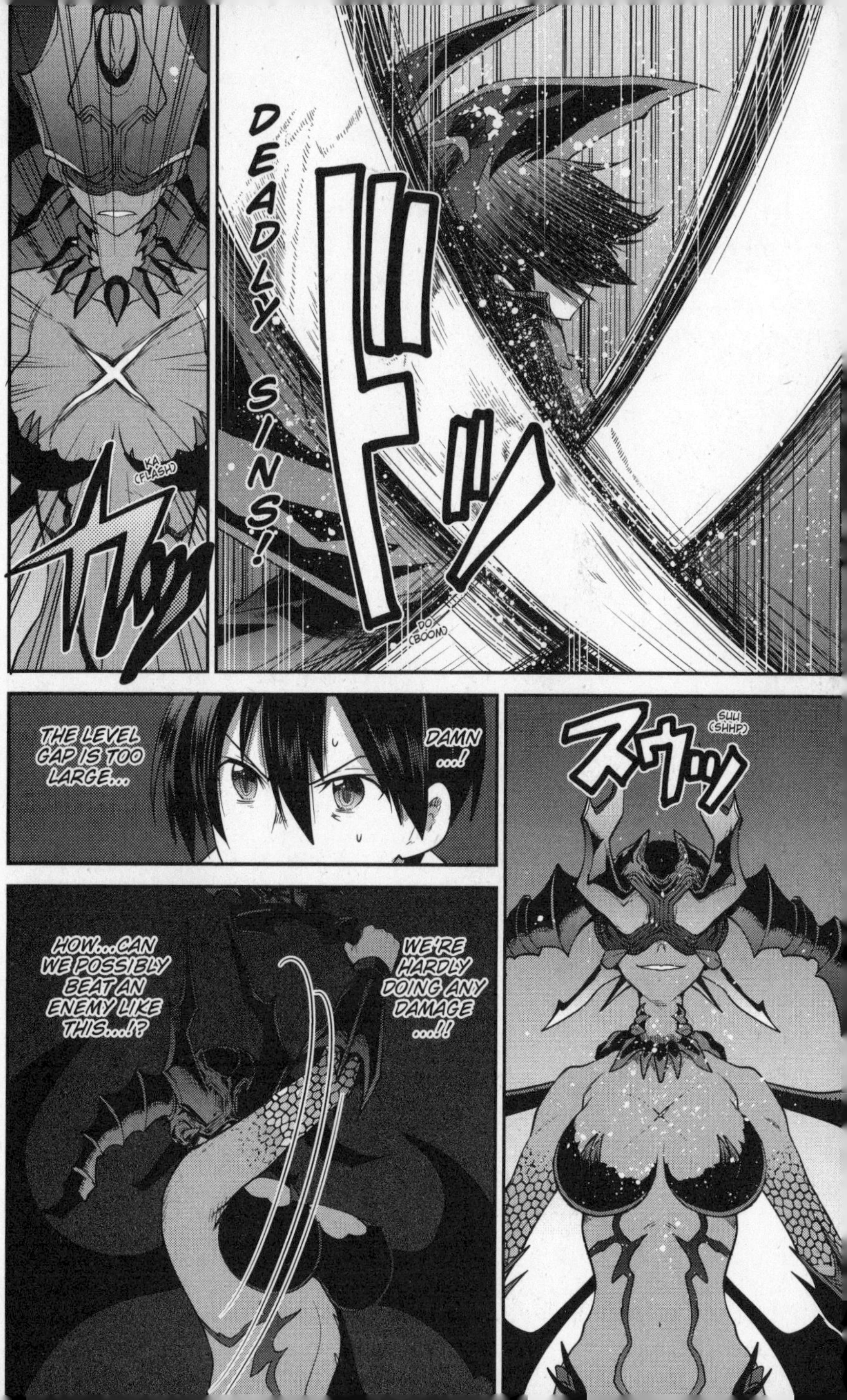
DEADLY SINS!
DO (BOOM)
KA (FLASH)
SUU (SHHP)
DAMN...!
THE LEVEL GAP IS TOO LARGE...
WE'RE HARDLY DOING ANY DAMAGE...!!
HOW...CAN WE POSSIBLY BEAT AN ENEMY LIKE THIS...!?

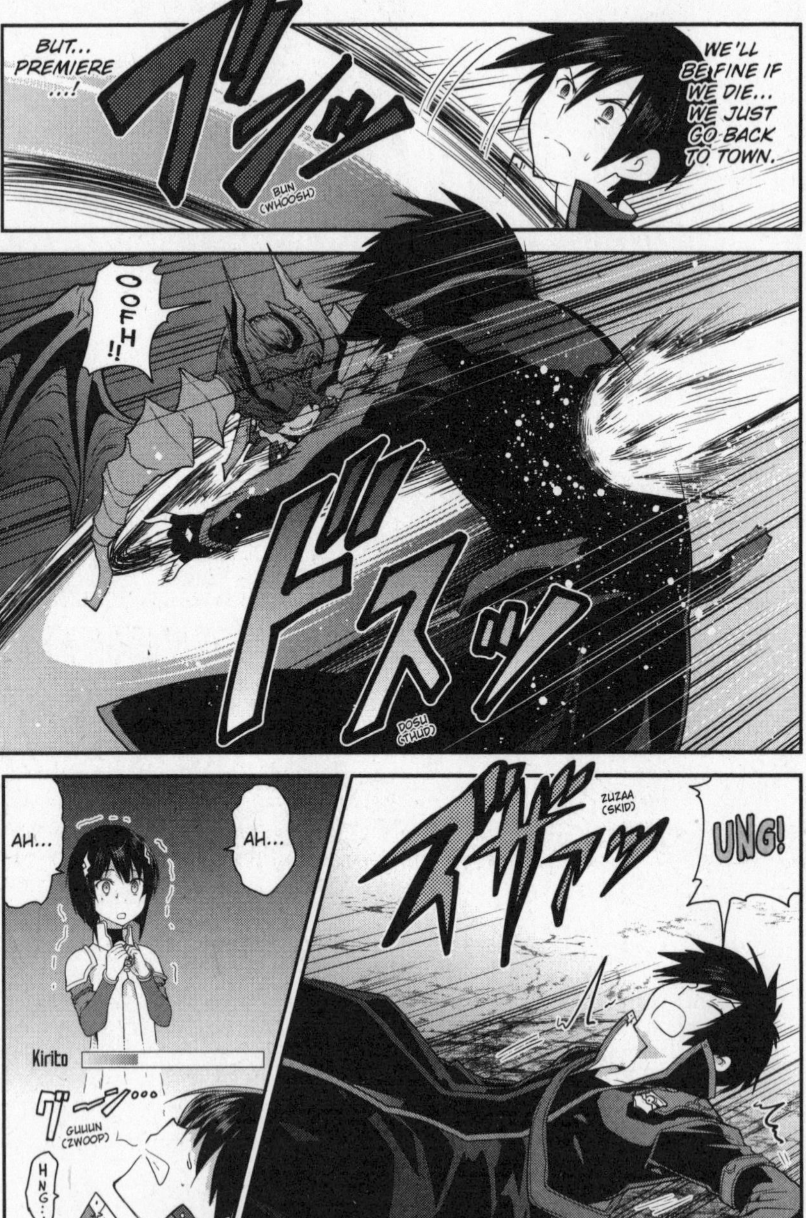
WE'LL BE FINE IF WE DIE... WE JUST GO BACK TO TOWN.
BUT... PREMIERE ...!
BUN (WHOOSH)
OOFH!!
DOSU (THUD)
ZUZAA (SKID)
UNG!
AH...
AH...
Kirito
GUUUN (ZWOOP)
HNG...

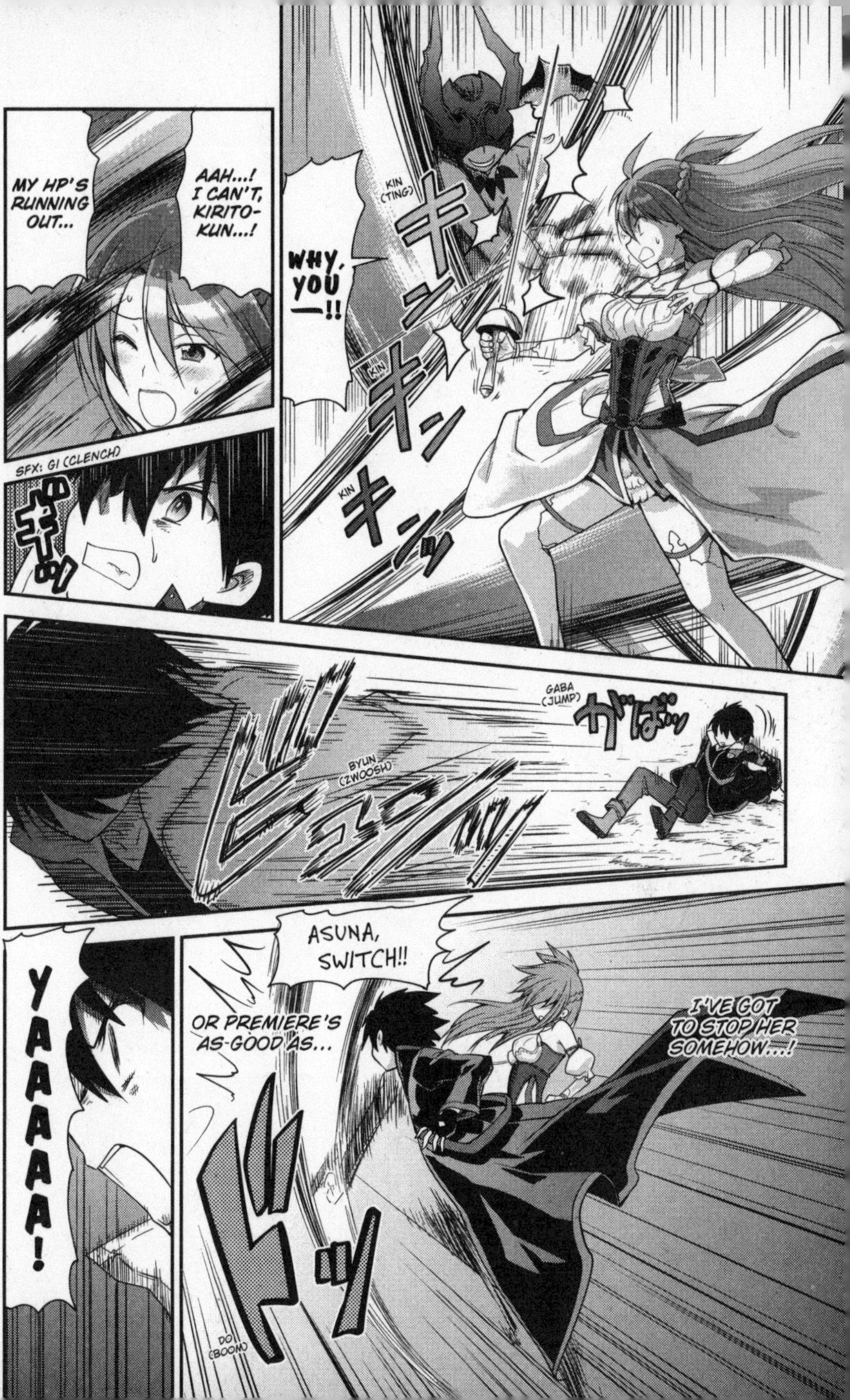
KIN (TING)
WHY, YOU—!!
KIN
KIN
AAH...! I CAN'T, KIRITO-KUN...!
MY HP'S RUNNING OUT...
SFX: GI (CLENCH)
GABA (JUMP)
BYUN (ZWOOSH)
I'VE GOT TO STOP HER SOMEHOW...!
ASUNA, SWITCH!!
OR PREMIERE'S AS-GOOD AS...
DO (BOOM)
YAAAAAA!

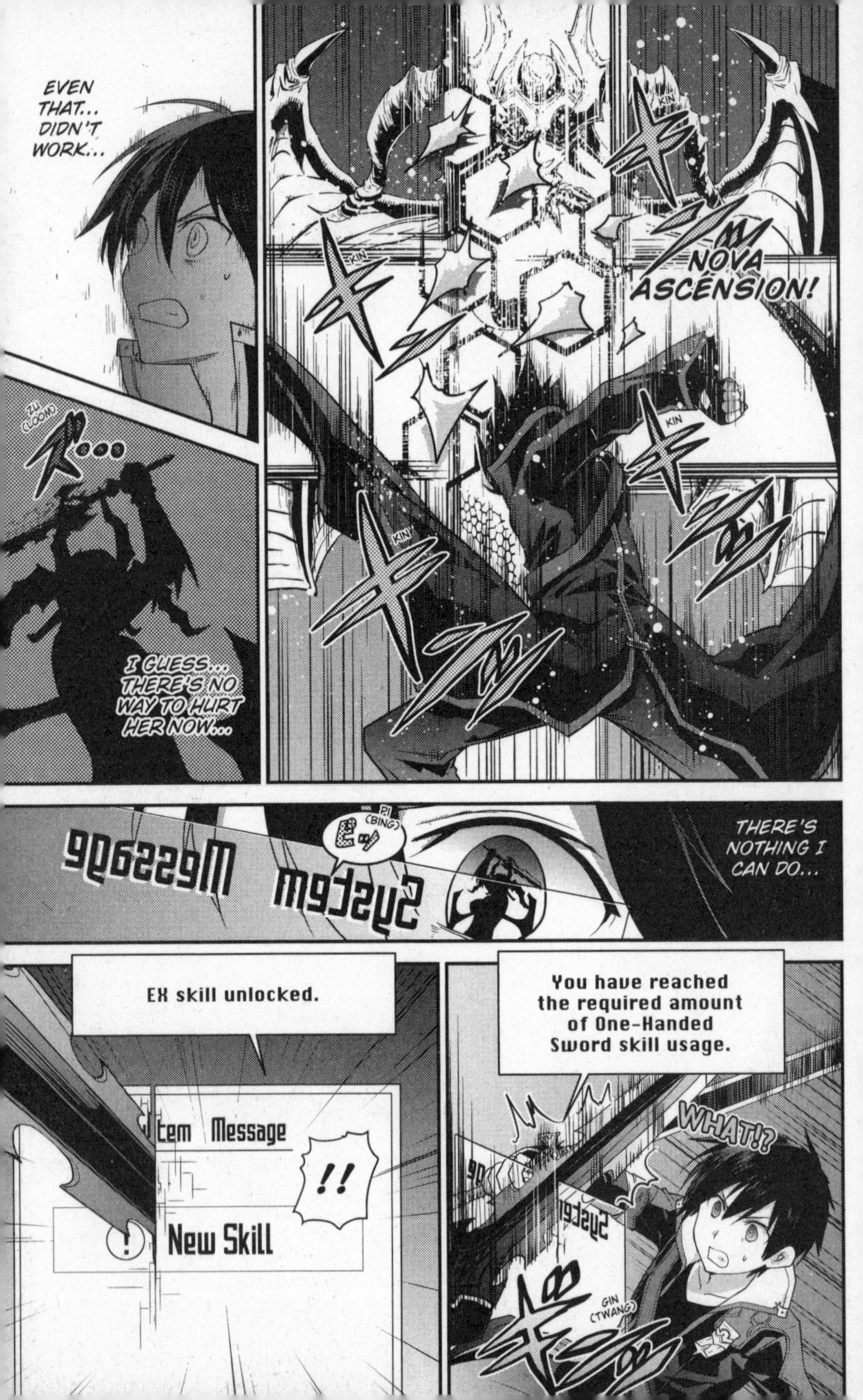
NOVA ASCENSION!
KIN
KIN
KIN
KIN
EVEN THAT... DIDN'T WORK...
ZU (LOOM)
I GUESS... THERE'S NO WAY TO HURT HER NOW...
THERE'S NOTHING I CAN DO...
PI (BING)
You have reached the required amount of One-Handed Sword skill usage.
WHAT!?
GIN (TWANG)
EX skill unlocked.
Message
!!
New Skill

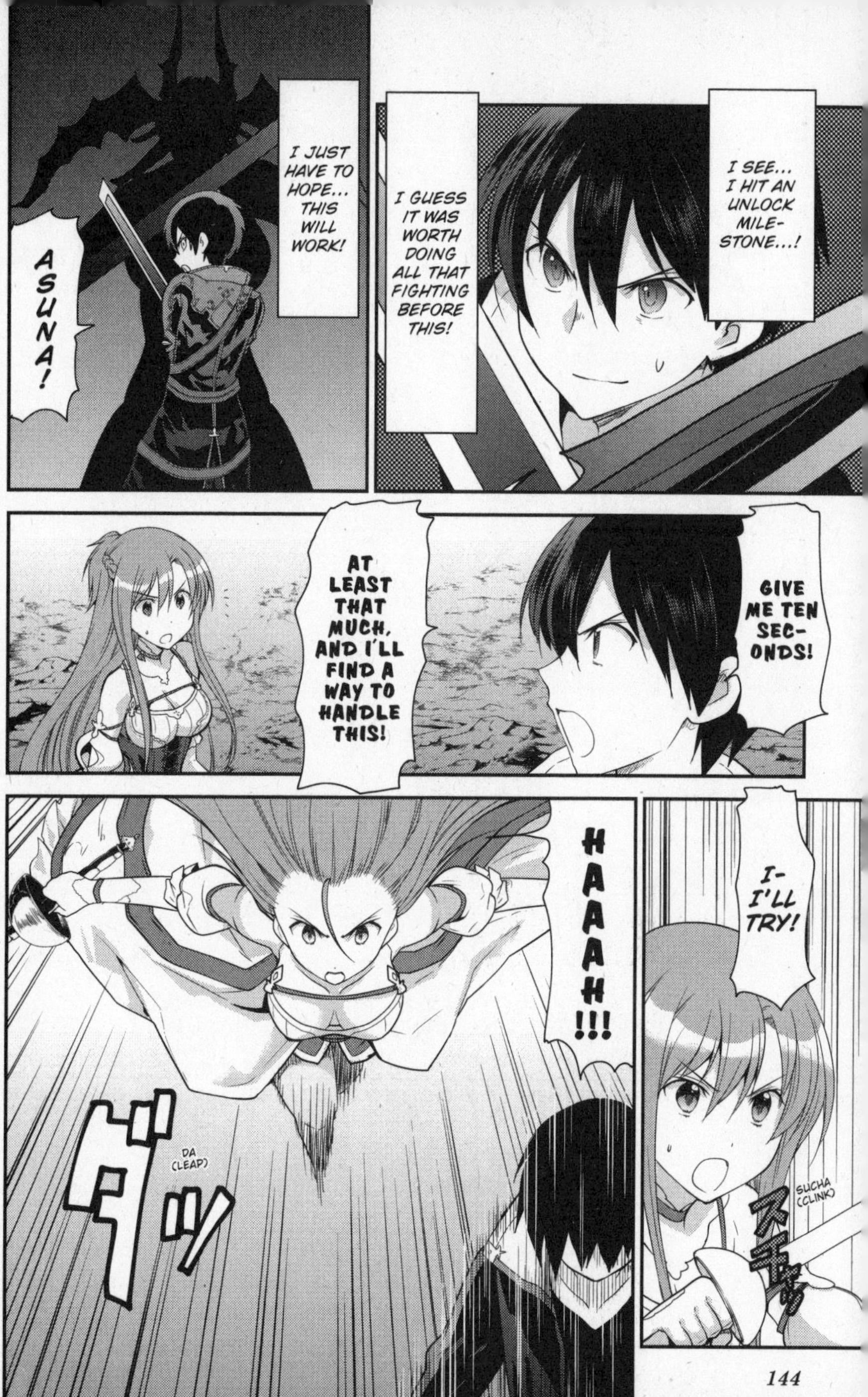

I SEE... I HIT AN UNLOCK MILE-STONE...!
I GUESS IT WAS WORTH DOING ALL THAT FIGHTING BEFORE THIS!
I JUST HAVE TO HOPE... THIS WILL WORK!
ASUNA!
GIVE ME TEN SEC-ONDS!
AT LEAST THAT MUCH, AND I'LL FIND A WAY TO HANDLE THIS!
I-I'LL TRY!
SUCHA (CLINK)
HAAAAH!!!
DA (LEAP)

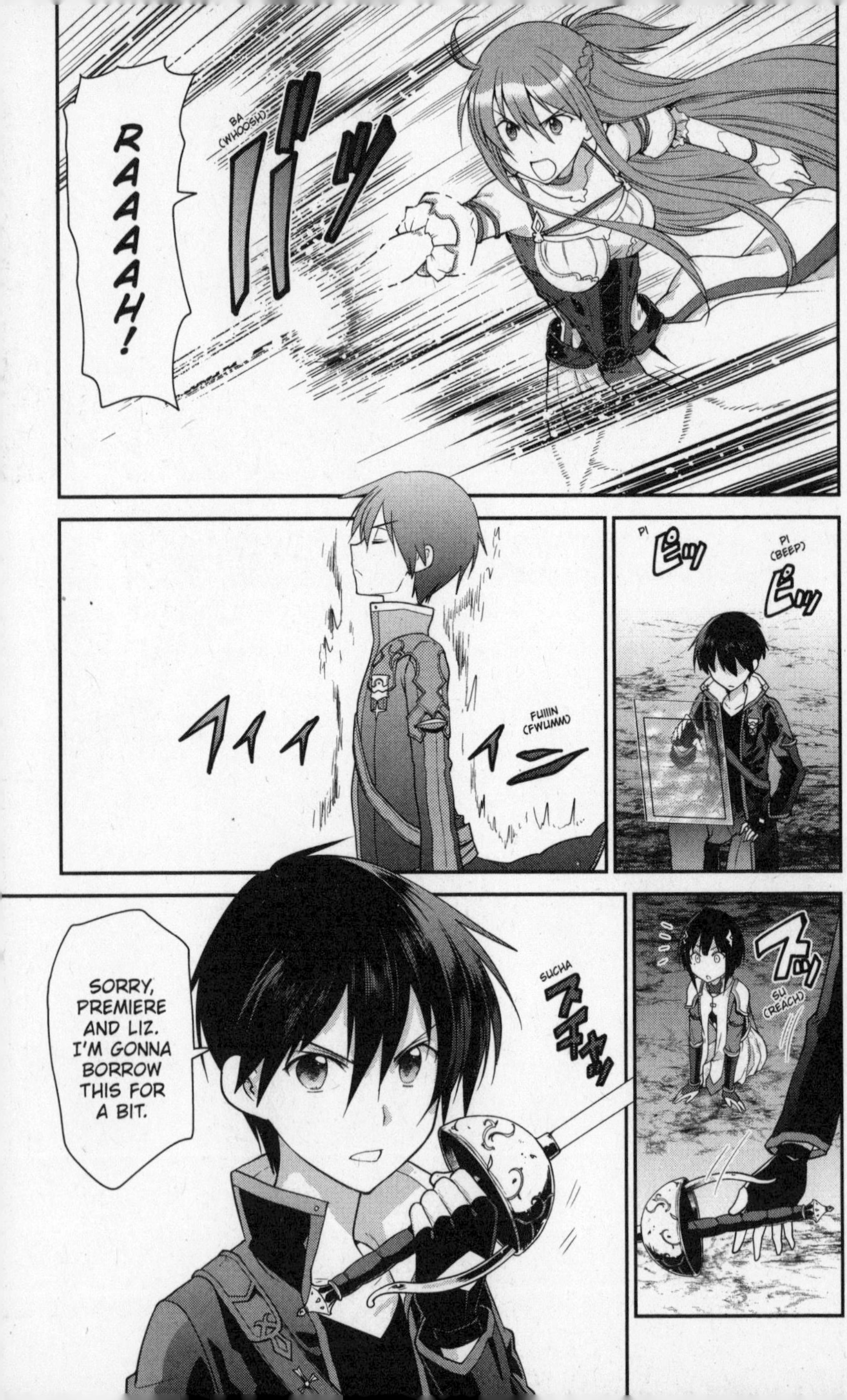
RAAAAAH!
BA (WHOOSH)
PI
PI (BEEP)
FUIIIN (FWUMM)
SU (REACH)
SORRY, PREMIERE AND LIZ. I'M GONNA BORROW THIS FOR A BIT.
SUCHA

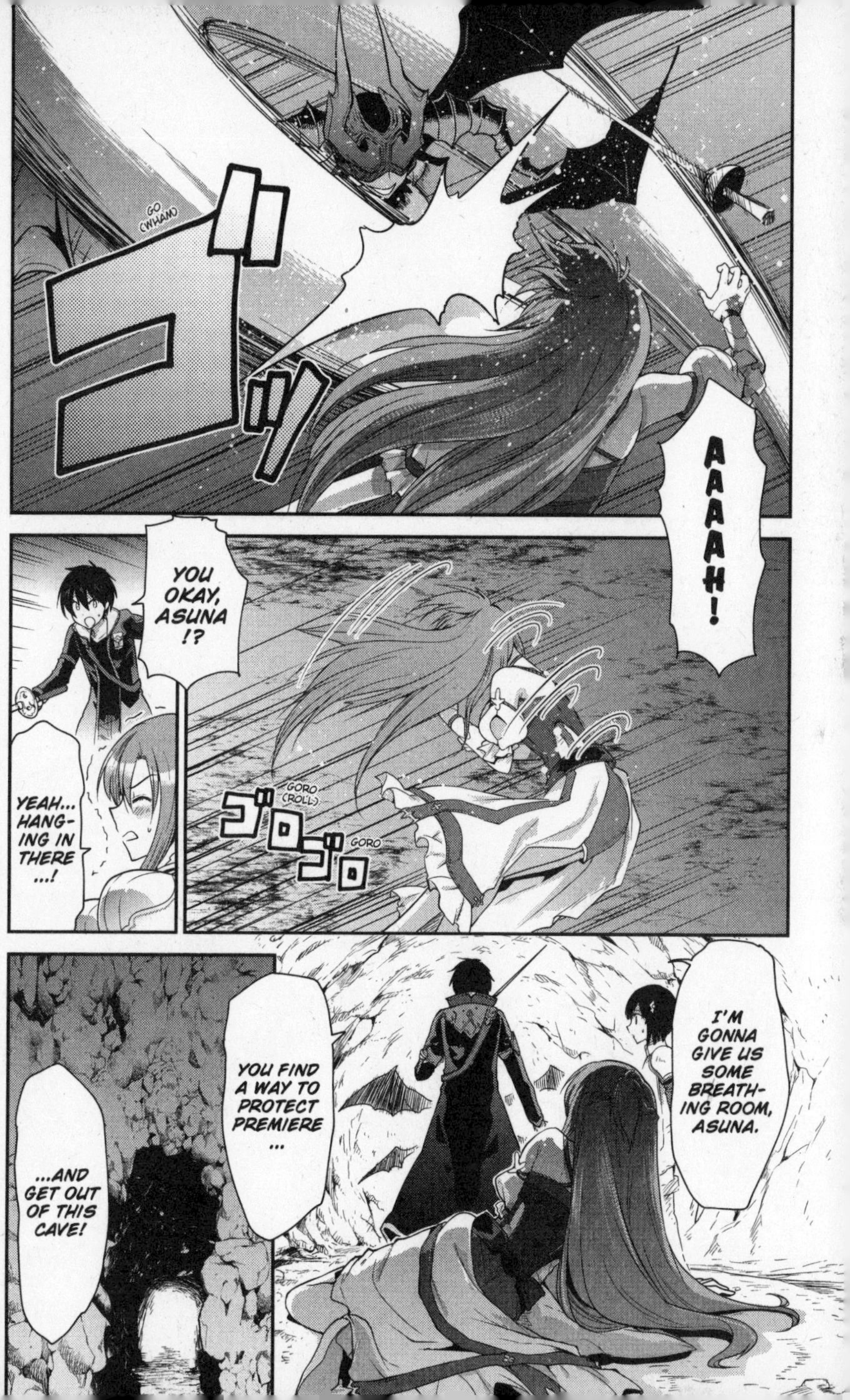
ゴッ
GO (WHAM)
AAAAAH!
ゴロゴロ
GORO (ROLL)
GORO
YOU OKAY, ASUNA!?
YEAH... HANG-ING IN THERE...!
I'M GONNA GIVE US SOME BREATH-ING ROOM, ASUNA.
YOU FIND A WAY TO PROTECT PREMIERE...
...AND GET OUT OF THIS CAVE!

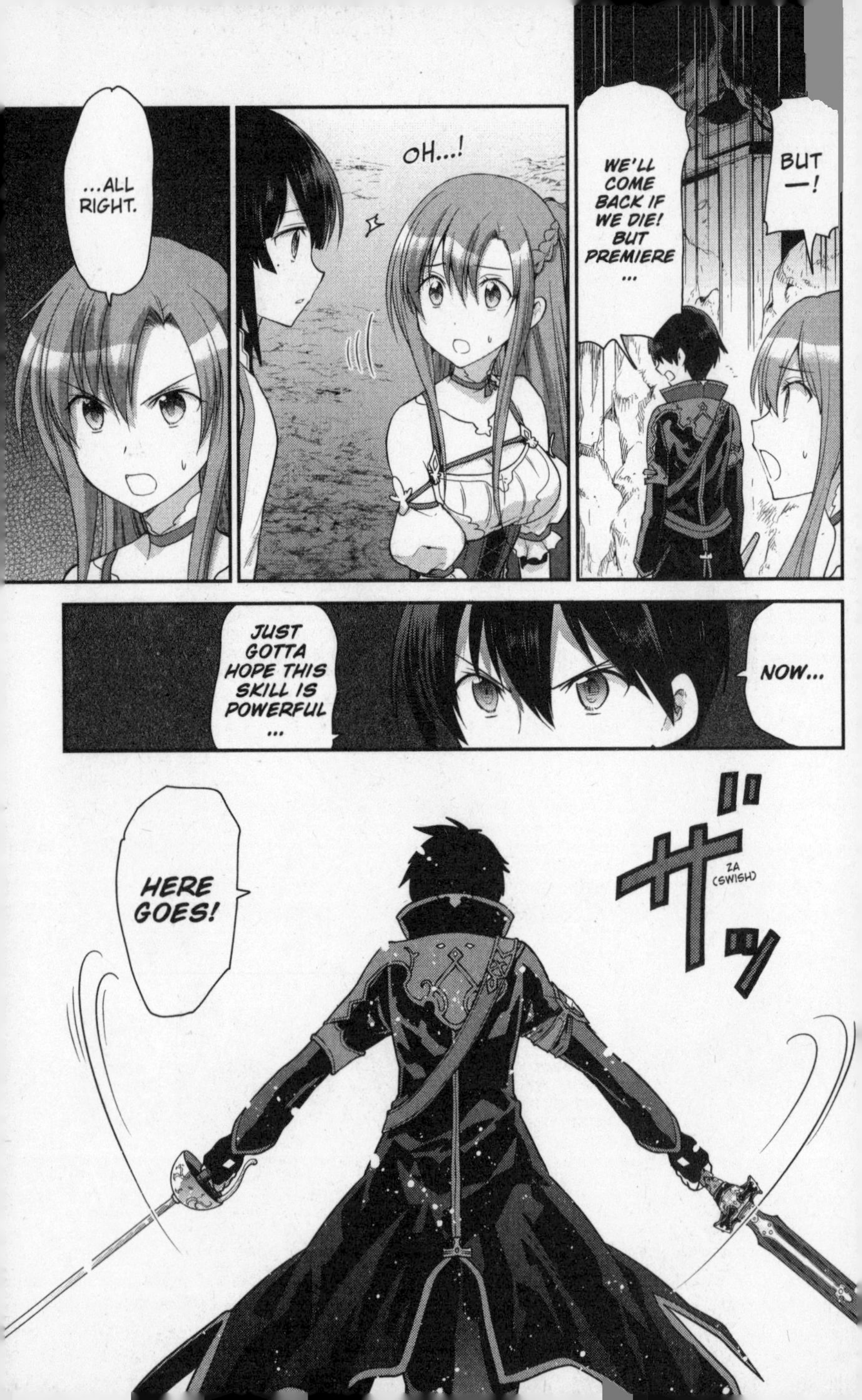
BUT—!
WE'LL COME BACK IF WE DIE! BUT PREMIERE ...
OH...!
...ALL RIGHT.
NOW...
JUST GOTTA HOPE THIS SKILL IS POWERFUL ...
ザッ
ZA (SWISH)
HERE GOES!

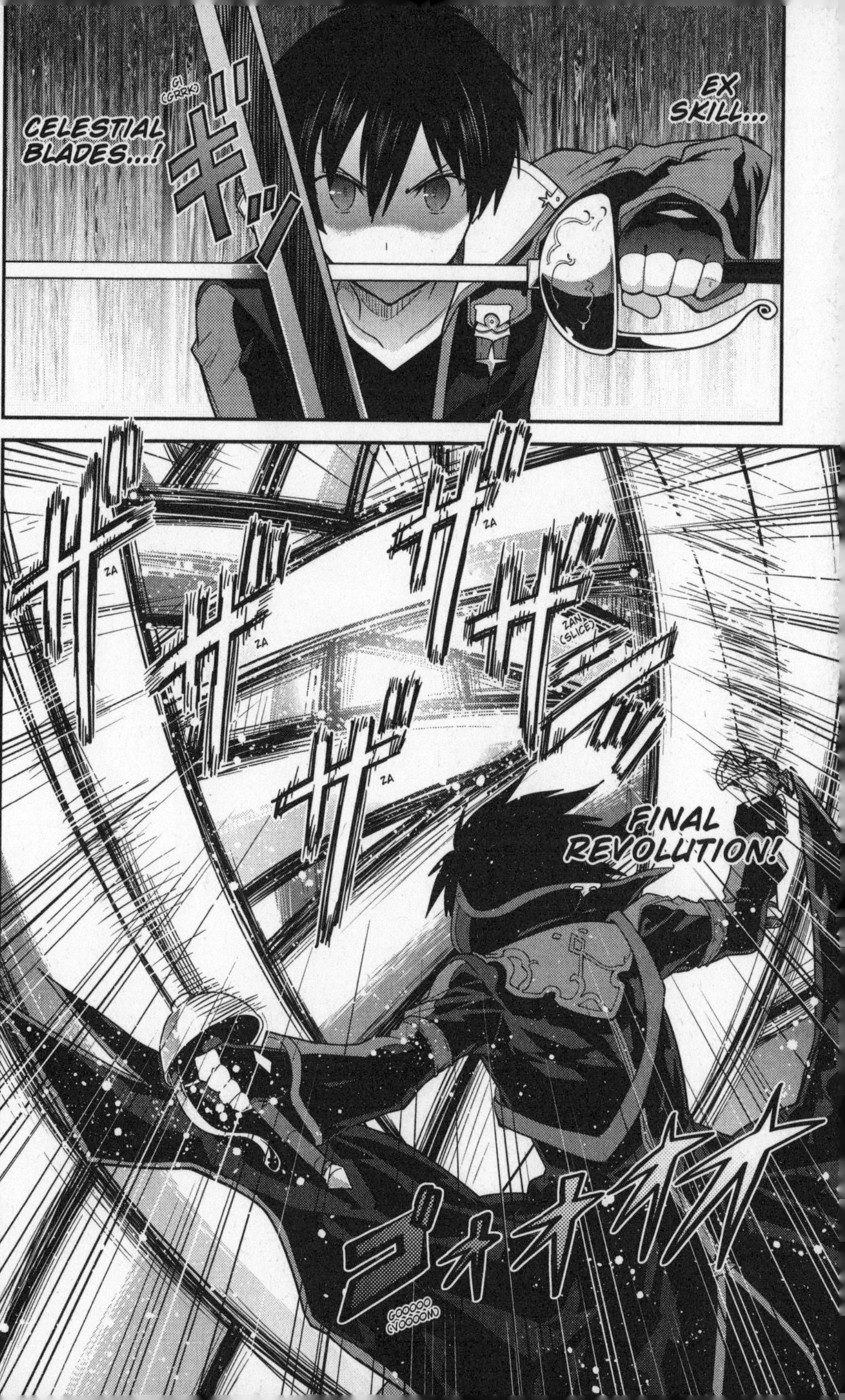
EX SKILL...
GI (GRRK)
CELESTIAL BLADES...!
ZAN (SLICE)
ZA
ZA
ZA
ZA
FINAL REVOLUTION!
GOOOOO (VOOOOM)

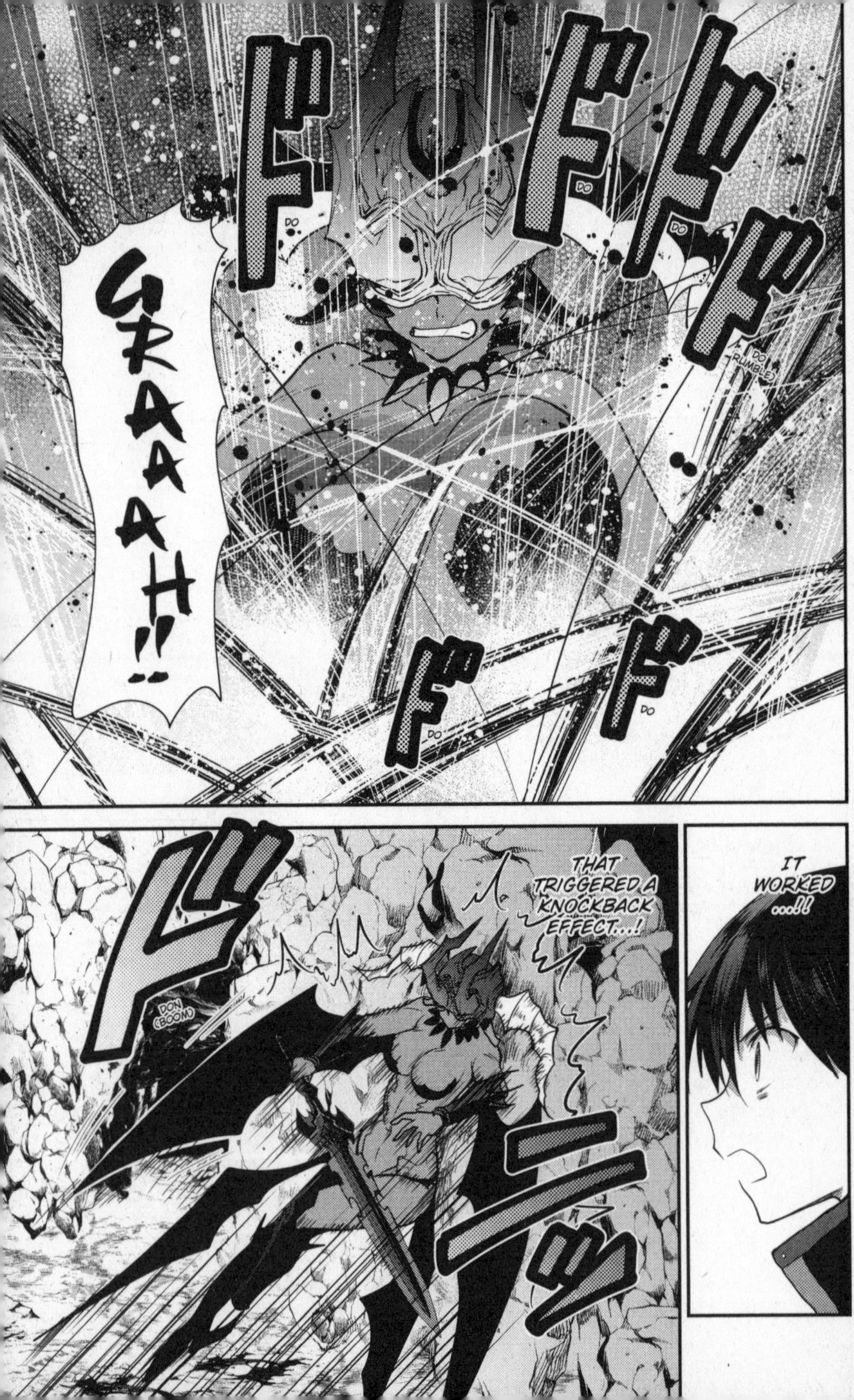

DO
DO
DO
DO
RUMBLE
GRAAAAH!!
DO
DO
IT WORKED...!!
THAT TRIGGERED A KNOCKBACK EFFECT...!
DON (BOOM)

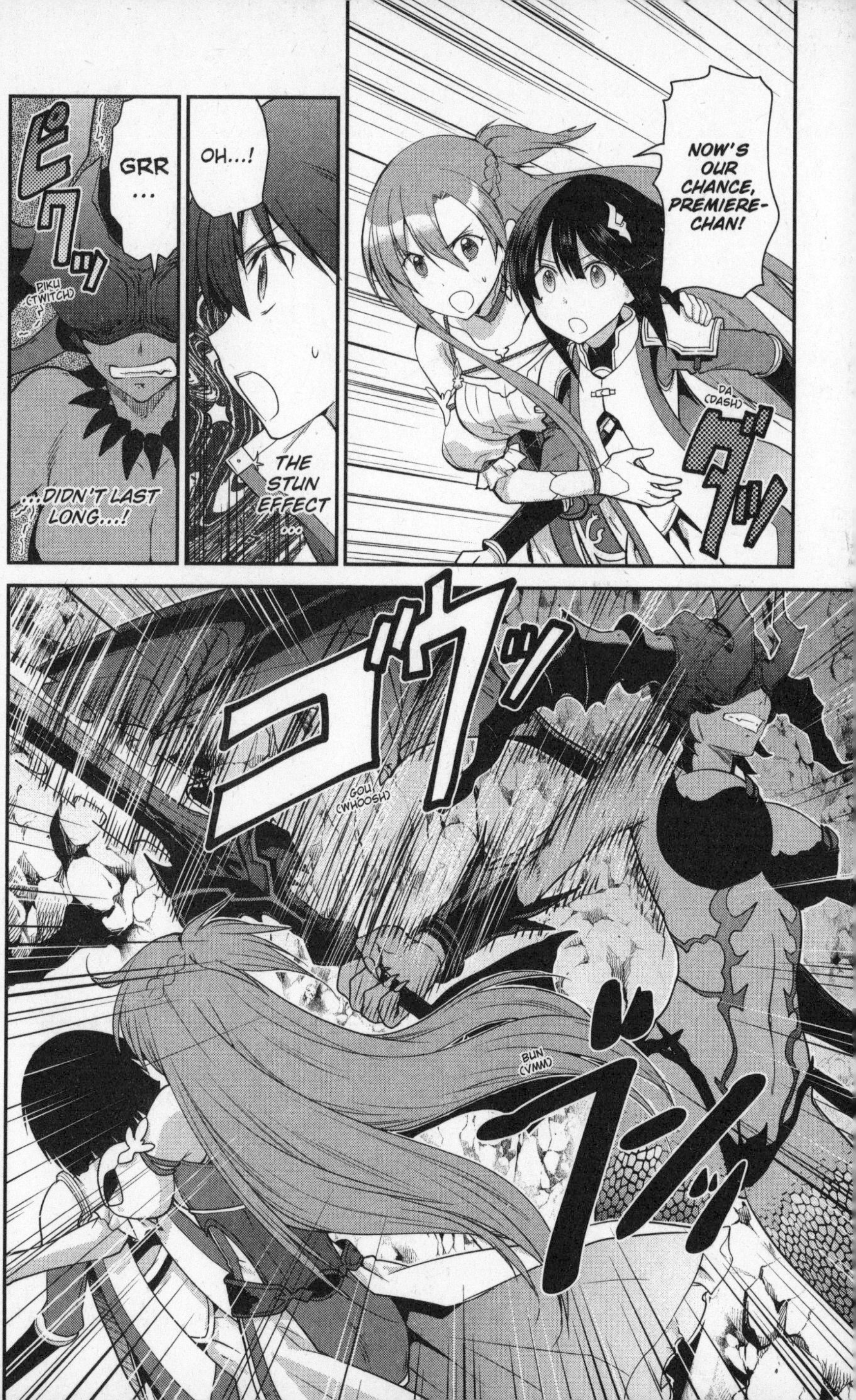
NOW'S OUR CHANCE, PREMIERE-CHAN!
DA (DASH)
OH...!
THE STUN EFFECT...
GRR...
PIKU (TWITCH)
...DIDN'T LAST LONG...!
GOU (WHOOSH)
BUN (VMM)

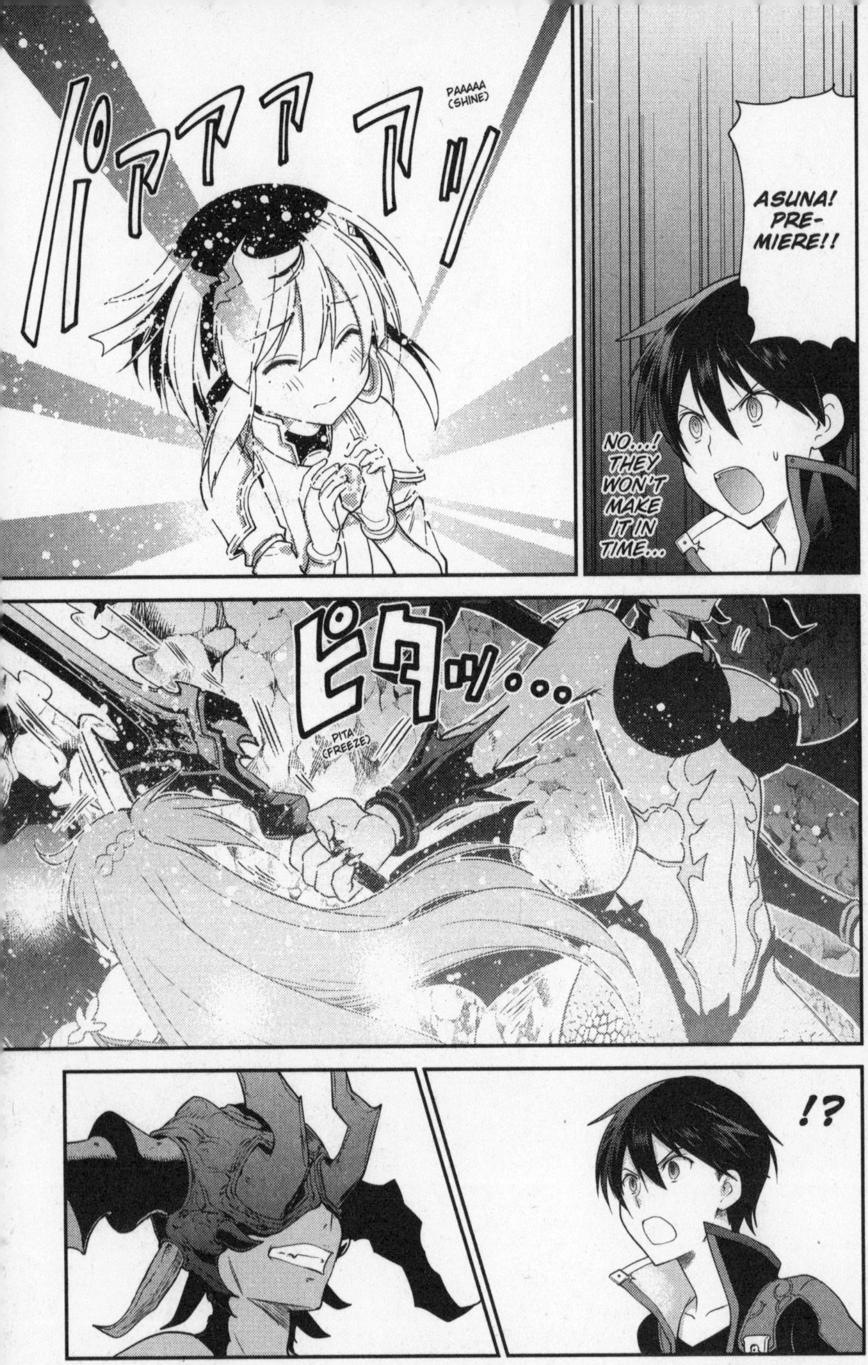
ASUNA! PREMIERE!!
NO...! THEY WON'T MAKE IT IN TIME...
PAAAAA (SHINE)
PITA (FREEZE)
!?

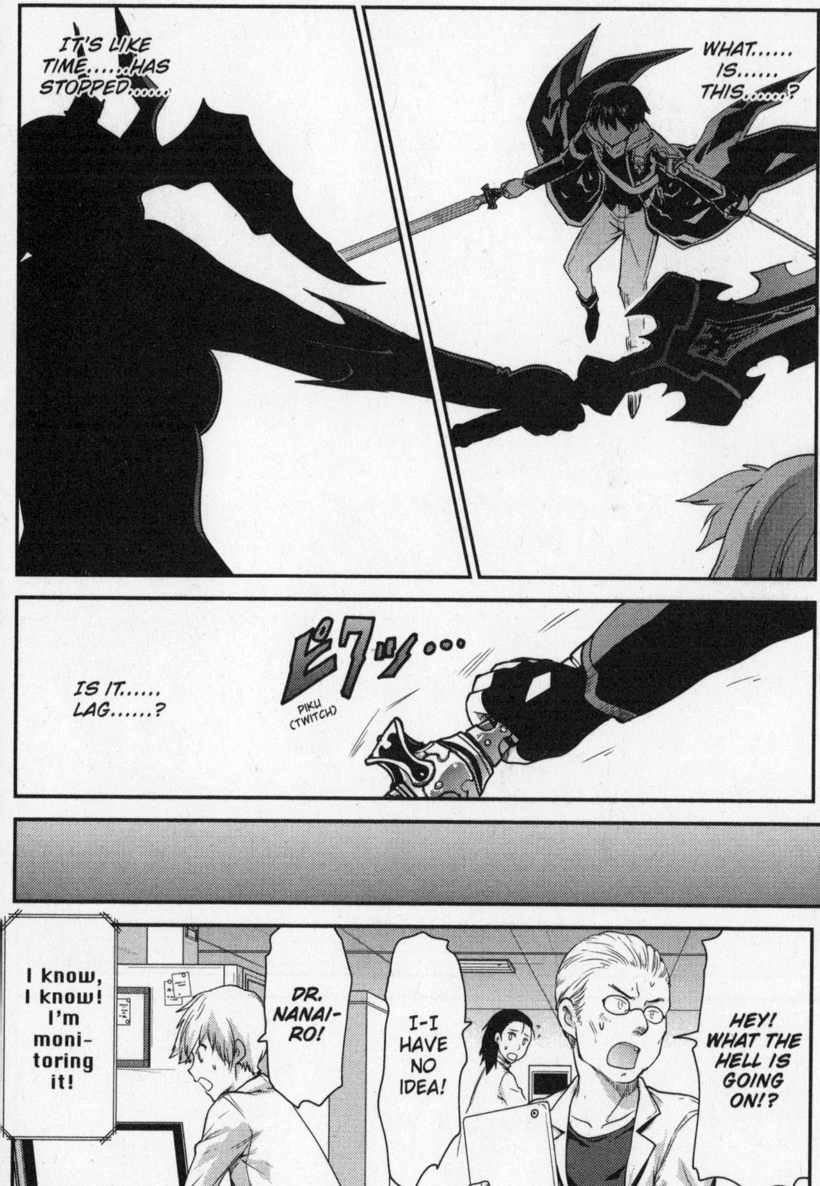
WHAT...... IS...... THIS......?
IT'S LIKE TIME......HAS STOPPED......
ピクッ…
PIKU (TWITCH)
IS IT...... LAG......?
HEY! WHAT THE HELL IS GOING ON!?
I-I HAVE NO IDEA!
DR. NANAIRO!
I know, I know! I'm monitoring it!

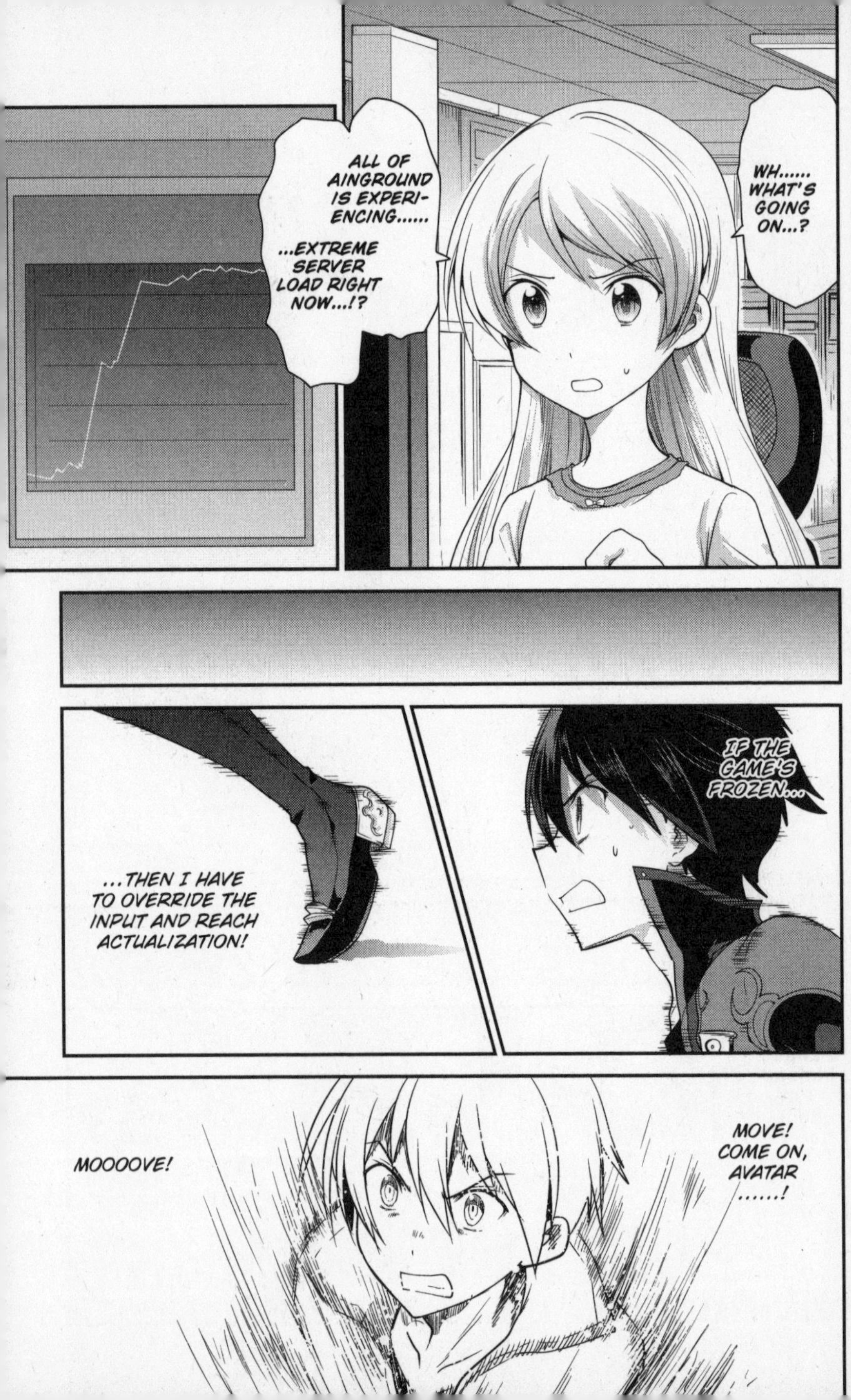
WH...... WHAT'S GOING ON...?
ALL OF AINGROUND IS EXPERI-ENCING......
...EXTREME SERVER LOAD RIGHT NOW...!?
IF THE GAME'S FROZEN...
...THEN I HAVE TO OVERRIDE THE INPUT AND REACH ACTUALIZATION!
MOVE! COME ON, AVATAR ......!
MOOOOVE!

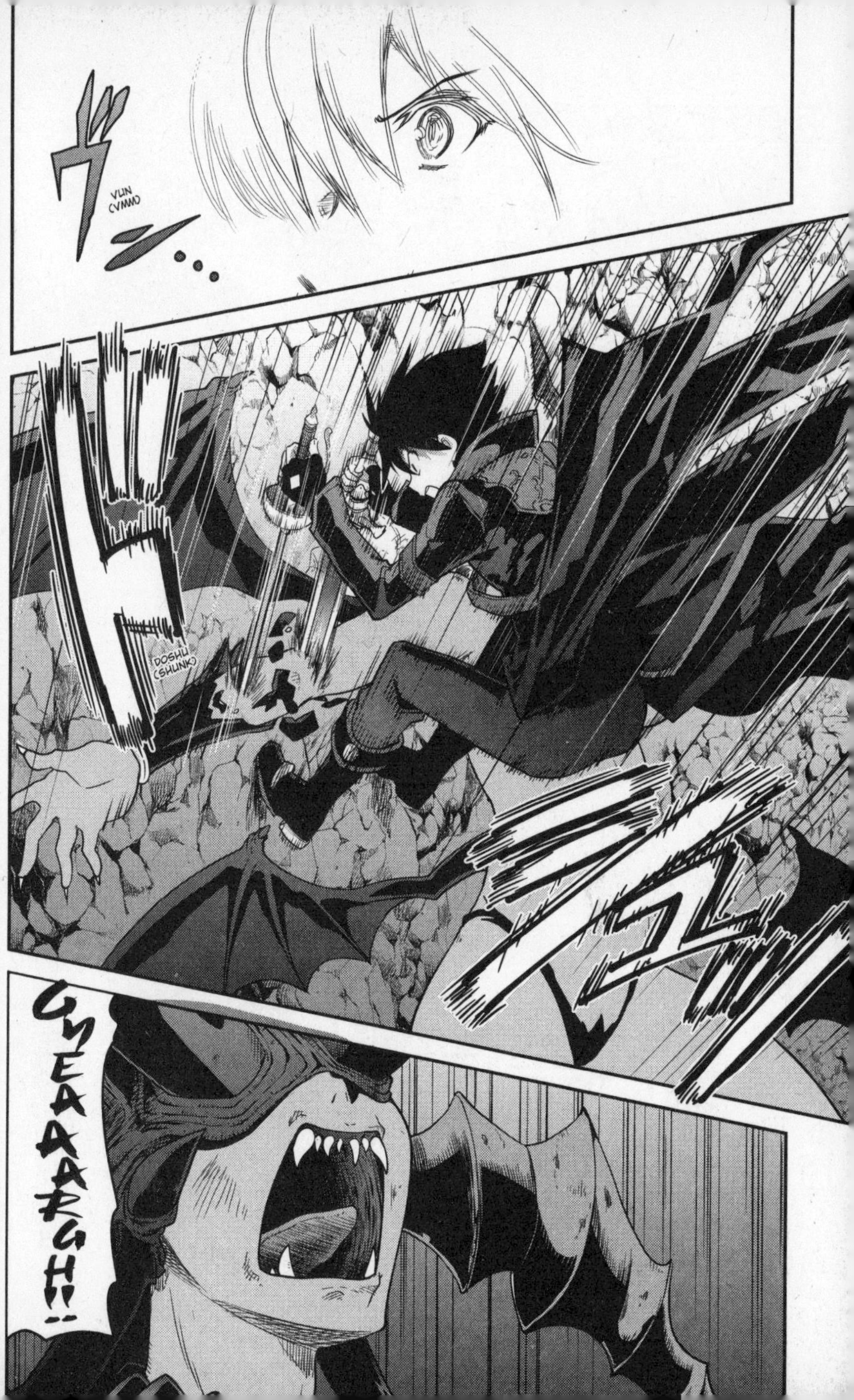
VUN (VMM)
DOSHU (SHUNK)
GYEAAAARGH!!

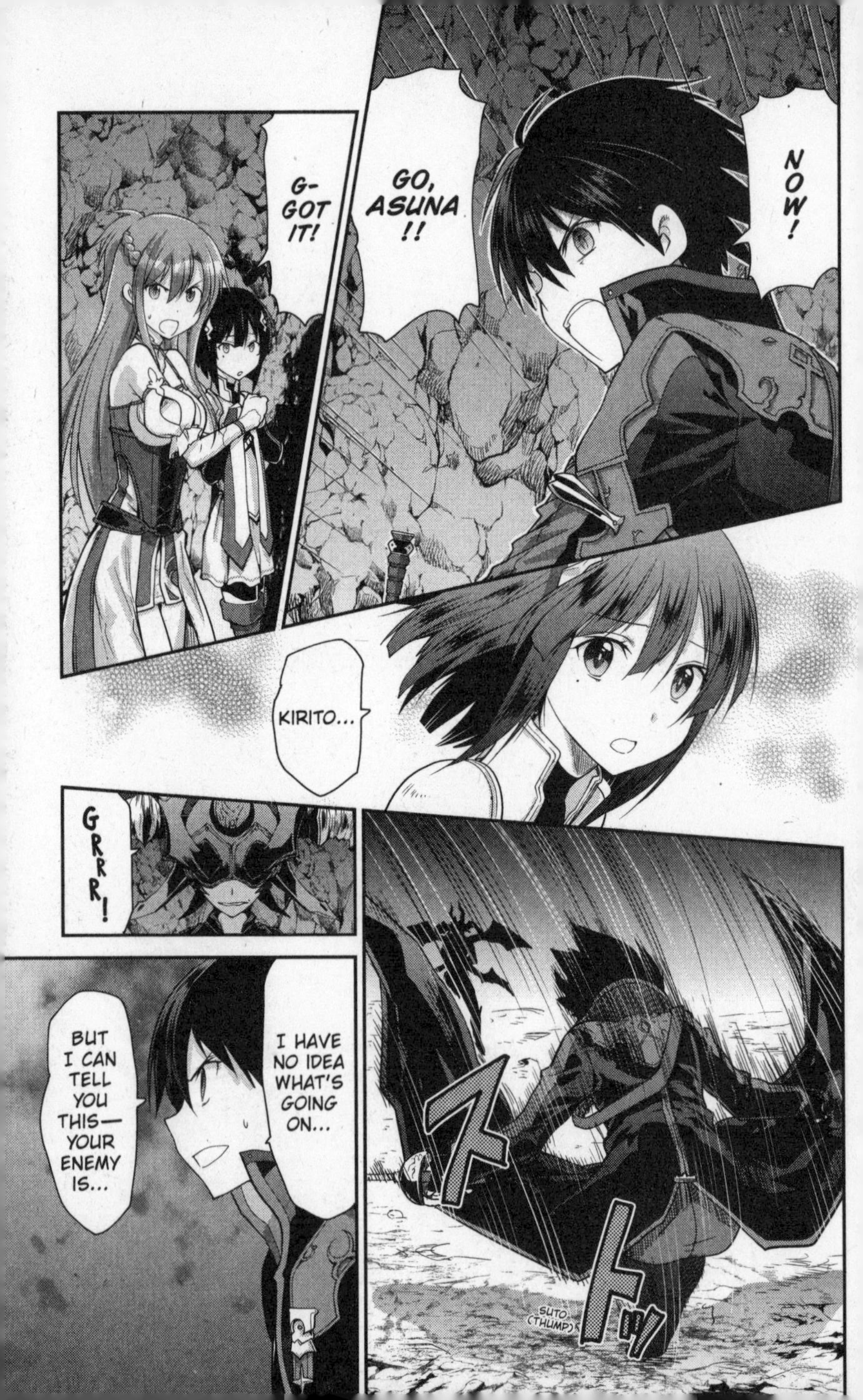
NOW!
GO, ASUNA!!
G-GOT IT!
KIRITO...
SUTO (THUMP)
GRRR!
I HAVE NO IDEA WHAT'S GOING ON...
BUT I CAN TELL YOU THIS—YOUR ENEMY IS...

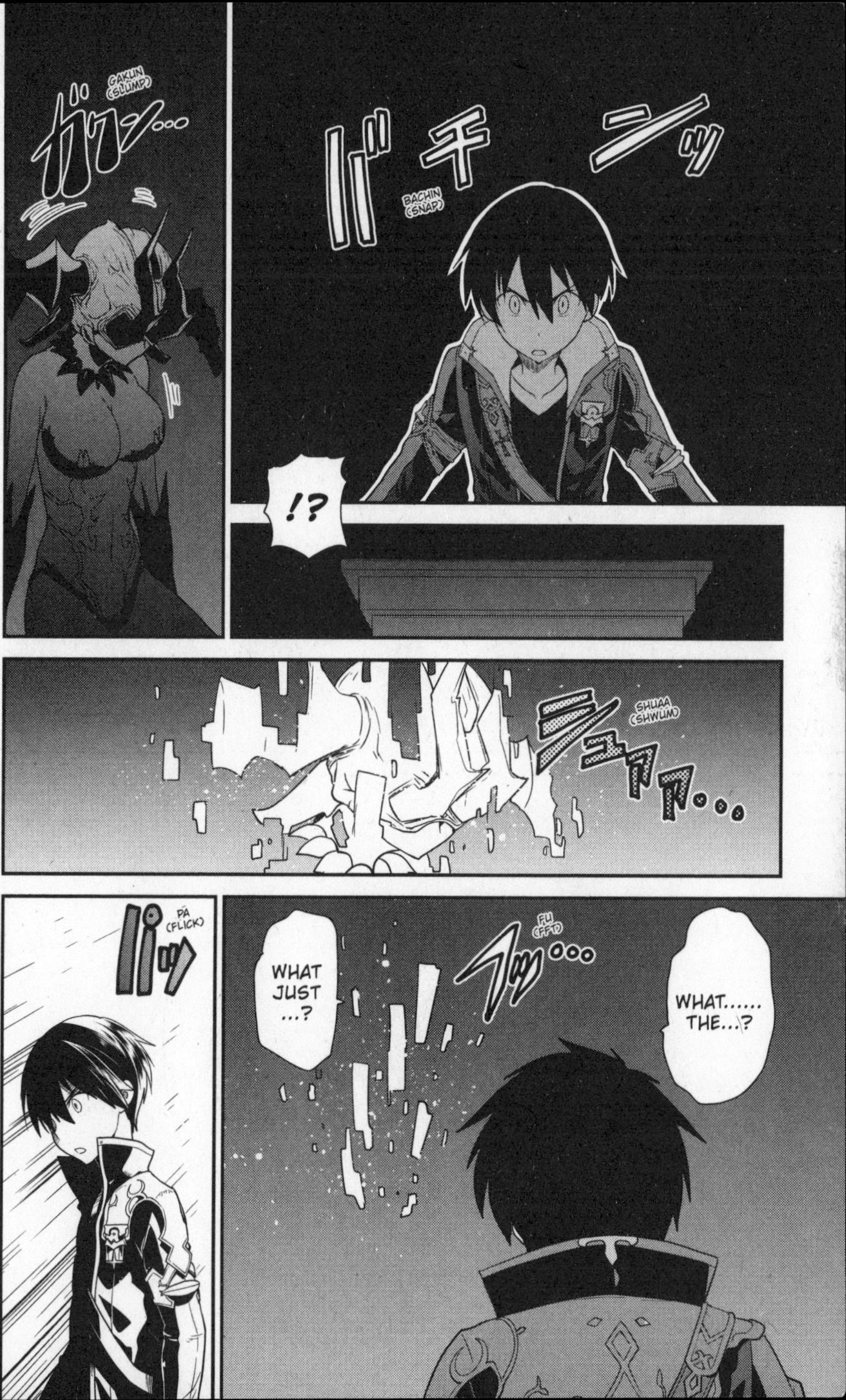
バチーンッ
BACHIN (SNAP)
!?
ガクン…
GAKUN (SLUMP)
シュアア…
SHUAA (SHWUM)
フッ…
FU (FFT)
WHAT...... THE...?
WHAT JUST ...?
パッ
PA (FLICK)

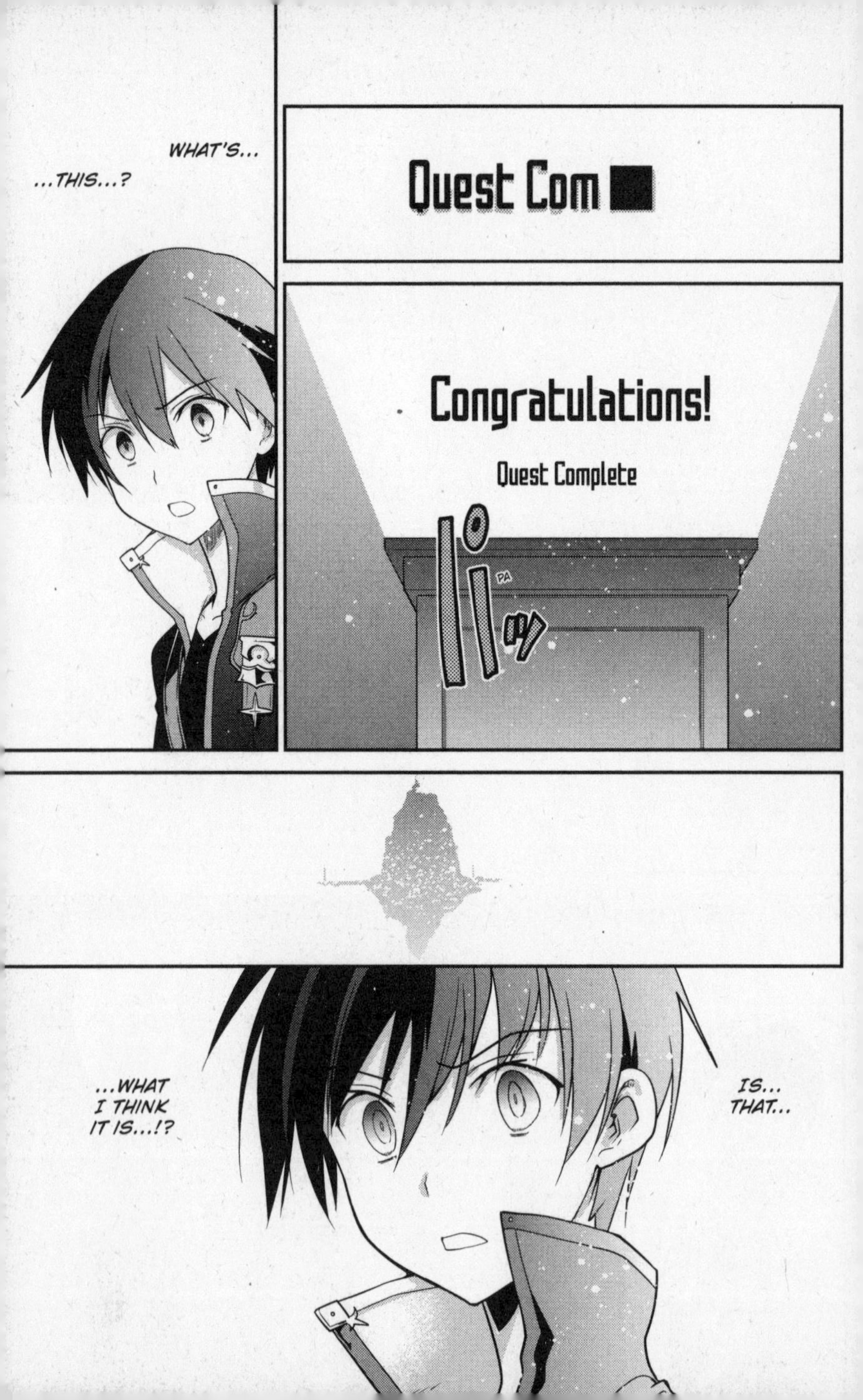
Quest Com
Congratulations!
Quest Complete
パッ
PA
WHAT'S...
...THIS...?
IS...
THAT...
...WHAT
I THINK
IT IS...!?

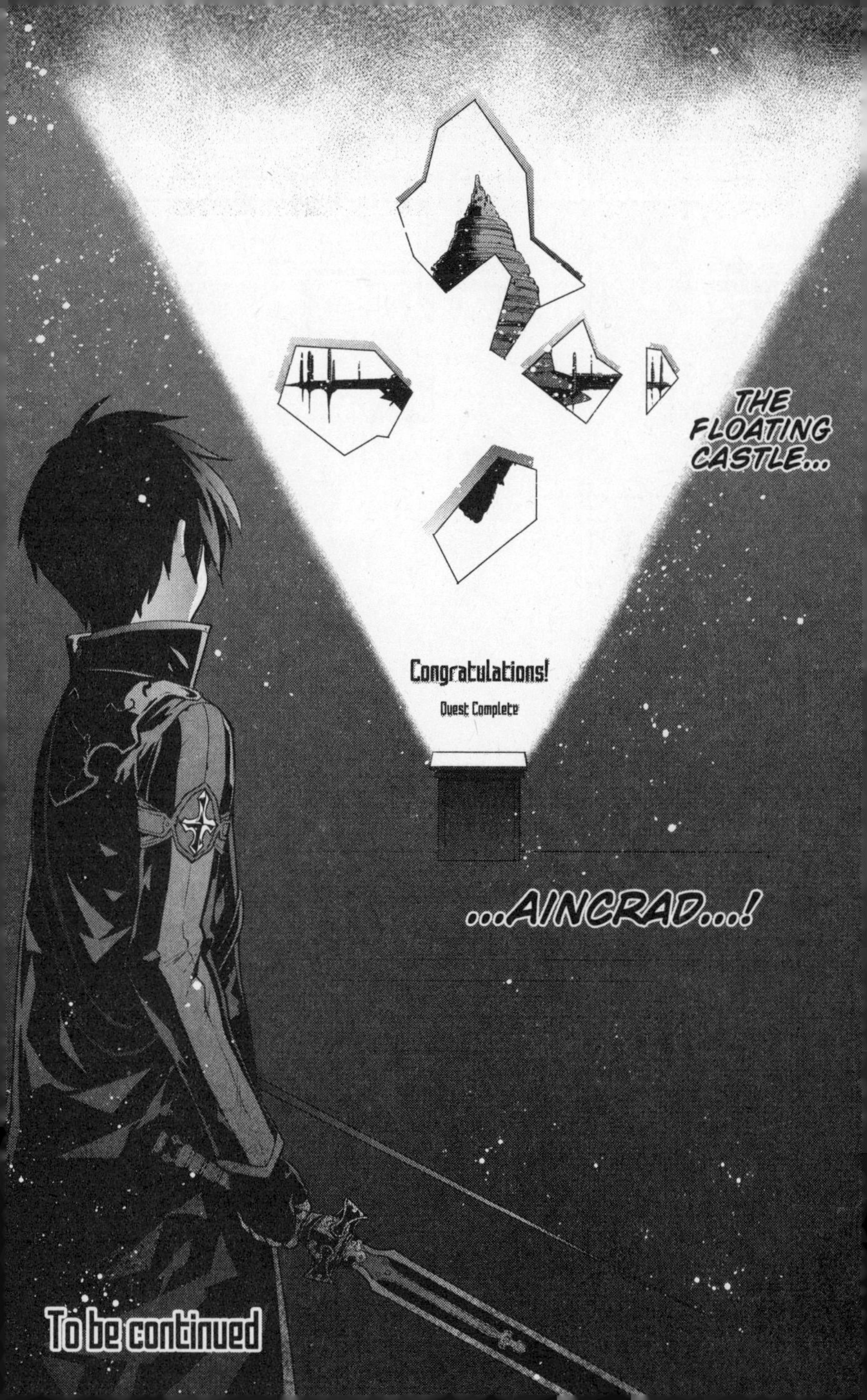
THE FLOATING CASTLE...
Congratulations!
Quest Complete
...AINCRAD...!
To be continued

AFTERWORD & MEMORIES

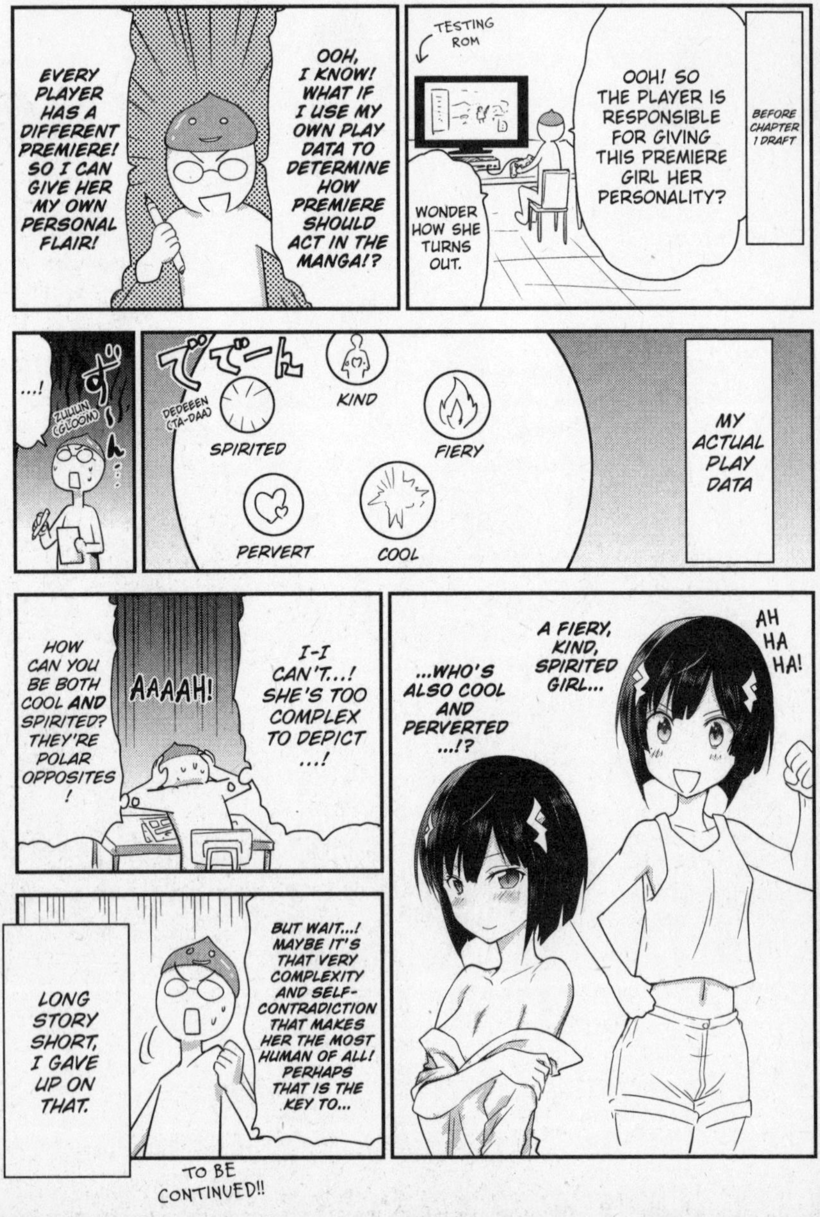
BEFORE CHAPTER 1 DRAFT
OOH! SO THE PLAYER IS RESPONSIBLE FOR GIVING THIS PREMIERE GIRL HER PERSONALITY?
TESTING ROM
WONDER HOW SHE TURNS OUT.
OOH, I KNOW! WHAT IF I USE MY OWN PLAY DATA TO DETERMINE HOW PREMIERE SHOULD ACT IN THE MANGA!?
EVERY PLAYER HAS A DIFFERENT PREMIERE! SO I CAN GIVE HER MY OWN PERSONAL FLAIR!
MY ACTUAL PLAY DATA
でで〜ん
DEDEEEN (TA-DAA)
KIND
SPIRITED
FIERY
PERVERT
COOL
ずぅ〜ん…
ZUUUN (GLOOM)
...!
AH HA HA!
A FIERY, KIND, SPIRITED GIRL...
...WHO'S ALSO COOL AND PERVERTED...!?
I-I CAN'T...! SHE'S TOO COMPLEX TO DEPICT...!
AAAAH!
HOW CAN YOU BE BOTH COOL AND SPIRITED? THEY'RE POLAR OPPOSITES!
BUT WAIT...! MAYBE IT'S THAT VERY COMPLEXITY AND SELF-CONTRADICTION THAT MAKES HER THE MOST HUMAN OF ALL! PERHAPS THAT IS THE KEY TO...
LONG STORY SHORT, I GAVE UP ON THAT.
TO BE CONTINUED!!

message

REKI KAWAHARA

Given that this is a manga adaption of a video game's alternate take on the original story, I have to imagine it was extremely difficult for Hirokawa-sensei to prepare for this project.

This is the first time we've done a manga of one of the *SAO* games too.

The entire story of *SAO* is based on video games, and the way this manga depicts a group of friends doing quests and going on battles really brings out that RPG flavor. I can't wait to see where this goes next!

SWORD ART ONLINE
—HOLLOW REALIZATION—
001

Congrats on the release of Volume 1 of *Hollow Realization*!

Hirokawa-sensei's delicate and adorable art brings this world to life...

I'm very much looking forward to the slightly more risqué versions of Asuna and the other girls from the game!

Oh, and if any of these designs seem complicated and hard to draw, blame Bandai Namco! Definitely not me!

message
abec
≫abec

KT-153-568

SWORD ART ONLINE: HOLLOW REALIZATION 1

ART: TOMO HIROKAWA
ORIGINAL STORY: REKI KAWAHARA
CHARACTER DESIGN: abec
STORY SUPERVISION: BANDAI NAMCO ENTERTAINMENT

Translation: Stephen Paul   **Lettering: Brndn Blakeslee**

SWORD ART ONLINE -HOLLOW REALIZATION- Vol. 1
© 2017 REKI KAWAHARA/TOMO HIROKAWA
© 2016 REKI KAWAHARA/PUBLISHED BY KADOKAWA CORPORATION
ASCII MEDIA WORKS/SAO MOVIE Project
© 2014 REKI KAWAHARA/PUBLISHED BY KADOKAWA CORPORATION
ASCII MEDIA WORKS/SAOII Project
© BANDAI NAMCO Entertainment Inc.
First published in Japan in 2017 by KADOKAWA CORPORATION, Tokyo.
English translation rights arranged with KADOKAWA CORPORATION, Tokyo,
through Tuttle-Mori Agency, Inc., Tokyo.

English translation © 2018 by Yen Press, LLC

Yen Press
1290 Avenue of the Americas
New York, NY 10104

Visit us at yenpress.com
facebook.com/yenpress
twitter.com/yenpress
yenpress.tumblr.com
instagram.com/yenpress

First Yen Press Edition: November 2018

Yen Press is an imprint of Yen Press, LLC.
The Yen Press name and logo are trademarks of Yen Press, LLC.

The publisher is not responsible for websites (or their content) that are not owned by the publisher.

Library of Congress Control Number: 2018950180

ISBNs: 978-1-9753-5474-9 (paperback)
        978-1-9753-2786-6 (ebook)

10 9 8 7 6 5 4 3 2 1

WOR

Printed in the United States of America